Date Due

APR 2 1990			
ILL 5/11/93			
MAR 21 1997			

BRODART, INC.   Cat. No. 23 233   Printed in U.S.A.

JAMES R. BETTMAN
University of California, Los Angeles

An Information Processing Theory of Consumer Choice

 ADDISON-WESLEY PUBLISHING COMPANY

Reading, Massachusetts
Menlo Park, California
London • Amsterdam
Don Mills, Ontario • Sydney

To Joan and David . . . .
My optimal choices

This book is in the
ADDISON-WESLEY ADVANCES IN MARKETING SERIES
Yoram J. Wind: Consulting Editor

ISBN 0-201-00834-3
ABCDEFGHIJ-MA-798

Foreword

Professor James R. Bettman's *An Information Processing Theory of Consumer Choice,* the first monograph in the Addison-Wesley *Advances in Marketing Series* is an excellent example of the type of monograph sought for the series—innovative, integrative, and relevant work that advances the science and practice of marketing.

The book is innovative in its effort to present a systematic theory of consumer behavior. It builds on and expands Bettman's early work in the consumer information processing area and suggests new concepts, findings, and hypotheses in this important area of consumer behavior. It integrates the relevant concepts, theories, and findings from psychology with previous works in consumer behavior and provides an excellent synthesis of the diverse approaches to consumer information processing. The book is also relevant to the researcher, student, and practitioner in providing a conceptual and operational framework for the evaluation of current research and theory, for the generation of new research ideas, and even for some thought-provoking hypotheses of relevance to marketing management and public policy decision makers.

Combining these features in a single readable book, Professor Bettman, a creative and careful scholar, offers a stimulating intellectual challenge to marketing and consumer behavior scholars and practitioners who are concerned with the better understanding of consumer behavior.

I hope you will enjoy and benefit from the book as much as I did. *An Information Processing Theory of Consumer Choice* is a significant advancement in our understanding of consumer behavior. Keith Nave, Senior Editor at Addison-Wesley, and I are proud to present this book to the marketing community.

Yoram J. Wind
Series Consultant

Preface

The purpose of this book is to present an integrated theory of consumer choice using an information processing perspective. The book is intended for researchers and advanced students of consumer behavior who desire an in-depth treatment of information processing research and theories as they relate to consumer choice. The underlying thread is the focus on the choices made by consumers: which brands to purchase, which information to examine, which stores to patronize, and so on. Each of these choices can be thought of as a selection process among some set of alternatives.

In attempting to understand choice, the approach taken is to focus on the information used by consumers and how that information is processed. In particular, the theory consists of several components, each necessary for understanding choice: processing capacity, motivation, attention and perception, information acquisition and evaluation, memory, decision processes, and learning. An overall view of the choice process is presented; then each of these components is discussed from an information processing perspective and related to this choice model. The major assertions made in these discussions are stated as a set of propositions about choice processes. These propositions are intended not only to provide a summarization of the theory, but also to give some direction for future research.

The theory grew out of earlier work I had done on decision net models of choice, particularly as summarized in "The Structure of Consumer Choice Processes," *Journal of Marketing Research,* November, 1971. It had become obvious to me that this earlier work was insufficient in many ways, especially in its lack of an adequate treatment of many choice-related concerns: motivation, processing capacity, memory, attention, and information acquisition, for example. The theory presented in this book was the outcome of my attempt to flesh out the skeleton developed in this earlier work.

This book owes a great deal to many others, without whose contributions it could never have been written. There is an obvious intellectual debt to the work of previous researchers on choice. I would especially like to acknowledge my own indebtedness to the pioneering work in human information processing of Professors Allen Newell and Herbert Simon of Carnegie–Mellon University.

Many colleagues have contributed in various ways to the development of this book. I would like to thank Professor Martin Shubik of Yale University for introducing me to information processing and other approaches to choice, and Professor Gerrit Wolf of the Georgia Institute of Technology for providing many insights into choice in his role as my dissertation chairman at Yale. Professor Wolf also provided helpful comments on the first draft of several chapters of this book.

My colleagues at the Graduate School of Management at UCLA have been a continuing source of ideas and support. I thank Professors Harold Kassarjian, Richard Lutz, Carol Scott, and Barton Weitz for reading and commenting on portions of the manuscript and for discussions on many related topics. I also thank Professor Kassarjian for his unflagging encouragement throughout the course of the project. I especially acknowledge my deep gratitude to a former colleague, Professor Masao Nakanishi, now at Kwansei Gakuin University. Professor Nakanishi not only read and provided extremely helpful comments on the entire manuscript, but has provided intellectual stimulation throughout my career. Many of his ideas are found in this book.

Others at UCLA have also played instrumental roles. I thank the students in doctoral seminars based on earlier drafts of this book for many vigorous discussions: David Arch, George Belch, Marian Burke, Terrie Hogue, Mary Jane Sheffet, John Swasy, and Michel Zins. Finally, I would like to thank Kathy Lutz for her suggestions on memory processes and cognitive approaches to learning.

Many colleagues at other institutions have also been most helpful. Professor Jacob Jacoby of Purdue University introduced me to research on information acquisition and furnished other useful ideas. Professors Jay Russo (University of Chicago), John Payne (Duke University), Joel Cohen (University of Florida), Franco Nicosia (University of California, Berkeley), John Howard (Columbia University), and James Engel (Wheaton College) read and commented on portions of the manuscript, and have also given me many other valuable inputs relating to choice process research. I owe Peter Wright (Stanford University) special thanks, as he read the entire manuscript and provided very thoughtful comments. Professor Wright has also supplied a substantial flow of ideas on choice processes throughout our careers. Finally, Professor Yoram Wind (University of Pennsylvania) assisted me in many ways in his role as Consulting Editor of the Addison-Wesley *Advances in Marketing Series*.

My secretaries at UCLA have been remarkably congenial in typing the manuscript. Ms. Judy Sternberg, Ms. Naomi Yano, Ms. Beverly Welsh, and Ms. Joanne Norris performed magnificently in processing many drafts.

Finally, I would like to make note of two very special sets of contributions to this book. First, my parents, Roland and Virginia Bettman, have been constantly loving and supportive throughout my entire educational process. Second, my wife Joan and son David have provided me a depth of love and understanding without which it would have been impossible to write this book. Their tolerance and encouragement during the process of writing were a great gift to me.

April 1978   J.R.B.
Los Angeles

Contents

CHAPTER 1

Introduction

The focus of this book is on gaining an increased understanding of consumer choice. Consumers make many different kinds of choices: which brand to purchase; which store to patronize; whether to spend or save; which information to examine; and so on. Although the specific focus of all these choices differs, the basic element of selection among alternatives is still present. Thus choice among alternatives provides the central unifying concept behind the theory that is presented. The specific components used in the theory are all tied to this unifying theme of choice.

The particular approach taken to understanding consumer choice is to view the choice process from an information processing perspective. This view is outlined briefly below. Following this introduction, the reason for selecting an information processing approach is examined. This rationale includes both a discussion of the basic phenomena characteristic of the consumer choice environment and a brief attempt to position the information processing view relative to past research on choice. Finally, an outline of the remaining chapters is given.

AN INFORMATION PROCESSING
APPROACH TO UNDERSTANDING CHOICE

The basic approach to studying choice taken in this book is to view the consumer as a processor of information; that is, the consumer is characterized as interacting with his or her choice environment, seeking and taking in information from various sources, processing this information, and then making a selection from among some alternatives. This interaction with the environment may be minimal in some cases, and extensive in others. The theory of choice presented here examines the components necessary for understanding these choice-related phenomena. The basic components of the choice process considered are processing capacity, motivation, attention and perception, information acquisition and evaluation, memory, decision processes, and learning. It is important to reemphasize that these elements are considered as they relate to choice; that is, choice provides the focal point to which these other components are tied. There is a great deal of research in each of the areas cited above. However, not all of this research is relevant for understanding choice. Hence, the focus on choice processes allows us to be selective in our treatment of these components. A brief and simplified description of the information processing theory presented in this book is now outlined.

Consumers make choices to accomplish goals. Therefore, motivation is an important component of the choice process. Given some set of goals, the consumer devotes attention to that information available which is relevant to attaining those goals. The consumer then interprets this information in light of previous knowledge and the context in which the information is obtained; that is, the consumer must decide what a particular piece of information means. For example, high price may be seen as signifying that an item costs too much, that the item must be of high quality, that the store in which the item is found has high prices, and so on. Although much of this attention is thus directed by current goals, this is not always the case. In some instances, consumers will be distracted, and notice information which is not relevant to current goals: an interesting item, something which was surprising or unexpected, and so on.

For some choices, the information already at hand may not be sufficient, and the consumer may actively seek additional information. This information search may be internal, of information stored in memory; or external, of information available from advertisements, brochures, packages, friends, salespeople, etc. Again, this information is interpreted and evaluated by the consumer. While taking in and processing this information, the consumer may be comparing alternatives. Consumers are depicted as having a limited capacity for processing information. That implies that in this process of comparing and making choices among alternatives, consumers do not typically undertake complicated computations or analyses or engage in extensive processing. Rather, consumers use simple heuristics, or rules of thumb, to help them in dealing with potentially complex choice situations. Such heuristics as "Buy what I bought last time" or "Find the brand with the highest protein content" may be used to select an alternative. The heuristics used appear to depend on individual differences (e.g., the consumers' processing abilities); specific properties of the particular choice task being undertaken (e.g., what information on alternatives is available and how it is presented); and on the type of choice situation (e.g., for some situations the consumer may have a great deal of prior knowledge and experience, whereas for others there may be virtually none).

Finally, after a choice has been made and the alternative chosen has been consumed, the outcomes experienced also provide information to the consumer. The impact of these outcomes on future choices depends on how these outcomes are interpreted. For example, if a product does not perform satisfactorily, the consumer may decide it was because the product itself was inadequate and should not be purchased again; or that it was because the directions for using the product were not followed properly and the product should be tried again; or that it was because the particular item was a "lemon" and the product should be tried again.[1]

The discussion above should not be taken to imply that all choices will be characterized by extensive search for and processing of information. In many cases the consumer may simply choose what was chosen previously, or may be so uninvolved with the purchase that very little effort is exerted. Thus the processes described may be extensively used in some cases and only minimally used in others.

In all of the above, the emphasis is on the *processes* underlying choice. The details of the processes used are the focus, not simply the outcomes which occur. Thus the consumer is depicted as having goals, taking in information, actively processing and interpreting that information, and selecting alternatives. The consumer has limited capacity, and hence uses simple heuristics in doing all of this. Choice provides the focal point for considering the other concepts of the theory (e.g., motivation, attention, and so on). Tying these concepts to the choice process provides an integrating framework. Thus the *purpose of this book is to provide an integrated view of choice from an information processing perspective.*[2]

WHY TAKE AN INFORMATION PROCESSING PERSPECTIVE?

Two basic types of reasons for adopting an information processing perspective are considered below: an examination of some of the basic phenomena characterizing the consumer choice environment, and a consideration of shortcomings in other approaches to choice.

---

1. Other postpurchase phenomena could also be examined using this information processing view of choice. For example, choices are made throughout the entire consumption process: how to use the product (e.g., whether to use butter for cooking or not); how to maintain the product (e.g., whether the consumer or someone else should maintain it, or whether to repair or scrap a damaged product); and how to dispose of the product (e.g., whether to throw it away or recycle it [Jacoby, Berning, and Dietvorst 1977; Nicosia 1974]). Although the theory appears to be quite relevant for understanding such choices, they will not be considered to any great extent below to limit the scope of the undertaking. Such areas appear to be fertile ones for future research, however.

2. Although the focus is on consumer choices, the concepts developed should in general be applicable to analyzing other types of choices. The choices made by organizations or executives in organizations seem to be particularly interesting potential application areas.

PHENOMENA CHARACTERIZING
THE CONSUMER CHOICE ENVIRONMENT

One reason for taking an information processing view of choice is that some of the major phenomena related to consumer choice are concerned with the provision of information to consumers by various sources and consumers' reactions to that information.

Information is provided to consumers in many ways. Marketers provide information to consumers directly, in advertisements, on packages, via in-store displays, or in brochures. In addition, information is indirectly conveyed by such elements as the price of the product or the types of stores in which the product is sold. Public policymakers may also provide information to consumers, in advertisements, on packages, and so on. For example, nutritional information is put on packages, mileage ratings for cars are developed, or energy consumption levels for appliances are provided. Finally, the consumer also receives inputs relevant to choices among alternatives from friends, salespeople, family, and so on. These inputs may be advice before the choice, or in the form of reactions to the choice.

Thus the consumer is constantly being bombarded with information which is potentially relevant for making choices. The consumer's reactions to that information, how that information is interpreted, and how it is combined or integrated with other information may have crucial impacts on choice. Hence, decisions on *what* information to provide to consumers, *how much* to provide, and *how* to provide that information require knowledge of how consumers process, interpret, and integrate that information in making choices. From this perspective, information processing is a central component of choice behavior.

SHORTCOMINGS IN PREVIOUS RESEARCH ON CHOICE

Another reason for taking an integrated information processing approach to choice is that previous research on choice, despite its many contributions, appears to have shortcomings in providing an account of the phenomena discussed above. Some of this prior work is considered below. It is beyond the scope of this introduction to consider this previous research in depth. For futher details, the references given should be examined. In particular, this book does not provide a comprehensive survey of consumer research results. Some prior familiarity with the major areas of consumer behavior research is assumed.

Psychological research on choice
One shortcoming of much psychological research related to choice is that only limited aspects of the choice process are considered in any particular research stream. For example, recent psychological work has considered such

topics as motivation (Weiner 1972); attention (Kahneman 1973); memory (Norman 1969); and learning (Estes 1975) from an information processing point of view, but these topics are not tied to choice; that is, there is no attempt to develop an integrated view of choice utilizing these concepts. This may certainly be a necessary strategy if one desires to thoroughly investigate the factors influencing some given psychological process. However, if the focus is on choice phenomena, only selected aspects of these influences may need to be examined and integrated.

Some psychological work has attempted to develop an overall view of choice. Three such approaches are considered here: stimulus–response theories of choice; expectancy–value theories; and information processing approaches.

Stimulus–response approaches to choice. One model of choice behavior in psychology has been the stimulus–response approach. In such an approach, the attempt is made to characterize the links between stimuli and responses to those stimuli. The most completely specified approach of this type has been drive theory (Hull 1952; Spence 1956). In drive theory, behavior is seen as instigated by the onset of stimuli, such as feelings of hunger or some event in the external environment, which then leads to a state of drive. Based upon past patterns of reward and punishment, the individual will have various levels of habit strength for potential responses to the stimulus (e.g., those responses rewarded most often in the past will have higher habit strength). Behavior is then basically determined by the interaction of the level of drive and habit strength (i.e., behavior is a function of Drive × Habit). Further elaborations of this model have been carried out, but these are the basic components of the approach. It is doubtful that many psychologists currently espouse such a choice theory in its strictest form. However, discussing some of the assumptions sometimes made within this paradigm is useful for bringing out features of the information processing approach. Hence, the discussion should be read in this light, since most theorists recognize that drive theory is an inadequate basis for studying choice.

There are problems with the approach described above. First, humans are viewed as *stimulus-bound*; that is, the instigation of activity is seen as coming only in *response* to some stimulus. The stimulus is seen as the source of activation, therefore. The human being is seen as being in an inactive state without the energy provided by the stimulus. However, as Atkinson (1964), Hunt (1963), Weiner (1972), and others have pointed out, human beings may be better viewed as being active, exploring the environment and molding it to more clearly suit their purposes rather than merely passively reacting to stimuli. This view of the active consumer is clearly a part of the information processing view above. The consumer is depicted as an active participant in the choice process, not only as a passive observer. Consumers may actively select and acquire information, actively decide how much processing to engage in, and so forth. Of course, there are instances where passive reactions are found (e.g., watching a television commercial, perhaps), but the point is that such passive reaction is not the *only* process.

A second point is that information must always be *interpreted* by the consumer in light of the situation at the moment. The meaning of particular pieces of information is not fixed (even for internal physiological stimuli), but must be developed. Drive theorists in general did not consider such interpretation processes. However, the information processing view would imply that one must *interpret* the meaning of internal stimuli such as hunger pangs. The internal stimuli provide only one source of information for this interpretation. Other factors in the environment are also important. Many studies have shown that internal states can be interpreted in many different ways depending upon the context in which the individual is placed (e.g., Brehm 1962; Nisbett and Kanouse 1968; Schachter and Singer 1962; Valins 1966; Weiner 1972). Thus, the drive theory notion that stimuli have a fixed, unambiguous meaning must be rejected. Individuals actively interpret stimuli, and these interpretations can vary across individuals or across situations for the same individual.

A final shortcoming of drive theory is that there is no consideration of the details of how particular pieces of information are combined and integrated to make a choice, what pieces of information are attended to, the processes of information search, and so on. However, as noted above, such questions as how consumers make choices, what heuristics are used, and what processes are considered are important areas of investigation for understanding consumer choice. It is difficult to see how one could understand and impact consumer choices without examining some of the information processing carried out.

Expectancy-value approaches to choice. A second general class of choice theories is expectancy–value approaches (e.g., Tolman 1932, 1955; Lewin 1938; Atkinson 1964). In these models, behavior is determined by two components, expectancy and value. The expectancy component refers to beliefs that actions will lead to certain outcomes, and the value component refers to the value of these outcomes. For example, if E_i is the expectancy that an action will lead to outcome i, and V_i is the value of this ith outcome, then the overall value for an action is given by $\Sigma_i E_i V_i$. The action chosen would be that action maximizing this expectancy-value summation. This model takes some important steps not found in drive theory toward providing an explanation of choice. Individuals are viewed as having anticipations about whether actions will lead to goals (expectancies), and are viewed as trying to evaluate alternatives. Thus there is some consideration of the processes underlying choice. However, there are still several shortcomings.

First, the model assumes a fixed method for comparing alternatives, and this method (the $E \times V$ summation) may require a reasonably high level of processing effort and calculation to undertake. As noted above, however, consumers use a variety of simple heuristics, depending upon the choice situation and other factors.

Second, the expectancy–value approach, as applied to choice, has tended to focus on static phenomena — given a set of alternatives, the individual evaluates expectancies and values from memory, and makes a choice.[3] The processes of attention, information search, memory, effects of outcomes, and so on are not considered. Thus only a limited portion of the overall choice process is examined. In addition, the processes through which expectancies are derived or evaluations formed are typically not considered, although some recent research has attempted to consider these phenomena (Weiner 1972, 1974).

In summary, expectancy–value models are inadequate bases for an integrated theory of choice because in general they fail to consider the variety of heuristics used in making choices; fail to consider phenomena related to choice (memory, attention, and so forth); and fail to consider the detailed processes underlying the formation of expectancies and values.

Information processing approaches. As noted above, many information processing approaches in psychology consider only limited ranges of phenomena and are not focused on choice. However, some work in psychology has taken an information processing view of choice. For example, McGuire (1976) outlines an approach to studying choice. He examines such aspects as exposure, perception, comprehension, agreement, retention, information search and retrieval, decision making, and action. The discussion of exposure considers the factors which influence to what kinds of information a consumer will be exposed, including both demographic and psychological characteristics. In his treatment of perception, McGuire examines attention levels and selective perception. Comprehension deals with issues of encoding and understanding, and the agreement component involves considering how information is evaluated. Retention and information search and retrieval are mainly concerned with memory and search strategies. McGuire also considers the use of choice strategies and how information is integrated in his decision-making component, and finally discusses the actual act of choice. McGuire presents these components as successive steps in the processing of information. His framework thus appears to include most of the notions relevant to understanding choice. However, the framework is very general, and there is limited consideration of the interpretation of outcomes and future impacts of outcomes. On the whole, though, McGuire's conceptualization is interesting and quite consistent with the theory presented in this book.

Newell and Simon (1972) also consider an information processing theory of choice. They conceive of the individual as having information input

---

3. This static approach does not characterize all expectancy–value work. In particular, Lewin (1938) emphasized the dynamic nature of choice.

and output mechanisms, processes for interpreting and processing information, and memories for storing and retrieving information. Their work has been very successful in modeling problem-solving behavior, such as solving logic problems or considering moves in chess. Their emphasis on the study of the detailed processes underlying problem solving, the use of simple heuristics, the impact of goals, and the impact of properties of the choice task all have influenced the present theory a great deal. Although many aspects of their theory have provided valuable insights, their work has focused largely on well-structured problems, such as chess, proving logic theorems, or solving cryptarithmetic problems, in which the information available is fairly unambiguous and precise. Thus there is a gap between the typical tasks studied by Newell and Simon and those characterizing consumer choice. Hence, the work of Newell and Simon, although very influential on and very compatible with the present theory, does not provide a readily usable framework for understanding consumer choice.

Thus research on choice in psychology, particularly the information processing approaches, provides some valuable inputs for the present theory. However, the frameworks reviewed do not seem sufficient in themselves for understanding consumer choice.

Consumer choice research

As was the case with much psychological research, a great deal of consumer research considers limited portions of the choice process. In the early stages of research on consumer behavior, the impact of demographic factors (income, age, education, etc.) on choice was considered. When this approach proved inadequate, studies of motivational factors (Dichter 1964, Martineau 1957; Newman 1957) on choice were carried out, followed by an emphasis on the impacts of personality factors (Kassarjian 1971). Major research efforts in brand loyalty (Jacoby and Kyner 1973) and scaling approaches to understanding choice (Green and Wind 1973) followed. Recently, work on attitudes (particularly expectancy–value models of attitude) has been a dominant interest (Wilkie and Pessemier 1973). In these endeavors, only a small portion of the choice process has been considered, and important findings have resulted. However, factors such as memory, attention, information search, and so on have not been studied, for the most part. There have also been more comprehensive attempts to model consumer choice and there has been some recent work on consumer information processing. Some of these efforts are now considered.

Comprehensive theories of consumer choice. Several major comprehensive theories of consumer choice have been proposed: Nicosia (1966); Engel, Blackwell, and Kollat (1978); Hansen (1972); and Howard and Sheth (1969). Howard (1977) has also recently proposed a more information processing oriented point of view. A detailed comparison of the theory presented in this book with these theories is presented in Chapter 12. However, a few summary comments can be provided at this point.

These earlier theories and the present theory all have certain common elements (Lunn 1974), such as a focus on choice as a process, the belief that choice has causes and can hence be explained (see Bass [1974] for an opposing view),[4] and the belief that consumers often actively search for and process information. However, there are also differences between these prior models and the present approach. First, none of these theories takes a very detailed information processing approach. Howard (1977) provides perhaps the most extensive treatment, but does not provide a detailed analysis. As another example, Howard and Sheth (1969) use a great many stimulus–response notions based on Hull's (1952) drive theory in their formulation. Second, these other consumer choice theories generally propose a limited range of heuristics for consumers. For example, Howard and Sheth and Hansen propose expectancy–value models. Howard (1977) and Engel, Blackwell, and Kollat (1978) consider more heuristics, but still do not discuss a broad range in detail. Third, the present theory provides a more comprehensive analysis of the impacts of properties of the choice task (e.g., how information is presented, where the choice process is carried out) than these previous theories.[5] Other differences exist and are discussed in Chapter 12, but it appears that these existing consumer choice theories, despite their impressive contributions to our understanding, do not provide a completely adequate framework for understanding consumer choice from a detailed information processing perspective.

---

4. The theory presented in this book holds that choice is conceptually deterministic. However, in application, due to problems of measurement error, definition of concepts, and so on, there will be a stochastic component. Thus it may be useful in some cases to consider a particular choice itself as the phenomenon of interest, and in others to consider probability or likelihood of purchase. In this book, the focus is generally on the choice itself rather than probability of choice. The implications of the concepts presented for studying likelihood of purchase are left for future research.

5. This impact of properties of the task on choice has been stressed by Newell and Simon (1972), as noted above. Man is viewed as using simple heuristics to adapt to the choice environment. As Simon (1969, p. 25) states, "A man, viewed as a behaving system, is quite simple. The apparent complexity of his behavior over time is largely a reflection of the complexity of the environment in which he finds himself." This notion of the dependence of choice processes upon task influences may appear to contradict the view of the individual as an active processor presented above. It is certainly true that the consumer's environment (what brands and information are available and how these are displayed, for example) will influence the choice process. However, the consumer must still actively interpret and utilize the information available in the environment in developing and implementing choice heuristics. The structure of this information may make particular interpretations and inferences more plausible or easier to form than others, but the consumer is still actively interacting with the environment in light of his or her goals. As Neisser (1967, p. 305) states, "Although we cannot always see only what we want to see, we can generally think what we like."

Previous work in consumer information processing. There has been a good deal of recent research into aspects of consumer information processing. This work has tended to make contributions to understanding relatively narrow aspects of the choice process, with no overall framework attempted. For example, some research has concentrated on the provision of information to consumers (e.g., Jacoby, Speller, and Kohn 1974a,b; Russo, Krieser, and Miyashita 1975; Wright 1973a; Wilkie 1975a; Jacoby 1975); other research on the particular heuristics used by consumers (e.g., Wright 1975; Alexis, Haines, and Simon 1968; Bettman 1970; Russ 1971; Payne 1976b); and still other research on information acquisition (e.g., Newman and Staelin 1972; Jacoby, Chestnut, Weigl, and Fisher 1976). This and other important research on consumer information processing is not reviewed in any detail here, as it is considered later throughout the book.[6]

Thus there is at present some valuable knowledge, but no integrated framework available for studying choice from an information processing perspective. It has been argued above that such a perspective can be extremely useful for understanding choice. The major goal of this book is to provide such a framework. Only the most relevant phenomena for that purpose are discussed, therefore. Other topics treated by consumer researchers which are not central to the choice process are treated tangentially, if at all.

AN OUTLINE OF FOLLOWING CHAPTERS

In Chapter 2 an overview of the theory is presented, providing a general framework for the following chapters, in which detailed components of the theory are examined. Several examples of consumer choice scenarios are presented, and each of the components of the theory is briefly outlined.

Chapters 3 through 9 discuss the major components of the theory. In each of these chapters, the major assertions made are stated as propositions about consumer choice. In addition, since the theory is dealing in many cases with phenomena which have not received much research in the consumer realm, each of the chapters attempts to outline the major areas where research is needed for the particular topic studied.

Given the importance of goals and motivation in consumer choice, the motivational mechanisms postulated are presented in Chapter 3. The flow of information provides a focus for the next several chapters. Chapter 4 considers

---

6. In a recent article, Chestnut and Jacoby (1977) attempt to provide a partial framework for applying information processing notions to consumer choice, focusing generally on perception and memory phenomena and in particular on encoding, conscious decision making, and long-term memory. They distinguish seven "sectors" of the consumer information processing system: automatic encoding, trace activation, conscious encoding, spectator behavior, participant behavior, operational memory, and long-term memory. Their framework seems quite compatible with portions of the theory presented in this book, and represents a promising effort toward developing an information processing view of consumer choice.

perception and attention, with Chapter 5 concentrating on processes of information acquisition and evaluation. Chapter 6 deals with the important role memory processes play in consumer choice. Chapter 7 considers decision processes, including a discussion of various types of choice heuristics, how these heuristics are implemented, methods for studying choice processes, and processing limitations to which consumers are subject. Research on decision nets, one particular type of choice heuristic, is presented in Chapter 8. Finally, learning processes are discussed in Chapter 9, particularly the impact of outcomes on future choices. Each chapter considers the effects of properties of the choice task and individual differences as appropriate.

Chapters 10 and 11 discuss implications of the model. Chapter 10 focuses on implications for public policy decisions, and Chapter 11 considers applications to marketing decisions. Finally, Chapter 12 compares the present theory to other major theories of consumer choice, and summarizes those aspects of the theory in most need of future research.

CHAPTER 2

Overview of an Information Processing Theory of Consumer Choice

It is useful in presenting the theory of consumer information processing and choice developed in this book to begin with an overview of the basic structure of the theory. Detailed examinations of the major concepts utilized are contained in later chapters. The overview begins with a brief discussion of the variety of choices made by consumers and the impact of this variety on developing a choice theory. Then several brief examples of hypothetical consumer choice processes are presented. Finally, each of the major concepts used in developing the theory is introduced and related to the choice scenarios.

One of the basic difficulties confronting the study of consumer behavior in general and the development of any theory of consumer choice in particular is that consumers make an enormous variety of choices. These choices often have different properties which make generalizations about the processes used difficult. For example, different choices may be characterized by different degrees of prior experience with the particular decision in question; by different amounts of information available in the shopping environment; by different amounts of time available for making the choice; and so on. Thus these differences can stem from properties of the individual consumer, properties of the existing set of alternatives, properties of the specific choice situation, etc. In addition, consumers make choices at many different *levels*. Choice of a particular brand from a set of alternatives, although the focus of most consumer research, is not the only type of choice made. Consumers must decide about whether or not to examine various pieces of information, which attributes to consider in evaluating brands, when to make a purchase, how to pay for purchases, how to use purchases, how to dispose of products, and so on.

The facts that choices are characterized by different levels and by different properties of other sorts can lead to difficulties, because the different types of choices which result may require different processes and strategies from consumers. One would expect different strategies, for example, between situations in which the consumer had made a choice many times previously and situations in which the consumer was making a choice for the first time. This makes depiction of a choice theory quite difficult. A general outline may be applicable, but detailed predictions will vary with the nature of the specific choice task considered. In an attempt to deal with this problem, several different choice scenarios are presented below. Then a general discussion of the theory is presented, with examples of how each specific scenario might require different emphases. Thus in general, a major contention of this book is that an understanding of the decision processes used by consumers requires careful analysis of the properties of the different types of choice tasks faced by consumers.

EXAMPLES OF CONSUMER CHOICE SCENARIOS

CHOICE SCENARIO 1

Jane Jones notes that she has used up a jar of mayonnaise. She puts mayonnaise on her shopping list. She has bought a particular brand for a long time and intends to buy that same brand when she goes shopping again.

CHOICE SCENARIO 2

Mary Smith, while reading through an issue of a magazine, sees a casserole recipe that looks interesting to her. She decides to try the recipe. One of the ingredients called for is a type of sauce mix she has not bought before. She puts the sauce mix on her list. When she goes shopping and finds the sauce mixes, she sees that there are several alternatives. She briefly looks at the packages and notices that the ingredients seem roughly the same, and the prices are also virtually identical. She feels frustrated that the package information is of no help. She thinks she recognizes the package for one mix, although she cannot recall where she has seen it before—perhaps in a commercial or at a friend's house, she thinks. She decides to buy this brand and try it. Later that week Mary makes the recipe and serves it. Unfortunately, it does not turn out well. The sauce, in particular, is too runny. Mary checks the sauce package and sees that she made a mistake and added too much liquid. She decides to try the recipe again and writes down the same sauce mix on her shopping list.

CHOICE SCENARIO 3

Jerry Baker and his family have just moved to a new home, and the family needs to purchase a washing machine. Since they will be moving into the house from their apartment in a few weeks, they must make a decision fairly quickly. Jerry and his wife have never purchased a washing machine before. They discuss the features desired, particularly the cycles available and color. Since Jerry approaches most choices with a great deal of thoroughness and prides himself on his ability to get the "best" brand at the best price, he decides to get some information about washing machines. He remembers that a friend, John Haskell, has recently purchased a washing machine, and also recalls that a recent *Consumer Reports* issue rated washing machines. Since the *Consumer Reports* issues are stored in the basement and he is upstairs, he decides to first call his friend. John is not there when he calls, so he leaves a message and goes downstairs and finds the *Consumer Reports* issue instead. He is reading the article when John calls him back. They discuss John's experience with his choice and also stores where discounts are available. In particular, John tells Jerry about two retailers who offer substantial discounts. Jerry returns to the *Consumer Reports,* and spends a good deal of time looking at the table in the article which summarizes the brands and their features. He decides that one brand looks best, based upon rough criteria about price, service record, and water usage. He shows this brand to Mary, who notices that the tub size is relatively small, which would lead to more washes. This feature leads them to reject this brand. Jerry then shows Mary another brand that he had felt looked good, and they decide on that brand.

Jerry now shifts to finding the brand they have chosen at the best price. He knows from previous experience that one discount store has very good prices, and he has found two other possible sources from his call to John Haskell. He calls these two and finds that one does not carry the brand he and his wife have chosen. He writes down the price and warranty terms for the other retailer. He and his wife now go to the discount store and see that their price is slightly more than that of the other retailer. They are about to leave when his wife notices that this store offers a two-year warranty in contrast to the one-year warranty offered by the other retailer. They decide to pay slightly more to get the longer warranty and order the machine from the discount store.

CHOICE SCENARIO 4

Sue Terry is faced with a decision about where to go to college. She is an excellent swimmer, and wishes to go to a school with a good women's athletic program. She has received letters from several schools that are interested in giving her an athletic scholarship, each accompanied by brochures on the athletic program at the school. She decides to apply to the four schools with the top-ranked women's swimming teams in the country. She is undecided about which school is her first choice. One school's swimming team has dominated women's intercollegiate swimming for several years. Sue wonders if she would be among the top swimmers in her event at that school. She believes that the coaching might be better there, but that she might not be able to swim in many meets. A second school, which is recruiting her very heavily, does not have quite as good a team, but has an excellent overall women's athletic program. They have brought in a new coach who had coached two Olympic medalists in Sue's event in the past. Sue is certain she can be the top or second best swimmer in her event on this team. Sue cannot decide which of the two schools she prefers, and finds it very hard to trade off the idea of a better team (which will probably win the national championship) and a school where she is more assured of competing. Sue vacillates back and forth as to which school she prefers. Finally the dominant school calls to say that they are sorry, but they will not be able to offer her a scholarship. Sue decides to go to the second school.

BASIC CONCEPTS OF THE THEORY

The brief scenarios presented above depict a range of choice processes. The general structure of an information processing theory of consumer choice is now presented. Following the introduction of the basic concepts of the theory, the application of the concepts to the scenarios will be considered.

Figure 2.1 presents an overview of the major concepts utilized in the theory. The basic elements of the theory are the concepts of processing capacity; motivation; attention and perception; information acquisition and evaluation; use of memory; decision rules and processes; and consumption and learning. Each of these concepts is defined more fully below. In addition, mechanisms for continually examining the environment (a scanner) and interrupting current behavior if necessary, and means for interpreting and handling conflict are needed.

Finally, although not shown specifically in Fig. 2.1, the operation of the theory is influenced by three other factors: individual differences, situational influences, and effects of different types of stimuli. Individual differences can impact the way most of the components are utilized. Different consumers will have different processing skills, goals, prior experience, and so on. For example, Jerry Baker in Scenario 3 goes through a very detailed search process for washing machines, which might not characterize many other consumers.

Situational influences can also play a role in the way the components of the theory operate. An individual may make different choices when shopping with a friend or when under time pressure, for example. Finally, the same individual in the same situation may react differently to different types of stimuli. For example, a viewer might react very differently to humorous and serious commercials for the same sponsoring company seen during the same television show. These three types of influences may modify how the various components might operate and interact for any specific choice. The major impacts are discussed in later chapters as appropriate.

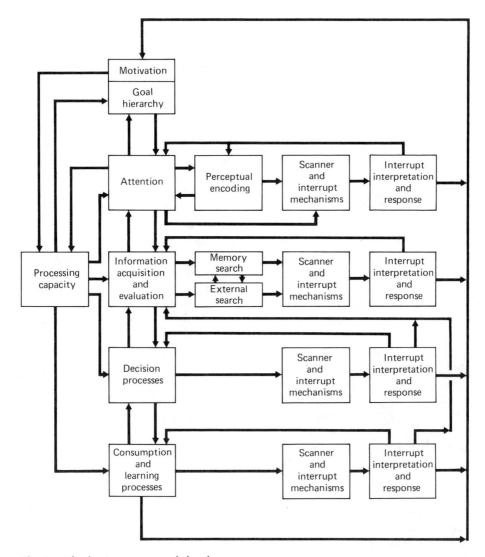

Fig. 2.1 The basic structure of the theory.

PROCESSING CAPACITY

Many authors have hypothesized that human beings have a limited capacity for processing information (e.g., Simon 1969; Norman and Bobrow 1975; Lindsay and Norman 1972; Slovic 1972a). This implies that in making choices humans cannot make complicated computations or engage in extensive processing without a good deal of effort. Also, human beings tend to be limited in the extent to which they can carry out many activities at the same time. These notions are very important for a theory of choice, because such limitations will affect the kinds of strategies or rules that are feasible for consumers to use in various choice situations.

This notion of effort or processing capacity impacts the various stages in the choice process; that is, such components of choice as motivation, attention, information search and retrieval, and so on are subject to the constraints imposed by the fact that consumers have limited processing capacity. This limited capacity must be *allocated* to the various activities engaged in by the consumer. Some basic questions (Kahneman 1973) which must be considered are then (1) what influences the demands upon capacity a particular task makes? (2) how is capacity allocated among competing activities? and (3) what are the effects when activities compete for capacity?

One very basic effect of capacity limitations that will appear again and again is that consumers develop heuristics, or simple rules of thumb, that enable them to deal with complex situations without requiring more processing capacity than is available. For example, consumers often limit the numbers of brands or attributes considered to simplify choice. In Choice Scenario 4, Sue Terry limits consideration to four colleges with excellent swimming teams rather than examining more of the huge set of colleges which exist and are potential alternatives for her. In Choice Scenario 1, the consumer chooses the same brand again and again, which requires little processing capacity. However, a great deal of processing capacity can be allocated to a choice process if the consumer so desires, as depicted by the extensive processing carried out by Jerry Baker in choosing a washing machine in Choice Scenario 3. Thus the major points are (1) that capacity exists and must be allocated, whether by a conscious decision or nearly automatically by learned rules and (2) that choice tasks are often so complex relative to the capacity available that simplifying heuristics are used.

MOTIVATION

Consumers are continually making choices. These choices are made to achieve certain purposes, or to accomplish some goals. Motivation is thus a crucial concept in any theory of choice. We will begin the presentation of an information processing theory of choice with a discussion of motivation, although the choice process is in essence continuous, without a real "starting" and "ending" point. A more detailed analysis of motivation is given in Chapter 3.

Motivation affects both the direction and the intensity of behavior; that is, motivation is not only directive, affecting choice of one behavior over another, but also refers to the energizing and influencing of the intensity of actions (e.g., the amount of capacity allocated to a particular activity). The concept of motivation used in the model is cognitive. Thought processes affect the structure and interpretation of one's goals. In this conception, how one interprets even basic biological processes can be affected by information processing considerations. For example, subjects' judgments about the meaning of internal phenomena (e.g., whether an aroused feeling is interpreted as hunger, anger, fear, joy, and so on) have been shown in many studies to be greatly influenced by the information given to subjects (examples are Schachter and Singer 1962; Valins 1966; Nisbett and Kanouse 1968). Thus, human beings interpret the meaning of events in light of the information available to them and how it is presented. The meaning is *not* inherent in the event itself.

In developing a specific notion of motivation, the choice process is depicted theoretically as a process of moving from some initial state toward some desired state (Newell and Simon 1972); that is, at the beginning of some choice process, the consumer is characterized as having some amount (possibly none) of information relevant to the choice, certain resources (e.g., money available to spend), and so on. The consumer must progress from this initial state to the desired state, which in most cases will be consummation of a purchase. In moving from the initial state, through intermediate states, and eventually to the desired state, the consumer uses strategies and heuristics.

Given this view of choice, motivation is viewed as a set of mechanisms for controlling this movement from one state to another (Simon 1967). In particular, two basic mechanisms are proposed: a hierarchy of goals, and an interrupt mechanism and "scanner." The scanner and interrupt mechanism are discussed below. For the moment the concept of a goal hierarchy is considered.

A *goal* is defined in this book as a specific state which, when attained, is instrumental in reaching the desired end state. This desired end state will be called the goal object. For example, if the consumer sets out to buy a washing machine, the desired end state, the goal object, is presumably to obtain the "ideal" washing machine, given the consumer's criteria. A set of goals may be seen as a set of intermediate states which need to be attained to move toward the goal object (e.g., "Decide what attributes are important to me" or "Find the cheapest store carrying this brand"). Then the choice process may be seen as the consumer's progress through such a set of goals. Goals thus specify purposive behaviors whose enactment is necessary to progress toward the goal object.

Since any goal can usually be broken down into more detailed units, the idea of a *subgoal* is necessary. A subgoal of a particular goal is simply a state which needs to be attained to obtain that particular goal; that is, for some specific goal, say "Find sources of information on product X," the subgoals relative to that goal might be "Look in the *Consumer Reports* index" and "Call store Y."

The concept of a subgoal is related to that of a plan. *Plans* are defined as those specific procedures or actions taken to achieve a goal (Miller,

Galanter, and Pribram 1960). But given the discussion above, a plan is equivalent to the *set* of subgoals of a goal. In the example of subgoals above, the plan is to look in *Consumer Reports* and call Store Y. Plans can also be considered goals (e.g., looking in *Consumer Reports* is a goal), just at a more detailed level than the original goal. Thus, depending upon the level of detail one chooses for analysis, a particular state can be seen as a goal or a plan. This again points up the need to specify carefully the level of analysis.

The essence of the concept of a goal, then, is that consumers progress through some sequence of goals and subgoals (states) in making a choice. Note that the emphasis is on relatively detailed states specifically related to the processing of information. More basic states (e.g., hunger, need for affiliation, salvation, and so on), which we will term *motives*, are not the focus.

The notions above can perhaps be clarified and the concept of a goal hierarchy best introduced by example. Consider the choice of a washing machine made by Jerry Baker in Choice Scenario 3. Let us begin not at the level of deciding on whether or not to purchase a washing machine, but at the point where Jerry has decided to make such a purchase and now wants more information about washing machines.[1] Jerry may have a sequence of broad goals such as those shown in the top portion of Fig. 2.2, "Determine which attributes are important," "Evaluate alternatives on these attributes," "Obtain the best alternative." To accomplish the goal of determining which attributes are important, Jerry decides to do three things: talk to his wife, call John Haskell, and look at *Consumer Reports*. These can be seen as subgoals of his original goal, dropping down one level of detail. This set of three subgoals is then his *plan* for attaining the goal, "Determine which attributes are important." Again, note that when we change the level of detail considered, those subgoals that were seen as a plan at one level become goals at the more detailed level. Each of these more detailed subgoals could now have further detail added. For example, to read the *Consumer Reports* article, Jerry has to go downstairs and locate the right article. The level of detail which is appropriate will depend upon the purpose of the analysis. For a study of use of information sources one would be quite interested in the second level of analysis in Fig. 2.2, the determination of the three sources used, but not with the third level.

Jerry must accomplish not only the goal of determining which attributes are important, but also his other goals. He must, in our example, evaluate alternatives on the attributes he has decided to examine, and decide

---

1. For simplicity the goal hierarchy does not show all of the goals which might be relevant. For example, one could imagine that at a more aggregate level goals related to having clean clothes or taking care of one's family might be relevant, whereas at a more detailed level one could consider goals related to how to trade off two attributes, and so forth. The decision about which way to get clothes clean (e.g., buy a washing machine versus use a laundromat) is also not considered, but is assumed to have already occurred.

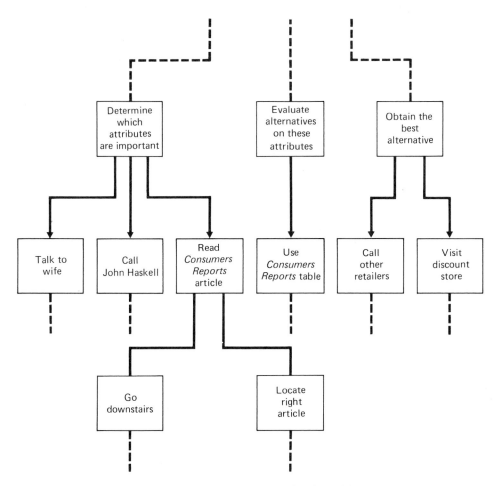

Fig. 2.2 Example of portions of a goal hierarchy. The dashed lines represent portions of the hierarchy not detailed in the example. For instance, the three initial goals might be subgoals of a goal "Purchase a washing machine." The subgoals given could be further subdivided, and so on.

where to obtain the alternative he has selected. Note that Jerry does not necessarily work on only one goal at a time. Although goals may have some natural sequencing, progress can often be made on several goals simultaneously (Reitman 1965). For example, while using the *Consumer Reports* table, Jerry may be evaluating alternatives at the same time he is deciding which attributes are important. Thus the current use of the term goal hierarchy differs from notions such as Maslow's (1954), whose hierarchy of motives implies that one motive *must* be satisfied before another becomes relevant. There will be some sequencing in the progress on goals, but also often some simultaneous progress. More detail could be added in this example, such as considering Jerry's choice of a store once he has chosen a brand, but the purpose of the example in introducing the concept of a hierarchy of goals has been served without adding further complications.[2]

The example above shows how a hierarchy of goals can be developed during a choice process. The hierarchy of goals existent at any particular time functions to guide behavior. The goals themselves may be developed through a procedure where goals at some level (e.g., "Determine which attributes are important") are considered as an end, and more specific plans (or sets of subgoals) are developed for attaining that end. This type of procedure has been called means-ends analysis by Newell and Simon (1963). Such a means-ends process would *also be a choice process* and follow the basic structure shown in Fig. 2.1. Thus the entire process of setting up a goal hierarchy can itself be a choice process. In many other cases, individuals would have learned strategies that they would use in developing these more detailed goals.

Several aspects relating to the concept of goal hierarchy should now be considered. First, the example above represents one kind of process for developing a hierarchy. In the example, Jerry was very thorough and developed a relatively detailed hierarchy. However, in many cases, consumers might develop only very broad goals, and develop subgoals only when they were actually shopping in the store. For example, in Choice Scenario 2, Mary Smith might only know that she wants a sauce mix before she goes to the store. In the store she may develop more detailed subgoals or plans while she is actually making the choice. Thus, these two scenarios depict one type of difference in choice processes, the degree to which the goal hierarchy is constructed outside of the store, prior to shopping, as opposed to being developed at the store, while shopping.

A goal hierarchy is probably in general continually being constructed and developed as a choice process proceeds, rather than being developed in its entirety, stored in memory, and retrieved as a whole. Development of the next steps in the hierarchy and progress on current goals probably occur simultaneously. Thus Jerry Baker presumably did not develop his entire hierarchy and only then begin processing; rather, he probably developed some initial goals and then developed further details of the hierarchy as he progressed. Almost nothing is known about how processing capacity is allocated to these two competing activities of current processing and development of future plans. There are undoubtedly differences in the extent to which consumers develop their hierarchies, whether one step at a time or several steps ahead. These differences probably occur both between individuals and between different choices for the same individual.

---

2. A consumer presumably will have many goal hierarchies relevant for various aspects of his or her life which exist or can be constructed. At any one point in time, goals relevant for consumer choices will be intermingled with hierarchies for other types of goals. This implies that there needs to be some mechanism for being able to shift from one set of hierarchies to another as the occasion demands.

A second important facet of goal hierarchies concerns the extent to which such hierarchies must continually be consciously constructed. For many choices, the consumer will have already worked out a strategy which has proven successful, and this strategy may simply be a learned unit that can be used. It need not be developed each time a choice is required. A common example of the effects of learning is shown in Choice Scenario 1, in which the goal hierarchy is essentially trivial, "Buy Brand X." More detailed subgoals such as "Drive to the store" and so on do not need to be explicitly considered, as the entire pattern of responses leading to the attainment of the goal has been learned. Consumers do have learned rules and simple strategies that they use for many situations, and in these situations complex goal hierarchies are not used. However, in other situations consumers may need to develop such hierarchies when their knowledge is limited and such development is deemed to be worth the effort required.

Thus there is a hierarchy of goals, and these goals direct the consumer's behavior during the decision process. This notion of a goal hierarchy speaks not only to the directional influence of motivation but also to the influence on intensity. The number and the complexity of the goals in the hierarchy will be related to the amount of processing needed to attain these goals. The intensity aspects can be accounted for in several ways. A consumer could have a general goal about how much processing to undertake that determines the intensity of behavior by affecting the details of the goal hierarchy formed. For example, in Choice Scenario 3, Jerry Baker decided to engage in an extensive information search. Factors that influence such general goals for the extent and depth of choice processes are discussed in more detail in Chapter 3 (such as time pressure and conflict). The important point is that the consumer may often *decide* how much processing capacity to allocate and how detailed a process to follow.

Such a conscious decision may not always be found, however. The choice environment itself may influence intensity. For example, in Choice Scenario 2, Mary Smith found that the information available on packages of sauce mix did not discriminate among the brands. Thus a great deal of processing of that information was not useful. Mary instead decided to simply try a brand she thought she recognized. Trial was a more effective source of information than more processing. In general the amount of processing will be a function of both the degree to which the choice environment allows various amounts and also of the amount of processing desired by the consumer *a priori*. Finally, degree of prior experience will also influence this processing intensity. For habitual decisions, a learned response strategy may be extracted from memory with little analysis. For unfamiliar decisions, on the other hand, more extensive processing might be carried out.

The notion of a goal hierarchy has now been examined. To complete the discussion of the motivation component of the theory, the notions of a scanner and interrupt mechanism need to be considered. The description above implies that consumers progress methodically along, carrying out goal after goal in completing a goal hierarchy and obtaining the desired goal object. This is an inadequate depiction without some procedure for interrupting progress toward a goal if demands so require, and without some procedure for distractibility. Human beings are not totally single-minded in their pursuit of goals (Neisser 1963; Simon 1967). Simon (1967) proposes a set of procedures. He postulates a *scanner*, or a mechanism for continually monitoring events occurring in the environment, for noticing when conditions require changes in current activities. In addition, Simon proposes that there is an *interrupt mechanism* which can actually carry out the interruption, stopping progress on current activities and initiating responses to the conditions encountered. In general the main function of the scanner and interrupt mechanisms is to allow for adaptation to changing conditions. Thus, the goal hierarchy, rather than being fixed, may change or be restructured in response to demands of the moment. For example, in Choice Scenario 3, Jerry Baker decides to call John Haskell before he reads *Consumer Reports*. John is not at home when he calls, however. At this point Jerry could wait for John to get home or go read *Consumer Reports*, and chooses the latter. When John calls, this is an interrupting event to his reading. Jerry could finish the article and call John back, but chooses instead to stop reading, talk with John, and then go back to *Consumer Reports*. A final example in Scenario 3 occurs when Jerry's wife notices the difference in warranties, and their criteria for choice are restructured as they make a trade-off between price and warranty length.

In general, a major source of interrupts is departure of environmental conditions from those expected or anticipated (e.g., John Haskell's not being home, the warranty's not being as expected, a store's being out of stock for an item, and so forth). Other sources are considered in Chapter 3. In the case of all of these interrupts, the consumer must decide whether current goals still make sense, and if not, must change the goal hierarchy. Thus, motivation is a pivotal concept: the goal hierarchy provides direction for other stages in the theory, and feedback from these other stages (e.g., events which lead to interrupts while processing) lead to changes in this hierarchy. Note also that although environmental factors often lead to interrupts, the consumer's *response* to these interrupts need not be determined solely by the interrupting condition itself, but may be the result of a choice process. For example, Jerry Baker and his wife had to decide what to do about the warranty difference they noticed. Thus the consumer's behavior is often goal-directed and shows active decision making, and is not necessarily passive and responsive only to the stimulus. The response resides in the consumer, not in the stimulus.

In summary, then, choice is seen as a process of moving from an initial state to some desired state. A goal hierarchy depicts the steps necessary to make this movement. In the course of carrying out the steps of the goal hierarchy, events may occur which lead to interruption of progress and changes in goals.

ATTENTION AND PERCEPTUAL ENCODING

Attention and perception are important elements in explaining choice behavior. The particular information attended to and perceived can have a great impact on choice. Kahneman (1973) distinguishes between two basic types of attention, voluntary and involuntary. Voluntary attention is now considered, with involuntary attention considered below.

Voluntary attention refers to the conscious allocation of processing effort to activities related to current goals and plans; that is, given a goal hierarchy, the particular goal being pursued leads the consumer to direct attention to those aspects of the environment relevant to attaining that goal. If one has a goal to "Find an economical freezer," for example, then one may attend to data on price, operating expenses, and so on if any information about freezers is obtained.

Perceptual encoding refers to the process by which the individual, having attended to some stimulus, interprets that stimulus; that is, the individual develops some notion of the meaning of the information he or she has devoted attention to. For example, a brand's symbol, say an automobile symbol, is interpreted in light of the consumer's knowledge, and may not be interpreted as an automobile symbol if the consumer is unfamiliar with that symbol. As another example, a particular protein level for a cereal is assessed in light of what the consumer knows about other cereals, or even other protein sources. Thus the interpretation of stimuli requires an analysis utilizing information stored in memory. Most theorists currently believe that this is a process in which an interpretation is actively constructed using both information from memory and the perceptual input itself (Lindsay and Norman 1972). One property of such a process, since the focus is on constructing interpretations quickly that are consistent with our concepts in memory, is that individuals tend to look for and see what they expect, to perceive expected configurations or patterns of stimuli. This type of process is termed an active-synthesis process by Lindsay and Norman.

The results of the perceptual interpretation of stimuli will often influence the subsequent direction of attention. For example, perception of a price figure on the package may lead to attention's being directed to a unit price shelf tag. Thus attention and perceptual encoding continually interact.

The description above assumes attention and perception are governed totally by the goal hierarchy. As noted above, this view of consumers as being nondistractible and unresponsive to external events is unrealistic. One also attends to events *not* directly related to current goals. Kahneman (1973) considers involuntary attention to be allocation of effort to stimuli based more upon automatic mechanisms than upon current goals. For example, most individuals will respond to a loud noise near them, a novel stimulus, and so on. As noted above, such events then lead to interrupts. The notions of scanning and interrupting mechanisms were introduced to deal with these events and conditions which lead to interruptions of current processing. Two types of interrupt-ing events seem most relevant to attention and perceptual encoding: conflicts, and learning about the environment. Each of these types of events is now dis-cussed below.

Conflict arises because an individual has competing and incompat-ible response tendencies (Berlyne 1957). Conflict during perceptual encoding and attention can arise from parts of the environment which are competing for attention (e.g., a man wishes to listen to an advertisement on his car radio and also sees a billboard he wants to read); disagreement between what was per-ceived and what was expected (e.g., a consumer is surprised when a price change is noticed or a package design has been changed); and so on. Berlyne (1961, 1968) argues that the impact of novel, surprising, and incongruous stimuli stems from the conflict induced by such stimuli.[3]

Conflict arising from perception and attention would ordinarily lead to an interrupt (Berlyne 1961). The specific effects of such an interrupt, the reactions to conflict, depend on the individual and his or her state at the time. Several theories (e.g., Hansen 1972; Howard and Sheth 1969) of consumer choice postulate optimal level theories; that is, there is some optimal level of conflict for an individual, and if conflict or some similar construct is below this optimal level, actions are taken to increase conflict. If conflict is above the optimal level, actions are taken to decrease conflict. The present theory does not assume a mechanistic response pattern. Instead, conflict is assessed, and decisions are actively made about whether it can be tolerated; and if not, how it can be handled. Of course, for conflicts arising from attention and per-ception, there are probably many cases where responses are more automatic and less dependent upon response strategies. For example, individuals will usually turn toward a loud noise or source of movement, and so on. In other cases, however, such as when a price is different from what was expected, re-sponse strategies will be used. The consumer may ignore the price change, switch to a cheaper brand, and so on. Thus the notion of active conflict re-sponse strategies, rather than some fixed pattern of responses, is central. This, of course, makes theorizing more difficult, since different response strategies may be used by different consumers, or by the same consumer in different situations.

There are many different sources of conflict: interpersonal, choice-re-lated (from many different choice conflicts), and so on. Reactions to conflict from any one source may depend on the levels of conflict from all the other sources. In any case, human beings are simply too flexible to be limited to a single pattern of responses to conflict. Many consumers *may* follow this pat-

---

3. Hunt (1963) points out that physiologically the effects of conflict among and frustra-tion of plans, and the effects of incongruity between inputs and expectations may be carried out by separate systems in the brain. This may mean that effects of conflict and incongruity should be separated in the model. However, physical distinctness does not necessarily imply psychological distinctness.

tern hypothesized in the earlier theories, but need not necessarily do so. Responses to conflict may include ignoring it, changing the emphasis on certain criteria, search for new information, reanalysis and reordering of goals in the goal hierarchy, and so on.

The second major type of interrupt event is different in its nature. Consumers may often learn about the purchasing environment, even if such learning is not directly relevant to current purchases. This type of phenomenon has been studied in psychology under the label of "latent learning" (Hilgard and Bower 1966). Learning about the environment can arise from interrupts when something happens to attract the consumer's attention. For example, a package may be explored because it "looks interesting." Such exploration would probably not occur under high time pressure, however. This exploration should probably be distinguished from learning that occurs because the consumer has a specific goal of learning about some aspect of the consumer environment, although a purchase is not planned in the near future. For example, a consumer may always read calculator advertisements in the newspaper, although purchase of a calculator may be far in the future.

Effects of interrupts, such as conflict and learning about the environment, on the choice process itself depend on the strategies followed by the consumer. Often, these interrupts may lead to changes in the goal hierarchy. Goals may be reordered, a goal may be added to the hierarchy, goals may be deleted, goals may be redefined, and so on. One class of responses resulting from interrupts that is particularly relevant for consumer choice is information search. Little research on interrupts and their effects on choice processes has been done. Mintzberg, Raisinghani, and Theoret (1976) provide some evidence on interrupts and their impacts in the context of organizational decision making, however.

There are two major sequences described above: voluntary attention to and perceptual interpretation of information relevant to current goals; and involuntary attention to and perceptual interpretation of interrupt events, particularly due to conflict and learning about the environment. Both of these sequences assume attention is allocated. However, there is also evidence that learning about the environment can occur with minimal conscious allocation of attention. Many researchers have studied this phenomenon, in different disciplines and under different labels: e.g., "low involvement learning" (Krugman 1965; Robertson 1976); "incidental learning" (McLaughlin 1965); "spectator learning" (Posner 1973). These approaches differ in their definitions and in their research methods, but all refer to the basic idea of learning about the environment passively, with little conscious involvement, and without such learning's being directly tied to some current goal. Thus learning about the environment can occur in two ways, through reactions to interrupts and through low attention passive processes.

Examples of the phenomena discussed above occur in the scenarios. In Scenario 1, Jane Jones' noticing that the mayonnaise is used up is an interrupt event that is easily resolved by putting the item on the shopping list. In this case the particular response strategy is one which has been carried out many times. However, such a standard response need not be carried out. If Jane is going on vacation she may decide not to replace the mayonnaise. Thus, although in many cases standard responses to interrupts may have been learned, interpretation of the meaning of the interrupt event and development of a response may be necessary. This latter case occurs in Choice Scenario 3 when Jerry and his wife must react to the departure from expectations on the washing machine warranty. In this case, an interrupt leads to changes in goals (the criteria for evaluating brands in this case).

Learning about the environment also occurs in Choice Scenario 2. Mary Smith notices a recipe for a casserole because it seems interesting. Her reaction is to decide to make the casserole, although it might have been to remember the recipe was there and vow to cook the casserole "sometime." Also, note that learning about the environment under low involvement may have occurred previously, since she can vaguely remember one brand, but not the source of this remembrance. Finally, note that in all scenarios the consumers attend to and perceive items of information which are related to attaining their goals.

Summarizing this component, consumers attend to and perceive those aspects of the environment relevant to attaining current goals in the goal hierarchy. However, interrupts can occur which may lead to changed goals and redirected attention. Conflict and learning about the environment are two major sources of interrupts. Learning about the environment may also occur with little conscious allocation of attention.

INFORMATION ACQUISITION AND EVALUATION

In making a choice, the consumer may retrieve information from memory, and in some cases search for further information if that in memory is not sufficient. The goals being pursued will clearly influence the direction of attention and hence the information examined. Thus, information acquisition and evaluation are heavily influenced by motivation, attention, and perception. In this section, acquisition and evaluation of information as components of choice are discussed. Further details are given in Chapters 5 and 6.

In simple habitual choice situations, a consumer may immediately make a decision, with no need for further information beyond that needed to actually choose the item (e.g., recall of the brand name or recognition of the package). In more complex choice situations, in which there is a specific goal for information search or in which an interrupt has occurred, more information may be needed.

Initially, search may be internal, with memory being searched for relevant information. Retrieval may not always require conscious effort, as information may be readily accessible through strong association with a stimulus. For example, the consumer with a favorite brand purchased frequently may not have to engage in complex retrieval strategies to obtain the brand name or to recall properties of the brand. However, in other situations, more conscious processing effort may be required. Jerry Baker may need to think for a minute to remember which friend had recently bought a washing machine, for example.

Upon searching memory, there may not be sufficient information. If so, more information may be sought externally. This may involve changing the immediate goal hierarchy (e.g., going to a store and looking, looking for another brand on the shelf, etc.), and redirecting attention and perceptual encoding. Also, memory is constantly searched in interpreting the external information found. The actual information found will heavily influence the future course of the search. Eventually, this process will be completed and information will be deemed sufficient for the moment. Information search is seen in several places in the scenarios. Jerry Baker calls a friend, reads *Consumer Reports*, calls two retailers, talks with his wife, and visits a store; Sue Terry examines brochures; and Mary Smith examines packages.

The decision about when information search should be stopped is influenced by many factors. For example, the original goal about the depth and extent of the process, discussed above, is relevant, as are information availability, the perceived "costs" of obtaining information (e.g., time costs, monetary costs, effort required), and the value of the information in helping to make a choice. The conflict response strategies used by the particular consumer will also be a factor. A detailed analysis of these factors and others is undertaken in Chapter 5. In the scenarios, Jerry Baker undertakes the most extensive search process. In essence he decided to invest a good deal of effort in analyzing his choice. Mary Smith decided to stop searching and simply try the product when she found that the information available was not helpful. Finally, Sue Terry did not search for more information in her attempt to resolve her school choice conflict. Rather than attempting to find out more about her chances of swimming at the dominant school, Sue made assumptions about her chances and pondered the choice as if those assumptions were true.[4]

The processes discussed above assume active search for sources of information, whether from friends, packages, advertisements, and so forth. How is information intake from advertisements handled in the model when the consumer is not actively searching for this information? For example, a television commercial may be seen for a product for which the consumer has no

---

4. Some consumers may search a great deal, and some may search very little or not at all. In these latter cases, the low amount of search could be due to prior knowledge, a cost–benefit trade-off, or even avoidance of information. It would be difficult to actually distinguish active avoidance from the results of making cost–benefit trade-offs, however.

purchase goal in mind. The earlier discussion of learning about the environment is relevant. In effect, the commercial is an interrupt from the television show. Given the interrupt, a goal reordering may occur. One possible goal is to input the information in the commercial, hence attending, encoding, interpreting the information in the light of what is in memory, and so on. Learning may even occur if no conscious effort is made at all, as discussed in the previous section (Krugman 1965; Robertson 1976; McLaughlin 1965; Posner 1973). Here the interrupt is built into the television show, and the response strategies to the interrupt are the important factor. Mary Smith's response to the recipe presented in her magazine is of this type. The fact that much of consumer learning may be of this type, without a specific information search goal, implies that studies of information search during the purchase process are very misleading if only external search is monitored. Internal search for previously learned information is also extremely important. Thus Jerry Baker, in Choice Scenario 3, *did not need to visit* several discount stores to check prices for his washing machine choice, because he already knew from learning on previous shopping trips unrelated to the washing machine choice that a particular discount store had the best appliance prices. He also knew that *Consumer Reports* had an article on washing machines, and thus did not search for other sources.

The discussion above focuses on intake of information. As information is acquired, it is also processed. In the low involvement learning cases just presented, this processing may be minimal. However, in general the incoming information is actively processed and evaluated. Consumers generate thoughts about the information they acquire while that information is being processed, namely their reactions to that information; that is, one may say to oneself that the arguments presented in an ad are good ones, misleading, not believable, and so on.

The information processed may also be put into memory. Factors affecting memory are complex and plentiful, as discussed in Chapter 6. Consumers may use memory in different ways in the process of choice. For example, Mary Smith uses *recognition* in making her choice, whereas the other scenarios present examples where *recall* is used for the most part. Recognition is often an effective strategy, since much detailed information need not be stored because the consumer can use the "external memory" (Newell and Simon 1972) of the package at the time of selection; that is, much information actually appears on the package, is available in the store, and hence need not be stored in memory in detail. This may narrow search processes, however, since examining a great deal of information from packages is time-consuming if more than a very limited number of brands is considered. Other examples of the use of an external memory are writing a shopping list or writing down prices or other data (e.g., Jerry Baker in Scenario 3).

Finally, the scanner and interrupt mechanisms may also impact information search and retrieval. One major cause of an interrupt could be conflicting information, whether from differing external sources, between an external source and what is stored in memory, or between expectations and an external source. Again the conflict is assessed and a decision is made about how to handle the conflict (e.g., the Bakers' decision about trading off length of warranty and price). This conflict handling might involve discounting a source or one's memory, seeking more information, and so on. A second major cause of an interrupt can be lack of information. In this case, the decision may be made either to proceed with this lack, or to pursue further information. In the case of Mary Smith, the information available did not allow her to make a distinction between brands, so she bought a brand based upon relatively hazy recognition, without further search. Finally, other interrupts might be due to encountering a cue which led to retrieval of previously "forgotten" information or a cue which reminded one of a goal which had been forgotten. These interrupts could lead to a revision in the goal hierarchy and recycling through the process.

Thus information search may be needed to attain specific goals in the goal hierarchy. This search may be internal, of memory, or external. Information is in many cases actively evaluated by consumers. The particular information found may lead to interrupts and changes in goals.

DECISION PROCESSES

Choices have been required in most of the previous components of the theory. For example, choices about which goals to pursue, what information to examine, and when to stop searching for information have been necessary. This presence of choice in these components implies that the entire choice process is a cycling procedure, rather than a simple sequential flow. For example, if a conflict arises at the perceptual stage, information search and a decision of some sort may be necessary to resolve the conflict, with possibly even changes in goals as a result. Then attention might be directed toward some new part of the environment, and so on. Thus the decision process component of the theory is a vital one, continually being used.

The major focus of the decision processes component is on comparison and selection of alternatives. Consumers use heuristics, or rules of thumb, to accomplish these comparisons. It could be argued that the detailed rules used for comparing alternatives are simply one level in the goal hierarchy, that eventually the subgoals developed are choice criteria. This conception is related to the notion above that choice occurs at many different places in the theory, in that choice of goals and choice among alternatives are seen as simply being different levels of detail of the same goal hierarchy. For example, in the case of Jerry Baker in Scenario 3, one could add subgoals to his goal "Use *Consumer Reports* table" depicted in Fig. 2.2. These more detailed subgoals might be of the form "Find all machines with water usage less than X," "Find all machines with better than average service records," and so on.

These subgoals, then, are factors used in comparing alternatives and eliminating some alternatives from consideration. Even more detailed subgoals might be considered. Thus choice among alternatives can be viewed as one level of the goal hierarchy, implying that there is no strictly separate decision process stage. However, given the interest in the specific choice rules used by consumers and the central role of decision processes in understanding choice, it was decided to examine decision processes as a separate component of the theory.

There are many different proposals for depicting the choice heuristics used by consumers, ranging from linear rules for combining ratings of attributes to branching flowcharts. As noted above, limitations in processing capacity lead to development of heuristics, or rules of thumb, rather than use of detailed or complex computations. Some alternative types of heuristics can be seen in the scenarios. For example, Jerry Baker appears to use some kind of rule where trade-offs are made among price, service record, water usage, tub size, and warranty length. One alternative is rejected because it does not have a satisfactory level for tub size. Note that when this alternative is rejected, Jerry goes back to another alternative he had processed earlier, rather than beginning the entire process of evaluating alternatives again with new criteria (Wright and Barbour 1977). Heuristics such as testing earlier selections to see if new criteria are met are common in consumer choice, since they allow complex tasks to be handled more simply than if extensive processing were undertaken. Sue Terry uses a simple one attribute rule to make her initial decision about where to apply for college: she chooses the schools in which the swimming programs are rated first through fourth. Alternative proposals for choice heuristics are reviewed and assessed in Chapters 7 and 8.

Different rules of thumb may be used by different individuals or by the same individual in making different choices. Thus there are in general important impacts of specific choice task properties and individual differences on how alternatives are compared. For example, in the washing machine scenario, Jerry Baker is able to use a relatively complex heuristic, partly because he has information easily available in tabular form in a *Consumer Reports* article. If the information had not been summarized in a table, but only in several manufacturers' pamphlets, or had been available only by reading tags on each machine while in the store, then the comparisons made would not have been so easy. In addition, Jerry might not have been able to get data on as wide a set of alternatives, but may have been limited to those in some particular stores. Thus the form of Jerry's decision process is intimately tied to properties of the choice environment, namely the information available and how that information is organized. Also, note the individual differences apparent in Jerry Baker and Sue Terry's contrasting approaches to making a choice. Effects of individual difference and choice task properties on choice heuristics are considered in detail in Chapter 7.

Specifying the heuristics used is not the only characterization of decision processes that is needed. One must also examine how a choice heuristic is implemented, or carried out. Any given heuristic can be carried out by using different methods. This concept of implementation method is best explained by presenting an example. One set of methods is discussed below. Other types are examined in Chapter 7, and determinants of the usage of each type of method are also considered.

One set of methods for implementing choice processes considers two views of the nature of the processing carried out. According to one view, one has available a repertoire of strategies or decision rules already existing in memory and some process which in effect calls these strategies when needed, much in the same manner as a computer program uses subroutines. Thus the heuristic to be used is already built, exists in complete form in memory, and is directly retrieved in choosing an alternative. Some calculation or processing may go on to carry out this preexisting rule but at no moment is this rule changed or built up. It is retrieved in its entirety. This might be called a *stored rule* method for implementing choice heuristics. Jane Jones is described by this kind of decision process in Scenario 1. A simple rule ("Buy Brand X") is directly retrieved from memory and implemented.

A second basic view regarding the implementation of choice heuristics is that a constructive method is used (Neisser 1967). In this case, heuristics for processing alternatives are developed from fragments or elements existing in memory. These elements may be beliefs, evaluations, combination rules, simple heuristics, and so forth: that is, choice heuristics may not be stored in their entirety in memory, but may exist only as fragments — subparts which are put together constructively at the time of processing, at the time of making a decision or a choice. The person may have only a general plan which guides the construction of a heuristic in a specific situation. The process is reconstructed each time needed, using the elements in memory. Thus rules may differ from one situation to the next, depending on how the fragments or elements are combined, and depending on which elements are more salient in the situation. Note that one implication of the notion of a constructive method, of the idea that rules are synthesized at the time of use, is that one cannot say decision rules are developed "following" information search. Rather, rules are probably often developed simultaneously with search: as information is examined, pieces of the rule are constructed, and this may lead to a new search. Thus there may be many information search-decision process-information search cycles. The decisions of Mary Smith (Scenario 2), Jerry Baker (Scenario 3), and Sue Terry (Scenario 4) all are characterized by some degree of construction, by some amount of development of the decision rule *during* the actual process of choice.

Both of these methods are probably used to implement choice heuristics. Processing may be constructive when a decision is made for the first few times or in a changed situation. In new or changed choice situations, rules will tend to be built up from elements rather than recalled as units. The constructive method will thus be most evident when there is little knowledge of the particular choice situation, or when previously developed rules are felt to be inapplicable. Under these conditions, the constructive elements are mainly built up from information available in the specific task environment, and rules for combining these elements are developed. In such cases the task environment, particularly the information available and how that information is presented, has a great effect on the resulting decision process which is constructed. However, if the consumer has had prior experience with a particular choice, elements may exist in memory and, if used frequently over time, the elements may become organized into an overall response strategy in memory. In this sense, use of stored rules is seen to be the result of learning as the constructive process is repeated. At any point in time a particular consumer will thus be engaged in construction for some decisions and usage of stored rules for others.

This distinction between constructive activity and use of learned, stored rules is related to the different types of choice processes postulated by almost all recent theories of consumer choice (e.g., Howard and Sheth 1969; Engel, Blackwell, and Kollat 1978; Hansen 1972; Howard 1977). In essence there is a habitual decision process, a process with moderate processing, and a process with extensive processing. For example, Howard and Sheth distinguish among routinized response behavior, limited problem solving, and extensive problem solving.[5] Howard (1977) presents the most detailed account to date of these three types of processing. These types of processes can be characterized by the types of implementation methods involved. In routinized response behavior, a stored rule is simply applied directly from memory (Jane Jones in Scenario 1). In limited problem solving there is some construction. Some elements may already exist in memory and can be utilized. Some information search may also be needed to determine how alternatives compare on those aspects considered by the choice heuristic used. Mary Smith's choice in Scenario 2 seems to be roughly of this type. She appears to have a notion that ingredients and price should be compared and attempts to do this, but decides, since these attributes will not discriminate, to rely on recognition of a brand seen previously. Some construction is undertaken, but not an extensive amount.

In extensive problem solving the decision rule may be constructed after a good deal of information search, including development of relevant criteria (Howard 1977). The elements for constructing a heuristic may be wholly or in large part developed from newly acquired data; these elements are not

---

5. A similar distinction was made for industrial buying in Robinson, Faris, and Wind (1967), who distinguish between straight rebuy, modified rebuy, and new task situations.

existing in memory. The decision by Jerry Baker in Scenario 3 is of this type. Extensive search (talking with his wife, calling John Haskell, reading *Consumer Reports*) is undertaken to determine criteria and develop some decision rule. In this case, much of the constructive activity takes place outside of the store, probably due in large measure to the fact that the information in the *Consumer Reports* table was more easily utilized than in-store information. In many choice situations, information available in the store might be easier to use, so that constructive activity would be carried out in the store.

The decision made by Sue Terry in Scenario 4 is difficult to categorize, as her process seems mostly passive. Brochures are sent to her, and she seems to make no further search. Her main action is to choose the four schools with the best swimming programs. Choice criteria are never firmly established, as she has great difficulty trading off being able to compete with quality of the team. Since the criteria issues are never really resolved, presumably this example is a kind of extensive problem solving. Although we have dealt extensively only with the stored rule-constructive distinction above, as noted earlier, other types of methods are also important, and are considered further in Chapter 7.

Finally, interrupts can also occur at the decision process stage. Conflict between criteria may occur. For example, Sue Terry, as noted above, had great difficulty with conflicting criteria. In this example, the mode of conflict resolution was passive. Sue never did resolve the conflict herself; events in the environment (the top school's decision not to offer a scholarship) led to its resolution. Also, Jerry Baker and his wife faced a conflict between warranty length and price. They resolved the conflict by trading off these criteria, deciding that an extra year's warranty was worth more than the price differential. Another type of interrupt may stem from the lack of information needed to develop a heuristic (i.e., feelings of "If I only knew X"). This type of interrupt can lead to search for the information, making of the decision in spite of the lack (if the information is not available or requires a good deal of effort to obtain), or perhaps even postponing or not carrying out the choice.

In summary, decision processes occur throughout the course of choice-determining goals, selecting information, comparing purchase alternatives. Consumers use various heuristics, depending upon both individual differences and choice task properties. Consumers may also use various methods for implementing choice heuristics, depending upon the choice situation and their degree of knowledge.

EFFECTS OF CONSUMPTION AND LEARNING

After a purchase is made and the alternative chosen has been consumed, the outcomes experienced can serve as a source of information to the consumer. The impact of any particular outcome on future choices depends on how the outcome is interpreted, on the specific *inferences* made about what caused the outcome. Differing inferences about the cause for an out-come can lead to differing actions on the consumer's part. For example, a consumer may determine that an undesirable outcome was due to not following directions properly or was due to a poor product. The actions taken as a result of the outcome might differ for these two inferences. Thus Mary Smith, in Scenario 2, decided that the poor results with the sauce mix occurred because she added too much liquid, and she decided to try the sauce again. If she had not bothered to check to see if she had followed the instructions properly, she may have decided not to try the recipe again or to try it with a different sauce mix. Thus the view of learning in this book is that outcomes provide information that can be interpreted. Future responses may not be impacted automatically by the outcome realized. Instead, consumers may make inferences about why particular outcomes occurred, and their future responses will in general depend upon what inferences were made.

After the consumer has decided why an outcome occurred, several types of action are possible, depending upon these inferences and upon the consumer's goals. The consumer may decide to do nothing, or may decide to make some changes in the choice heuristics used. Several types of changes in choice heuristics are possible. Two of the major types are simplification and elaboration.

If the consumption experience was as expected, simplifications may be made in the choice heuristics used. For example, certain patterns of attributes may be taken for granted. The heuristic will then become simpler. A common instance of this process occurs when the consumer reduces a more complex heuristic to "Choose Brand X" if experience with outcomes has been good and the inference is made that this is due to Brand X itself. Another instance might occur in which a consumer, after trying several brands, feels that they are roughly the same. Then more complex heuristics for comparing these brands might be simplified to "Buy the cheapest," for example.

A second type of change in choice heuristics may be an elaboration of a heuristic, as the buyer learns from outcomes to discriminate among brands. More criteria may be added to accomplish this increased discriminating power. In both of these types of learning, the actual extension or modification of the heuristic may not in fact occur until the next purchase occasion. The consumer may instruct himself or herself to "Remember to do X next time" or "Be sure to check Y." Details on the effects of consumption outcomes and learning are considered in Chapter 9.

OTHER FACTORS INFLUENCING CHOICE PROCESSES

As noted above, factors such as individual personality or predispositions, specific choice task or situational factors, and effects due to particular types of stimuli have not been explicitly represented. However, as the discussions of the sections above make obvious, the influence of these variables is very important. Such factors as choice of conflict management strategies, abilities to use memory, and so on are clearly personal factors. Different types of choice tasks may require different processes. Situational effects are seen in the interrupts as well as several other places. One would expect differences in choice processes for different people in similar situations, and for the same person in different situations. Finally, different types of stimuli might be treated differently. The effects of these aspects are discussed in later chapters as appropriate.

A SUMMARY OF THE CHOICE PROCESS

This chapter has examined the basic features of the consumer choice process from an information processing viewpoint. A goal hierarchy is seen as guiding the process, with interruptions for conflicting stimuli, unexpected events, etc. Thus the process is goal-directed, requiring active consumer participation. The hierarchy may be continually constructed, expanded, simplified, or modified as the process progresses. Attention is guided by these goals (subject to interrupts), and by perceptions. Memory retrieval is crucial in interpreting perception, guiding and interpreting the results of external search. Finally, decisions are continually being made at various points in the process.

The discussion has pointed out the complex interactive nature of the process. The process is not strictly sequential, but a continual branching and looping. For example, attention and encoding may be interrupted by an unexpected stimulus, which implies memory search to interpret it, perhaps decision processes, and cycling back to a revised goal hierarchy (Mintzberg, Raisinghani, and Theoret [1976] give examples of such cycling in organizational choice situations). A more detailed view of this process, based upon the discussions above, is presented in Figs. 2.3 and 2.4.

The concepts introduced have been presented within the context of understanding choice behavior. However, there are a great many interactions among the concepts. Goals direct other aspects of the process but may themselves be modified by feedback from these other aspects. The process, as mentioned, is a cyclical one rather than a strict goals-attention and perception-search-choice sequence. This raises the question of how one can make predictions using the theory. There are two basic difficulties. First, different types of choices may require different processes, as discussed above. Second, choices are made at many levels in the process, which leads to the cycling behavior. For example, choices must be made about which goals should be pursued next in constructing a goal hierarchy, when information search should be stopped, etc. The complications in the analysis of consumer choice in general may arise from attempting to treat different phenomena within one framework. Thus for making predictions one should concentrate on the particular type of choice and level of choice of interest; that is, different features of the general information processing approach may be more relevant for different

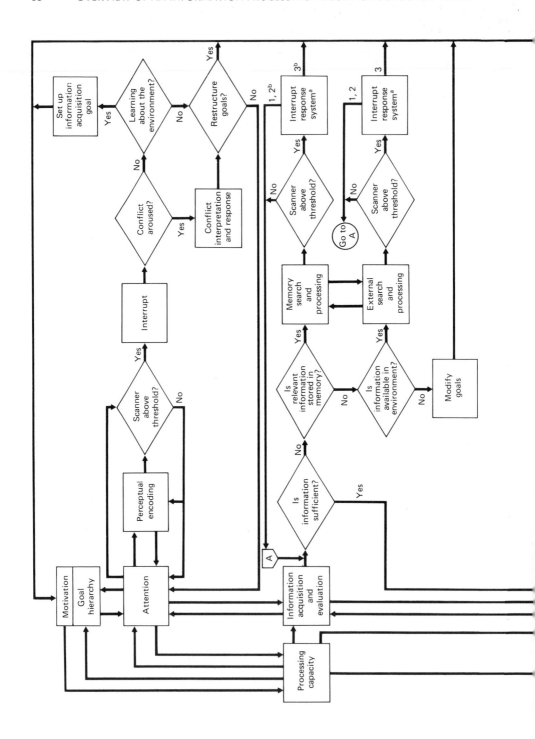

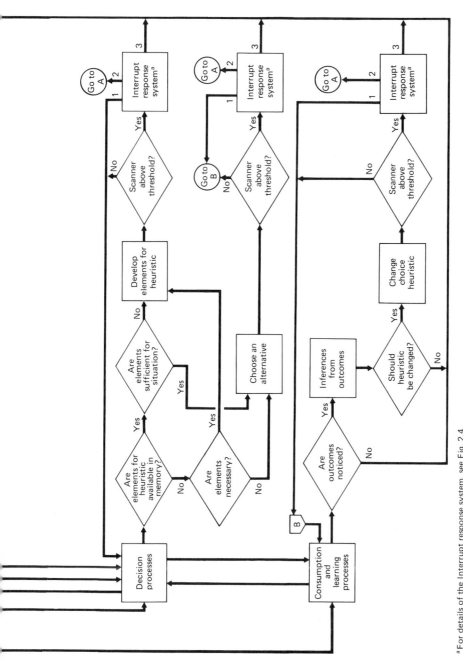

[a] For details of the Interrupt response system, see Fig. 2.4.
[b] These numbers are used to designate responses detailed in Fig. 2.4.

Fig. 2.3 The proposed theory in detail.

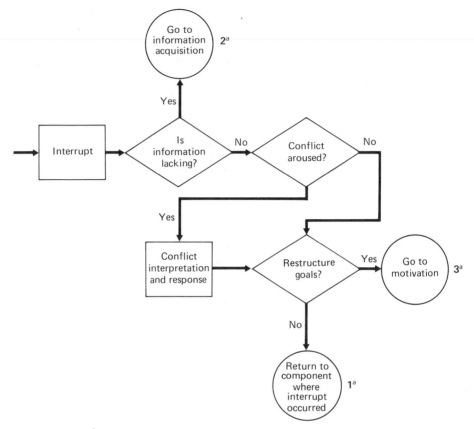

[a]These numbers are used in Fig. 2.3 to denote the appropriate responses.

Fig. 2.4 Details of the Interrupt response system.

choice problems. An analysis of the properties of the particular choice problem of interest can often yield insights into the kinds of decision processes which will be used (Newell and Simon 1972). Analysis of the multitude of different consumer choice tasks is obviously beyond the scope of this book. General principles guiding consumer information processing are presented. However, in the following chapters attempts will be made to examine some of the characteristics of choice problems which may lead to different types of choice processes.

One final point to be made is that the consumer is not always consciously making decisions about every choice and every piece of information encountered. The consumer would have time only for thought and not for action! Although conscious decision processes are often involved, there are also many situations in which learned rules and procedures are simply applied, in which reactions are in essence automatic. Different conditions may lead to varying degrees of conscious decison making. Such factors as degree of previous experience, importance of the choice, whether expectations are met, individual differences, and so on have been mentioned above as examples of these differences in conditions. Thus in general the choice process will take different forms for different people and even the same person in different situations.

Differences in the form of the choice process appear in the four Choice Scenarios presented. In Scenario 1, Jane Jones interrupts what she is currently doing when she notes she is out of mayonnaise. She forms a new goal of putting mayonnaise on her shopping list. When she shops she will need only minimal attention, perception, search, and decision process stages, as her goal is simply to "Buy Brand X."

In Scenario 2, the decision process is again characterized by an interrupt to learn about the environment, which leads to a set of goals relevant to making the recipe. Before Mary Smith goes to the store, only a simple goal hierarchy is developed (probably only a vague goal of getting a sauce mix). Attention is directed to the packages, and an interpretation of the meaning of the information found there is developed. The information search processes and construction of a choice rule seem to occur simultaneously. An interrupt occurs when Mary realizes the information available will not allow her to make a choice, and she deals with this by noting that she has a vague memory of one of the packages. After using the sauce mix, Mary's disappointing experience is interpreted as being a result of not following instructions.

The washing machine choice in Scenario 3 is probably the most complex process depiction. In this scenario almost all of the decisions are made consciously, as there is little prior experience. Goals are formed, attention is directed toward attaining these goals, external information search is carried out. Again the initial construction of a decision rule seems to be done simultaneously with search. Several interrupts occur (e.g., John Haskell is not at home when he is called, the warranty terms are not as expected), and goals are restructured in response. Decisions are made at many different levels, with a good deal of cycling. Also, Jerry's prior information is used many times in the process.

As noted above, Sue Terry's college choice in Scenario 4 is a very passive one. Information is received but does not appear to be sought, goals are formed but goal conflicts are never really resolved, and so on. In this process only limited search is carried out (e.g., she does read the brochures and apparently either knows or finds out which are the schools with the top four swimming teams). In this decision, environmental events (e.g., brochures arrive, one college decides not to offer her a scholarship, etc.) seem to basically determine the process.

In all four examples there is a commonality in that the basic components of the theory are utilized. The differences arise in the emphasis and extent to which each component is used and the degree of cycling involved. In the next chapters this commonality in information processing, the use of the basic components, is explored in more detail.

CHAPTER 3

Motivational Mechanisms in Consumer Choice

In examining choice, among the most basic questions are "Why was a particular choice made?" or "What was the purpose of that behavior?" Such questions have typically been dealt with as issues of motivation. The study of the motivation of behavior has elicited numerous and varied responses in psychological research. The major emphasis in most views of motivation is on explaining the determinants of the *direction* of behavior and of the intensity or *vigor* of behavior. In understanding consumer choice, it is clearly important to clarify the factors influencing preference for one alternative over another, the direction question. This may involve choice among items of information, choice of one brand over another for a particular product class, choice of one product class over another, or even choice of spending versus saving. In addition, consumer choice behavior can be characterized by different levels of intensity or vigor in the processing underlying a choice, ranging from minimal processing to a great deal. There are great differences in the amount of information sought, analyses performed, and in general in the amount of energy devoted to consumer choices, both across decisions for the same individual and across individuals for similar decisions.[1]

Surprisingly, there has been very little empirical research on motivational factors in consumer choice. Practitioners of motivation research in the 1950s attempted to analyze deep-seated needs and desires with some initial successes (e.g., Haire 1950), but methodological shortcomings led to the downfall of this research stream (Martineau 1957; Newman 1957; Dichter

---

1. Some writers consider additional questions for a theory of motivation. Atkinson (1964), for example, sees the persistence of behavior as crucial; that is, one must explain when one activity will stop and another begin. Hunt (1963) lists eight basic questions a theory of motivation should consider. Although additional questions can be raised, we will focus on direction and intensity for the most part.

1964). Other research, such as that on benefits sought in purchasing (Haley 1968), psychographics (Wells 1975), particular motives such as fear (Ray and Wilkie 1970; Sternthal and Craig 1974), or consumer values (Henry 1976; Vinson, Scott, and Lamont 1977), has examined issues relevant to consumer motivation, but has not systematically focused on relating motivation to choice. Given this overall lack of research, this chapter presents a general framework for portraying the structure and processes involved in consumer motivation. *Specific* motives, benefits, or goals underlying consumer choices are not considered in detail. Although many major theories of motivation have been proposed and researched in depth (e.g., Freudian theory [Freud 1948], drive theory [Hull 1952], expectancy–value theories [Lewin 1938]), the focus in the present theory of choice is on a cognitive approach, with an emphasis on the role of thinking processes in the selection and carrying out of one's goals. The rationale for this choice was presented in Chapter 1 and is not repeated here. For another general consideration of consumer motivation, see McGuire (1976).

OVERVIEW OF THE MOTIVATION COMPONENT

Before specific notions about motivation are presented, it is helpful to discuss the general nature of the choice process. The choice process may be characterized theoretically as a progression from some initial state relative to a choice to some desired state; that is, at any point in time the consumer may be characterized by what is known or what has been accomplished relative to the particular choice in question. Presumably the desired state is to select an alternative, i.e., to consummate the choice. The initial state might range from having virtually no knowledge about the choice to perhaps knowing the alternative to be selected and the steps needed to obtain it in cases where the same alternative is habitually selected. Given some beginning state, the consumer may use various strategies and heuristics (simple rules of thumb) to move from that state toward the desired state. This conception of choice is termed "search through a problem space" by Newell and Simon (1972). This notion is also similar to Lewin's (1938) field theory view of behavior as movement along a path toward a goal (Kassarjian 1973).

Motivation may be viewed in this context as the mechanism governing movement from one state to another (Simon 1967). The set of mechanisms proposed was outlined in Chapter 2. Basically, it is postulated that consumers develop a set of goals which are to be achieved in progressing from the initial state toward consummation of the choice. Since each goal may normally be broken down into more detailed subgoals, a hierarchical structure of goals, termed a goal hierarchy, results. The consumer is conceptualized as developing an initial goal structure, which may be quite general, and elaborating this structure as necessary throughout the choice process. Consumers are able to keep track of roughly where they are in the process at any point in time and are able to decide when to terminate facets of the process (e.g., when to stop looking for information).

At some points in the process, events may occur which were unanticipated, or the consumer may become distracted. A system which notices what happens in the environment (a scanner) and a system for stopping what one is currently doing to assess such happenings (an interrupt system) are also proposed. These systems allow one to examine changes in focus on the consumer's part. Interrupts which arise from other stages in the choice process (e.g., attention, information search, and so on) potentially lead to changes in goals, and thus shifts in the direction and perhaps even intensity of the choice process.

The mechanisms above account mainly for the direction of behavior. The intensity of choice processing is also a prime consideration. Intensity can range from minimal conscious processing (habitual choice), to extensive information search and analysis. In general, consumers develop heuristics, or rules of thumb, that they use in choice processing. For example, a consumer may use a rule of "Always look at *Consumer Reports* when considering an appliance choice" rather than deciding which of many potential sources of information to examine. Such rules may help to maintain the intensity of the choice process within reasonable limits.

The discussion above provides an overview of the motivational component of the theory. The relevant portions of the model for this motivational component are shown in Fig. 3.1. In the next section is a more detailed specification of the major concepts used—goals, goal hierarchy, development and carrying out of the goal hierarchy, and scanner and interrupt systems. Following this, the relation of the motivation component to other components of the theory is presented. Finally, more detailed aspects of the motivational component are examined. Throughout the chapter, an attempt is made to summarize the major proposals made as a set of propositions. This propositional format is followed for each of the major components of the theory.

MAJOR ASPECTS OF THE MOTIVATION COMPONENT

GOALS AND RELATED CONCEPTS

In the discussion above, choice was depicted theoretically as a progression from an initial state through intermediate states to some desired state. This is reflected in the following:

Proposition 3.1: Choice is viewed as a process of moving from some initial state to a desired state. Movement from one state to another is accomplished by applying strategies and heuristics.

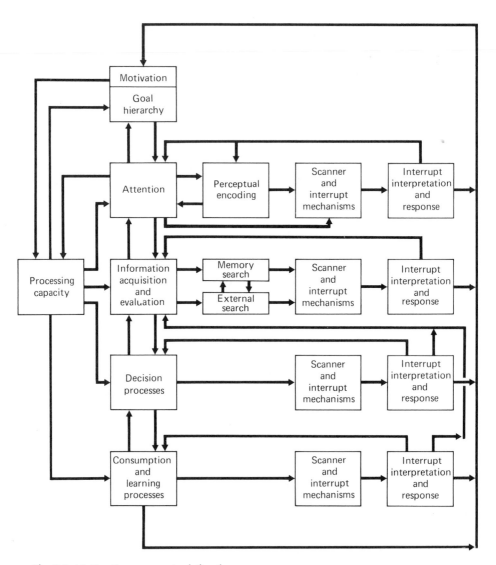

Fig. 3.1 Motivation segment of the theory.

Given this general view of choice, a *goal* is defined as a specific state whose attainment is related to achieving the desired end state. We will also call this desired end state the goal object (strictly speaking it should be possession or attainment of the goal object, but the simpler terminology is sufficient). Thus a set of goals can be viewed as a set of intermediate states the attainment of which is instrumental in moving toward the goal object. As an example, consider Choice Scenario 3 of Chapter 2, the washing machine decision. Initially, Jerry Baker's goals were to "Determine which attributes are important," "Evaluate alternatives on these attributes," and "Obtain the chosen alternative." Accomplishment of these goals would lead to purchase of a washing machine, the goal object. Goals are conceptualized in this example as specifying purposive behaviors or actions whose enactment is necessary to progress toward the ultimate act of choice.

Since any actions necessary to attain the goal object can usually be broken down into more finely detailed actions, the concept of a *subgoal* is also needed. A subgoal of a particular goal is simply a state whose attainment is necessary to achieve that particular goal. For example, in the washing machine choice example, "Read *Consumer Reports* article" is a subgoal under the goal "Determine which attributes are important."

The concept of a subgoal is related to that of a *plan*. A plan may be viewed as the specific procedures or actions taken to accomplish a goal (Miller, Galanter, and Pribram 1960). Thus a plan is equivalent to the *set* of subgoals for a particular goal. Note that the nature of choice processes leads to a problem with terminology. Due to the fact that desired actions can usually be broken down into finer units, what is considered to be part of a plan at one level (e.g., "Read *Consumer Reports* article" in our example) is a goal at a more detailed level, with its own plan (e.g., "Go downstairs" and "Locate right article"). Thus, depending on the level of detail chosen for analysis, a particular desired state might be either a goal or part of a plan. This is another instance of the problem of choices at different levels discussed in Chapter 2. If a specific level of analysis is chosen, the problem of terminology is less serious.

The focus of the particular definition of goal used above has been on relatively detailed states related to processing of information. Other consumer researchers have examined concepts which have a more general focus. For example, the benefits sought by consumers in purchasing a product have been considered (Haley 1968). This concept is related to that of a goal as used above in that the benefits desired may influence the specific types of goals chosen (e.g., a desire for a nutritious cereal may lead to a goal of examining the nutrition labels on cereal packages). Once again, the problem of levels of analysis arises, however. At some level, one must make a choice of those benefits desired, with the results of that choice influencing how more detailed goals and subgoals are structured. For example, in the washing machine example one could view the goal "Determine which attributes are important" as a choice among benefits. Then the next goal of "Evaluate alternatives on these attributes" requires relating these benefits sought to some evaluation of alternatives. One could push the level of analysis back beyond benefits, to needs or motives, which most researchers (see Kassarjian 1971 for a review) have viewed as more basic desired states (e.g., need for affiliation, hunger, need for achievement, and so on). Determining which needs are important (which may not be a process of which the consumer is consciously aware) may be seen as a precursor to determining which benefits will be sought. Thus the general term goal is defined more from the viewpoint of its role in the *process* of choice as a sequence of goals than from a content orientation. Depending upon the level of analysis chosen, goals could be related to basic needs and motives, benefits sought, or more detailed actions relevant to choice.

THE GOAL HIERARCHY

The ideas necessary for describing the concept of a goal hierarchy have been presented above. In essence a goal hierarchy consists of a series of goals, each of which may be divided into subgoals, with each subgoal potentially being further subdivided, and so on. A simple portion of a goal hierarchy was presented in Fig. 2.2 for the washing machine decision scenario. There were three initial basic goals: "Determine which attributes are important," "Evaluate alternatives on these attributes," and "Obtain the best alternative." In developing plans for attaining each of these basic goals, sets of subgoals were set up. For example, in determining attribute importance, Jerry Baker's plan was to talk to his wife, call his friend John Haskell, and read *Consumer Reports,* so his original goal had three subgoals. Each of these subgoals could be further subdivided, with plans being generated for their attainment, as shown for the "Read *Consumer Reports* article" subgoal. This concept of a hierarchy is thus simply a way of representing the structure of goals and subgoals. It is *not* a hierarchy in the sense used by Maslow (1954), for example, where an *a priori* ordering of motives is implied, stating that one motive must be satisfied before another becomes relevant. Consumers may have such orderings, which will then be operationalized in their goal hierarchies, but the concept of a goal hierarchy does *not* imply that this must be true.

Note that the level of detail depicted in the hierarchy is arbitrary, and depends upon the purpose of the analysis. For example, the subgoal "Locate right article" could be broken down to finding the right issue and locating the article in the issue. These could be even further broken down to the level of examining the physical movements involved in performing these tasks, if so desired.

A related issue is that breaking down a subgoal such as "Examine *Consumer Reports* table" would eventually lead to specification of the strategies and heuristics used by consumers for making comparisons among alternatives. For example, a further subgoal (possibly not attainable, of course) might be "Determine those brands with low water use, low price, and better than average repair records." Characterizing the decision strategies used by consumers can be viewed as characterizing a level of the goal hierarchy. Thus *specific comparisons among alternatives and progress toward attainment of more general goals are equivalent phenomena in terms of the goal hierarchy notion.* The only distinction is which level of the hierarchy is being considered. The recursive nature of the hierarchy (i.e., subgoals at one level are goals at the next level) implies that motivation and choice phenomena are very closely related. In this chapter we will discuss motivation in general, and defer consideration of specific strategies for choosing among alternatives to Chapters 7 and 8. The discussion above may be summarized as the following proposition:

> *Proposition 3.2:* The motivational mechanism used to carry out a particular choice process is a goal hierarchy, specifying those goals and subgoals that must be attained to progress from the initial state of the choice process to the desired state.

Note that the directional aspects of motivation appear as the specific goals and subgoals in the hierarchy, and the intensity aspects refer to the extensiveness of the processing needed to progress through the hierarchy.

Different choice processes may result in goal hierarchies of varying degrees of complexity. In the simplest case, the initial goal in the hierarchy is simply "Buy Brand X" where a habitual choice is being made, and little processing is required. At the other extreme may be complicated decisions such as choosing a house, where many goals and subgoals might be present. In such cases, where a framework for making the choice must often be developed because present knowledge is limited, a decision may be characterized by large amounts of processing and a long decision time (Howard 1977). Determinants of choice process intensity are discussed later in this chapter. For purposes of describing the major aspects of the motivation component it suffices to state:

> *Proposition 3.3:* Choice processes may be characterized by different degrees of intensity; that is, different amounts of processing effort may be carried out in different choice processes.

DEVELOPMENT AND PROCESSING OF GOAL HIERARCHIES

Development of goal hierarchies
Development of a goal hierarchy can be viewed as a constructive process; that is, pieces of the hierarchy may be put together as the choice process progresses. We assume that the consumer is capable of constructing many hierarchies for different choices, and that while working on a particular choice, the hierarchy for that choice is being developed. In many cases an initial set of goals may be developed which provides an overall outline for the choice. In some cases this outline may be as broad as "Buy a washing machine"; in other cases it may be more detailed, such as "Choose a model of Brand X washing machine." As the consumer begins developing plans (sets of subgoals) to implement these initial goals, the hierarchy becomes more de-

tailed.[2] Whether the degree of detail developed is just that required for the processing at the moment or is instead a more extensive blueprint for future processing is undoubtedly a function both of individual differences and differences in choice situations. For example, a consumer having a party may, in implementing the choice of what to have for dinner, simply go to the store with a broad goal of getting something for dinner; may find a recipe and write down the ingredients needed on a shopping list; or may even develop a seating arrangement for the guests as well as a shopping list. In general, therefore, the concept may be expressed as:

> *Proposition 3.4:* Consumers develop goal hierarchies constructively, first developing general goals and then elaborating these goals into more specific subgoals as choice progresses.

Four further aspects of the development of goal hierarchies are now considered to more carefully delineate the scope of Proposition 3.4. First, as noted above, consumers may use heuristics, or rules of thumb, in developing goal hierarchies; that is, the consumer may use a heuristic such as "Always look at *Consumer Reports* when considering an appliance choice." Such a heuristic can then become a guide for creating certain goals and subgoals in the hierarchy for some particular appliance choice (e.g., "Read *Consumer Reports* article" and its subgoals in the washing machine scenario). Such rules or strategies can result from prior experience, both within the same product class as the current choice being considered, or from previous choices in other product classes; that is, a consumer's prior choice experiences with toasters and hair dryers may lead to the "Look at *Consumer Reports*" rule stated above, and this rule may then be applied in developing goals for another purchase of a toaster or for the consumer's first purchase of an iron or washing machine. This discussion can be summarized as:

---

2. A general heuristic method for elaborating broad goals into more detailed subgoals has been proposed by Newell and Simon (1963). They call this method means–ends analysis. The basic concept is that the individual notes the difference between the current state and the desired state, and develops subgoals of applying strategies that he or she has learned or feels will reduce such differences. For example, in the washing machine example, Jerry Baker's initial goal "Determine which attributes are important" might be elaborated as follows: Jerry notes that the major difference between his current state and the state of having accomplished that goal is that he has no information on attributes of washing machines. Jerry's standard strategies for gathering information relevant for such choices may be reading *Consumer Reports,* talking to his wife, and talking to friends who have been faced with similar choices. Subgoals of implementing these strategies are formed. For a more formal treatment of means–ends analysis see Newell and Simon (1963) and Ernst and Newell (1969). They examine a general model for means–ends analysis called the General Problem Solver (GPS).

Proposition 3.4.i: Strategies and heuristics formed from previous choice experiences can provide a set of general guides for the development of goals and subgoals for current choices.

Second, over time various segments of a goal hierarchy for a repetitive decision may become learned units. For many choice situations, the consumer may have already developed from previous experience a sequence of actions that results in attaining the desired state. Eventually such a sequence becomes a learned unit that is used without needing to be developed piece by piece (e.g., such a simple act as driving to a particular store, which initially required some conscious processing to get directions right, will become a nearly automatic act). When a certain type of choice problem occurs, the consumer may use such learned strategies without consciously considering that action. As long as the choice environment remains as expected, the learned strategy is a useful way of limiting the amount of conscious processing necessary. The notions above may be expressed as another elaboration of Proposition 3.4:

Proposition 3.4.ii: Segments of goal hierarchies can become learned units with increased experience for a particular type of choice.

A third consideration in the development of goal hierarchies is that consumers may use different modes to construct them. One such distinction is that construction of a goal hierarchy may be carried out either outside of the store, prior to the actual shopping trip, or while actually in the store. In general, the amount of construction performed prior to shopping might vary from the lowest level of recognition of some broad goal alone (e.g., "Get something for dessert"); to goals related to product class only (e.g., "Get a frozen pie"); to goals related to both product class and brand (e.g., "Get a Brand X apple pie") (Kollat and Willet 1967). For example, Udell (1966) found that for small appliance purchases, 73 percent of his sample claimed to have decided on what product (not necessarily model or brand) to buy before they went to the store, although this figure is probably biased upward by consumers' desires to appear rational.

The distinction between *a priori* and in-store construction appears to be an important one, as in-store construction implies there may be more effects of in-store stimuli (e.g., package information, special displays) on what criteria and alternatives are examined. In particular, when goals and subgoals are constructed in the store, one might expect the particular information used to reflect how information is organized and presented in the store. Information which was easy to process would tend to be utilized, while that which was difficult would be ignored (Russo, Krieser, and Miyashita 1975; Russo 1977). Thus processing might be influenced by not only the availability of information in the store but also by the form in which the information was presented. Of course, even when in-store construction is used, over time the goal hierarchy would tend to be less dependent on the immediate processing situation, and more use of learned strategies would be expected. In summary,

> *Proposition 3.4.iii:* The extent to which goal hierarchies are developed outside of the actual shopping environment or while actually in a store shopping will vary across individuals and types of decisions. In general, the greater the amount of in-store processing, the greater the impact of both the in-store information available and the way in which that information is presented.

Finally, a fourth aspect of the development of goal hierarchies which should be considered is that progress may not always be from general goals to more detailed subgoals. If for some reason a person cannot carry out some specific subgoal, then general goals may be changed, and new subgoals elaborated. For example, if an individual has a preferred alternative which he or she usually purchases, the goal hierarchy may be trivial, "Buy Brand X." However, out-of-stock situations, price changes, being asked by a child for another brand, and so on, may lead to having to develop new broad goals (e.g., choosing between buying some new brand or waiting if an out-of-stock has occurred) which may then be elaborated. These are examples of interrupts, discussed more fully below. Thus we have,

> *Proposition 3.4.iv:* Unexpected events may lead to abandonment of previously developed detailed goals and development of new broad goals.

Processing of goal hierarchies

No attempt has been made to characterize how processing of a hierarchy occurs, how the various goals and subgoals are attained and the entire choice process carried out. A set of goals and subgoals is not carried out automatically. Rather, the consumer must keep track of what goal is being worked on at the moment, must decide when to stop work on some goals and when to start work on others, and so forth. In general, the consumer must have some kind of system which enables him or her to organize and carry out behavior toward the goals developed. Mischel (1973) proposes that human beings have what he terms self-regulatory systems for carrying out goals.[3] He postulates

---

3. This concept seems very similar to the notion of an executive processor postulated by Newell and Simon (1972). However, the concept of a self-regulatory system seems more useful than borrowing the notion of an executive from computer science.

that human beings have capabilities for giving themselves instructions and for reinforcing or admonishing themselves in the course of carrying out these instructions; that is, individuals may be able to keep track of where they are in a choice process, may remind themselves what must be done next, congratulate themselves on completing various tasks, and so on. Such processes may be used by consumers to regulate themselves while carrying out a choice. Very little research exists on such self-regulatory systems (but see Patterson and Mischel 1975, 1976; Mischel and Patterson 1976; Bandura 1978).

Given such a system, how might a goal hierarchy be processed? One conception, quite rigid and mechanistic, is that one goal in the hierarchy is selected (e.g., "Determine which attributes are important" in the washing machine scenario), all of the subgoals leading to this goal are processed, then another goal is selected (e.g., "Evaluate alternatives on these attributes"), and so on. It seems unlikely that people process in this fixed a fashion. It seems much more plausible that the consumer performs some actions which are relevant to the general problem, but not necessarily in any rigid order. There will be some sequence constraints needed (e.g., one obviously cannot buy the chosen alternative if it has not yet been chosen), but in general these constraints may allow some flexibility in arranging the order of processing. Then one might predict that the action which is most "available" will be performed. For example, in the washing machine decision, if John Haskell had not called back and his wife were not home, Jerry Baker may very well have read *Consumer Reports* rather than waiting for his wife or the return call. Note also that while reading *Consumer Reports* to learn about criteria, Jerry is probably also evaluating alternatives at the same time. Thus one action can achieve progress on several goals simultaneously. In fact, behaviors which allow progress on several goals at once may be viewed as more desirable. Finally, a goal or subgoal need not be attained by starting to work on it and then continuing until it is attained. It seems much more likely that partial progress is made, other goals are worked on, the first goal is then worked on some more, and so on. The entire notion of how a goal hierarchy is carried out is one which has seen virtually no research.

Implicit in the discussion above is the notion that one "knows" when a goal or subgoal is attained, or when it cannot be attained and processing should cease. However, more specific criteria need to be developed. Simon (1967) lists several examples of types of criteria for terminating processing: (1) achievement of aspiration levels, where processing will cease when the level of performance aspired to has been attained (the consumer may stop searching through a stack of *Consumer Reports* when an article sought is found, for example); (2) satisficing, in which processing may terminate if a goal or subgoal has been achieved "well enough" (a consumer may stop searching for information on prices of appliances after looking in three stores because this is "sufficient" based upon his or her subjective cut-off levels); (3) impatience, a situation in which only a certain amount of processing will be done (a consumer, for example, may decide to spend only one hour looking for a dress); (4) discouragement, in which processing may stop if a certain number of actions have been tried without success. Before this number has been tried, attempts will continue.

These termination criteria represent mechanisms for attempting to explain *persistence* toward a goal. These criteria can also be thought of as allocation rules for determining how much processing capacity will be given to the particular goal in question. Note that in all of them a threshold or standard is involved; that is, if some activity (e.g., time spent shopping, number of stores visited) is above a certain standard, the activity is terminated; if not, it is continued. Thresholds occur in many other places in the theory presented here (e.g., thresholds needed for interrupts, whether attributes are seen as meeting certain standards or not) and determinants of the particular standards or threshold levels used need more study (Bettman 1974b; Reitman, Grove, and Shoup 1964).

The discussion above may be summarized as two propositions:

Proposition 3.5: Consumers possess self-regulatory systems for carrying out the actions implied by a goal hierarchy. Such systems keep track of progress to date and what activities remain to be accomplished.

Proposition 3.6: Consumers develop criteria for determining when activity related to attaining a particular goal should be terminated. Such criteria as aspiration levels, satisficing, impatience, and discouragement may be used.

Thus far we have proposed that choice is a progression from a starting state to some desired final state, and that consumers develop a hierarchy of goals, which represents an overall strategy and more detailed substrategies, for attaining the desired final state. The goal hierarchy may be constructed and elaborated as progress toward the desired state is made, and consumers have the ability to monitor their own progress toward this state. This discussion has assumed that consumers begin a choice process and continue this process with no interruptions, unexpected events, or distractions. Let us now consider the impact of such factors on the motivational aspects of the choice process. As discussed above, the major mechanisms involved in the impact of these factors are scanner and interrupt mechanisms.

SCANNER AND INTERRUPT MECHANISMS

As Neisser (1963) has pointed out, the description above of processing a goal hierarchy seems much too single-minded and nonadaptive. People are frequently distracted, and rearrange goals and plans if more pressing needs arise. Thus some sort of adjustment process is needed. Two components seem necessary for such a process: "(1) A certain amount of processing must go on continuously, or almost continuously, to enable the system to *notice* when conditions have arisen that require ongoing programs to be interrupted. The noticing processes will be substantially in parallel with the ongoing goal-attaining program of the total system, although this parallelism may be realized, in fact, by the high frequency time sharing of a single serial processor. (2) The noticing program must be capable of *interrupting* and setting aside ongoing programs when real-time needs of high priority are encountered" (Simon 1967, p. 34). These two components are labeled the *scanner* and *interrupt mechanisms,* respectively.[4]

Such mechanisms seem necessary in a theory of choice to enable adaptation or adjustment of goals to changes in the choice situation; that is, in order to make changes in the goal hierarchy, the consumer must be capable of monitoring the choice environment, detecting events of potential interest (e.g., price changes, out-of-stock conditions, new brands, and so on), and interrupting current activities to react to these events if necessary. Thus the goal hierarchy can be responsive to demands of the moment. This discussion leads to

> *Proposition 3.7:* Consumers possess both a scanner, which monitors the choice environment, and a mechanism for interrupting activity on current goals if events in the choice environment warrant.

There are three broad types of events that may be noticed by the scanner and lead to interrupts (Simon 1967; Hansen 1972): (1) events in the environment which depart from expectations, such as noises, new objects (for example, new brands), or changes in previously experienced conditions (e.g., price changes, rearrangement of the selling area of a store, and so on); (2) physiological events, such as hunger, thirst, or fatigue; and (3) cognitive events, such as remembering a forgotten task (e.g., a product which was used up but was not put on the shopping list is recalled and the need for purchasing it is remembered). Hansen (1972) claims that most interrupts in consumer choice processes stem from environmental stimuli; that is, new alternatives, new prices, or changes in some other feature of the shopping situation. In this sense, the onset of an interrupt can be seen as stimulus-bound or, in other words, as dependent upon the stimuli in the choice environment. Reactions to

---

4. There is some physiological evidence for these scanner and interrupt mechanisms. Lindsay and Norman (1972, pp. 622–626) discuss evidence showing that the diffuse thalamic projection system of the reticular arousal system in the brain seems to be sensitive to changes and may play a basic role in monitoring and interrupts. Although such a physiological mechanism provides suggestive evidence that the proposed systems may exist, the focus in this book is on the psychologically meaningful aspects of the scanner and interrupt mechanisms.

the interrupt event need not be determined by the environment alone, however, but reflect the assessment of the interrupting event in light of the available information. For example, noticing a price increase for a product may lead to no particular reaction if prices have been generally rising during an inflationary period.

Proposition 3.8: Interrupting events are of three main types:

a) Environmental events which depart from expectations

b) Physiological events

c) Cognitive events

Reactions to these events depend upon the consumer's interpretation of the significance of the event.

Thus far, the consumer has been characterized as progressing toward goals until some event occurs which is noticed and causes an interruption of ongoing activity. Note that these interrupts may, in general, arise in other components of the choice process (e.g., attention and perception, information search, decision processes), rather than directly in the motivational component. To see the tie between interrupts and motivation, the question of effects of an interrupt must be considered.

Effects of interrupts seem to be of two major sorts: (1) physiological effects, and (2) assessment of and possibly changes in the current goal hierarchy. Physiologically, an interrupt event, often an unexpected event of some sort, can lead to increased arousal.[5] However, the major interest for the present is the effect of interrupts on the goal hierarchy. The general effect may be to cause the consumer to assess the adequacy of current goals, to decide whether these goals still make sense in light of the interrupting event. The consumer may stop activity on the choice process and begin activities directed toward dealing with the interrupt, may decide that the interrupting event can be ignored, and so on. For example, in the washing machine choice example of Chapter 2, an interrupt occurred when the difference in warranty lengths between the other retailer and the discount store was noticed. The reaction to this interrupt could have been to ignore it and continue with the proposed activity of ordering the washing machine from the other retailer. However, Jerry Baker and his wife instead stopped that activity (i.e., they did not leave the discount store and call the other retailer) and set up a new goal of trading off the warranty and price differences, leading ultimately to purchase from the discount store.

---

5. Arousal refers to the state of *internal* physiological activity of an individual. Typical measures include pulse rate, eye pupil dilation, galvanic skin response, brain wave measurements, and others. Levels of arousal will vary across situations for the same individual, and across individuals for the same situation (Duffy 1957).

Proposition 3.9: Interrupting events have two main types of effects:

a) Increased physiological activity, such as arousal

b) Assessment of the adequacy of the current goal hierarchy, with changes in the hierarchy implemented if it is found inadequate.

Thus motivation is closely tied to the other concepts in the theory. The goal hierarchy provides direction and intensity information to the other stages, and feedback from these other stages in the form of interrupt events can lead to changes in the goal hierarchy. The scanner and interrupt mechanisms provide a crucial link between the motivational and other components.

SUMMARY

Consumer choice is viewed as progress through a sequence of states, from an initial state to some desired state. The specific activities to be carried out to attain this desired state are represented as a set of goals and their subgoals, or in other words, a goal hierarchy. Consumers develop these goals as they are working on the choice, with broad goals developed and then elaborated. Unexpected events may lead to interruptions in the current activity, and perhaps to changes in the goals to be pursued. The hierarchy of goals thus may be continually changing in response to changing conditions, changing both with respect to the specific goals included and with respect to the number of goals and subgoals included.

LINKAGES TO OTHER COMPONENTS OF THE THEORY

As argued in several places above, the motivational constructs postulated play a central role in the theory. The specific goals and subgoals in the goal hierarchy will be a major force in the direction of processing capacity and attention to the information available in the environment, since in general different goals may require different information; that is, progress toward attaining some particular goal may require certain information. A subgoal of obtaining that information would probably be developed and processing capacity would be allocated toward that end. The amount of capacity allocated, the intensity of the process, may be in part a function of the specific goals and subgoals involved. Thus the direction and extent of attention, perception, and information search (both in memory and the environment) seem to be strongly dependent on the structure and content of the goal hierarchy. Decision processes are utilized to attain the goals and subgoals developed, and hence reflect this goal hierarchy as well.

The linkages do not run solely from motivation to the other components, however. As argued above, interrupt events which originate in the other components may lead to changes in the goal hierarchy. The current hierarchy may be modified (e.g., a new attribute may be considered), or it may even be abandoned for the moment because other events are more pressing (e.g., a consumer stops considering alternatives in a store because he remembers he has left the lights in his car on). Also, processing capacity, since it is limited, must be allocated between processing directed toward current goals and processing involved in scanning the environment; that is, both progress toward goals and monitoring environmental events require processing capacity. Thus in general there will be a trade-off—the more capacity is allocated to current goals, the less active will be the scanning function, and hence the fewer interrupts will tend to occur. This impact of allocation rules for processing capacity on the motivation component is discussed further below. Thus motivation affects and is affected by the other components of the theory. These links can be seen by referring to Fig. 3.1.

MORE DETAILED ASPECTS OF THE MOTIVATION COMPONENT

The accounts above are intended to introduce the major features of the motivational component of the theory. In several places more detailed expositions were omitted because they would potentially interfere with gaining an overall view of the concepts introduced. Now that this overall view has been given, these more detailed considerations are presented.

EFFECTIVENESS OF HIERARCHICAL ORGANIZATIONS

A basic proposition of the motivational component is that consumers use goal hierarchies to carry out choice processes (Proposition 3.2). There seems to be little direct evidence for this proposition. However, several theorists have argued for the plausibility of hierarchical arrangements in general because of the efficiency of such structures as a basis for carrying out information processing. Thus the evidence is indirect: goal hierarchies are plausible because they seem as though they would be effective.[6] We may state:

> *Proposition 3.2.i:* Hierarchies allow effective information processing.

Simon (1969, pp. 84–118) has presented the most detailed discussion in support of this proposition. He proposes that the key property of hierarchical organizations as far as their effectiveness is concerned is that there are intermediate steps, so that a complex problem can be effectively broken down into parts; that is, having a hierarchical goal structure makes progress toward the ultimate goal easier because subgoals serve as intermediate steps. An entire

---

6. Some related evidence from the organizational behavior literature suggests that merely setting goals facilitates performance (Locke 1968; Organ 1977).

path to the goal need not be developed at once. Subgoals serve as intermediate points that are general guides to constructing still further subgoals. Also, a consumer may develop general goals for the choice process and defer generating more detailed subgoals until actually shopping.

Bower (1970) also argues that hierarchical organizations are efficient for the processing involved in memory operations. Bower, Clark, Lesgold, and Winzenz (1969) find that subjects presented with words to memorize which are arranged hierarchically are able to recall and recognize those words at a much higher level than can subjects who received the same words arranged essentially at random. In addition, they show the important result that words at one level of the hierarchy serve as general cues for retrieving the next lower level of the hierarchy (e.g., the word "metals" as part of the hierarchy on minerals would become a clue for the subject to recall types of metals). This provides empirical support for the notion that intermediate goals provide guides for constructing more detailed goals. Finally, Dawes (1966) presents results which suggest that recall of sets of statements that are not easily represented as hierarchies in memory is distorted so that these sets of statements are seen as hierarchical.

DETERMINANTS OF CHOICE PROCESS INTENSITY

It was postulated above that choice processes vary in intensity, in the amount of processing carried out (Proposition 3.3). However, intensity of a choice process is a complex phenomenon. First, it is not clear how one should operationalize intensity. There are at least two basic components involved: extent, or number of criteria, trade-offs, etc. involved; and number of alternatives processed. These seem to be conceptually independent dimensions. One may process a few alternatives in great detail or a great many alternatives through a simple set of criteria. Whether these two forms of extensive processing differ in their determinants or effects is not known. Since the number of alternatives and/or dimensions will vary across different choice environments, this variation leads to operational problems in comparing intensity across situations. Finally, operationalizing intensity is also complicated by the fact that some individuals will be more skilled and/or efficient than others in their choice processes, and hence will accomplish more for some given level of effort.

In addition to the problem of measurement or operationalization, there seem to be at least two relevant types of intensity one might consider for a choice process. The first type refers to the total extent of the choice process. The second type refers to the extent of processing that might be done *a priori,* before shopping, as opposed to what will be done while shopping. In general, therefore, intensity is a phenomenon which is very elusive. In the following discussion of the determinants of intensity, intensity is probably best viewed as a general notion rather than as a specifically defined construct.

The major determinants of intensity are expressed in the following proposition:

> *Proposition 3.3.i:* Intensity of a choice process is dependent upon
>
> a) Properties of the choice environment
> b) Estimation of the benefits of extensive processing versus the costs
> c) Degree of experience with the choice in question
> d) Degree of conflict present
> e) Individual differences

Each of these determinants is now discussed.

Properties of the choice environment

The structure of the choice environment itself can have a great impact on the intensity of choice processes. Such structure would include the number of alternatives, the number of dimensions per alternative, the complexity of these dimensions, and so on. If there are few alternatives, each with few dimensions which are not complex, then a great deal of processing may not be possible. On the other hand, where a great many alternatives exist, a greater range of discretion in extent of processing may exist.

Even if the consumer decides to perform a good deal of processing, the specific type of processing done can also depend upon the structure of the choice environment. If information on dimensions of the alternatives is difficult to obtain and alternatives are plentiful, the consumer may process many alternatives using a relatively simple set of criteria. If information on dimensions is easy to obtain and alternatives sparse, the few alternatives may be processed in great detail. Intermediate degrees of availability of information on dimensions and alternatives may lead to choice processes where both alternatives and criteria are processed fairly heavily. This discussion highlights Simon's (1969) stress on the role of the task environment, since people adapt to their environments. Observing processing strategies in the environments above, where the form is more or less forced, may tell us more about these task environments than about the person. Thus the psychologically interesting phenomenon to study may be the intensity the individual desires, rather than the actual intensity, if this actual intensity is forced by the structure of the task environment.

Benefits versus costs of processing

There is some suggestive evidence that a rough estimate of the processing effort required versus the benefits expected is performed in determining the intensity of processing. Bucklin (1966) found that where the effort needed to shop in more than one store is low, more stores in fact tend to be visited, and that more stores tend to be visited for higher priced goods. Udell (1966) also found this relationship between product price and number of stores visited.

Kiesler (1966) presented subjects with choices of two equally attractive alternatives, four equally attractive alternatives, or four alternatives with two equally attractive and two less attractive choices. He found that choice times were about the same for two and for four equally attractive alternatives. In addition, when the set of four alternatives was given where two of the four alternatives were *less* attractive, there was an *increase* in decision time over the four equally attractive alternative cases. Kiesler argued that this increase occurred because subjects were willing to process the two attractive alternatives out of four, but gave up if there were four, thus suggesting that any benefits which might accrue were not worth the added processing. Hendrick, Mills, and Kiesler (1968) attempted to refine this finding by manipulating the processing effort required to compare alternatives. The manipulation was the number of dimensions stressed as relevant for the choice (one or fifteen). For subjects' first choices, decision times were longer for four equally attractive alternatives if one dimension was stressed. Decision times were longer (although the difference was not statistically significant) for the two attractive, two unattractive set if all 15 dimensions were stressed, however. Thus there was apparently a tendency to give up trying to compare all four alternatives when the comparison was seen as complex and the benefits slight. The data for second choices did not yield this pattern, however. Pollay (1970a) explicitly modeled this choice situation, using a Bayesian analysis of expected utility versus expected cost of processing. The crucial variable in the theory is how difficult it is to discriminate alternatives. The easier alternatives are to discriminate, the more processing will be done. The theoretical reasoning behind these studies is quite provocative. However, as intimated above and analyzed in detail by Wright (1977), the empirical evidence is not adequate. These notions should perhaps best be considered as interesting hypotheses in need of further tests.

A related analysis is provided by research on predicting the degree of effort an individual will exert on a given task (Kukla 1972b; Weiner 1972). According to these researchers, an individual's level of effort for a given task may depend on the individual's perceptions of his or her own level of ability for that type of task and perceptions about the degree of difficulty of the task. In terms of the consumer choice process, degree of processing effort might be influenced by the perceived difficulty of the choice task and one's perceived abilities for that type of choice. The specific prediction relating effort to these perceptions is that "performance level is relatively low when the task is perceived to be very easy because subjects believe that great effort is not necessary in order to succeed. When the task is thought to be very difficult, performance is again low, this time because subjects believe that great effort will be of no avail. It is just when the task is perceived to be neither extremely easy nor extremely difficult that effort is seen as the crucial determinant of success or failure. Thus performance level is highest at tasks of intermediate perceived difficulty" (Kukla 1972b, pp. 461–462). Weiner, Heckhausen, Meyer, and Cook (1972) report results supporting these contentions.

The analysis above predicts an inverted U-shaped function between intensity of the consumer choice process for a particular choice task and the perceived difficulty of that choice task. Additional predictions are made by Kukla (1972b, p. 466). This approach seems to have merit, and implies that measures of the perceived difficulty of shopping tasks and of ability in such tasks should be developed.[7]

Prior choice experience

The notion that amount of processing engaged in depends on product class experience has been presented earlier and will not be explored in depth here. It suffices to say that, in general, as experience for a particular choice accumulates, more learned strategies are invoked and less effort devoted to processing is needed. However, there are complicating factors. As experience accumulates, the individual is more knowledgeable about the dimensions of alternatives and how to compare alternatives. If the choice environment *changes* (e.g., a new alternative is introduced or the preferred alternative is no longer available), such a consumer may actually process more than a consumer with limited experience, since the processing task might be moderately difficult for him or her but very difficult for the consumer with little experience (see the last section for the basis for this hypothesis).

Degree of conflict present

Conflict, as noted briefly in Chapter 2, arises because the consumer has competing and incompatible response tendencies. Conflict may arise in the choice process because the consumer has competing tendencies for buying several alternatives, but only needs one of them, or because various goals the consumer has for the purchase conflict (goal conflict is discussed in more detail below). The consumer is not only faced with the conflict induced by the choice process itself. Other sources of conflict abound in daily life. It is presumably the *total* level of conflict impinging upon the individual which must be dealt with at any one point in time. Different reactions to the *same amount* of choice-related conflict may occur depending upon the level of conflict from other sources, how easily each source of conflict can be handled, which sources are controllable by the individual, and so on.

In general the individual faced with a conflict may assess that conflict, interpret it, and decide upon a conflict handling strategy given this interpretation. Thus there may be no single standard response to conflict. Little is known

---

7. The measure of need for achievement has been used in these studies to measure ability (Kukla 1972a). Perhaps this instrument could be adapted for use in measuring ability for consumer tasks.

about such adaptive conflict handling strategies, however. The bulk of the work on conflict handling strategies has proposed that there is a single broad strategy. An optimal level of conflict (or some related phenomenon such as incongruity) is assumed to exist. If total conflict is below the optimal level, goals for increasing conflict may be developed. If total conflict is above the optimal level, but not too far above, goals for decreasing conflict may be constructed. Finally, if conflict is far above the optimal level, simple rules may be used (Berlyne 1960; Hunt 1963; Driver and Streufert 1964; Howard and Sheth 1969; Howard 1977; Hansen 1972).[8]

If consumers do use such strategies, then in the case of both conflict below the optimal level and conflict moderately above the optimal level increased processing might ensue. For conflict below optimal, the consumer may search for a new brand to try, to seek variety (Howard and Sheth 1969; Bettman 1971b; Venkatesan 1973). Howard and Sheth (1969) term this diversive exploration. A second type of activity might be to look for information about other product classes not to be purchased on the current trip while in the store shopping. This phenomenon, termed epistemic behavior by Howard and Sheth (1969), can lead to stored information and learning about the environment. Also, when conflict is low consumers may develop only broad goals before shopping and wait to construct the remaining goals in the store. The in-store processing may be used to increase conflict.

If total conflict is moderately above the optimal level, then goals for reducing conflict may be developed. Such goals might involve increasing the intensity of the decision process, as reflected in search for additional information relating to criteria or alternatives.

Finally, if total conflict is too far above the optimal level, extended choice or search processes may not be used, but rather simple rules. If the magnitude of the effort appears too great, a simple decision may be the easiest way to escape the situation. Another method of escape is to simply postpone the decision if possible. Note that this notion implies that if other sources of conflict are high, high choice conflict may *not* lead to an extended decision process, but to a simple one. Time pressure can be one source of increased levels of conflict, so under time pressure we may find simple choices if total conflict is too high.

The mechanisms above may be plausible. However, they imply a fixedness of reaction patterns and lack of flexibility uncharacteristic of human behavior. Hence, more work should be done on characterizing strategies for reacting to conflict.

---

8. Looft (1971) claims that the unimodal patterns (one local optimum point) typically used in optimal level theories to depict response as a function of degree of conflict (or of some other related variable) are artifacts of averaging data over individuals. He examined response patterns of individual subjects and found that many subjects had bimodal (two local optima) response patterns. When these subjects were averaged, the unimodal curve resulted for the group data.

Individual differences

Individuals differ in terms of the degree to which they wish to make the best decision possible as opposed to a satisfactory one. Pollay (1970c) has performed empirical work in this area, reporting rank correlations of decision times with various personality variables. Unfortunately, the sample size used was very small. Other research has shown increased search if the consumer desires an "optimal" choice (Swan 1969; Claxton, Fry, and Portis 1974). These findings are only suggestive, and more research is needed into those individual differences impacting choice process intensity.

ALLOCATION OF PROCESSING CAPACITY BETWEEN CURRENT GOALS AND THE SCANNER AND INTERRUPT MECHANISMS

In the course of a choice process, the consumer may be simultaneously performing two types of activities: working on goals related to the choice at hand, and monitoring or scanning the environment to see if events occur which might require interruption of current processing on goals. A basic question is how the consumer allocates limited processing capacity between current goal processing and scanning. One conception of this allocation is that there is a threshold that must be surpassed before an event will lead to an interrupt; that is, an event must depart from expectations beyond a certain amount before an interrupt will occur. Then in effect the allocation is accomplished by the level of the threshold. A higher threshold, for example, would imply interrupts would be less frequent (less capacity allocated to scanning and interrupting) and there would be more concentration on current goals (more capacity allocated to goal processing).

If we assume that the consumer may have some latitude in setting the level of this threshold, various factors may affect this decision.[9] In particular, we postulate

> *Proposition 3.7.i:* Processing capacity is allocated between processing on current goals and the scanner and interrupt mechanisms. This allocation may be accomplished by setting a threshold for the degree of departure from expectations needed for an interrupt to occur. This threshold may be a function of:
>
> a) Importance of the current goal
>
> b) Time pressure
>
> c) Developmental stage
>
> d) Importance of goals for learning about the environment

---

9. Consumers may not be able to vary this threshold. An alternative view is that the threshold is fixed, but reactions to events above the threshold are varied. For some interesting views on how to implement interrupts in artificial intelligence programs using various triggering devices, see Rieger (1977).

The more important the goal one is currently processing, the higher the threshold, and hence the more persistent should be the efforts toward that goal. With respect to time pressure, Kahneman (1973, pp. 24–26) cites a good deal of evidence that the effort (processing capacity) needed to accomplish a given task is greatly affected by time pressure, with higher pressure leading to need for allocation of greater capacity to processing that given task. Thus, for any particular goal, higher time pressure may imply less capacity should be made available for the scanner and interrupt mechanisms, and hence that a higher threshold might be used.

Children are normally more distractible than adults. Hence developmental stage may be related to the level of the threshold, with lower thresholds at younger ages. Finally, an individual may have a goal of learning about the choice environment in general, even if what is learned is not relevant to the immediate choice at hand. Then the person may *lower* the threshold. For example, one may be bored and desire novelty or variety, and hence *want* to be interrupted, or one may simply wish to learn about aspects of the choice environment that may be useful for future choices. This latter example is quite important for consumer choice, as many consumers appear to examine broad features of their shopping environment, even if they are unrelated to their current shopping goal (e.g., noticing prices for stereos in a discount store although one is buying some film). In general a low threshold for interrupts, and hence a higher probability of interruption, is adaptive where such learning about the environment is important. As the features of the environment become more known, then selectivity becomes relatively more important and the threshold may be increased.

Thus many factors can affect the allocation of capacity between current processing and interrupts. Relationships have been postulated above, but no research currently exists in this area.

GOAL CONFLICTS AS A SOURCE OF INTERRUPTS

In the earlier discussion of sources of interrupts, it was noted that unexpected events or departures from expectations may be major sources. One type of departure from expectations that can arise in the course of developing or processing a goal hierarchy is goal conflict, or incompatibility among goals. Goal conflict can arise in developing a goal hierarchy, when incompatible goals are noted. This conflict might lead to an interrupt, depending on the threshold for interrupts, of course. Conflict can also arise when actually processing goals. In other words, the conflict may not be inherent to the goals themselves or seen beforehand, but may only be discovered. For example, a man may decide to purchase a lawn mower that performs well in cutting grass and is durable. He may discover in examining the available alternatives that the lawn mowers that perform best are least durable. Hence, the goals conflict, although the consumer did not know this until actually processing the available alternatives. Finally, Howard and Sheth (1969, pp. 114–116) also consider a case where goal conflict may *always* be present, claiming the house-wife is always conflicted between family needs and her own needs within a fixed budget. In general we postulate:

> *Proposition 3.8.i:* Goal conflicts are an important class of interrupt events. Reactions to goal conflicts depend on individuals' conflict handling strategies.

In discussing examples of goal conflicts, the framework of Lewin (1938) will be useful. Conflicts may be classified as approach–approach, approach–avoidance, and avoidance–avoidance.[10] In an approach–approach goal conflict, two desired goals are present, but not simultaneously obtainable. This type of goal conflict could arise when choices are made involving normally separate parts of a person's value system which are inconsistent. For example, in choosing whether or not to engage in a food storage program (keeping a supply of food stored for one's family in case of an emergency), goals of providing for the self-sufficiency of one's family and goals of helping others in need, both valued by the individual, may be seen as being in direct conflict. Another way in which an approach–approach goal conflict could arise is from being able to attain only one goal at a time. For example, a consumer may want to go on a vacation to France and a trip to Mexico, but has only a one-week vacation, so cannot do both.

Approach–avoidance conflicts are those where the same goal has both positive and negative features. Often this leads to a situation in which goals lead to subgoals, and the subgoals conflict, some being positive and some negative in light of other goals. An example is the goal of purchasing a car, with subgoals of choosing a make and paying for it. The person wants the new car, but does not want to spend that much money.

Avoidance–avoidance conflicts involve situations in which two goals to avoid something conflict. An instance would be where a consumer does not want to go to the store at the last minute to buy some wine for guests, but also does not want to have a dinner with no wine.

Given that a goal conflict has led to an interrupt, how might the individual respond? The theory presented here argues that individuals assess the conflict, interpret it, and decide upon a conflict handling stategy. Thus, there may be no single strategy or theory of response to conflict applicable. If two goals conflict, individuals may search for some rationale that will allow them

---

10. The major work on goal conflict done in a consumer research context was that of Bilkey (1951, 1953, 1957) who applied Lewin's vector psychology to consumer choice. Mostly approach–avoidance conflicts were considered. A formal approach to approach–avoidance, approach–approach, and avoidance–avoidance conflicts is presented in Coombs and Avrunin (1977).

to resolve apparently conflicting goals (e.g., in the example about food storage above, individuals may reason that they will not be able to help in an emergency if they are worrying about where their next meal is coming from); may eliminate one goal from consideration; or may trade off one goal against another (e.g., price vs. quality). If the conflicting goals arise from properties of the set of alternatives examined, individuals may search for new alternatives, and so on. As Kiesler (1975) states, individuals are extremely flexible in resolving goal conflicts, and we know little about the process. Most research on conflict resolution has examined conflict between individuals or groups, not conflict within a single individual.

INDIVIDUAL DIFFERENCES IN THE MOTIVATION COMPONENT

In the foregoing sections many individual difference variables have been indicated which may lead to differences in aspects of the motivational component (e.g., the way goal hierarchies are constructed and carried out, and in the way interrupts occur and are handled). Those individual difference variables which seem to be potentially most significant are summarized below. Since the basic areas involved have been discussed in previous sections, the variables are only listed. Note that these variables are not only relevant across individuals, but also could be useful for examining differences in processing for the same individual across different situations.

Proposition 3.10: Individual differences can affect aspects of the motivational component. Significant individual difference variables may be:

a) The particular array of learned heuristics or strategies available to the consumer.

b) The degree to which the goal hierarchy is constructed before versus during shopping, and the degree to which construction is carried out outside versus inside the store.

c) The type of self-regulatory system (self-instructions, etc.) used.

d) The specific rules and criteria used for terminating processing on a particular goal.

e) The degree to which optimal rather than satisfactory choices are desired.

f) The methods used to estimate the effort needed for accomplishing particular goals.

g) The threshold level necessary for an interrupt.

h) The reaction strategies used to respond to interrupts in general, and to conflict in particular.

SUMMARY OF THE PROPOSITIONS

The discussion of the motivational component has now been completed. In this section the propositions are repeated so that they appear together, as a means of providing a more easily accessible overview of the major assertions made in the chapter.

Proposition 3.1: Choice is viewed as a process of moving from some initial state to a desired state. Movement from one state to another is accomplished by applying strategies and heuristics.

Proposition 3.2: The motivational mechanism used to carry out a particular choice process is a goal hierarchy, specifying those goals and subgoals that must be attained to progress from the initial state of the choice process to the desired state.

> *Proposition 3.2.i:* Hierarchies allow effective information processing.

Proposition 3.3: Choice processes may be characterized by different degrees of intensity; that is, different amounts of processing effort may be carried out in different choice processes.

> *Proposition 3.3.i:* Intensity of a choice process is dependent upon:
>
> a) Properties of the choice environment
> b) Estimation of the benefits of extensive processing versus the costs
> c) Degree of experience with the choice in question
> d) Degree of conflict present
> e) Individual differences

Proposition 3.4: Consumers develop goal hierarchies constructively, first developing general goals and then elaborating these goals into more specific subgoals as choice progresses.

> *Proposition 3.4.i:* Strategies and heuristics formed from previous choice experiences can provide a set of general guides for the development of goals and subgoals for current choices.
>
> *Proposition 3.4.ii:* Segments of goal hierarchies can become learned units with increased experience for a particular type of choice.
>
> *Proposition 3.4.iii:* The extent to which goal hierarchies are developed outside of the actual shopping environment or while actually in a store shopping will vary across individuals and types of decisions. In general, the greater the amount of

in-store processing, the greater the impact of both the in-store information available and the way in which that information is presented.

Proposition 3.4.iv: Unexpected events may lead to abandonment of previously developed detailed goals and development of new broad goals.

Proposition 3.5: Consumers possess self-regulatory systems for carrying out the actions implied by a goal hierarchy. Such systems keep track of progress to date and what activities remain to be accomplished.

Proposition 3.6: Consumers develop criteria for determining when activity relating to attaining a particular goal should be terminated. Such criteria as aspiration levels, satisficing, impatience, and discouragement may be used.

Proposition 3.7: Consumers possess both a scanner, which monitors the choice environment, and a mechanism for interrupting activity on current goals if events in the choice environment warrant.

Proposition 3.7.i: Processing capacity is allocated between processing on current goals and the scanner and interrupt mechanisms. This allocation may be accomplished by setting a threshold for the degree of departure from expectations needed for an interrupt to occur. This threshold may be a function of:

a) Importance of the current goal

b) Time pressure

c) Developmental stage

d) Importance of goals for learning about the environment

Proposition 3.8: Interrupting events are of three main types.

a) Environmental events which depart from expectations

b) Physiological events

c) Cognitive events

Reactions to these events depend upon the consumer's interpretation of the significance of the event.

Proposition 3.8.i: Goal conflicts are an important class of interrupt events. Reactions to goal conflicts depend on individuals' conflict handling strategies.

Proposition 3.9: Interrupting events have two main types of effects:

a) Increased physiological activity, such as arousal

b) Assessment of the adequacy of the current goal hierarchy, with changes in the hierarchy implemented if it is found inadequate

Proposition 3.10: Individual differences can affect aspects of the motivational component. Significant individual difference variables may be:

a) The particular array of learned heuristics or strategies available to the consumer

b) The degree to which the goal hierarchy is constructed before versus during shopping, and the degree to which construction is carried out outside versus inside the store

c) The type of self-regulatory system (self-instructions, etc.) used

d) The specific rules and criteria used for terminating processing on a particular goal

e) The degree to which optimal rather than satisfactory choices are desired

f) The methods used to estimate the effort needed for accomplishing particular goals

g) The threshold level necessary for an interrupt

h) The reaction strategies used to respond to interrupts in general, and to conflict in particular

NEEDED RESEARCH

It has become evident in this chapter that there has been very little research that specifically examines the mechanisms proposed for the information processing view of motivation presented. The research areas outlined below represent an assessment of the more important questions to be examined. The presentation is organized around the propositions presented in the chapter.

Proposition 3.1 postulates that choice processes can be viewed as movement from one state to another. Exactly how consumers do perceive choice processes needs to be examined, as these perceptions will influence how choice is carried out. Also, it was hypothesized that consumers use heuristics to move between states. Delineation of the major types of heuristics used (e.g., "Buy the cheapest," "Talk to friends who have purchased one," "Buy large sizes") would be an important step. Suggested methods for approaching this and the other research areas to be proposed are outlined below.

Determinants of the intensity of choice processes, as noted in Propositions 3.3 and 3.3.i, are another major research area. Of the classes of determinants noted, two areas appear most in need of research. First is classification of the properties of choice environments (e.g., what are the numbers of alternatives and dimensions available, what other aspects of the choice environment affect the degree of processing needed or types of processing required?). The second area is examination of the processes by which consumers estimate how much effort attaining a given goal will require.

Virtually nothing is known about the process of developing goal hierarchies (Propositions 3.4, 3.4.i, 3.4.ii, 3.4.iii, 3.4.iv). The use of strategies and heuristics as guides for developing goals, the processes by which initial goals are elaborated into more detailed subgoals, and the processes by which portions of the hierarchy become learned units seem to be important areas for research. Also, the extent of in-store versus out-of-store processing needs study.

The properties of the self-regulatory systems hypothesized (Proposition 3.5) for carrying out plans need to be characterized. In particular, the role of instructions to oneself, self-imposed standards, and the mechanisms needed for self-reinforced sequences of behavior are appealing topics (Mischel 1973, p. 275).

The types of rules used for terminating processing on a given goal and the criteria (thresholds) used in these rules (Proposition 3.6) require research. Another important area is an analysis of what factors influence the threshold level for interrupts, i.e., what conditions lead to greater or lesser concentration on the current task as opposed to consideration of interrupt events (Propositions 3.7 and 3.7.i). The most significant determinants to examine appear to be time pressure and goals for learning about one's environment.

Analysis of consumer choice environments to see what are the most prevalent types of interrupt events should be undertaken (Propositions 3.8, 3.8.i). A second area of great importance, which will arise again in later chapters, is characterization of the types of strategies used by consumers to deal with conflict and the determinants of those strategies.

Study of the effects of interrupts (Proposition 3.9), particularly classification of those interrupt events which tend to lead to changes in goal hierarchies, would be useful. Finally, there are many important individual difference variables to study (Proposition 3.10). Several of these have been mentioned above. The most important seem to be depiction of differences in heuristics available, the degree of in-store versus out-of-store processing, types of self-regulatory systems used, and strategies used for reacting to interrupts in general and to conflict in particular.

The list above represents a formidable amount of research. In addition, the methods necessary for studying such questions are not those typically used in consumer research. Two general approaches which are useful for studying some of the problems above are outlined below. Further details on methods for studying processes are given in Chapter 7.

For examining properties of particular choice environments or choice tasks the notion of a task analysis is quite useful. Newell and Simon (1972) argue quite forcefully that the structure of the task being undertaken by a subject greatly influences what processes will be used; that is, the task itself imposes certain constraints on what types of processes will work in accomplishing that task. Newell and Simon argue that a thorough task analysis, a consideration of what the task *requires* for successful completion, yields a great deal of knowledge about how behavior must be structured to be adaptive in the particular task environment. Much of the difficulty in building models of consumer choice stems from the inability to perform a detailed task analysis for a "typical" consumer task, given the wide range of tasks undertaken by consumers. Thus one must concentrate on some particular choice task or class of choice tasks of interest (e.g., choice among magazines as sources of information, choice among alternatives when processing is done in the store, and so on) and attempt to specify the properties of that task which affect information processing. Some examples of task analyses are presented in later chapters.

A second general approach is directed to those research areas above that attempt to examine processes, use of strategies, and so forth. For such studies research methods which *directly* examine processing seem very useful, rather than methods where details of processing are not observed and only indirect inferences are attempted. A typical approach would be to have the subject actually perform the behavior of interest (e.g., to examine the process of goal hierarchy development, the consumer could be presented with a choice task and asked to determine how he or she would accomplish that task). Then the processes used are observed while the subject is doing the task. Several methods for attempting to observe process are available. One method used in several consumer research studies (e.g., Alexis, Haines, and Simon 1968; Bettman 1970; Russ 1971; Payne 1976a,b) is protocol analysis. In using this method, the consumer is instructed to think out loud while actually performing the task of interest. This verbal record is termed a protocol. It may be distinguished from introspection or retrospective rationale in that the subject is supposed to verbalize thoughts as they occur during the course of processing. These protocol data are then used to gain insights into the processes and strategies used. The major advantage of the method is that a great deal of data on internal processing events are made available for inspection. The major disadvantages are the difficulty of gathering and analyzing the data. Further discussion of this method is presented in Bettman (1974a) and in Chapter 7. Other methods for observing process are available, such as studying eye movements and monitoring information selected. These methods seem more relevant to research needs of different types than those discussed above, and discussion of these methods is thus postponed for the present.

Attention and Perceptual Processes

Choices are often made in environments in which an enormous amount of information is potentially available for processing, ranging from information directly relevant to the choice (e.g., information in memory, package information, advertisements) to the vast array of other stimuli constantly present in the everyday environment (e.g., buildings, other people and events, or internal stimuli such as feelings of hunger). In understanding the processing underlying some choice, therefore, one must examine how the individual manages to make sense out of this potentially confusing array. In particular, two basic questions must be addressed. First, one must consider which aspects of the environment are attended to, which particular stimuli are processed. Second, given that some piece of information is the focus of attention, how that information is perceived and interpreted is crucial, as any piece of information can usually have several different meanings. Answers to these two questions are vital for understanding consumer choice, as which pieces of information are selected for attention will influence the direction of future behavior, and it is the stimulus *as perceived* which affects choice, not the objective stimulus itself.

The goal of this chapter is to examine the processes underlying attention and perception. The emphasis is clearly not on the structure of existing perceptions, as in multidimensional scaling studies of perceptions (Green and Rao 1972); rather the focus is more on underlying processes.

OVERVIEW OF THE ATTENTION AND PERCEPTION COMPONENT

Attention to some stimulus is defined as the allocation of processing capacity to that stimulus, as devoting processing effort (Kahneman 1973). A basic question, given this definition, is to which particular stimuli is processing capacity allocated? There seem to be two answers to this question, leading Kahneman to distinguish between voluntary and involuntary attention. Allocation of voluntary attention is considered first, with involuntary attention considered below.

73

In Chapter 3 the consumer engaged in making a choice was characterized as having a set of goals to be attained. Such goals provide a basis for
determining what aspects of the environment are attended to. In this context,
voluntary attention refers to the allocation of processing efforts related to current goals and plans; that is, given the relevant goal hierarchy for a choice, the
particular goal being considered directs attention to those pieces of information in the environment (both external to and internal to the consumer) relevant to attaining that goal. For example, if one has a goal to "Determine protein content for cereal brands," then attention to information on cereal
packages or to existing information in memory about cereals is likely.

Given that attention has been devoted to some piece of information
thought to be relevant to current goals, the process of perceptual encoding
must be carried out. Perceptual encoding refers to the process of interpreting
the stimulus, of ascertaining the meaning of it; that is, the same piece of objective information, say a price, may have different meanings to different individuals, or even to the same individual at different times. A particular price may
be interpreted as too high, too low, as denoting quality or lack of it, as being
more than one currently has to spend, and so on. The interpretation developed
will depend upon information stored in memory, on those beliefs already held
by the individual, and by the context of the situation. In particular, perceptual
encoding is seen by many theorists as a process in which an interpretation is
constructed, based on both memory and the actual stimulus, with the context
provided by memory being a crucial element. In fact, individuals often develop expectations for what will be seen, based upon what is stored in memory,
and tend to look for and see what they expect. This entire process of construction and interpretation is termed an active–synthesis process (Lindsay and
Norman 1972). Finally, the results of perceptual interpretation of some
stimulus will often influence the subsequent direction of attention. Perception
of protein content of a brand of cereal as being low may lead to attention's
being directed to protein contents for other brands of cereal, for example.
Thus attention and perceptual encoding continually interact.

Thus in the basic sequence outlined above, current goals lead to direction of attention to relevant aspects of the environment, and then to interpretation of the meaning of the stimulus selected for attention.[1] This sequence
is not the only one possible, however. There can also be attention to stimuli
not directly related to the current choice or current goals. Kahneman (1973)
notes that there can be involuntary attention, which refers to allocation of
capacity to stimuli based more upon automatic mechanisms than upon current goals. For example, individuals will respond to loud noises near them, to
novel or interesting stimuli, to unexpected events, and so forth. As outlined
previously in Chapter 3, such events can lead to interrupts, which may result in
changes in goals and perhaps shifts in the focus of current processing. In such

---

1. This notion of attention followed by perception may be too rigid. It is plausible that
some very general perceptual interpretation of a stimulus, to see if it really appears
relevant, is carried out before a great deal of attention is allocated to the stimulus.

cases, attention is allocated to stimuli related to the interrupting event, and perceptual interpretation of these stimuli ensues to determine the meaning of the interrupt and plausible responses to it. Thus the interrupt sequence just described seems more relevant when the individual is *confronted* with information, and the goal-directed sequence seems more relevant when *seeking* information. Two major sources of interrupts are conflicts and learning about certain aspects of the purchasing environment, even though those aspects may not be relevant for current purchases. These are each discussed in more detail in later sections. For now, it suffices to note that the effects of such interrupts will depend on the way the consumer interprets the interrupting event and the strategies used by the consumer to react to the event. There may be physiological effects such as heightened attention. Interrupts can also often lead to changes in the goal hierarchy, with goals being reordered, added, deleted, and so on. Thus the focus of behavior may change.

These two sequences described above, voluntary attention to and perceptual interpretation of stimuli relevant to current goals, and involuntary attention to and perceptual interpretation of interrupting stimuli, both assume that attention is allocated and actively directed. However, there is also evidence that some learning about the choice environment occurs with little conscious allocation of attention, passively rather than actively (Posner 1973; Krugman 1965). This phenomenon is also considered. Thus learning about the environment that is not directly related to current goals can occur in two ways: through reactions to interrupt events and through low involvement passive processes.

The discussion above gives an outline of the attention and perceptual encoding components of the theory, and the relevant portions of the overall model are shown in Fig. 4.1. A more detailed examination is now carried out for the major concepts discussed above—attention, perceptual encoding, the role of expectations, interrupts due to conflict and learning about the environment, and processes in which little conscious attention is involved. Then the relationship of the attention and the perception component to other parts of the theory is discussed and more detailed aspects of the attention and perceptual component are considered.

MAJOR ASPECTS OF THE ATTENTION AND PERCEPTION COMPONENT

ATTENTION

As noted above, attention to some stimulus is defined as the allocation of processing capacity or effort to that stimulus.[2] There are both selective

---

2. There are processes that are postulated to operate prior to the actual devotion of processing effort to a stimulus, processes which do preliminary analyses of the stimulus without conscious direction of attention. Neisser (1967) calls these processes preattentive. Two major types of preattentive processes are global processes which group the entire stimulus field into coherent units; and control of head and eye movements. These processes are conceptualized as being outside of the voluntary control of the individual and as requiring minimal if any processing capacity (Neisser 1967, 89–93).

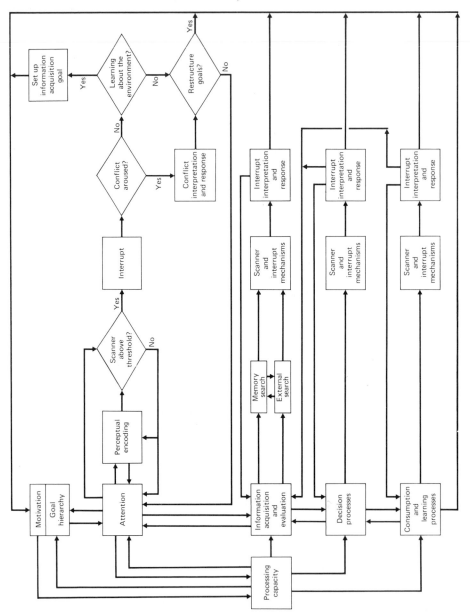

Fig. 4.1 Attention and perception segment of the theory.

and intensive aspects to such a definition of attention; that is, allocation of processing capacity is selective, in that some stimuli are attended to in preference to others; and allocation is also intensive, in that different amounts or degrees of capacity can be allocated. These notions can be summarized as

> *Proposition 4.1:* Attention to a stimulus is the allocation of processing capacity or effort to that stimulus. Such an allocation of effort has both selective and intensive aspects.[3]

Consideration of factors influencing the allocation of effort to some particular stimulus, the selective aspect of attention, leads to a distinction between two major influences: goals and unexpected events. As discussed in Chapter 3, one of the most basic aspects of consumer choice is its goal-directed nature. Consumers form goal hierarchies in the course of making choices. Given a particular set of goals, potential sources of information in the environment can be evaluated for usefulness in the light of these goals. Thus goals provide one main basis for the selective aspects of attention. For example, a consumer may have a goal which leads to "looking for a brand with no sugar added," "looking for a blue shirt," "looking for information about mufflers," or "trying to remember what I was told about which dentists are good." Such goals lead to attention to some specific subset of the information available at any one point in time, what Kahneman (1973) terms voluntary attention. This selective aspect of attention is necessary in that it allows processing information which is relevant and of interest for current goals out of the total set of all stimuli simultaneously present. This is necessary to allow progress toward these goals; input would otherwise be chaotic. However, selectivity also narrows one's focus so that some potentially important events may be missed. One function of the second influence on selectivity, described below, is to provide a mechanism for noticing crucial events which are not related to current goals.

Research in looking behavior, how people acquire information from a visual display, has shown the selectiveness of attention. Areas of a picture containing more information seem to be fixated most often (Antes 1974), with fixations made first to these informative areas and then explorations made in the neighborhood of these areas (see also Parker 1978 and Rayner 1978). Chase and Simon (1973) and Simon and Barenfeld (1969) report a similar phenomenon in looking behavior for chess positions, in which chess masters' fixations concentrate on patterns of pieces that form meaningful and familiar positions. Finally, Van Raaij's (1976b) eye movement studies of consumer choice indicate that consumers select some pieces of information and ignore others.

---

3. Howard and Sheth (1969) define attention in a roughly similar way as "the degree of openness of the buyer's sensory receptors for a particular feature of a specific stimulus display and a consequent narrowing of the range of objects to which the buyer is responding" (Howard and Sheth 1969, p. 415). Howard's (1977) definition is very similar.

While important, goal-directed processes are not the only influence on the selective aspects of attention. Attention is also allocated to events in the environment which are surprising, novel, potentially physically threatening, and so on. For example, loud noises, movement, flashes of light, and departures from expectations will often lead to direction of attention to the stimuli involved. In the consumer context this might involve price changes, new brands, changed package designs, and so on. Kahneman terms this type of attention involuntary, in that it seems to be a function of more automatic, built-in mechanisms, rather than current goals. As noted above, these mechanisms are adaptive, in that too narrow a focus on current goals could potentially be detrimental. In summary,

> *Proposition 4.1.i:* Two major influences on the selective aspects of attention are
>
> a) Current goals, leading to voluntary attention.
>
> b) Surprising, novel, potentially threatening, unexpected, etc. events, leading to involuntary attention.

For the present we will focus on goal-directed, or voluntary, attention. Involuntary attention is discussed below when interrupts are considered.

Attention also has intensive aspects; that is, there can be degrees of attention. A consumer may respond to a question about a commercial by saying "I wasn't really paying close attention," for example. Different amounts of processing capacity can be allocated to any particular stimulus in the course of processing that stimulus. Kahneman (1973, p. 4) sees this capacity allocation decision as made by the individual, not by the environment per se, although some tasks demand more effort than others if the individual decides to undertake them: "The effort that a subject invests at any one time corresponds to what he is doing, rather than what is happening to him." Pribram and McGuinness (1975), citing physiological evidence, also consider the level of attention to be related to information processing capacity. However, they relate processing effort to changes in representation or organization, to increasing the *competence* of the processing capacity by forming larger chunks[4] in memory, rather than directly relating effort to the *size* of the capacity allocated as Kahneman does. Thus effort would be most demanded during concentrated problem solving, where coordination and integration of various pieces of information might be most required. In more habitual decisions, little effort would be required, as existing organizations in memory would suffice. Thus, in Kahneman's view, more capacity (effort) is allocated as the individual decides to give more attention; in Pribram and McGuinness'

---

4. A chunk is roughly defined as "any configuration that is familiar to the subject and can be recognized by him" (Simon and Barenfeld 1969). In essence, a chunk is an organized cognitive structure that can grow as information is integrated into it.

view, effort is used to create a more "effective" processing capacity. Although these formulations clearly differ, the basic idea in both is that increases in processing capacity (as actual capacity or as capability) roughly correspond to increases in attention.

> *Proposition 4.1.ii:* The intensity aspects of attention refer to the degree to which processing capacity is allocated. Increases in processing capacity correspond to increases in attention.

PERCEPTUAL ENCODING

The previous section describes the allocation of attention to some particular stimulus. Once a stimulus has been given some level of attention, the next question is how is the stimulus processed to ascertain its meaning or interpretation? As noted earlier, the meaning of a stimulus resides in the assessment of that stimulus by the individual, in how the individual interprets that stimulus, rather than in the stimulus itself. What is important is what is perceived, not necessarily what is.

There seem to be two main stages in this interpretive process. The first stage is a feature analysis, an extraction from the sensory input of the main features present (Lindsay and Norman 1972; Gregg 1974; Hunt 1971). Such an analysis can range from basic features such as angles, contours, brightness, depth, and so on up to more complex features which reflect patterns or configurations of objects familiar to the individual. Based upon the feature analysis, a rough classification of the pattern is made.

Analysis at this very detailed level of features is probably not the most fruitful level for examining the development of perceptual interpretations in consumer choice. The second main stage of the perceptual process, termed the active-synthesis stage, seems to be a more valuable focal point, as it more directly involves the consumer's knowledge about choice alternatives. This stage is now described.

Lindsay and Norman (1972, p. 131) point out that feature analysis is not sufficient for developing interpretations. Context is extremely important. We *construct* interpretations, given our view of the current context of events. Thus memory plays a crucial role in synthesizing meaning. "A large part of the interpretation of sensory data is provided by the knowledge of what the signal must be, rather than from information contained in the signal itself. This extra information comes from the *context* of the sensory event" (Lindsay and Norman 1972, p. 133). In other words, based on what has just been observed and knowledge of context, expectations are developed for what should come next. Kahneman (1973) terms this "perceptual readiness." These expectations are continually being constructed and changed as the course of information processing goes forward. Lindsay and Norman (1972) refer to this as an active-synthesis model of perceptual interpretation. They describe this model as attempting "to convert the sensory evidence into an interpretation consistent with our knowledge about the world. It is continually constructing, testing, and revising hypotheses about what is being perceived. When the predictions fail or the context is lacking, it proceeds slowly, relying heavily on the sensory data. When operating in a familiar and highly predictable world, it can move quickly and efficiently, sampling only enough data to confirm current expectations and reconstructing what it does not see according to the rules of its internal model" (Lindsay and Norman 1972, pp. 146–147). Such a system is very efficient: only limited processing needs to be carried out if events are proceeding in accord with expectations, with more extensive processing required only if expectations are lacking or not met. Thus for choices where there is a good deal of consistent previous experience and hence strong expectations exist about the alternatives available, their properties, and so on, a perceptual interpretation may be almost automatic, developed with very little effort (see Schneider and Shiffrin [1977] and Shiffrin and Schneider [1977] for a discussion of such automatic processes). Another property of such a system is that often consumers will perceive stimuli as they expect them to be, even if that expectation is in fact not valid (e.g., for a choice with a good deal of previous experience, one may not notice a price change, or a new alternative, since one expects the choice situation to be the same as it was previously). Since the role of expectations is so central in the active-synthesis model, the next section will consider this role in more detail. Summarizing the discussion above, we have

> *Proposition 4.2:* Perceptual interpretations may be developed by an active-synthesis process where context and prior expectations are important elements. Interpretations may be guided by what a stimulus seems to be based on context and expectations as well as by the actual features of the stimulus.

THE ROLE OF EXPECTATIONS IN PERCEPTUAL ENCODING[5]

Expectations about what the environment is like played a central role in the perceptual mechanisms discussed above. In essence, perceptual interpretation is partially guided by the actual properties of the stimulus and partially by the individual's expectations about what the stimulus should be.

---

5. The use of expectations as a construct in this section is essentially the same as the usage of the term schema in psychology (Bartlett 1932; Piaget and Inhelder 1973). A schema is "an internal structure, developed through experience with the world, which organizes incoming information relative to previous experience" (Mandler and Parker 1976, p. 39). Bobrow and Norman (1975) provide a thorough account of the interrelations among schemata, processing resources, goal-directed processing, and processing initiated by interrupt events. Bregman (1977) uses a similar concept, ideals, to describe processes underlying perception and behavior. Finally, Abelson's (1976) concept of the use of scripts in decision making is also related. Thus many theorists have postulated that humans use organized patterns of expected events in decision-making situations.

There are several lines of evidence which support the role of expectations in perceptual analyses. First, Pribram and McGuinness (1975) cite physiological evidence stating that expected patterns have a physiological representation. These patterns seem to be built up over time as a result of experience with the particular phenomenon for which the pattern is relevant. When the expected pattern is in fact encountered, processing proceeds normally. When there is a mismatch between input and the expected pattern, an interrupt may occur. Lindsay and Lindsay (1966) support these notions about expected patterns and the role of experience in developing these expectations. Their results suggest that frequently occurring patterns may be recognized as gestalts, as total configurations, without being analyzed into their more underlying dimensions. Patterns which are not frequently occurring, on the other hand, may be identified only after an examination of the underlying dimensions. Thus there are important impacts of degree of experience and familiarity on perceptual processes.

A second line of evidence, from studies in marketing, shows that what is perceived depends upon expectations based on what is in memory. For example, Allison and Uhl (1964) show how perceptions of beers are different depending upon whether one is told the identity of the brand of beer one is drinking or is given an unlabeled bottle. One interpretation of this result is that knowledge of the brand name leads to expectations about taste and other attributes, and that these expectations are stronger than subjects' abilities to actually discriminate differences on these attributes. Another example in a marketing context is a study by Preston and Scharbach (1971). Consumers were more prone to make illogical generalizations from advertisements than from other forms of communication. The reasons for this seemed to be that the consumers had expectations about what advertisers would *like* to say, and perceived the ads to say this even if the ads did not. Other work has shown perception and expectations to be influenced by need states (see Engel, Blackwell, and Kollat 1978, pp. 342–344 for a review).

A final area of research related to the use of expectations in developing perceptual interpretations has studied the perceptual skills of subjects. Such skills have been related to the amount of prior knowledge possessed about some task and the complexity of the expectations developed on the basis of that knowledge. Studies of perception in chess have shown these phenomena most dramatically (Simon and Gilmartin 1973; Chase and Simon 1973). Chess masters are able, after viewing an actual chess position containing about 20 pieces for five seconds, to almost perfectly reconstruct the position. Players below the master level do not come close to this performance. In addition, when pieces are placed randomly on chessboards, no differences are observed between pieces correctly placed by masters and nonmasters. This discounts an explanation in terms of sheer memory ability. The explanation appears to be in the *units* of perception: the masters perceive certain *configurations* of pieces as a whole. In other words, the masters have larger or more complex chunks or patterns in memory than nonmasters, and can thus perceive more individual pieces although only recalling the same number of patterns. Thus the more complex the expectations, the more efficiency is shown in these recall situations. In consumer research, brand name can be seen as a chunk which summarizes expected patterns or attribute configurations (Bettman and Jacoby 1976; Jacoby, Szybillo, and Busato-Schach 1977). Consumers may then learn over time to base choices on such expected configurations or chunks (e.g., on brand name) rather than performing detailed analyses (Bettman 1971b). Howard (1977) notes that during extensive problem solving, expectations are not yet present, and processing is slower and much more difficult than when expectations are available. The basic role of the formation of chunks in learning in general is discussed by Buschke (1976).

These facets of the role of expectations in perceptual processes can be summarized as

> *Proposition 4.2.i:* Expectations based upon beliefs stored in memory can influence several aspects of perceptual encoding:
> a) Expectations develop over time, based upon experience with a phenomenon
> b) If expectations are met, encoding proceeds normally. If expectations are not met, an interrupt may occur
> c) Perceptions may depart from reality if expectations are strong
> d) Perceptual efficiency may depend on the complexity of expectations held, the size of the patterns one can recognize

The discussion thus far has assumed that attention and perception are goal-directed processes, that aspects of the environment relevant for the attainment of current goals are attended to and perceptual interpretations of such aspects are developed. However, as stated above and in Chapter 3, consumers do not always behave in such a single-minded fashion. We now turn to a discussion of what happens when expectations are not met, or when environmental events indicate that different needs from those underlying current goals and plans must be addressed.

The notions of scanning and interrupting mechanisms were introduced in Chapter 3 to deal with events and conditions that can lead to interruptions of current processing. Two major types of interrupting events seem most relevant to the attention and perceptual encoding component: conflict and learning about the environment. Thus we state

> *Proposition 4.3:* Interrupting events during attention and perception are of two main types:

a) Conflict

b) Learning about the environment

Reactions to these events depend on the consumer's interpretation of the significance of the event.

Each of these two classes of interrupts is now discussed in turn.

INTERRUPTS DUE TO CONFLICT

Within this section are four major subsections: an examination of the nature of conflict, a rationale for focusing on conflict rather than some other construct, a consideration of different types of conflict interrupts, and a discussion of reactions to conflict interrupts.

The nature of conflict

The essential notion underlying the construct of conflict is that an individual is faced simultaneously with competing and incompatible response tendencies (Berlyne 1957); that is, there are several responses which might be given, but these responses are incompatible, so that only one can be performed. For example, a consumer may be attempting to decide among four brands of automobiles from which only one will be purchased. Note that it is conflict as *perceived* by the consumer that is important, not actual conflict or conflict as seen by others.

Berlyne (1957) hypothesizes that degree of conflict is related to four factors: (1) the *number* of competing tendencies, with conflict increasing as the number of competing tendencies increases; (2) the *nearness to equality* of the competing tendencies, with increased conflict the nearer the tendencies are to equality; (3) the *absolute strengths* of the response tendencies, with higher conflict the higher these strengths; and (4) the *degree of incompatibility* of the responses, with higher conflict the more incompatible the responses. Thus, in the consumer choice example above, the more the consumer is equally and strongly favorable to each of the four cars, the higher the conflict. Also, the conflict tends to be greater for the four car case than if the consumer were only considering three cars. Finally, the four potential responses (purchase of each car) also seem very incompatible, with purchase of one car probably precluding purchase of the others. The notions above are expressed as

Proposition 4.4: Conflict is a result of competing and incompatible response tendencies. Four factors may underlie conflict:

a) The number of competing response tendencies

b) The nearness to equality of the competing response tendencies

c) The absolute strengths of the response tendencies

d) The degree of incompatibility of the responses

These notions have been subjected to experimental test by Berlyne and others, and some problems have arisen. For example, Kiesler (1966) and Hendrick, Mills, and Kiesler (1968), in studies reported in Chapter 3, argue that in some cases increasing the number of alternatives appears to lessen conflict, although it should be noted that their results are weak and that what they observed was the *response* to conflict and not the degree of conflict itself. In addition, Worell (1962) found that degree of conflict seemed to vary with the difference in strength between competing tendencies, but not with their absolute level of strength. Thus Berlyne's notions, although they have provided most of the framework for research on intraindividual conflict, are not without controversy.

Choice of conflict as a focus

One question which should be addressed before proceeding further is why perceived conflict should provide the focus for interrupts and responses to them. Alternative constructs, such as level of arousal (Hebb 1955; Howard 1977) or level of incongruity (Hunt 1963) have been proposed by other theorists, for example. We will argue, however, using arousal and incongruity as examples, that conflict is a more appropriate construct for the purpose of modeling properties of interrupt events.

Arousal, as a measure of physiological activity, seems inadequate for several reasons. First, there are many sources of arousal—conflict, fear, drugs, anxiety, and so forth. Thus high arousal in itself may not correspond to a conflict event. Second, physiologically there seem to be several distinct types of arousal (Kahneman 1973, pp. 32–33; Pribram and McGuinness 1975). The third reason, however, is probably most important. We are concerned with the *perception* of a state, not the state itself; that is, it is conflict as perceived and interpreted, or arousal as perceived and interpreted, that influences behavior. Actual levels of arousal are often interpreted by subjects in different ways, depending upon the information given to them, so that actual levels of arousal may not be relevant (e.g., Schachter and Singer 1962; Valins 1966). Driscoll and Lanzetta (1964) and Hawkins and Lanzetta (1965) showed that actual arousal did not correlate with information search, for example. One could of course use perceived arousal, but this seems to move further from the labels for subjective experience probably used by individuals, which is undesirable for a measure of a perceived phenomenon. Finally, Hansen (1972, pp. 288–290) found that perceived conflict and an index of perceived motive arousal did not correlate highly.

Incongruity is not used as a focus because conflict seems more general. Berlyne (1961, 1968) has argued that what he calls the collative variables (e.g., novelty, incongruity, complexity, surprisingness) work through conflict;[6] that is, these variables are seen as generating conflict. For example,

---

6. They are called collative variables because collation or comparison of elements is involved in generating the effects.

incongruity between expectations and actual events will involve competing response tendencies, one generated by the expectations, the other by the input received. Thus, on the whole, conflict appears to be a useful construct for attempting to characterize this one major class of interrupting events in the attention and perception component. This is stated as

> *Proposition 4.5:* Conflict seems to be the most appropriate construct for characterizing one major class of interrupting events. Such constructs as arousal and incongruity are not completely adequate.

Types of conflict interrupt events

Given the background above on conflict, we can now consider more directly the role of interrupts in the attention and perception component. There seem to be three major causes of conflict-based interrupts which are relevant for attention and perceptual processes: (1) parts of the environment or perceptual field competing for attention (e.g., the consumer sees a package he wants to look at, but at the same time remembers something about the product that he wants to think about; or a consumer sees a billboard she wishes to read while at the same time an advertisement she wants to hear is on the car radio); (2) disagreement between what was perceived and what was expected (e.g., a price change for one's favorite brand is noticed); and (3) competing interpretations of the stimulus are possible (e.g., the consumer may be able to interpret a complex advertisement in many ways). Note that all of these can be seen as related to competing and incompatible response tendencies — i.e., conflict. The origins of a system for interrupts may reflect the fact that attention to such phenomena, allowing interruption of current processing, may be adaptive for survival (e.g., respond to sudden movements or novel events). Summarizing this discussion, we postulate

> *Proposition 4.6:* Three major causes of interrupts due to conflict in attention and perception are
>
> a) Parts of the environment or perceptual field competing for attention
>
> b) Disagreement between what was perceived and what was expected
>
> c) Competing interpretations for a stimulus

More detail can be provided on each of the three major causes above. Parts of the environment which are competing for attention can arise in many ways. Information relevant for consumer choices is embedded in the ongoing activities of everyday life, and television commercials, radio advertisements, and so on, may be present at the same time the individual is trying to do something else. Then the individual may choose to attend to the commercial, for example, or the other task at hand. Such *reactions* to an interrupt are discussed more fully below. In addition, one final point should be made about parts of the environment which compete for attention. *Internal* stimuli, such as recall of some information in memory or feelings of hunger, are part of the environment as well as external stimuli such as advertisements. Thus internal and external stimuli can compete, or two internal stimuli, as well as two external stimuli.

Disagreement between what was perceived and what was expected seems to be a particularly important cause of interrupts. As noted above, individuals form expectations about products and these expectations influence one's perceptual interpretations. Thus in some cases reality may depart from expectations, but the departure may not be perceived. However, if the departure is noticed then an interrupt will occur, and the reaction to the interrupt will involve interpreting the meaning of this departure. Thus an important issue is *how much* of a deviation from expectations is necessary to cause an interrupt, the threshold discussed in Proposition 3.7.i. As noted in this earlier proposition, the threshold probably varies over individuals and situations (e.g., higher time pressure may lead to less noticing of deviations). There is some evidence in the marketing literature relevant to departure from expectations and interrupts. Kohan (1968) found, using physiological measures, that physiological activity was highest when changes occurred in a commercial (e.g., when a voice began more than halfway through a previously silent commercial). Other studies have shown that changes in advertisements (Grass and Wallace 1969) or novel advertisements (Bogart, Tolley, and Orenstein 1970) seemed to initially attract high attention.[7]

Finally, competing interpretations from a stimulus can arise for a stimulus which contains elements which are inconsistent. For example, Greeno and Noreen (1974) had subjects read consistent and inconsistent sets of sentences, and reading time was recorded. Inconsistent sets of sentences took longer to read than consistent sets of approximately equal lengths. One implication might be, then, that extra time is spent in noticing and interpreting the inconsistency. In a similar vein, complexity of a stimulus may also be related to competing interpretations, as a more complex stimulus allows more interpretations. Morrison and Dainoff (1972), using subjects' assessments of the complexity of advertisements, found that time spent looking at the advertisement was positively related to complexity. Let us now turn to analysis of the reactions to interrupts generated by conflict.

Reactions to conflict interrupt events

General notions about reactions to interrupt events have been presented in earlier chapters. Briefly, the individual is seen as assessing the

---

7. For a review of the effects of other factors on attention to advertisements, such as size, color, etc., see Diamond (1968). These factors may be related to collative properties, but the relationship is not clear.

meaning of the interrupt and then deciding how to handle the interrupt.[8] Thus the specific effects depend upon individuals' reaction strategies. However, one can characterize the effects in general. There seem to be two major types of reactions to conflict interrupt events: increased physiological activity, and assessment of the adequacy of the current goal hierarchy in light of the information conveyed by the interrupt event. If warranted by the interrupt event, current goals may be changed, dropped, or redefined, and some new activity initiated. For example, if one notices a price increase on one's favorite brand, then instead of picking up that brand, one may decide to look at other brands. Thus one important type of goal change in reaction to a conflict interrupt event may be to set up a goal for information search. One may also decide to ignore the price change, however, so reactions to conflict interrupt events depend on the person's assessment of the conflict, decisions about whether the conflict can be tolerated, and if not, how it can be resolved. As a summary, we propose, parallel to Proposition 3.9,

> *Proposition 4.7*: Conflict interrupt events have two main types of effects:
>
> a) Increased physiological activity
>
> b) Assessment of the adequacy of the current goal hierarchy, with changes in the hierarchy implemented if it is found inadequate. One particular change of importance is that goals for information search may be developed.

Further analyses of reactions to conflict interrupt events are presented in the more detailed treatments of aspects of the theory given later in the chapter. At this point, we turn to an overview of interrupts leading to learning about the environment.

LEARNING ABOUT THE ENVIRONMENT THROUGH INTERRUPTS

In some instances, consumers appear to learn about their purchasing environment, even if the specific knowledge gained has no direct relevance to current purchases. For example, while in a store to buy a washing machine, a consumer may notice prices for refrigerators and stereos, or may notice which brands of electronic calculators the store carries. Thus if the consumer later makes a choice in a product category in which such learning took place, there may be a store of knowledge that can be used. The phenomenon of learning about the environment may be a partial explanation, therefore, for the low

---

8. For conflict interrupt events related to attention and perception, there are also cases where responses probably are more automatic and less dependent upon response strategies. For example, when consumers were faced with advertisements for Salem cigarettes that ended with "You can take Salem out of the country, but . . . ," the tendency to silently complete the jingle is probably more or less automatic (the need for closure).

amounts of information search observed for consumers choosing durables (e.g., Newman and Staelin 1972).

Such learning about the environment could arise from several different types of interrupting events. First an interrupt may occur if something happens to attract the consumer's attention. For example, a package may be explored because it "looks interesting." Note that this type of interrupt is also related to interrupts due to conflict, since "interestingness" may engender conflict. The distinguishing feature of learning about the environment, however, is that the exploration is unrelated to *current* purchases, but is rather aimed at gathering information for potential future use. A second type of interrupt event, related to the first, may occur when the consumer decides *a priori* to "look for something interesting," to have a predisposition to explore. Finally, a third type of learning about the environment is where the individual has a goal of learning about some product if time permits, but is not planning a purchase in the near future. For example, a consumer may usually stop and look at stereos while shopping, although purchase of a stereo may be far in the future.

One major stream of research relevant to learning about the environment is research in psychology on latent learning. Latent learning refers to learning which is carried out that is incidental to the main task, and the effect of which appears only at the time of "reward"; that is, exploratory behavior can lead to learning that is not relevant to the current goal, but that may be useful at some future time. "The latent learning experiments show that an animal can learn by exploring the maze, without food reward, so that, when reward is later introduced, performance is better than rats without this exposure, and sometimes as good as that of rats with many previously rewarded trials. The 'latent learning' consists of knowledge of the maze, not revealed in choice of the shortest path from entrance to exit until the rat is motivated to make that choice" (Hilgard and Bower 1966, pp. 199–200). This latent learning research documents the existence of the phenomenon and also conditions under which latent learning should occur. In particular, the argument can be made that learning about the environment should be most prevalent under low levels of conflict in the current choices being made by the consumer. The higher the level of conflict involved in the choice that is one's current focus, the less likely one is to look at something that is interesting, but irrelevant for the present. Simon (1967, p. 39), after reviewing the latent learning literature, comes to roughly the same conclusion: "latent learning should occur principally under conditions of low irrelevant drive." Thus, we propose

> *Proposition 4.8:* There are several types of interrupt events leading to learning about the environment. The major effect of such events is information search. Learning about the environment should be most prevalent in low conflict situations.

The sections above all assume that conscious allocation of attention is necessary for perceiving and learning about aspects of the consumer environment. However, some studies suggest that such active involvement is not necessary. Thus learning about the environment can occur in two ways, through conscious allocation of attention due to interrupt events and through low involvement processes.

LEARNING ABOUT THE ENVIRONMENT
THROUGH LOW INVOLVEMENT PROCESSES

Several researchers, working in different areas and using different paradigms, have postulated that individuals can learn about their environment without necessarily consciously allocating much attention. Three streams of research in particular are examined below: the "low involvement learning" work carried out in marketing (Krugman 1965; Robertson 1976); work on "incidental learning" (McLaughlin 1965; Postman 1975); and research into "spectator learning" (Posner 1973).

Low involvement learning

Krugman (1965) claims that much learning and persuasion may occur under low involvement, particularly for television commercials. Krugman defines involvement as the number of connections, or personal references, that persons spontaneously make between their own lives and the advertising stimulus. Thus his concept of involvement seems closely related to the idea of allocation of processing capacity. Under low involvement (and hence low allocation of capacity to the advertising message), Krugman hypothesizes that perceptual defenses are absent, that which attributes are seen as salient may shift with repeated viewing of an advertisement, and that attitude does not change until after the catalyst provided by making a choice. Low involvement and high involvement processing are seen as requiring different models. Robertson (1976) develops this viewpoint more fully, discussing the impacts of low commitment on many aspects of consumer choice, but emphasizing the passive rather than active nature of the process.

This notion of low involvement processes has also generated research on the effects of media. Krugman (1971) sees print media as requiring more attention or effort than television; with print requiring more active processing, and television confronting us with the information and enabling more passive processing (see also McLuhan 1964). Wright (1974a), on the other hand, sees content as the source of attention, with media moderating the way attention operates. For example, print allows a greater response if the consumer desires, since one can control the information rate, as opposed to a television commercial. On the other hand, print allows the consumer greater freedom to ignore the message if it is not involving. Thus television may be more effective for content with low involvement for most consumers. For further research and thinking on low involvement processes, see Maloney and Silverman (1978).

Incidental learning

The work done on incidental learning, while related to the idea that lower levels of attention can still result in learning, is more appropriately classified as research performed within a particular methodological paradigm. A typical study of incidental learning might be carried out as follows. Several groups of subjects (divided into "intentional learning" groups and "incidental learning" groups) are asked to go through a list of words and perform a task, called the "orienting task." Typically, different sorts of orienting tasks have been used. Two common types are semantic tasks, in which semantic processing and comprehension of the word are required (e.g., rating a word for its pleasantness or unpleasantness); and nonsemantic tasks, where semantic processing is not necessary (e.g., check whether there is an "s" in the word). Each intentional group and each incidental group is then given one of the orienting tasks to perform. In addition, the intentional groups are told that they will be tested for their memory of the words on the list, but the incidental groups are *not* told. Then a memory test of some sort (recall or recognition) is given after the list has been presented. Thus the memory test is presumably unexpected by the incidental groups. The typical results are that intentional learners do better than incidental learners, but that the nature of the orienting task has a large impact. Incidental groups learn more with semantic orienting tasks than with nonsemantic tasks. Thus the implication is that if consumers are confronted with information, say in a commercial, then if the commercial induces the consumer to react in ways which cause "semantic" analysis of the ideas involved, learning can take place even if there is no conscious intention to learn. This notion, although related to low involvement processes, is not quite the same. The major distinction between intentional and incidental learning is whether or not there are specific instructions to learn.[9] Even without such instructions (the incidental groups), learning can occur if "semantic" involvement is somehow induced. Thus the learning is not without involvement, but learning in which there is involvement that may not be consciously directed by the individual.

Spectator learning

Posner (1973) summarizes research in concept formation that makes the distinction between subjects who use what he calls spectator learning and those who engage in participant learning. The task is one where subjects are shown some positive and negative instances of a concept, and are to learn to classify further instances as being positive or negative. Subjects who engage in spectator learning appear to passively examine the first series of positive and

---

9. The distinction that learning is intentional when subjects have instructions to learn the relevant material and incidental when there are no instructions to learn would seem to imply that almost all nonlaboratory learning is incidental learning. However, this definition was developed to apply to laboratory paradigms in which the experimenter "controls" instructions; the basic concept, although difficult to operationalize, is one of "set" or "preparedness" for learning. In this sense, although some human learning may be incidental, there are certainly many instances of goal-directed learning, guided perhaps by *self-instructions,* rather than by externally imposed instructions.

negative instances, can later correctly classify new instances, but cannot state any rule for differentiating positive and negative instances. Subjects engaged in participant learning, on the other hand, are actively generating and testing hypotheses and develop rules for classifying instances. Thus some subjects are able to passively learn, while others are much more active. Posner (1973, p. 83) argues that in some instances where complex patterns are to be learned (e.g., much of human pattern recognition in general) the passive approach may be more effective than an active approach.

The three areas of research briefly summarized above all deal with learning about one's environment. Krugman's notions actually postulate learning under low levels of involvement and attention to the advertising message. The incidental learning and spectator learning notions do not present such a clear picture. In both cases the focus seems to be on whether or not the learner is actively trying to learn, or is merely taking events in passively. It is not clear what levels of attention are postulated, although it seems most likely that low to moderate levels of attention are involved rather than high attention levels. Thus the conclusion seems to be that learning about the environment can occur under conditions of low attention and under conditions of passive rather than active processing. Although some notions about the conditions under which such phenomena occur have been advanced (e.g., Robertson [1976] claims much of consumer learning is of this sort, Krugman [1965] specifically cites television advertising, and use of spectator versus participant learning strategies seems to be an individual difference variable), the actual role of such processes relative to more active ones is not well understood at present. McKeachie (1976) discusses factors influencing under what conditions active and passive learning processes are likely to be most effective, but the research done to date is very limited.

> *Proposition 4.9:* Learning about the environment can occur under conditions of low involvement and low attention and under conditions where stimuli are passively rather than actively processed.

SUMMARY

Attention and perceptual processes are the processes involved in selecting a stimulus for processing and interpreting that stimulus. Attention is seen as allocation of processing capacity to a stimulus. Attention is given to stimuli either because the stimuli are instrumental in reaching current goals, or because the stimuli have led to an interrupt. If a stimulus is attended to, then an interpretation of the meaning of the stimulus is developed. This interpretation is heavily influenced by prior expectations about the stimulus. Interrupts are of two major types: interrupts due to conflict, and interrupts leading to learning about the environment. Such interrupts can lead to changes in the goals to be pursued. Learning about one's environment can also occur under conditions of low attention and conditions where one passively takes in information.

LINKAGES TO OTHER COMPONENTS OF THE THEORY

Attention and perceptual processes have important linkages to other components in the theory. As argued above, motivation (particularly current goals) plays an important role in determining which particular stimuli are attended to and interpreted. The attention and perception component also can influence the motivational component, however, since interrupts generated from the attention and perceptual component can lead to changes in goals.

Attention and perception themselves interact. The results of a perceptual interpretation of one stimulus may lead to direction of attention to some other stimulus. Thus there is a continual cycling between attention and perceptual processes.

Attention and perception are also closely linked to information search and memory. If the consumer has a goal of obtaining some piece of information, then attention and perception are essential mechanisms in the process of information search. Stimuli are scanned and interpreted until the appropriate one is found. In addition, the very process of perceptual interpretation requires information search, particularly internal search in memory. Prior expectations or expected patterns, stored in memory, play a vital role in interpreting the meaning of stimulus input. One must interrelate the input with what one already knows. Finally, interrupts will often lead to goals for information search; thus attention and perception indirectly influence search through the motivation component.

The above are some of the major linkages to other components in the theory. There is also a link to decision processes, since decisions are being continually made about what to attend to next, what interpretation of a stimulus makes the most sense, etc. Finally, attention is rather directly linked to processing capacity by its definition. On the other hand, perception of simple or familiar stimuli seems to require little processing capacity (Kerr 1973). Kahneman (1973, p. 191) points out that relative to choices, decisions, rehearsal, or mental manipulation of symbols, routine perceptual processes should require little effort. However, under interrupts, perceptual processes should require more capacity. Pribram and McGuinness (1975) present evidence that when expectations are not met, more effort is necessary.

MORE DETAILED ASPECTS OF THE
ATTENTION AND PERCEPTION COMPONENT

The major features of the attention and perception component have now been presented. More detailed elaborations of some of the notions introduced above are now presented.

MEASUREMENT OF ATTENTION

A good deal of research on attention in the context of consumer behavior has focused on measuring attention, particularly attention to television commercials and print advertisements. Dalbey, Gross, and Wind (1968) present an overview of the alternative measures which can be used. Verbal responses, usually to questions attempting to tap awareness, recall, familiarity, and so forth for some particular stimulus, are one class of commonly used measures. These measures assume that the greater the attention to a communication, the more likely one is to remember it. Another important class of measures is nonverbal, particularly physiological measures. Such measures as pupil dilation, galvanic skin response (GSR), salivation, and others have been utilized. One of the most researched areas has been studies of pupil dilation. Hess and Polt (1960) and Hess (1965) first suggested that increases in the size of the pupil of the eye while viewing a stimulus corresponded to interest or affective (pleasantness or unpleasantness) reactions. A major advantage of the technique for marketing and advertising researchers was thought to be the technique's reduced bias in measuring a consumer's feelings (Krugman 1964). Krugman showed that pupil responses to pictures of various products were roughly related to sales data, and more so than traditional verbal measures. However, Blackwell, Hensel, and Sternthal (1970) review recent research which suggests that pupil dilation does not measure pleasantness or affect, but instead measures the degree of active processing of information (Beatty and Kahneman 1966; Hess and Polt 1964; Kahneman and Beatty 1966, 1967). Thus pupil response measures may tap the degree of processing effort or attention devoted to a stimulus, but not the evaluative results of that processing (see also Goldwater 1972).

Finally, Krugman (1968) presents some fascinating results of using pupil dilation measures to study consumers' abilities to evaluate how much processing a commercial will require and then allocate that amount. About four to ten seconds after the onset of a 60-second commercial, a peak pupil dilation response occurs (a peak for that first ten seconds) and this peak correlates at .83 with average response for the total commercial. As Krugman states, this "appears to be an evaluative event accompanied by commitment of a specific degree of energy to the ensuing experience" (p. 251). Thus such pupil dilation measures may be useful for measuring the allocation of attention to stimuli and then assessing influences on such allocations. For example, effects of information load on attention to advertisements could be studied, or effects of particular design parameters of advertisements.

> *Proposition 4.1.iii:* Attention has been measured in many ways, using mainly verbal awareness and recall responses or physiological measures. Pupil dilation measures seem particularly useful for tapping the amount of processing effort (attention) being allocated.

MODELS OF CONFLICT

Four determinants of conflict were presented above in Proposition 4.4. Berlyne (1957) proposed a formal model of conflict which would be consistent with these determinants. In particular, Berlyne assumes that if there are n alternative responses, each can be characterized by some measure E_i of response strength or tendency. He further assumes that one can convert these measures of response strength into a response probability P_i for each response. Then the overall measure of conflict, C, is given by

$$C = -\bar{E} \sum_{i=1}^{n} P_i \log_2 P_i, \tag{4.1}$$

where $\bar{E}$ is the mean response strength. The portion of this formula given by $-\Sigma_i P_i \log_2 P_i$ is the information theory measure for entropy or uncertainty. Note that it increases as n increases, and increases as the P_i approach equality (Determinants a and b in Proposition 4.4). The multiplication of entropy by the mean response strength means that conflict increases with absolute response strength, Determinant c in Proposition 4.4. The fourth determinant, the degree of compatibility among the responses, is essentially ignored. Other researchers have equated uncertainty with entropy and importance with the absolute level of response strength, and have postulated a multiplicative model of conflict as uncertainty X importance (Hawkins and Lanzetta 1965; Lanzetta and Driscoll 1968; Hansen 1972). Since it is conflict as *perceived* by the individual which is important, not actual conflict or conflict as seen by others, the implication is that *perceptions* of uncertainty and importance are the relevant variables. Conflict as a perceived phenomenon is not well modeled currently. There are no good measures for perceived conflict (physiological measures will not suffice, since individuals interpret internal states differently depending on context and other factors as discussed previously). There is also no underlying model of the constructs relating to uncertainty and importance if these are even the two main conflict determinants.[10] Thus modeling and measuring perceived conflict is a crucial area for research.

> *Proposition 4.4.i:* Formal models of conflict, as currently formulated, appear to be inadequate.

---

10. This is clear from examining the notion of perceived risk (Cox 1967b), which also uses the notions of uncertainty and importance. However, risk and conflict seem to be distinct phenomena. For example, an approach–approach conflict does not seem to be necessarily a risky choice. Also, Bettman's (1973) model of perceived risk measures certainty as percentage of acceptable brands and Cunningham (1967) measures certainty as how certain you are a brand you haven't tried before will perform as well as your present brand. If there are many acceptable brands, or if one is certain the unknown brand will perform as well, there can still be conflict, defined as competing response tendencies, but there would tend to be low risk. Before progress in understanding risk or conflict can be made, better conceptual models of what comprises each phenomenon need to be developed.

REACTIONS TO INTERRUPTS DUE TO CONFLICT

As noted in Proposition 4.7, conflict interrupt events have two main types of effects: physiological, and assessment of the meaning of the conflict and reacting to it. Let us consider each of these in turn.

Physiological effects

One of the first effects of an interrupt due to conflict is the occurrence of an innate reaction, the orientation reaction (OR) (also sometimes called the orientation response or reflex). Such a reaction has been shown to occur when expectations are not met (Pribram and McGuinness 1975; Berlyne 1961). The OR consists of a pattern of responses that helps prepare the individual to respond to the interrupting stimulus: (1) orientation (physical adjustments such as turning one's head, etc.) toward possible sources of significant information; (2) increased efforts to process and analyze the stimulus which led to the interrupt; (3) inhibition of ongoing activity so that capacity (attention) can be allocated to the interrupting event; and (4) an increase in arousal (Kahneman 1973, pp. 42–49). Lindsay and Norman (1972, p. 611) and Simon (1967, p. 35) argue that any interrupt leads to arousal increases. Increases in arousal can have affects on attention. Under moderately high arousal, attention may become more narrow, focused on fewer aspects of the situation (Kahneman 1973, pp. 37–42). If arousal is extremely high, however, response patterns may be disrupted and extreme distractibility is reported (Korchin 1964). Finally, note that although conflict leads to arousal, the reverse need not be true. Physiological arousal can occur without necessarily increasing conflict, depending on one's beliefs about the source of the arousal. For example, arousal caused by drugs may be attributed to the drug if subjects are made aware that the drug causes arousal (Schachter and Singer 1962; Driscoll and Lanzetta 1964).

Over time, even if conflict is not handled, a conflicting stimulus will habituate from sheer repetition, and cease to evoke an OR. New expectations form over time.

> *Proposition 4.7.i:* Major physiological effects of an interrupt due to conflict are occurrence of the orientation reaction (OR) and an increase in arousal. Over time the stimulus leading to conflict will habituate if repeated, and will cease to evoke an OR.

Thus the overall effect of the OR, as a first reaction to an interrupt, is to try to analyze the instigating stimulus and prepare for future actions. The next step for the individual, having noted the conflict, is to assess its magnitude and meaning and decide what to do.

Response strategies to conflict interrupt events

The specific impact of an interrupt, the reaction to conflict used by an individual, is assumed to depend upon the individual and the individual's state at the time; that is, the individual will interpret and assess the conflict in light of his or her understanding of the current situation. Then decisions may be actively made about whether the conflict can be tolerated and if not, how it can be dealt with. Although there are certainly instances where responses to conflict are learned and nearly automatic, for many choice conflicts of interest an active assessment may be made. Other theorists, as noted in Chapter 3, have assumed optimal level theories, where there is an optimal level of conflict. This notion of an optimal level and associated response strategies seems too mechanistic, however. The notions of an active assessment, interpretation, and decision about how to handle a given conflict are central to the present theory, rather than an assumption of a fixed response pattern. This unfortunately makes study of responses to conflict more difficult, since different strategies will in general be used by different individuals and by the same individual in different situations.

Little is currently known about response strategies for conflict. Kelman and Baron (1968a) develop a typology of response modes for resolution of inconsistency, however, based upon a functional approach; that is, the response chosen is assumed to depend on the functions each mode serves. This typology may be useful for enumerating different possible response modes, and for generating hypotheses about when each mode will be used. Even though inconsistency is the focus of their analysis, as argued above and by Berlyne (1968), inconsistency generates conflict.

Kelman and Baron classify modes for resolving inconsistency along two dimensions. First, the process used in handling the inconsistency may be avoidance of the inconsistency or confrontation of the inconsistency. Second, the nature of the outcome of the process may be reduction of the instigating inconsistency or maintenance of it. These two dimensions can be combined to yield a four-fold classification. We now consider each of the four types in more detail.

Reaction strategies which reduce and avoid inconsistency are those which attempt to eliminate the inconsistency by treating inconsistent information in such a way as to avoid seeing its implications. Modes which reduce and avoid are denial, distortion, rationalization, or source derogation. Strategies which attempt to reduce and confront the inconsistency differ from those above in that the discrepant elements are actively processed and changed to be consistent. For example, changes in attitudes, behaviors, or standards are examples of these strategies.

Reactions which maintain the inconsistency while seeking to avoid its implications are those that do not directly alter the inconsistent elements themselves. Rather, the context within which the discrepancy is viewed is varied, in particular by avoiding making the discrepancy salient. An example of such a mechanism is compartmentalization in which an individual can hold two inconsistent beliefs by keeping the areas of his or her life to which each belief refers separate from one another. Finally, modes which maintain and confront are characterized by active restructuring of the context in which the discrepant elements are embedded. Bolstering (adding new elements that are consistent with one of the original inconsistent elements), differentiation (seeing something as having several different facets, some positive and some negative), and transcendence (introduction of a higher principle which justifies the original inconsistency) are examples of such reaction modes. See Kelman and Baron (1968a, pp. 670–675) for further details on the modes outlined above.

Kelman and Baron not only classify modes but also offer some hypotheses about when the various types of modes will be used. One set of hypotheses refers to the choice of reduction modes versus maintenance modes. Kelman and Baron hypothesize that to the extent that inconsistent elements are tied to the same goal, rather than different goals, they are most likely to be handled by inconsistency reduction mechanisms; if tied to different goals, maintenance mechanisms are more likely. Thus if an interrupt resulted from a conflict between spending money on oneself or the family (Howard and Sheth 1969, pp. 114–116), one might argue that a maintenance mode such as compartmentalization or bolstering might be used. On the other hand, if a conflict arose because price for an item was not as remembered, but had increased, reduction mechanisms might be most likely, such as rationalization or change in attitude, action, or standard of what price one is willing to pay. In addition, Kelman and Baron propose that inconsistency maintenance is fostered to the extent that the goals to which the inconsistent elements are tied are independently and equally important to the individual.

For the choice between avoiding the inconsistency or confronting it, Kelman and Baron propose two main determinants. First, choice of a mode depends upon availability, or which aspects of the conflict are controllable and which are not; that is, one may not be able to avoid, because of the situation (e.g., a highly respected source may be hard to derogate). Second, emphasis on short-term goals may tend to generate avoidance modes, whereas emphasis on implications for long-term goals may lead to confronting mechanisms. Confronting mechanisms may involve search for information. Also, time pressure would seem to imply emphasis on short-term goals in most cases, and hence lead to avoidance modes. Kelman and Baron also claim that choice among methods in the same cells of the typology will be based upon which method requires the least changes and adjustments for the individual, and which method requires only peripheral rather than central changes. Finally, Abelson (1968) hypothesizes that under high conflict more "primitive" types of modes, such as denial, are used.

Thus the Kelman and Baron work provides an array of possible strategies for reacting to conflict, and also some hypotheses about the conditions under which various types of strategies might be used. At present there is virtually no empirical research in which conflict reaction strategies have been measured and the conditions favoring one or another strategy examined. Summarizing the above, we propose

Proposition 4.7.ii: Strategies for reacting to conflict may be characterized by whether they reduce or maintain conflict and by whether they avoid or confront the conflicting elements. Use of one type of mode rather than another depends on such factors as

a) The degree to which the conflicting elements are tied to the same goal or different goals

b) The extent to which the goals to which the conflicting elements are tied are independent and equally important

c) The availability of each mode in the particular situation

d) The degree to which long-term or short-term goals are emphasized

INDIVIDUAL DIFFERENCES
IN THE ATTENTION AND PERCEPTION COMPONENT

Those individual difference variables mentioned in earlier sections which seem to be most significant are listed below.

Proposition 4.10: Individual differences can affect aspects of the attention and perception component. Significant individual difference variables may be:

a) The particular expectations possessed, the "vocabulary" of familiar patterns or chunks held

b) The threshold level necessary for an interrupt

c) The reaction strategies used to respond to conflict

d) The degree to which *a priori* goals for learning about the environment are present

e) The degree to which passive versus active learning strategies are used

SUMMARY OF THE PROPOSITIONS

The propositions developed in the chapter are repeated below to provide a summary of the major points made.

Proposition 4.1: Attention to a stimulus is the allocation of processing capacity or effort to that stimulus. Such an allocation of effort has both selective and intensive aspects.

Proposition 4.1.i: Two major influences on the selective aspects of attention are

a) Current goals, leading to voluntary attention

b) Surprising, novel, potentially threatening, unexpected, etc. events, leading to involuntary attention

Proposition 4.1.ii: The intensity aspects of attention refer to the degree to which processing capacity is allocated. Increases in processing capacity correspond to increases in attention.

Proposition 4.1.iii: Attention has been measured in many ways, using mainly verbal awareness and recall responses or physiological measures. Pupil dilation measures seem particularly useful for tapping the amount of processing effort (attention) being allocated.

Proposition 4.2: Perceptual interpretations may be developed by an active-synthesis process where context and prior expectations are important elements. Interpretations may be guided by what a stimulus seems to be based on context and expectations as well as by the actual features of the stimulus.

Proposition 4.2.i: Expectations based upon beliefs stored in memory can influence several aspects of perceptual encoding:

a) Expectations develop over time, based upon experience with a phenomenon

b) If expectations are met, encoding proceeds normally. If expectations are not met, an interrupt may occur

c) Perceptions may depart from reality if expectations are strong

d) Perceptual efficiency may depend on the complexity of expectations held, the size of the patterns one can recognize

Proposition 4.3: Interrupting events during attention and perception are of two main types:

a) Conflict

b) Learning about the environment

Reactions to these events depend on the consumer's interpretation of the significance of the event.

Proposition 4.4: Conflict is a result of competing and incompatible response tendencies. Four factors may underlie conflict:

a) The number of competing response tendencies

b) The nearness to equality of the competing response tendencies

c) The absolute strengths of the response tendencies

d) The degree of incompatibility of the responses

> *Proposition 4.4.i:* Formal models of conflict, as currently formulated, appear to be inadequate.

Proposition 4.5: Conflict seems to be the most appropriate construct for characterizing one major class of interrupting events. Such constructs as arousal and incongruity are not completely adequate.

Proposition 4.6: Three major causes of interrupts due to conflict in attention and perception are

a) Parts of the environment or perceptual field competing for attention

b) Disagreement between what was perceived and what was expected

c) Competing interpretations for a stimulus

Proposition 4.7: Conflict interrupt events have two main types of effects:

a) Increased physiological activity

b) Assessment of the adequacy of the current goal hierarchy, with changes in the hierarchy implemented if it is found inadequate. One particular change of importance is that goals for information search may be developed.

> *Proposition 4.7.i:* Major physiological effects of an interrupt due to conflict are occurrence of the orientation reaction (OR) and an increase in arousal. Over time the stimulus leading to conflict will habituate if repeated, and will cease to evoke an OR.

> *Proposition 4.7.ii:* Strategies for reacting to conflict may be characterized by whether they reduce or maintain conflict and by whether they avoid or confront the conflicting elements. Use of one type of mode rather than another depends on such factors as

> a) The degree to which the conflicting elements are tied to the same goal or different goals

> b) The extent to which the goals to which the conflicting elements are tied are independent and equally important

> c) The availability of each mode in the particular situation

> d) The degree to which long-term or short-term goals are emphasized

Proposition 4.8: There are several types of interrupt events leading to learning about the environment. The major effect of such events is information search. Learning about the environment should be most prevalent in low conflict situations.

Proposition 4.9: Learning about the environment can occur under conditions of low involvement and low attention and under conditions where stimuli are passively rather than actively processed.

Proposition 4.10: Individual differences can affect aspects of the attention and perception component. Significant individual difference variables may be:

a) The particular expectations possessed, the "vocabulary" of familiar patterns or chunks held

b) The threshold level necessary for an interrupt

c) The reaction strategies used to respond to conflict

d) The degree to which a *priori* goals for learning about the environment are present

e) The degree to which passive versus active learning strategies are used

NEEDED RESEARCH

Propositions 4.1, 4.1.i, 4.1.ii, and 4.1.iii all refer to the notion of attention as allocation of processing capacity, and note that one good measure of attention seems to be pupil dilation. One stream of research that seems promising, therefore, is to examine those factors influencing the degree of processing carried out on marketing stimuli, advertisements or packages in particular, using pupillary dilation measures as measures of processing effort. Such studies would be particularly useful for public policy research, where factors such as the amount of information presented, source of a corrective advertisement, and modes for presenting some piece of required information on a package could be varied to examine the effects on the degree of processing undertaken. In particular, comparisons of degree of processing with some measure of desire to process would be helpful in assessing whether a contemplated action would lead to usable information for consumers. A related area for research is examination of the degree of attention paid to various portions of advertisements or other information displays by examining eye movements in conjunction with pupil dilation measurements. One could vary factors similar to those mentioned above. For example, one might examine which segments of an ad are fixated most often under time pressure or under varying degrees of information load. Such questions would aid in the design of information displays. Thus methodologies which track eye movements and pupil dilation are particularly relevant for studying attention processes.

A second major focus for research is on the role of expectations in shaping perceptions (Propositions 4.2 and 4.2.i). One interesting question relates to the "vocabulary" of existing familiar patterns or chunks consumers hold in memory, the prior knowledge used in forming expectations about the choice environment. Are there wide differences in the complexity and number of familiar patterns stored by consumers, as there are in chess? Could one devise tasks such as the reproduction of positions by chess players to examine chunking behavior and the "vocabulary" of chunks? One might present information relevant to consumer products (say a package label) and ask consumers to reproduce it, for example. Knowing which factors come together to form familar patterns would provide insights into how consumers develop concepts about products. Very little is also known about how such familiar patterns develop over time. Is there some kind of hierarchical formation pattern, where groups of elements are chunked together and then these chunks are combined? If so, then hierarchical clustering schemes (Johnson 1967) may offer good models for analyzing data on attribute relationships. Other promising research questions include how repetition of an advertisement affects building of familiar patterns of information from that ad; and how the effects of repetition on the building of familiar patterns vary with the level of information load imposed by the ad. This latter question is of great importance for designing consumer information programs (Bettman 1975b). Study of these questions might require examination of eye movements, as well as methods which can assess which elements are being grouped together to form a more complex pattern (see Chase and Simon [1973] and Reitman [1976] for discussions of proposed methods for measuring chunks involving time between responses, and see Buschke [1976], Friendly [1977], or Sternberg and Tulving [1977] for a discussion of methods for measuring chunks involving organization of recall over repeated trials).

Another major area for research is the modeling and measurement of perceived conflict (Propositions 4.4, 4.4.i, 4.5). There are many constructs discussed in the literature—uncertainty, importance, involvement, arousal, conflict, risk, and so on—with no theoretical notions as to how they relate. In addition, there is no underlying theory relating to determinants of these components, i.e., what determines uncertainty, importance, and so on. There is also controversy about the combination rule for constructs leading to conflict. Berlyne (1957) postulated a multiplicative relationship, but Lanzetta and Driscoll (1968) support a linear model. The major problem is the lack of a validated criterion measure for perceived conflict. Physiological measures may be insufficient because it is conflict *as perceived* that is relevant. It is possible that perceptions of conflict would vary monotonically with some physiological measure, but this is an empirical question. Development of some kind of behavioral criterion for conflict would be very useful. Choice time, typically used in psychological studies, seems to be inadequate because it confounds response strategies for handling conflict with the level of conflict. Thus the priorities seem to be development of a firm conceptual base, which would include notions about the interrelationships of the various constructs and components in the literature (perhaps tested empirically in a multitrait–multi-method study [Campbell and Fiske 1959]); theoretical bases for developing a criterion measure for perceived conflict; and rationale for specific combination rules, which could then be tested (e.g., Bettman 1975a). The important need is for the development of an integrated theoretical and measurement scheme.

Another potential research area related to interrupts due to conflict is understanding how much of a departure from expectations is needed for an interrupt (Propositions 4.3, 4.6). One would first need to conceptualize and determine how to measure the distance of some event from one's prior expectations about that event. Then one could examine whether some contemplated changes in marketing stimuli would lead to interrupts, and for how many consumers.

Research is also needed into strategies for responding to conflict (Propositions 4.7, 4.7.i, 4.7.ii). The Kelman and Baron (1968a) framework provides a preliminary notion of what the range of strategies might include, and under what circumstances usage of various strategies might be expected. Development of ways to measure response strategies seems to be the necessary first step, and one proposal for such measurement is presented in Chapter 5.

Finally, research is needed on how consumers engage in what has been termed "learning about the environment" above (Propositions 4.8, 4.9). First, studies which examine the extent of the phenomenon would be useful. Second, one could examine whether there is greater learning about the environment in low conflict situations. Finally, the extent to which attention and active learning are relevant to consumer choices as opposed to low involvement and passive learning seems to be a very important question, as different processes may occur for high and low involvement (Krugman 1965; Robertson 1976; Maloney and Silverman 1978).

CHAPTER 5

Information Acquisition and Evaluation

In the pursuit of particular goals in their goal hierarchies, consumers attend to, perceive, and process information. Some choices are habitual and nearly automatic, and little information may be acquired and processed. For other less routine decisions, consumers may need to make choices about information gathering: which pieces of information should be acquired, from what sources; how much information should be acquired; what strategies should be followed in the actual acquisition process; what should be the response to conflicting sources of information, or to lack of available information; how is information to be integrated into the consumer's current structure of beliefs about products? Such questions form the focus for this chapter, which discusses the processes of acquiring and evaluating information.

Acquisition of information is viewed at its most general level. Information can be acquired by actively *seeking* it or by being *confronted* with it, as in a television commercial (Donohew and Tipton 1973). Thus information acquisition is *not* synonymous with information search, but includes information consumers obtain without actively looking for it. Information search is further broken down into two components: information sought from memory, or *internal search and retrieval*; and information sought through outside sources, *external search*.[1] Finally, evaluation of information is concerned with the processes by which a consumer integrates a piece of information into an existing belief structure.

---

1. Engel, Blackwell, and Kollat (1978) and Nicosia (1966) also distinguish between internal and external search. In addition, Hansen (1972) uses the term deliberation to refer to phenomena related to internal search, and exploration to denote external search.

OVERVIEW OF THE INFORMATION
ACQUISITION AND EVALUATION COMPONENT

In making a choice, the consumer examines relevant information in memory, and in some cases may acquire additional information from the external environment (e.g., from friends, salespeople, packages, advertisements) if that in memory is not sufficient. In general, the goals being pursued will exert a strong influence on the particular pieces of information attended to and perceived. In effect, particular goals or subgoals for information acquisition exist in the consumer's goal hierarchy. Thus information acquisition can be seen as one level in the goal hierarchy, as one particular type of goal. It is an extremely important level, however, and hence is examined as a separate component of the theory. Information search processes are considered first below, then processes that are relevant when the consumer is confronted with information.

It is proposed that information search generally begins with internal search, with memory examined for relevant information. The degree to which this internal search is a conscious process varies with the type of choice being considered. In choice situations in which the consumer has a great deal of experience, a simple habitual choice may be made. In such a case, no information may be needed beyond that necessary to actually implement the choice (e.g., recall of the brand name or recognition of the package), and such implementation is virtually automatic. Thus the internal search process is essentially trivial. However, for more complex choice situations, the consumer may need to think actively about what is in memory, to exert more conscious processing effort. The detailed processes of storage and access to information in memory are important enough that a separate discussion of memory is presented in Chapter 6. For the present, internal search is characterized in more general terms.

As the consumer examines information in memory, that information may prove to be sufficient for the purposes at hand, and no further search may be undertaken. However, there can also be interrupts during internal search. Several pieces of information may conflict, information may be lacking, and so forth. Although responses to an interrupt can vary, as noted in previous chapters, one major type of response to insufficient or conflicting information is external search.

During external search, the consumer may examine the environment to see if relevant information is available. The consumer in general uses different search patterns and searches for different amounts of information in different choice situations. Information acquired during external search may lead to further internal search to interpret or elaborate that information. Thus there can be a continual cycling between internal and external search processes. Interrupts due to conflicting information or lack of information may also occur during external search. Again, reactions will vary, but more external search may ensue. Eventually, of course, the consumer will cease searching for information and make a decision.

The proposed sequence of internal search, possibly followed by external search, applies only to cases where information is actively sought. The consumer can also be confronted with information, as in an overheard conversation, a billboard, or a television commercial, for example. This notion was examined in some detail in Chapter 4 under the label of learning about the environment. Such learning can occur through interrupts (one is confronted with information that leads to a goal of further exploring that information) or through low involvement, passive processes. In the latter case, information can be taken in, even though a great deal of active processing is not undertaken. This type of information acquisition, from being confronted with information, will be considered where relevant below, but the more detailed discussions have been given in Chapter 4.

The sections above discuss information intake. As information is acquired, however, it is also processed to some extent. In the low involvement passive learning cases noted above, such processing is minimal. However, in the other cases the incoming information may be actively processed and evaluated. Consumers generate responses and reactions to information they acquire. These reactions may determine to a great extent the impact of any particular information input.

The basic aspects of the information acquisition and evaluation component have been discussed above. The relevant portions of the overall model are shown in Fig. 5.1.[2] The major concepts are each considered below: internal search, external search, and evaluation of the information acquired. Then the relationship of the search and evaluation component to the other components of the theory is considered, and more detailed facets of the search and evaluation segment are examined. Figure 5.2 provides a more detailed outline of the basic phenomena related to information acquisition discussed below, as there are many areas discussed and some initial structure may prove useful.

MAJOR ASPECTS OF THE INFORMATION
ACQUISITION AND EVALUATION COMPONENT

INTERNAL SEARCH

Internal search refers to the acquisition of information that is available in memory. It is hypothesized that when faced with a choice to make, consumers in general first engage in internal search, examining memory for

---

2. Donohew and Tipton (1973) develop a similar model, with decisions about sufficiency of information, how to handle conflicting pieces of information, and so on. They devote more attention to selection of sources of information and to particular processing styles than does the model shown in Fig. 5.1.

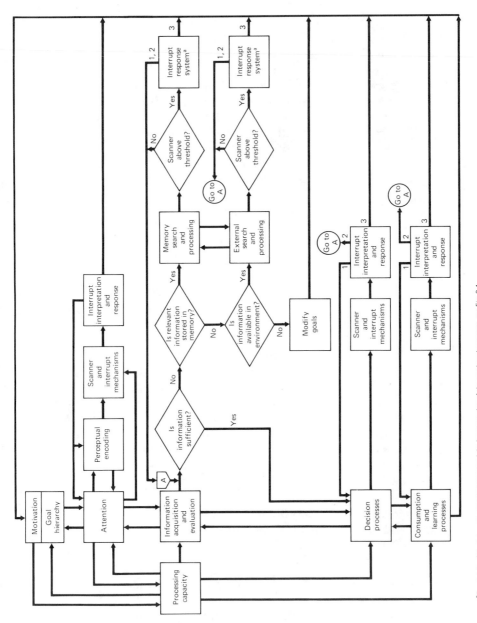

[a]For details of the Interrupt response system and the interpretation of the numbered responses, see Fig. 2.4.

Fig. 5.1 Information acquisition and evaluation segment of the theory.

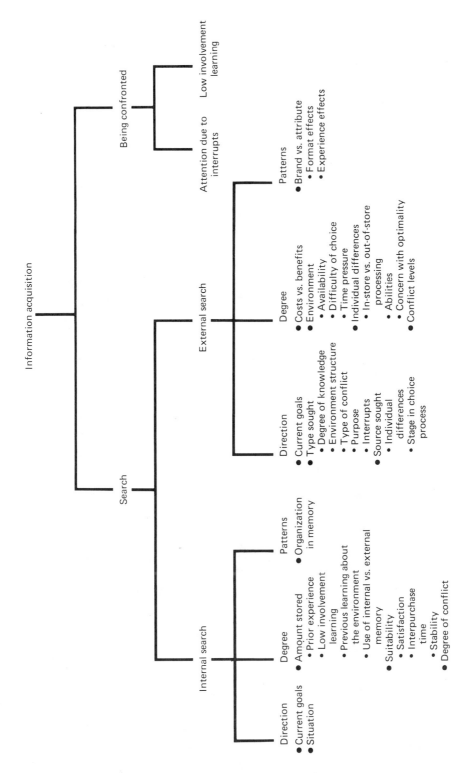

Fig. 5.2 A framework for viewing consumer information acquisition.

available information.[3] There are two aspects of internal search: direction and degree; that is, the researcher may be interested in *which* pieces of information are examined, or the *direction* of search; and *how much* information is sought, or the *degree* of search. The direction of internal search may in large part be determined by the particular goals currently relevant to the consumer, by what is useful for the choice at hand. Although what is in memory clearly depends upon the structure of the particular choice environment within which the consumer acts, the course of search through memory may be more under the control of current goals and less directly influenced by the choice environment itself. In addition to generally examining which pieces of information are sought from memory, one can also characterize details of the actual *sequences* of data retrieved during search, the patterns of memory search. The consumer's general strategies for searching memory would influence these patterns.

Various degrees of internal search are possible, ranging from virtually automatic responses in habitual choice situations to more extensive searches of what is in memory. In many cases, the initial internal search may not be exhaustive or comprehensive; the purpose of the search may be to ascertain what is *not* known, to provide a guide for external search. Then there may be cycles between external and internal search, as noted above. In general, it is proposed that the major determinants of degree of internal search are the amount of information stored in memory; the suitability of that information or its usefulness for the current choice; and level of decision conflict.

> *Proposition 5.1:* Active information search initially may be internal search of information stored in memory. Such search can be characterized by direction (which pieces of information are sought); by degree (how much is sought); and by more detailed patterns in the sequences of information sought (what acquisition strategies are used).

In the course of internal search, interrupts may occur. Information may be found to be lacking, for example. The lack may not be recognized until some processing is done. For example, the consumer may discover that he or she cannot remember a price. In addition, conflict may be aroused in other ways during internal search. For example, if the consumer's weights for various attributes have changed since the last choice in a product class, and if previously preferred brands would not be preferred given these current attribute weightings, perceived conflict might increase. The consumer might not even be aware of this conflict until the actual internal search was performed. Finally, during the course of internal search, the consumer may be reminded of

---

3. In situations in which the consumer has no prior knowledge, in which an interrupt has occurred (e.g., a commercial has just come on that caught the consumer's attention), then external search with little or no internal search may ensue.

goals other than those relevant to the purchase being considered. Such interrupts can lead to restructuring of goals. Although responses to interrupts vary, as noted in Chapters 3 and 4, one major type of response to such interrupts arising during internal search may be formation of a goal for external search. In summary,

> *Proposition 5.2:* During internal search interrupts can arise based upon lack of needed information, conflicting information, or recall of previously forgotten goals. One major response to such interrupts may be formation of a goal for external search.

EXTERNAL SEARCH

External search is the acquisition of information from sources other than memory, such as friends, packages or other in-store displays, advertisements, magazines such as *Consumer Reports*, and so forth. In the theory, external search is postulated to follow internal search, but the internal search need not be complete to lead to external search. A brief internal search may suffice for the consumer to ascertain what is not known, or an interrupt of internal search due to a lack of information or conflict may lead to external search. Periods of external search, followed by internal search, then more external search, and so on are probably typical. In many cases, however, decisions to be made are trivial and habitual, and very little internal or external search may ensue for such choices where there is a great deal of prior knowledge and experience.

As with internal search, both direction and degree aspects can be examined for external search. These direction and amount questions lead to broad characterizations of the search process. Consumers have more detailed strategies for acquiring information that can also be considered by examining the actual sequences of information acquired from some information display.

> *Proposition 5.3:* Following initial internal search, there may be external search for information. Such search is characterized by direction (which pieces of information are sought); by degree (how much is sought); and by more detailed patterns in the sequences of information sought (what acquisition strategies are used).

As was the case for internal search, the influence of current goals is a major factor determining which pieces of information are sought by the consumer; that is, those pieces of information most useful for the current choice will tend to be sought. Several influences other than current goals on the direction of external search can also be considered, such as prior experience or structure of the choice environment. External search can also be of varying degrees, as well as in different directions. The influences upon degree of search are numerous (e.g., costs vs. benefits of search, choice environment factors, individual differences, conflict), and the amount of research on these influences is substantial and will be discussed below.

External search is also subject to interrupts due to novel or surprising events, conflicting information, lack of information, and so on. Such interrupts may lead to further external search; some of the determinants of degree of search discussed below, particularly conflict and reactions to it, are relevant. In general, we propose

> *Proposition 5.4:* Interrupts can arise during external search. Responses to these interrupts depend on the consumer's interpretation of the significance of the interrupts in light of current goals.

One final aspect which must be considered is the relationship between internal and external search, particularly with regard to amount of search. The most simplistic conception is that internal and external search are compensatory, that the more is done of one, the less must have been done of the other. However, it is also possible that the degrees of search are positively correlated, that if one tends to do a good deal of internal search, one also tends to do a good deal of external search. The relationship found may depend on level of conflict. It might be hypothesized that under low perceived conflict, internal and external search would be compensatory. In high conflict choices, however, it may be that degree of internal and external search are positively, rather than negatively, correlated. The relationship would also presumably depend on individual differences.

> *Proposition 5.5:* The relationship between amount of internal search and amount of external search performed is currently not well understood. Possible influences on the form of the relationship are level of conflict and individual differences.

EVALUATION OF INFORMATION

The previous sections have considered the input of information, but not any details of its processing. Evaluation of information refers to the consumer's processes for relating incoming information to his or her existing structure of beliefs and values. The consumer's responses and reactions to the incoming information can influence the ultimate impact of the information on the existing structure—whether this information will be integrated, ignored, distorted, and so on. The discussion below assumes active processing of information which is being acquired; that is, the consumer is consciously analyzing and interpreting the message, actively reacting to it. Thus the discussion is more relevant for cases in which attention is devoted to a piece of information, in which the consumer is highly involved, than for cases in which the consumer is confronted with information and responds with low involvement, such as discussed in Chapter 4. Howard (1977) proposes that factual learning may occur during low involvement, with active evaluation requiring higher involvement.

Wright (1973a, 1974a, 1974c) has done a good deal of work in analyzing active processing of advertising messages. He postulates that a consumer, in performing an analysis of a message and relating it to his or her existing cognitive structure, generates cognitive responses to the message; that is, the consumer actively generates thoughts and ideas triggered by the assertions made in the message. Such thoughts can be elaborations of ideas in the message or evaluative reactions. These cognitive responses are seen as underlying the effects of the advertising. This approach is emphasized in this section because it explicitly recognizes the nature of consumers as active processors, interacting with and interpreting incoming information in light of their current beliefs, values, and goals. Krugman (1965) also uses the cognitive response idea in his notions of high involvement processing, emphasizing the spontaneous "connections" a viewer makes between his or her own life and the message. Finally, Calder (1978) relates cognitive responses to script notions of attitude (Abelson 1976), and argues that cognitive response theory can be expanded to take memory structure and visual imagery into account.

There is a vast array of other communication studies that examine message acceptance (McGuire 1969). However, these studies seem to offer fewer insights into the nature of consumer processing than does the cognitive response approach, because the detailed responses are not examined. Thus this vast literature is beyond the scope of this section.

To study whether cognitive responses to messages underlie the effects of these messages, major types of cognitive responses must be identified and modes for measuring the degree of these responses devised. Wright (1973a) suggests three major responses: (1) counterarguments, or refutations of claims made in the message; (2) source derogations, or negative characterizations of the source of the message; and (3) support arguments, or agreements with the claims. To measure individuals' usage of these responses, Wright (1973a) proposed use of a thought-monitoring approach. Immediately after receipt of a message, subjects are instructed to list all thoughts relevant to the product or advertising message that occurred to them during exposure, ignoring spelling and grammar. Time is limited to three minutes to balance the experimenter's desire for obtaining a complete set of responses with the goal of avoiding the generation and listing of thoughts not actually occurring during the message as increased time is allowed. Then coders use explicit definitions of the three types of responses cited above to code the thought-monitoring protocols. Wright (1974c) undertakes a careful analysis of the strengths and weaknesses of this method.

Wright (1973a, 1974a) used this thought-monitoring procedure to examine acceptance of an advertising message. The medium used (audio or print) and involvement levels (high and low) were manipulated. The results of Wright's analyses (1973a, 1974a) are quite striking. Counterarguments emerge as the most important response, being negatively related to acceptance. Media and involvement levels have interesting effects also. For audio presentation, in which information sequence and the rate of information transmission are not under the consumer's control, counterargument emerged as the only important cognitive response influencing acceptance. There was less source derogation and support argument. For print presentation, involvement effects were important. Under high involvement, more counterarguments were observed, and less source derogation. Finally, support arguments were higher under print presentation, regardless of degree of involvement. Thus both media differences in opportunities for response and involvement levels impact the mix of cognitive responses used by the individual. Involvement seems to be required for counterargument. When involvement is low and the medium allows consumer control (print), responses requiring less effort than counterarguing (source derogation and support arguments) are used.

Other research has also used the thought-listing approach. Wright (1974c, 1978) reviews the relevant studies. One study of interest in the current discussion on evaluation of information is that of Osterhouse and Brock (1970). They explain the result that distraction during the reception of a message leads to increased acceptance by showing that distraction inhibits counterarguing. Thus studies of cognitive responses seem to be quite fruitful for examining consumer message processing.

> *Proposition 5.6:* Consumers appear to evaluate incoming information in situations in which there is some degree of involvement by actively generating responses to the message presented. Such responses typically can be categorized as counterarguments, source derogations, and support arguments. Counterarguments are the most prevalent response under most conditions, and are negatively related to message acceptance. The medium through which the message is presented impacts the pattern of cognitive responses.

SUMMARY

Information acquisition and evaluation processes refer to the gathering of information needed for choice from either memory or the external environment. If information is actively being sought to carry out some goal, internal search of memory is usually performed first, followed by external search if the information in memory is not sufficient. As information is taken in, the consumer is actively responding to that information. The reactions which are generated may have an important bearing on the ultimate impact of the information. Interrupts can occur during search, and further search or changes in goals may result. Finally, the consumer is also confronted with information at times when no active search is under way. Reactions in such situations may include low involvement or passive response processes, as outlined in Chapter 4.

LINKAGES TO OTHER COMPONENTS OF THE THEORY

Motivation has important linkages to information acquisition and evaluation. Information is often acquired in the light of what is needed to accomplish current goals. As noted above, goals for information search are an important type of goal in most goal hierarchies. Hence, examination of information search can be thought of as study of one particular type of goal. The information acquisition and evaluation component also impacts motivation, as interrupts can lead to changes in the goal hierarchy.

Attention and perception are also very interrelated with information acquisition and evaluation. Given some goal, attention is allocated to aspects of the environment relevant for attaining that goal, and the meaning of those aspects is then developed. If the goal is one of information acquisition and evaluation, then attention and perception are in effect mechanisms for carrying out such a goal. Acquisition and evaluation of information are closely tied to memory as well. Memory is examined directly in internal search, but in external search as well as in evaluation processes the consumer must use data stored in memory to interpret incoming information.

Information acquisition and evaluation processes are complexly intertwined with processes of decision among alternatives; that is, choice and acquisition processes can go on simultaneously. As information is acquired and evaluated it may be used to aid in developing a decision rule, or in evaluating an alternative using a rule. The decision rule is *not* necessarily developed and applied only after all information is gathered. Also, choices are always being made, at different levels: which information to examine as well as which product or brand to choose, for example. Thus informational and choice processes are continually cycling.

Finally, processing capacity is also related to the acquisition and evaluation component. Studies have shown that the way information is presented (Russo, Krieser, and Miyashita 1975; Russo 1977) and the rate of presentation of information (Wright 1974a; Seibel, Christ, and Teichner 1965) are related to demands on processing capacity, for example.

MORE DETAILED ASPECTS OF THE INFORMATION ACQUISITION AND EVALUATION COMPONENT

MEASURES OF INFORMATION SEARCH

Before one can examine influences on search, one must be able to measure the degree of search undertaken. This has proven to be a difficult undertaking. In one of the rare attempts to measure phenomena related to internal search, Hansen (1972, p. 281) used the scale "When faced with a problem of this kind, how carefully would you think that most people would consider the alternatives?" This measure does not directly examine internal search, however, but examines deliberation, and includes several other aspects of prechoice processing in addition to internal search.

More previous work has been carried out in measuring external search. Many measures of degree of external search have been used: number of stores visited, number of shopping trips, time spent, number of sources of information used, and so on (Newman and Lockeman 1975). Several studies have also combined scores on items such as those above to form an overall index. For example, Newman and Staelin (1972) measured the number of kinds of information sought (e.g., for various attributes or stores), the number of sources of information consulted, and the number of retail outlets visited. They then combined these measures into an overall search index. Although such measures seem relatively straightforward, recent research has indicated that these measures may be suspect. Newman and Lockeman (1975) measured degree of external search using both the typical survey methods described above and an unobtrusive in-store direct observational method for a sample of women's shoe buyers. They found very low correlations between the observational and survey measures, with the highest of eight such correlations being .12. In addition, the survey measures severely understated the amount of search actually observed. Future studies should thus be very careful in attempting to measure degree of external search.[4]

As noted earlier in Proposition 5.5, the relationship between the degree of internal and external search carried out is not clear. Partially this problem has been one of lack of measures for both processes. Only one study has measured phenomena related to both internal and external search (Hansen 1972, p. 291). He found that the average amount of deliberation (related to internal search) was perfectly rank correlated with the average amount of external search over six situations varying in level of perceived conflict. Data on the correlation of the search and exploration indices *within* each conflict situation were not reported. However, as stated above, Hansen does not actually measure internal search itself.

> *Proposition 5.7:* Current measures of degree of internal and external search do not seem adequate. More precise measures need to be developed.

INFLUENCES ON THE DEGREE OF INTERNAL SEARCH

Three general determinants of degree of internal search are the amount of information stored in memory, the suitability of that information

---

4. The information monitoring and eye movement techniques to be discussed in Chapter 7 provide measures of external search, but these techniques may not be easily applicable to measuring search in actual choice environments.

for making the choice, and degree of conflict. The greater the amount of stored information (Woodruff 1972), the more suitable that information is, and the greater the degree of conflict (if not too high), the greater the amount of internal search. Let us now state

> *Proposition 5.1.i:* Degree of internal search may be higher
> a) The more relevant information is stored in memory
> b) The greater the suitability of that information
> c) The greater the degree of perceived conflict (up to some maximum level of conflict which can be handled)

Each of these three factors can now be examined in more detail. One difficulty in most of the research reported below is that internal search was not directly measured, so only indirect inferences can be attempted. The outline in Fig. 5.2 may be useful in providing additional structure for this and following sections.

Amount of stored information

The amount of information in memory reflects the degree of prior learning relevant for the choice in question. There are several sources of information in memory about a product class. First, past purchase experiences in a product class may lead directly to learning about criteria and/or alternatives. Bennett and Mandell (1969) examined search behavior for new car purchases, and found that the number of previous purchases of the *same* make as that eventually bought was negatively related to degree of external search. This *may* imply a greater reliance on internal search. As noted above, lower external search need not imply higher internal search, but such indirect evidence is all that is available. They found, however, that *total* number of previous purchases, without regard to make purchased, was not related to degree of external search. Thus not all previous purchase experience is necessarily instructive.

A second source of information in memory is low involvement learning (Krugman 1965), from information with which the consumer is confronted (e.g. in television commercials), rather than from information which is actively sought. Such information, Krugman hypothesizes, would mainly affect attribute saliences, or whether attributes come to mind during the choice process.

A third source of information in memory is from previous learning about the environment, or learning that has been gleaned about the product class currently under consideration in previous situations where that product was not itself being considered. Brands available and general price levels for specific retail stores are among the types of information which might be gathered in this manner.

Finally, a fourth influence on the amount of information actually stored in memory as a result of prior experiences is an individual difference variable, the degree of reliance upon in-store displays as an external memory

(Newell and Simon 1972); that is, a consumer may not try to remember items of information, but may use the package or shelf tags while in the store. Thus these become an external memory, making efforts to retain data internally less crucial. Consumers undoubtedly differ in terms of the degree to which they use the product display in this manner. This may be related to the distinction between prior planning versus in-store decision making made in Chapter 3. Some individuals may prefer to do as much decision processing as possible outside of the actual store, and hence would attempt to retain more in memory; others would prefer to process in the store itself, and might retain less.

Thus there are four main sources of information stored in memory: prior purchase experiences (including previous acquisition activities, word of mouth, etc.), previous low involvement learning, previous learning about the environment ("latent learning"), and the degree to which one uses internal (one's own memory) as opposed to external (packages or lists) memory. All of this stored information can of course be used by consumers to generate new information by deduction or inference.

Suitability of stored information

The sheer amount of information stored is not the only determinant of degree of internal search. As pointed out above, for example, Bennett and Mandell (1969) suggest that the total amount of prior purchasing experience may not necessarily be relevant. Another crucial determinant is the suitability, appropriateness, or usefulness of the stored information for the current decision (Engel, Blackwell, and Kollat 1978, p. 239). One factor influencing suitability is satisfaction with previous purchases. Presumably, the more satisfactory these purchases, the more relevant is one's stored information based upon past purchases. Newman and Staelin (1971) show that satisfied users take less time to make a decision. They also show in a later study (Newman and Staelin 1972) that buying the same brand as before is associated with less external search. Again, this evidence is only indirect about degree of internal search.

A second factor influencing suitability is length of interpurchase time. The longer the interpurchase time, the greater the likelihood of forgetting relevant information. In addition, the longer the interpurchase time, the greater the likelihood of changes in the mix of alternatives, such as the appearance of new brands or the occurrence of changes in price or other attributes. Swan (1969) found that more external search ensued when different mixes of brands were offered over time in his experiment than when the mix of brands remained the same. Also, Krugman (1965) hypothesizes that under low involvement learning, which attributes are salient can change. The longer the interpurchase time, the greater the likelihood of such switches in salience of attributes. These switches might lead to the necessity for more external search if different attributes than the consumer had previously considered are of increased salience. Thus the two major determinants of information suitability are satisfaction with previous purchases and interpurchasing time. Interpurchase time is related not only to ease of remembering but also to the degree of stability one might expect in the choice environment.

Degree of perceived conflict

As discussed in previous chapters, response modes to conflict can vary. However, Hansen (1972 pp. 280–294) found that amount of deliberation (which may be related to internal search), as measured by a projective question, was higher under higher perceived conflict. Hansen also found somewhat weaker support for more external search under high conflict.

INFLUENCES ON THE DIRECTION OF EXTERNAL SEARCH

As noted above, the influence of current goals is a major factor in understanding the direction of external search. However, other factors are relevant as well. In this section two areas of research on the direction of external search are considered. In one stream of research, different *types* of information (e.g., how to weight criteria, attribute ratings, available retail outlets) are sought, depending on several factors; in the second stream, influences on which *sources* (e.g., stores, mass media, friends, salespeople) of information are used is considered. Each of these streams is now considered in turn.

Influences on type of information sought

In the following, five factors which may influence type of information sought are considered. One factor which may influence how useful a particular kind of information is relative to current goals is the degree of knowledge already held about the product class being considered. If there is little knowledge about a product class, then Howard and Sheth (1969) hypothesize that information that aids in weighting and developing criteria for evaluating brands is most desired (this is their phase of extensive problem solving). Only after such criteria are developed is information on properties of alternatives the focus. The information must help the consumer to develop a framework for making a choice (Howard 1977). However, this notion seems too narrow, as information on properties may help to shape the criteria. If the consumer knows what criteria are to be applied, but does not know which alternative best meets these criteria (limited problem solving), then data on how the alternatives perform relative to the criteria would be sought. Thus Howard and Sheth postulate that search aimed at developing plans (i.e., ascertaining criteria) can be separated from the search needed to implement those plans (i.e., comparing alternatives on the criteria). These processes will probably tend to go on in parallel, however, since determining what the attributes or criteria are for a product class often involves examining some set of alternatives. Finally, if the alternative desired is known (Howard and Sheth's routinized response behavior phase), the consumer may search for information about prices and stores where that alternative is available (e.g., price levels, hours, locations, service capabilities). See Howard (1977) for a more detailed discussion.

The Howard and Sheth analysis thus provides specific notions about what types of information are sought when knowledge resulting from prior experience is lacking. These notions may be too specific, however. In choice situations in which the consumer has had little prior experience, so that the goal hierarchy may initially be composed of broad, vague goals, consumers may engage in a relatively general search for information relevant for the choice, in hopes that such information may later prove useful. In such a situation the consumer may not know at the time exactly how or if the information will be used later (Greeno 1976; Howard 1977). The point is that, in general, the type of information sought depends on what is already known.

A second factor influencing what type of information is sought is the structure of the particular choice environment, the relative availability of various kinds of information. For some product classes, there may be only a few attributes and many alternatives, or vice versa. Particular alternatives may be carried at only one particular store. These features of the environment would limit search for various types of information. For example, if one desired to buy a particular make of automobile for which there was only one dealer in the area, search for a retailer would be trivial. On the other hand, in a large city, where usually many dealers for any particular make are available, the search for the dealer from whom the car should be purchased might be quite extensive. In addition to these general factors of task environment structure, there are factors specific to individual stores. Some consumers, as noted earlier, tend to rely on little prior planning, and keep little product information in memory. Instead, decision making is done within the store, using the in-store display as an external memory and making only general plans *a priori*. This individual difference variable may affect the degree of environmental influence on type of information sought. For individuals who make decisions in the store itself, the type of data sought may be greatly influenced by the particular set of alternatives available. If few alternatives for a particular product class are available in the store, processing may tend to concentrate on more attributes, relative to alternatives, than if the store carried a wide assortment of brands.

The type of conflict occurring in a particular choice situation (e.g., approach–approach, approach–avoidance, avoidance–avoidance) is a third factor that influences the type of information sought. March and Simon (1958, pp. 116–118) discuss these influences. Approach–approach conflicts, where competing alternatives are desirable, would tend to result in short decision times, with situational factors relating to what captures one's attention in the moment or order of presentation of alternatives influencing choice. Thus little search might be performed; rather, some feature of the particular situation might tip the balance for one alternative or the other. For avoidance–avoidance conflicts, the tendency would be to search for new alternatives. These alternatives might be other alternatives within the same product class, or alternatives to choice of the product class itself. For example, if a consumer is attempting to choose between two outfits for a baby present, neither of which is really liked, the consumer may decide to search for more outfits, perhaps at a different store, or decide to choose a toy instead of an outfit. March and Simon make no direct hypotheses about approach–avoidance conflicts.

A fourth influence on the type of information sought is the purpose for which the information will be used. Mazis (1972) used the framework of cognitive tuning developed by Zajonc (1960) to study this issue. Zajonc differentiated between transmission tuning, in which a person expects to communicate to others; and reception tuning, in which the individual expects to receive information for personal use only. Earlier research (Cohen 1961; Brock and Fromkin 1968) had shown that receivers accepted more discrepant information than did transmitters. This is consistent with the view that receivers tried to process as much information as they could, in order to form an accurate impression, whereas transmitters were more concerned with structuring the message they would present to others. Mazis manipulated the expectations of his subjects by telling "decision makers" they would be asked to provide an overall evaluation of a car after acquisition of information about it and by telling "nondecision makers" they would communicate their impression of the car to another person who would then make an evaluation. Mazis also gave subjects control over how much familiar or novel information they sought. The results showed that "decision makers" chose significantly more novel information than "nondecision makers." Thus the task for which the information will be used affects what type of information will be gathered. This finding may be applicable to word of mouth: consumers who engage in word of mouth but do not intend to buy a product themselves may differ in the kinds of information they transmit from those consumers who both buy the product and transmit word of mouth.

Finally, a fifth influence on type of information examined is that interrupts can lead to goals for external search. In general, the interrupting event itself provides the focus for which information would be examined (e.g., for an interrupt due to a novel stimulus, the initial focus is presumably on that stimulus and its surrounding context). The discussion above has been lengthy, with five main determinants of type of information sought being considered. This may be summarized as

> *Proposition 5.3.i:* The type of information which will be sought in external search may be influenced by
>
> a) The amount and type of knowledge held in memory
>
> b) The structure of the particular choice environment, the relative availability of various types of information
>
> c) The type of conflict occurring
>
> d) The purpose for which the information will be used
>
> e) The particular nature of interrupt events

Influences on the source from which information is sought

Consumers can choose varying mixes of sources of information—advertisements, in-store shopping for several brands, multiple store shopping for one brand, and so on. Several studies have examined aspects of these patterns. Two major factors appear that influence these patterns of sources sought: individual differences and stage in the choice process.

Several studies suggest that consumers display wide individual differences in the patterns of sources they consider. For example, Donnermuth (1965) proposed that consumers could be put into a two-fold classification scheme, based upon number of brands considered and number of retail outlets shopped. By combining these two dimensions, he developed a "shopping matrix." Some consumers may shop in many stores for a single brand, others in one store for many brands, or some may consider both several stores and brands. In an empirical study using the matrix, Donnermuth found that in general there was little shopping across stores for one brand, but there was some examination of many brands in one store for appliances. Many consumers visited one store and examined one brand; when more effort was expended, it usually led to consideration of both more brands and more stores.

Claxton, Fry, and Portis (1974) examined patterns of information source usage, using a cluster analysis based upon three major variables: total number of sources used, number of stores visited, and total deliberation time (time from first consideration until purchase). Furniture buyers and appliance buyers formed two samples for their analyses. The results were similar in both cases. One group (roughly 5 percent of the samples) was labeled thorough (store intense). This group took a long time to decide, used many sources, and visited a very large number of stores. The second major group was labeled thorough (balanced), 44 percent of the sample for furniture and 27 percent for appliances. This group took a long time and used many sources, but only a moderate number of stores. There were two subgroups of this group, slow and fast. These subgroups are interesting in that the slow group took more time but visited fewer stores, and the fast group was the opposite. This may suggest tradeoffs between deliberation over time and store visits, although Claxton, Fry, and Portis point out that long decision time may simply indicate procrastination. Finally, the third main group, labeled nonthorough, was 34 percent of the sample for furniture and 65 percent for appliances. This group used few sources, made few store visits, and took less time. Again, subgroups were found based upon deliberation time. These groupings were then related to other variables. Higher income and education were associated with thoroughness, as were price paid and concern with selecting the right product. Immediacy of need was related to lack of thoroughness, and existence of financial constraints to thoroughness. This research is important in emphasizing the idea of a multidimensional profile of search activities, rather than a single summary measure.

One final set of findings on source patterns is the temporal patterns of source usage found in innovation research. Rogers (1962) states that mass media sources tend to be used during the earlier awareness and interest stages of adoption whereas word-of-mouth communication tends to be most used during later evaluation and trial stages. Kohn Berning and Jacoby (1974) reviewed the evidence for this proposition and found mixed support. They then applied a new methodology to study of this issue. Five product categories were selected, and subjects were asked to select a brand from a set containing both "old" and "new" (recently introduced) alternatives for each category (actual brands were used). Information of five types could be obtained: (1) ads; (2) price; (3) package information; (4) comments attributed to "friends"; and (5) comments attributed to sales personnel. This information was available on index cards that could be selected by the subjects in any order desired. When the subject was ready to choose a brand, she stopped searching the available information and made her choice. There were no limits set on degree of search. The findings showed that innovators (those who chose a new brand) selected more information than noninnovators, mostly attributable to greater use of the "friends" cards. Also, it was found that more personal information was acquired in later portions of the total card sequence, supporting Rogers (1962). The above can be summarized as

> *Proposition 5.3.ii:* The source from which information will be sought is a function of
> a) Individual differences
> b) Stage in the choice process

This finishes the discussion of influences on the direction of external search. Now influences on the degree of external search can be considered.

INFLUENCES ON THE DEGREE OF EXTERNAL SEARCH[5]

Many factors influence the amount of external search performed by the consumer. The major determinants of the degree of external search are now presented, followed by a summary of the research related to each determinant.

> *Proposition 5.3.iii:* Degree of external search is influenced by
> a) The costs vs. benefits of information
> b) Choice environment factors such as availability, difficulty of the choice task, and time pressure
> c) Individual differences, such as use of in-store vs. prior processing, abilities, and concern with optimality of the choice
> d) Conflict and conflict response strategies

---

5. See also the recent review by Newman (1977).

Costs vs. benefits of the information

A common notion, developed from economic theories of search, is that consumers weigh the costs of obtaining information against the benefits which might be expected from using that information. Although the trade-offs implied by rational theories of search (e.g., Stigler 1961) may not be made in such an optimizing fashion, there is some evidence that consumers may heuristically trade off costs and benefits. Costs of search may include time and effort, money, frustration and other psychological costs, and delay of the decision (Engel, Blackwell, and Kollat 1978, pp. 242–243). Benefits might include increased satisfaction with the purchase or psychological benefits such as feeling one did a thorough job (Engel, Blackwell, and Kollat 1978, pp. 238–241). The consumer must assess whether the information is beneficial. Finally, note that one form of search is to simply *buy* the product and try it. For low cost products, the costs versus benefits of this strategy may be appealing.

Several models exist which are related to the costs versus benefits of search. Burnkrant (1976) proposes and presents a preliminary test of an expectancy–value model which focuses on benefits from a source of information. In particular, need for information on a topic, expectancy that processing a stimulus will lead to information on that topic, and the value of that information on the topic determine search tendency. Literature is reviewed which supports the notion that more useful information is preferred, regardless of whether or not it is supportive of the individual's beliefs. In preliminary research testing the theory, Burnkrant found only an effect due to need for information. Feather (1967) presents evidence for a different expectancy–value model which focuses on seeking consistency and avoiding inconsistency.

These two expectancy–value models, although considering elements of a costs versus benefits approach, do not provide complete examples of that approach. Pollay (1970 a, c) presents an explicit Bayesian model of costs versus benefits of search and uses the model to predict decision times. If difficulty of discriminating alternatives is high, the model predicts decision time will shorten, as the higher costs of processing will outweigh the benefits at an earlier time. This notion is partially borne out by Pollay's studies and those of Kiesler (1966) and Hendrick, Mills, and Kiesler (1968), discussed in more detail in Chapter 3.

Other empirical work has focused on the components of the cost-benefits model, particularly the cost component. Lanzetta (1963) and Lanzetta and Kanareff (1962) found that as cost of information increased, less information was purchased. Bucklin (1966) found that lower shopping costs (as inferred from the geography of the area where shopping was done) were related to greater external search of stores. Swan (1972) found that if trying a brand were the only means of gathering information, a greater cost for switching brands led to less switching and hence less search. Lutz and Reilly (1974) found that in purchase situations where perceived risk was low, and hence costs of search relative to benefits might be high, the subjects' stated prefer-

ences were for simply buying and trying a brand rather than seeking information from other sources. Green (1966) reported similar results. Winter (1975)
found that greater search ensued if subjects had no attractive alternative task
to search behavior (and hence opportunity costs were lower). Finally, Chestnut
and Jacoby (1976) found less search for any one choice the greater the total
number of choices to be made.

Some work has also been done relative to benefits from search. Swan
(1969) found that if subjects received payoffs only if optimal rather than satisfactory choices were made, search increased. In his study, benefits were thus
directly related to search. Donnermuth (1965), Bucklin (1966), and Katona and
Mueller (1955) found consumers searched more for higher priced products.
Also, Claxton, Fry, and Portis (1974) showed that presence of financial constraints for a consumer implied more search. If finances are tight, presumably
cost savings (a benefit) are more important, and search may be seen as potentially leading to cost savings.

Finally, there is work which suggests that costs and benefits are
weighed against each other. Lanzetta (1963) and Driscoll and Lanzetta (1965)
found that search continued until uncertainty was reduced to a certain level,
when a decision was made. Lanzetta (1963) calls this a "commitment threshold." Hansen (1972) postulates that either conflict will be reduced to a tolerable level, or search will stop when the conflict generated in choosing search
alternatives is greater than the product choice conflict. These notions imply
that there is a point below which it simply is not worth the effort to further
reduce uncertainty or conflict, indirectly supporting the notion that perceived
benefits and costs are weighed against one another.

Choice environment factors

Since human beings adapt their behavior to reach goals, and goals are
sought in particular choice environments, the characteristics of the choice
environment may greatly influence the amount of information search. This
influence of the shopping environment may be more potent for external
search than for internal search. In general there are three major properties of
choice environments considered below: availability of information, difficulty
of the choice task, and time pressure.

The first major influence, availability, is to be taken in its most general
sense; that is, availability refers to not only whether the information actually
exists, but whether it is more or less accessible. One obvious influence on
amount of search is how much information exists in the choice environment. If
there is little or no information relevant to a consumer's goals, extended
search may not be possible. The consumer may need to modify goals for
search, change his or her acceptable level of conflict, postpone the purchase,
and so on. Even if there is a great deal of information, it may not be in the form
desired by the consumer. For example, there may be many alternatives, each
with values for several attributes, but no information available for developing

criteria; or there may be much information relevant to determining criteria, but few available alternatives. If the consumer wants information on criteria in the former case and on alternatives in the latter, then even though there is information available, it is not the type needed, and thus search might be reduced.

A second choice environment factor influencing degree of search is difficulty of the choice task. Two types of research are relevant here: research related to how easy the information itself is to process, and research related to the sheer amount of information presented, the information load. Ease of processing is heavily impacted by the format utilized for presenting information. Information may be present, but in a form which consumers cannot process effectively. This would tend to lower information search. Russo, Krieser, and Miyashita (1975) and Russo (1977) show that the lack of use of unit price information may be due in part to the difficulties inherent in processing such information as it is typically presented. By changing the mode of presentation to make the unit price information more processable, usage (and hence external search, presumably) increased. Day and Brandt (1974), examining truth in lending information, and Bettman (1975b), examining proposals for presenting nutritional information, also cite the need for information that is presented in more easily processable form. Finally, Howard (1977) discusses several factors relating to processability: simplicity of the language used, abstractness, and redundancy. He notes that processability is perhaps most important for extensive problem solving, since the consumer has little knowledge and few prior expectations to guide processing.

Another aspect related to the difficulty of the choice task is the amount of information available. Typical component measures of amount of information available used in consumer research are the total number of brand alternatives available and the number of attributes given for each alternative. Several researchers have argued that as task difficulty (measured as the total amount of information, or information load) increases, there will first be increases in search, but then eventually decreases as too high an information load is imposed. Studies reporting such as "information overload" include Schroder, Driver, and Streufert (1967), Streufert, Suedfeld, and Driver (1965), and Sieber and Lanzetta (1964) (Note that Jacoby, Speller, and Kohn [1974a,b] also report overload, but do not measure information search).

However, not all researchers find that search eventually declines as load increases. Lussier and Olshavsky (1974), for example, in a design which included up to 12 brands with 15 attributes per brand, found that the number of pieces of information referenced increased (at a decreasing rate) as the numbers of attributes and brands increased. These conflicting results are difficult to reconcile. However, Seibel, Christ, and Teichner (1965) present results supporting the notion that high input rate in itself is *not* the crucial factor. Rather, the factor limiting performance is whether a *high rate of internal processing* is required. Thus the more complex the manipulations *required* for a set of data in some fixed time span, the greater the potential for an information overload. In several types of consumer situations (e.g., in which the in-store display may be used as an external memory or in which the consumer is reading print advertisements) the time available for processing and hence the rate of internal processing can be controlled by the consumer, and processing can be done at a more leisurely rate. The sheer amount of information may not be a crucial factor, since consumers can select subsets of the information and can devote as much time as they desire to processing it. On the other hand, in cases in which the required internal processing may be complex and the rate of information input cannot be controlled by the consumer, as in listening to radio or television commercials, for example, performance may deteriorate as load increases (Wright 1974a). This notion of whether or not the rate of processing required is controllable seems to reconcile the results of the studies cited above, as the tasks of all of the studies seem to require high internal processing. Lussier and Olshavsky (1974) allowed subjects to control rate of information input, whereas the other studies had some aspect of the flow of information outside of the subjects' control. Shwartz (1976) presents other evidence for this notion that processing time is a crucial element. Thus the amount of information processing necessary *per unit time* seems to be the crucial factor in leading to information overload effects, not the sheer amount of information itself. (See Scammon [1977] for similar arguments.) This coincides with the first factor related to choice task difficulty discussed above, in that in both cases the ease of processing information, or *processability*, is positively related to amount of search.

Finally, the third choice environment factor related to degree of search is time pressure. Since time pressure influences the degree of control the consumer can have over internal processing rate, such pressure may affect search behavior. In general, as time pressure increases, search should decrease. Several researchers have shown that the more immediate the need for purchase (e.g., because the currently owned product has broken down), the less the information search (Claxton, Fry, and Portis 1974; Katona and Mueller 1955). Also, Donohew and Tipton (1973) point out that in many situations search is cut off by running out of time, rather than by a decision on the part of the individual about whether or not information is sufficient.

Thus three factors related to difficulty of the choice task influence amount of external search. The more easily available the information is, the more processable information is, and the less time pressure there is, the more external search there will tend to be.

Individual difference factors

As noted in Proposition 5.3.iii, several types of individual differences may be related to degree of external search. First, individuals may use the external memory provided by in-store displays to different extents, and differ in the amount of prior planning done before entering the store. Individuals who rely on in-store processing to a greater extent will tend to display greater external search. However, one cannot imply that this necessarily means greater overall search for such individuals as compared to individuals who rely on out-of-store processing, since those relying on in-store processing may use less internal search. A related issue is that individuals differ in terms of the degree of prior latent learning or other sources of learning about the environment for different purchases. The fact that low external search has been observed in studies of durable purchases (Katona and Mueller 1955; Newman and Staelin 1972) may mean only that internal search is used, not that consumers are irrational or lazy. Measures of the *total* amount of search carried out, both internal and external, need to be utilized in such studies.

A second source of individual differences is the abilities of consumers. Abilities which seem particularly relevant are those Mischel (1973) refers to as cognitive and behavior construction competencies. By this is meant the ability needed to ascertain and carry out appropriate behaviors. There is a good deal of research on ability factors associated with carrying out external search. Several researchers have found that more educated and affluent consumers engage in more search (Thorelli, Becker, and Engeldow 1975; Miller and Zikmund 1975; Claxton, Fry, and Portis 1974; Katona and Mueller 1955). However, Newman and Staelin (1972) found that external search was not monotonically related to education. Those consumers with advanced degrees engaged in little external search. This may be due to increased time pressures; a higher degree of past knowledge and hence higher internal search; greater effectiveness of search for such consumers; or that such consumers don't care as much about the choices studied. The Newman and Staelin data do not allow for tests of these hypotheses. Other factors related to processing abilities have been examined in studies not related to consumer research. For example, Sieber and Lanzetta (1964) show that degree of conceptual complexity is related to search, with more complex subjects searching more. Lanzetta and Kanareff (1962), in related research, show that for tasks with a fixed time span, processing abilities are related to external search. For low speed processors, less information will be gathered. Time needed for processing apparently competes with the time available for acquisition. Thus, in general, greater abilities, defined in various ways, may lead to greater search. The main caveat to this generalization is that greater abilities may also mean more efficient search or more use of internal search. These factors might in some cases lead to lower external search.

A third major type of individual difference variable related to degree of external search is the consumer's concern with optimality of the choice. As noted in Proposition 3.6, consumers may develop criteria for determining when activity related to goals should be stopped. One such criterion may be satisficing, stopping when an alternative is "good enough," even if it is not necessarily optimal. Individuals with higher standards for what is "good enough" will tend to engage in more external search. Both Swan (1969) and

Claxton, Fry, and Portis (1974) found that greater concern with optimality of choice was associated with greater amounts of search. Other individual difference factors related to external search are summarized in Engel, Blackwell, and Kollat (1978, pp. 243–244) and Howard (1977, pp. 166–167).

Thus, in general, greater use of in-store processing, less prior knowledge, greater abilities, and greater concern with finding an optimal alternative tend to be associated with higher external search.

Conflict and conflict response strategies

A great deal of research has attempted to relate conflict and conflict response strategies to degree of external search. Under the optimal level theories described in Chapter 3, for example, external search would be expected under both moderate levels of conflict and under low levels of conflict. For moderate levels of conflict, external search is seen as a way out of the dilemma posed by the conflict, as a way of reducing the general level of conflict (e.g., Howard and Sheth 1969 and Howard 1977;[6] Hansen 1972), although some researchers note that information can increase conflict as well as decrease it (Woodruff 1972). Under low levels of conflict, novel or discrepant information may be sought (Howard and Sheth 1969; Hansen 1972; Venkatesan 1973). Most of the research cited below has examined the moderate conflict case.

A large body of research by Driscoll, Lanzetta, and their associates has examined level of conflict and external search behavior. In these experiments, conflict is defined as uncertainty times importance. Uncertainty was usually measured by the entropy measure suggested by Berlyne (1957), and discussed in Chapter 4. That is, if P_i is the probability of choice of alternative i, then uncertainty is measured by $H = \Sigma/+ _i(P_i \log_2 P_i)$. Various experimental manipulations were carried out to vary importance. Sieber and Lanzetta (1964) found that search was directly related to uncertainty, but curvilinearly related to importance: the higher importance condition had lower search levels. Hawkins and Lanzetta (1965) found that search increased with uncertainty, but decreased with importance. There was also no interaction between uncertainty and importance, contrary to the hypothesis of a multiplicative model for conflict. Driscoll, Tognoli, and Lanzetta (1966) found that search was directly related to the H measure of uncertainty and also to subjective measures of uncertainty generated by the subjects. Finally, Lanzetta and Driscoll (1968) showed that search increased with uncertainty and importance, but again found no importance by uncertainty interaction.

This series of studies supports uncertainty as a determinant of search, but obtains varied results for importance. Heslin, Blake, and Rotton (1972)

---

6. Howard and Sheth (1969) and Howard (1977) use variables of Confidence and Stimulus Ambiguity, not conflict per se. However, lower Confidence and higher Stimulus Ambiguity would seem to imply higher conflict.

criticize these studies for using responses of different judges to the same stimuli to compute the H measure of uncertainty (i.e., P_i was estimated from how many judges chose response i). Thus interjudge disagreement was used to measure a construct which purportedly reflects within-subject uncertainty. Heslin, Blake, and Rotton performed a study using a within-subject method to measure uncertainty, and also varied response importance. The results showed that both uncertainty and importance led to higher search, and that inter-actions between uncertainty and importance did occur. Thus the relationship of uncertainty and importance to conflict and search is still unclear. Criterion measures for perceived conflict and more standardized measures of impor-tance and uncertainty seem necessary to clarify these issues. As noted in Prop-osition 4.4.i, current models of conflict, such as those tested in these experi-ments, seem inadequate.

In consumer research settings, Hansen (1972) related conflict (mea-sured as uncertainty times involvement) to internal and external search. Internal search increased with perceived conflict, but the support for increases in external search was weaker. Although perceived risk is a different phenomenon from conflict (see Chapter 4), it may be related to conflict. There has been some research relating risk to information search which provides weak evidence that word-of-mouth is sought more by high risk perceivers (Cox 1967b, p. 610; Lutz and Reilly 1974). Sheth and Venkatesan (1968) also report high risk perceivers search for more information. Finally, although not directly measuring conflict, Westbrook (1977) found that those consumers expressing the most dissatisfaction prior to making a purchase had the most extensive plans for searching for more information. As emphasized in Chapter 4, the nature of conflict and the theory underlying it need to be studied in more detail, and appropriate measures devised for conflict and related variables. There is no clearly supported relationship between level of conflict and degree of external search.

Variations in response modes to conflict may also influence search. The typology of Kelman and Baron (1968a) for modes of response to incon-sistency was outlined in Chapter 4. The most important distinction in their typology for information search seems to be that of avoiding versus confront-ing an inconsistency or conflict. Those consumers who confront conflict may be more likely to search for information as a result of conflict. The deter-minants of when confrontation will be used, rather than avoiding, are twofold (see Proposition 4.7.ii): (1) emphasis on long-term goals rather than on short-term goals; (2) the relative availability of confrontation and avoidance. The first of these refers to an emphasis on the usefulness of information for future goals. The more useful, the more likely information will be confronted and sought. Burnkrant (1976) summarizes research supporting the confronting of and search for information when it is useful in attaining goals. The second of these factors refers to the relative "availability" of the two modes. For exam-ple, if a highly respected source has presented inconsistent information, avoidance may be difficult. Confrontation might be more likely.

This ends the discussion of determinants of amount of external search. In all of the research cited, the implicit assumption that degree of internal search could be assumed to be either constant or to not affect degree of external search has been made, since conclusions were drawn about degree of external search without measuring degree of internal search. This assumption seems suspect, and should be directly researched in future studies by attempting to measure both internal and external search.

ANALYSIS OF DETAILED PATTERNS OF INFORMATION ACQUISITION

The discussions above have concentrated on general features of the information acquisition process: how much information is acquired, or broad characterizations of what types of information are selected. However, recent research has begun to examine in detail the strategies individuals use in acquiring information from information displays, the sequences of information examined and the structure of such sequences. This research, more detailed in focus than that discussed above, is now examined.

Some recent research in both cognitive psychology and consumer decision making has begun to examine detailed patterns of external information search. Simon and Barenfeld (1969) examined how an expert chess player perceives the features of a position, and developed a program, PERCEIVER, based upon information about relations among pieces and recognition of learned configurations of pieces (chunks). In Russ's (1971) study of small appliance choices, protocols were gathered and subjects obtained information by requesting it from the experimenter. Svenson (1974) examined protocols obtained from six subjects in making a decision among seven hypothetical houses, where information on houses was presented in booklets. Lussier and Olshavsky (1974) studied decisions among hypothetical typewriter brands, where information on each brand was typed on a card. Jacoby, Szybillo, and Busato-Schach (1977) studied brand choice, with information covered by tape on a display arranged as a brands x attributes array. The information could be examined by removing the tape from any given attribute row in the array. Russo and Rosen (1975) examined choices among six used cars, each characterized by three attributes, by studying sequences of subjects' eye fixations over the data, displayed on a cathode ray tube. Russo and Dosher (1975) also examined choices among several sets of alternatives by examining eye movements. Jacoby, Chestnut, Weigl, and Fisher (1976) and Bettman and Jacoby (1976) studied choice of brands of cereal by using an information display board, where cards containing information on cereals were arranged in a brands x attributes array. Subjects could select as many cards as desired. Van Raaij (1976a, b) studied choices of coffee using both eye movement data and display board analyses. Finally, Payne (1976a, b) studied choices of apartments in two experiments, where information was presented in a number of envelopes attached to a board in brands x attributes array. He varied number of alternatives and number of attributes to study task effects on processing.

In all of this research, the data include a detailed description of the sequence of information actually acquired by the subject. Thus external information seeking responses are measured, but not necessarily internal processing, although the two may be congruent (see, for example, Just and Carpenter 1976). These external search sequences can be analyzed to see if any patterns emerge. Some stable findings have emerged from these studies. First, there are individual differences in the order of external information search. Some subjects search by examining one "brand" (strictly speaking, alternative) at a time; that is, they choose a brand and gather information on several attributes of that brand. Then they may choose a second brand and gather information on several attributes (not necessarily the same as those for the first brand) and so on. This strategy may be called Choice by Processing Brands (CPB). A second group of subjects acquires information by choosing an attribute and determining values for each of several brands on that attribute, choosing a second attribute and determining values for several brands and so on. This may be called a Choice by Processing Attributes (CPA) strategy. Other strategies exist, but the two major strategies are those related above. As noted in more detail in Chapter 7, several of the studies have found more processing by attribute than by brand (e.g., Russ 1971; Russo and Rosen 1975; Russo and Dosher 1975), with others finding more brand processing (e.g., Bettman and Kakkar 1977). The relationship of these two major strategies to the decision rules used by consumers is also discussed in Chapter 7.

A second set of findings from several of the studies above is that some subjects use one of the basic strategies above in a uniform manner, i.e., they do not change their strategy during the course of the search. Other subjects use phased strategies (Wright 1974e), in which the type of processing varies over the search. One type of phased strategy observed is one in which the first phase is information input, either by brands or attributes, and the second phase is a set of paired comparisons among specific alternatives (Svenson 1974; Lussier and Olshavsky 1974; Russo and Rosen 1975; Payne 1976a, b).

Third, some studies have attempted to relate processing strategy to other consumer behavior variables. For example, Jacoby, Chestnut, Weigl, and Fisher (1976) found that processing by brands was related to high consumption frequency, and processing by attributes to low consumption frequency and low brand loyalty. Bettman and Kakkar (1977) also suggest that greater experience with the alternatives is associated with greater use of brand processing.

Finally, a fourth factor that has been considered is the effect of the structure of the task environment (i.e., how the information display is arranged) on search processes in the above studies. A brief task analysis indicates that the tasks in many of the studies (e.g., matrix displays or tables) make it equally easy, in terms of the effort needed to *acquire* the information, to process by brands or by attributes. However, this property is not true of the real world, except for perhaps tasks such as reading a table in *Consumer Reports*. For a choice of brands from a supermarket shelf, information is organized by brand, facilitating brand processing. Bettman and Kakkar (1977) attempted to directly test the effect of display format on the structure of the resulting acquisition sequences. They examined three groups of consumers, each presented with a different display format: one which was the standard matrix array, with either brand or attribute processing being equally easy; one was a display that encouraged attribute and discouraged brand processing; and one was a display that encouraged brand and discouraged attribute processing. The results showed that consumers acquired the information in the fashion that was easiest given the display. For example, attribute processing was observed when the format encouraged it, and not when the format discouraged it. Implications of this task analysis and these research findings are considered in later chapters. The sections above can be summarized as

> *Proposition 5.3.iv:* Detailed patterns of external information search can be examined by measuring the sequence of information acquired from an information display. Analyses of such sequences show
>
> a) Two major acquisition strategies are processing by brands and processing by attributes
>
> b) Phased strategies may be used in which the type of processing varies over the course of search
>
> c) Processing strategies may be related to other consumer variables
>
> d) The type of processing strategy used seems to be strongly affected by the format of the information display

The discussion above documents impacts on the structure of external search processes. Processing in internal search can also be influenced by various factors. Perhaps the most important of these is how information is stored in memory. As Calder (1975a) points out, the type of processing used may depend very closely on the way information stored in memory is organized. Payne (1976a) distinguishes between two possible ways (among many other possibilities) of representing attribute-brand data in memory: where the organization is by brand or by attribute. Internal search might presumably proceed in ways congruent with this organization—i.e., if information is stored by brand, internal search might be by brand; if stored by attribute, search might be by attribute. Johnson and Russo (1978) provide evidence based on recall response times that the organization of internal storage is also heavily affected by the format in which the information was presented, congruent with the external search results noted above. If information was presented by brand, it tended to be stored by brand; if presented by attribute, it tended to be stored by attribute.

Proposition 5.1.ii: The detailed patterns of internal information search may depend on the way in which information is stored in memory.

INDIVIDUAL DIFFERENCES IN THE INFORMATION ACQUISITION AND EVALUATION COMPONENT

Those individual difference factors which seem to be most important for the information acquisition and evaluation component are given below:

Proposition 5.8: Individual differences can affect aspects of the information acquisition and evaluation component. Significant individual difference variables may be:

a) The amount of product-related information held in memory

b) The organization of that information in memory

c) The degree to which in-store processing is used rather than out-of-store processing

d) Processing abilities

e) The degree to which optimal rather than satisfactory choices are desired

f) The patterns of information sources used

g) The reaction strategies used to respond to interrupts in general and conflict in particular

SUMMARY OF THE PROPOSITIONS

As an aid in summarizing the major assertions made in the chapter, the propositions are summarized below:

Proposition 5.1: Active information search initially may be internal search of information stored in memory. Such search can be characterized by direction (which pieces of information are sought); by degree (how much is sought); and by more detailed patterns in the sequences of information sought (what acquisition strategies are used).

Proposition 5.1.i: Degree of internal search may be higher

a) The more relevant information is stored in memory

b) The greater the suitability of that information

c) The greater the degree of perceived conflict (up to some maximum level of conflict which can be handled)

Proposition 5.1.ii: The detailed patterns of internal information search may depend on the way in which information is stored in memory.

Proposition 5.2: During internal search interrupts can arise based upon lack of needed information, conflicting information, or recall of previously forgotten goals. One major response to such interrupts may be formation of a goal for external search.

Proposition 5.3: Following initial internal search, there may be external search for information. Such search is characterized by direction (which pieces of information are sought); by degree (how much is sought); and by more detailed patterns in the sequences of information sought (what acquisition strategies are used).

Proposition 5.3.i: The type of information which will be sought in external search may be influenced by

a) The amount and type of knowledge held in memory

b) The structure of the particular choice environment, the relative availability of various types of information

c) The type of conflict occurring

d) The purpose for which the information will be used

e) The particular nature of interrupt events

Proposition 5.3.ii: The source from which information will be sought is a function of

a) Individual differences

b) Stage in the choice process

Proposition 5.3.iii: Degree of external search is influenced by

a) The costs vs. benefits of information

b) Choice environment factors such as availability, difficulty of the choice task, and time pressure

c) Individual differences, such as use of in-store vs. prior processing, abilities, and concern with optimality of the choice

d) Conflict and conflict response strategies

Proposition 5.3.iv: Detailed patterns of external information search can be examined by measuring the sequence of information acquired from an information display. Analyses of such sequences show

a) Two major acquisition strategies are processing by brands and processing by attributes

b) Phased strategies may be used in which the type of processing varies over the course of search

c) Processing strategies may be related to other consumer variables

d) The type of processing strategy used seems to be strongly affected by the format of the information display

Proposition 5.4: Interrupts can arise during external search. Responses to these interrupts depend on the consumer's interpretation of the significance of the interrupts in light of current goals.

Proposition 5.5: The relationship between amount of internal search and amount of external search performed is currently not well understood. Possible influences on the form of the relationship are level of conflict and individual differences.

Proposition 5.6: Consumers appear to evaluate incoming information in situations in which there is some degree of involvement by actively generating responses to the message presented. Such responses typically can be categorized as counterarguments, source derogations, and support arguments. Counterarguments are the most prevalent response under most conditions, and are negatively related to message acceptance. The medium through which the message is presented impacts the pattern of cognitive responses.

Proposition 5.7: Current measures of degree of internal and external search do not seem adequate. More precise measures need to be developed.

Proposition 5.8: Individual differences can affect aspects of the information acquisition and evaluation component. Significant individual difference variables may be:

a) The amount of product-related information held in memory

b) The organization of that information in memory

c) The degree to which in-store processing is used rather than out-of-store processing

d) Processing abilities

e) The degree to which optimal rather than satisfactory choices are desired

f) The patterns of information sources used

g) The reaction strategies used to respond to interrupts in general and conflict in particular

NEEDED RESEARCH

Areas where research seems most needed are summarized below, organized in terms of the propositions presented above. One major area of research concerns the measurement of both internal and external search (Propositions 5.1, 5.3, 5.7). As noted above, there are serious questions about the adequacy of current measures. Measures of external search are probably easiest to develop. However, measures of internal search are also very important, as measures of external search have been used as surrogates for total search. This approach can be very misleading, since little external search may be done if a comprehensive internal search has been carried out. One way to proceed in measuring internal search might be to measure the amount of information the consumer has stored in memory that is relevant for a specific choice. This amount may be monotonically related to degree of internal search. If degree of internal search is measured, then measures of total search can be constructed. These total search measures should then be applied to purchase situations (e.g., for durables) to see if prior research findings about lack of search are valid.

Studies of the relationship between degree of internal and external search are also needed (Proposition 5.5). Are these search modes compensatory or do increases in one tend to be accompanied by increases in the other? The form of the relationship may be contingent upon the degree of involvement or conflict in the choice facing the consumer, and on individual differences.

The notions above refer mainly to amount of search. Studies are also needed to distinguish the quantity of search from the quality or effectiveness of search. Little work has been done on search quality, which may be roughly defined as the amount of relevant information attained for a given amount of search effort. Defining such a variable would be difficult, but it seems necessary, since sheer amount of search may not be a good indicator of the degree to which information has influenced criteria or the decision itself, or of the degree to which search has allowed "adequate" comparison of alternatives.

These suggested studies attempt to more clearly define the nature of internal and external search. Research on the amount of search performed and factors affecting that amount is also needed. For internal search (Proposition 5.1.i) two areas seem most important: development of measures of the amount of relevant information stored in memory, and factors influencing whether a piece of information is deemed suitable or not. For external search (Propositions 5.3.i, 5.3.ii, 5.3.iii), the major research areas are again measurement of the information stored in memory, categorization of the structure of consumer choice environments (in particular, the relative availability of various types of information), and study of conflict response strategies.

Wright's cognitive monitoring (1973a, 1974a, 1974c) approach provides a possible methodology for the latter area, examination of response modes to conflict. Subjects in an experiment where choices involving various amounts of conflict had been made could be asked to list their spontaneous responses to these conflicts. Examination of the elicited responses could be used to generate both types of responses and coding rules. Finally, experimental manipulations could be used to examine how responses to conflict are related to various factors such as level of conflict, type of conflict, and so on. This research direction seems very exciting, although difficult. Measures of the degree of perceived conflict are needed to fully explore this research area. The approach above could also be used to examine the responses to interrupts in general (Propositions 5.2 and 5.4).

Wright's (1973a, 1974a, 1974c) work on information evaluation (Proposition 5.6) could also be extended. His research measures the link from a cognitive response to a message to acceptance of that message. However, he does not examine the link from the particular pieces of information in a message to the resulting cognitive responses. Also Wright's work examines only very broad types of cognitive responses. One could examine these responses in more detail, to examine more directly what inferences consumers make from communication messages. Lutz and Swasy (1977) propose one method for doing this more detailed analysis, and Olson, Toy, and Dover (1978) report some initial research results.

Research on detailed acquisition strategies (Propositions 5.1.ii and 5.3.iv) has recently been quite prevalent. Major research areas are study of those factors which might impact the acquisition strategies used (e.g., time pressure, degree of prior knowledge of the alternatives); examination of how the external search patterns relate to any internal information processing of the alternatives examined; and study of how information is organized in memory.

Finally, some individual difference variables in need of research (Proposition 5.8) are the amount and organization of relevant information held in memory, use of conflict response strategies (mentioned above), and differences in the degree to which in-store processing is used. Differences in in-store processing may affect the degree of internal and external search, and also may affect the amount of influence the task environment exerts on choice.

CHAPTER 6

Memory Functions

Memory plays a major role in several of the other components of the theory. For example, consumers use information held in memory in the process of perceiving and interpreting incoming stimuli. In addition, information stored in memory is constantly being examined by the consumer in the course of making choices. Memory thus is a slightly different component of the theory than any discussed thus far. In essence, memory is necessary for carrying out the functions described in other components—perception, search, choice and so on—and is utilized by these other components rather than being a separate "stage" of the choice process. However, it is important in understanding the functioning of the other components to understand the properties of memory, how memory works. Thus the structure and operation of memory are considered in detail in this chapter.

OVERVIEW OF THE MEMORY COMPONENT

Since memory is a component that can be used in many different ways by other components in the theory, rather than attempting to describe how memory is typically used, we will first consider the general structure of memory, and then how memory might be utilized.

One concept of memory that has recently been very influential is that there are different types of memory storage systems, each with different functions and properties. A typical model of this type, shown in Fig. 6.1, hypothesizes a set of sensory stores (SS), a short-term memory store (STS), and a long-term store (LTS) (Atkinson and Shiffrin 1971; Shiffrin and Atkinson 1969; Greeno and Bjork 1973). The basic sequence of processing is that information passes from the sense organs to the appropriate sensory store. Each sensory store is hypothesized to be very short-lived, losing information within fractions of a second unless the information is further processed (i.e., unless attention is

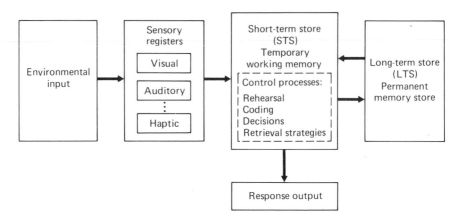

Fig. 6.1 Information flow through the memory system is conceived of as beginning with the processing of environmental inputs in sensory registers (receptors plus internal elements) and entry into the short-term store (STS). While it remains there the information may be copied into the long-term store (LTS), and associated information that is in the long-term store may be activated and entered into the short-term store. If a triangle is seen, for example, the name "triangle" may be called up. Control processes in the short-term store affect these transfers into and out of the long-term store and govern learning, retrieval of information and forgetting. (From Richard C. Atkinson and Richard M. Shiffrin, 1971. The control of short-term memory *Scientific American* **225** (August): 82. Copyright © (1971) by Scientific American, Inc. All rights reserved.)

allocated to the stimulus). If the information in the sensory store is attended to and processed, it is transferred to the short-term store. The STS has a limited capacity, and information can be kept active in the STS by further processing. Information which is active in the STS can be retrieved quickly and almost automatically. Also, information in the long-term store may be brought into the STS as needed to interpret the input information. Thus the STS is the locus of current processing activity, where information from the sense organs and long-term memory can be brought together and processed. Finally, a portion of the information in the STS, if adequately processed (a discussion of the meaning of "adequate" in this context is given below), can be transferred to the LTS. The LTS is hypothesized to be of essentially unlimited capacity and a permanent repository of information. Thus information enters the sensory store from the sense organs and, if actively processed, goes to the short-term store. The STS is then the locus of current processing on a stimulus, using information from the long-term store as necessary to interpret the stimulus input. If sufficient processing is carried out, some of the new information input may become part of the long-term store.

In addition to this characterization of the basic structure of memory, one must also consider how individuals *use* memory; that is, individuals have various strategies for how and what to process, for what to store in long-term memory and how to store it, for how to retrieve information from long-term memory, and so on. Such strategies are often called control processes (Atkinson and Shiffrin 1968, 1971; Shiffrin and Atkinson 1969). Although in many cases storage of and access to items in memory may be nearly automatic, with little conscious thought, retrieval and storage can also be involved and difficult processes.

Finally, there may be an *external* memory in many cases in consumer choice, where information is available without needing to be stored in the consumer's own memory. Such phenomena as package information, shopping lists, buying guides, or ads clipped out by the consumer and brought to the store are part of this external memory.

Thus there is a memory system and a set of control processes that can be used to interact with that memory system. In general, two very basic kinds of usage of memory occur. In one case, information that is currently in long-term storage or external memory must be retrieved to be used in interpreting incoming information or to be used in current processing; that is, information must be gotten *out* of memory. In the second case, incoming information is processed and stored *in* memory for later use. These two functions are of course not independent; they are simultaneously occurring at almost all times. These functions form the basis for the interactions of the memory component with other components of the theory. The relevant portions of the theory are shown in Fig. 5.1.

The basic concepts of the memory component are now presented in more detail below: the multiple store view of memory, control processes, properties of short-term and long-term memory, and the impact of different types of consumer choice tasks on memory usage.

MAJOR ASPECTS OF THE MEMORY COMPONENT

THE MULTIPLE STORE APPROACH TO MEMORY

As noted above, one prevalent view of memory is that there are different types of memory stores. However, recent research has begun to cast doubt on the strict interpretation of the multiple-store concept, particularly the distinction between the LTS and the STS as separate memories. Postman (1975) provides a thorough and critical summary of the evidence, and concludes that the distinction is not well supported. Other conceptions of memory have been advanced which do not postulate multiple stores.

In one such conception, Craik and Lockhart (1972) propose that human beings have limited processing capacity, and that this capacity can be allocated to processing incoming information. In particular, they argue that capacity can be allocated to yield various *levels of processing*. Levels of processing might range from a simple sensory analysis (e.g., noting that the information is printed in red type) to more complex semantic and cognitive elaborations of the information (e.g., relating the information to other information in memory and seeing how it fits with previous beliefs). Presumably the "lower" levels of processing (e.g., sensory analysis) would require less processing capacity to be allocated than the "higher" or "deeper" levels (e.g., semantic analyses). It is then hypothesized that the level of processing attained determines the future retention of the information. In particular, "deeper" levels of processing (and hence greater use of processing capacity) are hypothesized to be associated with more elaborate and longer lasting memory for the information (see Craik and Tulving [1975] for supporting evidence and extensions to the theory, and Nelson [1977] and Baddely [1978] for critiques of this approach). The fact that there is limited overall processing capacity to be allocated accounts for the finding that only a small amount of information can be processed in depth at any one time. Note that this explanation assumes only a single memory, not several different memory stores. Rather than postulating several distinct memories, the theory assumes there is an overall processing capacity and the ability to engage in different levels of processing.

Another general conception of memory that does not require multiple stores is the activation model. In this model, there is one memory store, but only limited portions of that store can be activated at any one point in time; that is, there is a limitation on the capacity for activation. Only the activated portion of memory can be used for current processing. Thus, at any point in time, there is a currently activated portion of memory, which is being used for current processing, and a remaining unactivated portion. Activation is temporary, and will die out unless further effort is devoted to maintaining the activation. The exact nature of activation is typically unspecified; however, the concept is one of rate, or intensity. Therefore, notions of effort (Kahneman 1973) or allocation of processing capacity can also be viewed as concepts of activation. A general model of this type is outlined by Collins and Loftus (1975). The limited capacity for dealing with incoming information which led to postulation of the STS is thus handled in this model by the limitation on total amount of activation.

The three models described to this point, multiple-store, levels of processing, and activation, do not seem incompatible. The multiple-store theories do not strictly require that there be physiologically separate stores; the *functions* of each store are what is important. Shiffrin and Atkinson note that their system is "equally as consistent with the view that stores are separate physiological structures as with the view that the short-term store is simply a temporary activation of information permanently stored in the long-term store." (Shiffrin and Atkinson 1969, pp. 179–180) Bower (1975) makes the same point. Thus the multiple-store model can be viewed as an activation model. Also, a liberal view of the Craik and Lockhart (1972) model allows it to be viewed as an activation approach, since the allocation of processing capacity is a major mechanism of their model.

Thus it seems that all three models of memory cited above are consistent with the idea of a limited processing capacity and a single memory store, with allocations of that capacity to the processing of incoming information. The phenomena of the limited STS seem perfectly explainable in these terms, since there is a limitation on the total amount of processing capacity available for allocation. The STS is the locus of current processing, the limited portion of memory that is activated at any point in time. This concept of a limited capacity that is allocated to processing incoming information is the memory model espoused in the theory of this book. In examining the properties of memory below, the terminology of short-term memory (STM) and long-term memory (LTM) will be utilized to escape from the notion of separate stores, rather than defining new terms for the currently activated portion of memory and the entire memory itself. However, these terms are to be understood in the light of the discussion above.

> *Proposition 6.1:* The internal memory system consists of a set of sensory stores, a short-term memory, and a long-term memory. Each of these memories has different properties and functions.

>> *Proposition 6.1.i:* Short-term and long-term memory are not necessarily physiologically separate memory stores. Rather, a single memory is postulated, with a limitation on how much of that memory can be simultaneously activated.

The propositions above deal with the consumer's own internal memory system. However, as noted above, external memory devices are often available, ranging from package information to detailed shopping checklists. The presence of an external memory can serve to reduce the burden on the consumer's internal memory. Thus the availability of external memory in any particular choice situation can be an important factor characterizing that situation. In summary,

>> *Proposition 6.1.ii:* In addition to the internal memory system, consumers may have access to an external memory, comprised of package information, written shopping lists, buying guides, and so on. The availability of external memory devices may vary over choice situations.

Before considering the properties of short-term and long-term memory in more detail, we must examine the basic methods used by human beings in interacting with memory. Such processes are termed memory control processes.

MEMORY CONTROL PROCESSES

Memory control processes are the strategies used by people to control the flow of information into and out of memory (Shiffrin and Atkinson 1969; Atkinson and Shiffrin 1968, 1971). These processes can be under the active control of the individual. There are certainly many habitual, nearly automatic, processes used by individuals in inputting and outputting information. Individuals undoubtedly possess a repertoire of such processes, and decisions are *not* made on every input to or retrieval from memory. However, in some cases, such conscious decisions are made, so an understanding of the strategies involved is important.

> *Proposition 6.2:* Memory control processes are the strategies used by individuals for controlling the flow of information into and out of memory. Important control processes are
>
> a) Rehearsal   b) Coding
>
> c) Transfer   d) Placement
>
> e) Retrieval   f) Response generation

Rehearsal

After a stimulus has entered short-term memory, processing effort may be needed to further analyze the stimulus. Rehearsal is this process of further analysis, and is carried out in the short-term memory. The two roles usually assigned to rehearsal are maintenance of information (keeping it activated) in the STM; and ultimate transfer of information to the LTM from STM.

The initial concept of rehearsal was that of rote repetition of the information in STM, usually verbal in memory experiments; that is, the individual was viewed as silently repeating the information being considered. Retention in long-term memory was postulated to be a direct function of the amount of time spent in rehearsal. However, this notion has been shown to be inadequate. Many studies have shown that retention in LTM does not necessarily vary directly with amount of rehearsal time. Instead, retention can vary with the form of the rehearsal itself (Woodward, Bjork, and Jongeward 1973; Craik and Watkins 1973; Postman 1975), whether mere repetition (less retention) or more detailed analysis of the information (more retention). Thus rehearsal can probably best be characterized as allocation of processing capacity, which will be done in accordance with the goals of the individual and the requirements of the task at hand (e.g., to remember a phone number only while one dials it probably requires only rote repetition, but learning a complex concept may require more elaborate processing, such as relating the concept to other concepts in memory).

Coding

Rehearsal strategies are intimately related to coding strategies. Coding refers to the way the individual *structures* information for rehearsal; that is, associations may be formed between the information and data from long-term memory. It is now well known that subjects in verbal learning studies use mnemonics, associations, images, and many other strategies of encoding the inputs they receive to facilitate memory (Bower 1970; Reitman 1970). For example, a subject given the nonsense syllable pair BAQ-GYF to remember may come up with a mnemonic of "give back" (GYF-BAQ) or may even develop a mental image of football back Frank Gifford in an attempt to remember the item. Bower and Winzenz (1970) manipulated subjects' coding strategies directly by instructing different groups how to rehearse in a paired-associate learning task: simple repetition; reading aloud of a sentence containing the two paired associates; generation of a sentence containing the two words; and imagery formation involving the two words. Recall increased monotonically from the repetition to the imagery group.

Transfer

A third control process is the transfer process, the decision of *what* to store in memory and the form in which to store it. Information that is important for attaining goals and information that is easily stored are likely to be given highest priority (Shiffrin and Atkinson 1969). These properties need not coincide; that is, information needed for goals may be difficult to process, for example. Trade-offs must be made in such a case. Also, what is to be stored and the form of storage may depend on what the individual expects to do with the information if such expectations are present. More or less detail may be required depending on the task to be performed when the information will be used. For example, differences in what may be stored when individuals expect to have to recognize or recall information are discussed below. In situations in which individuals do not have firm expectations about how the information will be used, the easiest transfer strategy in that situation will probably be used. Finally, as discussed in earlier chapters, events which are surprising, novel, inconsistent with expectations, and so on will often be given priority for processing and storage.

Placement

Placement deals with where an element is stored in memory. Where an item is stored depends on the existing organization of memory and the particular associations utilized in coding the item. In this sense the "where" question does not refer to a physical location, but the association structure developed when the item was processed. This association structure is affected by the context of presentation: e.g., if words are presented in categories, recall tends to be grouped by those same categories (Bower 1970). The importance of the placement decision is that later retrieval may depend on the likelihood that the particular placement strategy used can be reconstructed. (See Landauer [1975], however for a contrasting view of memory as being randomly organized.) In addition, a placement decision may lead to *reorganization* of a portion of memory, based upon the particular concept being stored (Rumelhart, Lindsay, and Norman 1972; Lindsay and Norman 1972, especially Chapter 11).

Retrieval

Retrieval of items from memory is a crucial memory control process. Retrieval processes can range from almost immediate access for familiar items to involved problem-solving search processes for other items. The control processes discussed above interact with retrieval. If the basis used for coding, transfer, and placement cannot be retrieved, the item itself may not be accessible. Forgetting is seen, therefore, in light of the view of the LTM as a permanent memory store, as a failure of the retrieval process rather than the decay or loss of items. The basic underlying notion can be best seen intuitively by considering cases in which an item cannot be remembered, and then some event occurs which gives the "clue" needed to immediately retrieve the item. This phenomenon implies that the correct retrieval strategy just could not be found at first.

Failure of the retrieval process may result from searching in the wrong "part" of memory (i.e., in the wrong set of associations), from running out of time to perform the search, or from losing one's place in the search. This latter possibility reflects the limited capacity for short-term memory; that is, only a small portion of memory can be activated at any one point in time. This may result in one's not being able to keep track of one's place in a complex search for an item which one finds hard to retrieve (Olshavsky 1971). Use of some external device (e.g., paper and pencil) as a memory aid is often tried by individuals in such cases. Finally, differences in the extent of retrieval processes are also hypothesized to characterize different types of memory tasks, particularly recognition and recall. Some theorists argue that a retrieval search process is not required for recognition, that the presence of the to-be-recognized item generates an immediate contact with that item in memory (Kintsch 1970; Anderson and Bower 1972). Others (e.g., Shiffrin 1970; Tulving and Thomson 1971) argue that search is needed in the case of both recognition and recall.

Response generation

A final set of control processes is that of response generation. The view of many theorists is that remembering is a constructive process; that is, items are reconstructed from memory. Partial recollections are used as the basis for reconstructing what "must have been." Items are *not* stored in memory exactly as they were entered and aroused in toto when desired. Neisser (1967, pp. 285–286) calls this latter view the "reappearance hypothesis," and rejects this view in favor of a constructive approach: "The present proposal is, therefore, that we store traces of earlier cognitive acts. . . . The traces are not simply 'revived' or 'reactivated' in recall; instead the stored fragments are used as information to support a new construction." Bower (1970) and Norman (1969) develop similar views, all based upon the earlier ideas of Bartlett (1932). Jenkins (1974) and Cofer (1973) summarize other research supporting a constructive approach to response generation in memory. This constructive view implies that memory may be subject to biases, since reconstructions will be based partly on what was and partly on individuals' expectations or schemas for what "must have been."

This completes the discussion of control processes in memory. An overview of the memory system has now been presented. Further details about the functioning of the short-term and long-term memories are presented next.

PROPERTIES OF SHORT-TERM MEMORY

The properties of short-term memory are now examined. These properties fall into three major categories: capacity, the times needed to transfer information to long-term memory, and the type of information thought to be analyzed in short-term memory.

Capacity

As discussed above, the STM is of limited capacity. This constraint derives from the limited overall processing capacity, so that only a small portion of memory can be activated at one time.[1] Miller (1956) first formulated the hypothesis that STM was limited, and reviewed evidence that showed that approximately seven chunks of information could be processed at any one point in time. A chunk was defined to be a configuration that was familiar to an individual and could be manipulated as a unit, in essence an organized cognitive structure that could grow as information is integrated into it.[2] For example, a brand name can summarize a good deal of more detailed information for a consumer familiar with that brand, and hence the brand name and all it stands for can be thought of as a chunk. The actual amount of underlying material that can be processed simultaneously can thus be expanded by formation of larger chunks. This notion of a capacity for chunks is consistent with a memory model in which the constraint is on processing capacity or amount of activation if the assumption is made that the processing capacity needed to manipulate a chunk is independent of the size of the chunk. That seems to be in fact the essence of the chunking concept, that it is the organization of the chunk that allows for ease in processing.

The capacity of STM is lowered if other processing demands are made. This follows immediately from the notion of the limits on STM as processing capacity limits. If part of total capacity must be used for another task, that leaves less for processing chunks of information. The normal capacity of seven

---

1. The notion of the STM as a "box," with a fixed number of "slots," has also been used, but is rejected on the basis of the arguments above denying the need for the distinction between the long-term and short-term stores.

2. Bower (1975) points out that this definition is circular: a chunk is something that can be processed as a unit, and the capacity of STM is inferred from examining units of information that are processed, which units are then called chunks.

chunks or so may be reduced to a capacity of two or three chunks if other tasks are undertaken simultaneously, such as search processes or counting tasks (Simon 1969; Newell and Simon 1972; Waugh and Norman 1965; Olshavsky and Gregg 1970; Olshavsky 1971).

Transfer times

Another property of short-term memory concerns the amount of time required to transfer an item from STM to LTM, assuming suitable processing is performed (i.e., if the type of coding needed to allow retention in LTM is performed, or if the form of rehearsal leads to retention, as discussed above). Simon (1969, pp. 35–42) and Newell and Simon (1972, pp. 793–796) cite evidence that suggests that from five to ten seconds are required to fixate one chunk of information in LTM if one must later *recall* the information. If *recognition* only is required, times on the order of two to five seconds may be needed (Simon 1969, p. 39; Shepard 1967). This task difference follows from the fact that for recognition, discrimination of the item from others is all that is needed, not reconstruction of the information. The main source of evidence used for these assertions is that on the so-called total-time hypothesis, a fixed amount of time is needed to learn a fixed amount of material (Cooper and Pantle 1967; Bugelski 1962; Wilcoxon, Wilson, and Wise 1961). However, this hypothesis may not hold true in general. The time required per chunk may vary with the efficacy of the rehearsal and coding strategies used. Hence the times above are guides rather than precise estimates.

If information is not rehearsed at all, it is lost from STM in about 30 seconds or less (Shiffrin and Atkinson 1969). Whether this loss is due to decay (Shiffrin and Atkinson 1969) or displacement by new items being allocated capacity (Waugh and Norman 1965) is still under debate. As Postman (1975) notes, it is very difficult to distinguish between these two alternatives experimentally.

Type of information analyzed

STM was originally hypothesized to be an acoustic store; that is, items were represented acoustically by their sounds, rather than semantically. Recent evidence increasingly shows that this counterintuitive notion is not correct, in the sense that the information is not *necessarily* acoustic. There is evidence for both acoustic and semantic coding in STM. As Postman (1975, p. 300) wryly notes, "Hopefully the question of whether words can be encoded semantically in short-term memory situations is now settled. The idea that people would mouth the sounds of words for several seconds at a stretch without knowing what they were saying was always a bit unsettling."

The sections above are summarized as

Proposition 6.3: Short-term memory is characterized by the following properties:

a) A limited capacity of about seven chunks, with capacity falling to two or three chunks if tasks other than the memory task are simultaneously imposed

b) Times for transferring one chunk from short-term to long-term memory of five to ten seconds if recall of the information being transferred is required and of two to five seconds if recognition is required. If information is not rehearsed, it is lost from STM in about thirty seconds or less

c) Items are coded both acoustically and semantically in STM

PROPERTIES OF LONG-TERM MEMORY

Long-term memory is hypothesized to be an essentially unlimited and permanent store, with both semantic and some auditory and visual storage. The basic questions about LTM are what are the elements stored, and what is the organization of that storage.

Elements in long-term memory

There seems to be some agreement that an important part of what is stored in LTM is semantic concepts and the associations among them (Quillian 1968; Rumelhart, Lindsay, and Norman 1972; Anderson and Bower 1973). Concepts may include events, objects, processing rules, attributes of objects and events, and so on. Underwood (1969) particularly emphasizes that various attributes of objects and events can be stored and used to discriminate items and aid in retrieval. Such attributes as temporal sequence information, information about the spatial aspects of events, modality through which the information was obtained (e.g., audio, visual, smell, etc.), affective data, and contextual data can potentially be stored. This notion of contextual data, particularly time context, has been suggested by several authors, who cite Koffka's (1935) original notion of a "trace column," a kind of time line memory for the sequential occurrence of events (Russo and Wisher 1975; Posner and Warren 1972; Hintzman and Block 1970).

Storage of processing rules is also important. Newell and Simon (1972) and Rumelhart, Lindsay, and Norman (1972) see processing rules as being stored in the database and being able to be operated on and activated like other data. Finally, it seems clear that in addition to memory for semantic concepts there is substantial memory for visual images and auditory events in LTM, but the mechanisms are currently not well understood (Paivio 1975).

The structure of long-term memory

There is also general agreement on the structure of the storage in LTM for semantic information. Semantic storage is thought to be organized as a network of nodes and links between nodes, with the nodes representing concepts and the links denoting relationships among concepts; or as some organization which is structurally equivalent to a network formulation (Frijda 1972). Note that this does not imply there is a corresponding physiological network. In fact, John (1972) argues that it is the *pattern* of neurological activity at any moment that constitutes a memory, not a specific pathway between sets of neurons.[3]

Collins and Loftus (1975) present a network model, originally based on Quillian's (1968) work, in which there are nodes representing concepts and several kinds of links between concepts. Each link has a strength corresponding to how essential that link is to the meaning of the concept. Processing a concept corresponds to activating the node corresponding to that concept, with activation spreading through the network along the links. Collins and Loftus (1975) show how the theory can explain effects of perceptual set and other data. The Argus model of Reitman (1965) is also a network of nodes with activation operating over the network.

Anderson and Bower (1973) see memory as a network of concept nodes interconnected by associations and also use the concepts of activation. Finally, Rumelhart, Lindsay, and Norman (1972) develop a network of concepts and relations, with particular emphasis on the coding of actions and events.

Other models have been proposed, but they can be viewed as equivalent to network models. Newell and Simon (1972) see memory as an organization of list structures (a list structure is a list the elements of which can also be lists). A list structure can be easily transformed into an equivalent network. Smith, Shoben, and Rips (1974) present a set-theoretical model, where concepts are described by a set of features or properties. As Hollan (1975) points out, their model can also be reduced to a network model. Finally, within the marketing literature, Nakanishi (1974) proposed a model he called a contiguous retrieval model. In this model, concepts are stored in clusters rather than in lists, and retrieval of concepts is based upon the closeness of associa-

---

3. A recent model of memory, in a sharp departure from these network organization notions, posits random storage and undirected retrieval, in essence a memory without organization (Landauer 1975). Landauer postulates a memory consisting of a three-dimensional space with a large number of homogeneously distributed storage loci. A "pointer" moves through the space in a three-dimensional random walk over time. Data entry occurs at the location of the pointer when the data is perceived, so that if time between entries is short, the storage locations will be close together. Search is undirected, starting from the location of the pointer. Search spreads uniformly in all directions, as an expanding sphere, up to a limited radius. Landauer shows how this simple model can account for standard learning and forgetting curves, effects of spacing of practice (massed versus widely spaced), and effects of word frequency. The importance of the model is that phenomena that appear to require active strategy selection are explained by essentially random mechanisms. In essence, the temporal organization of events in the environment provides the only organization to memory, a totally passive organization (due to the relation of storage distance and time between storage for any pieces of data). This model points out once again the need to carefully study which features of observed behavior are attributable to the internal mechanisms of the subject and which to the texture of the external environment.

tion or contiguity of concepts in the cluster. This model is essentially equivalent to the Collins and Loftus (1975) model discussed above in that the cluster of concepts can be defined by nodes and links with the notion of closeness or contiguity being modeled by the strength of the links.

In these models, new information is integrated by developing a configuration of links between the new concept and already stored concepts, or by adding links to already existing concepts. Also, inferences can be made by following paths of links and nodes. Such inferences allow us to construct responses, and also to test inputs for consistency with what we already know. The above notions can be expressed as

> *Proposition 6.4:* Long-term memory is a permanent and essentially unlimited store, characterized by the following properties:
> a) Semantic concepts, associations among concepts, visual images, and auditory events may be stored
> b) The form of storage for the semantic concepts can be viewed as a network, with nodes representing concepts and links representing the associations between concepts

One final point should be made. The description above, with storage, retrieval, processing, and so on, seems to imply that a person is viewed as a computer, an IBM 360 with skin. This is not true. A person is an information processor, as is a computer, and as such both will have certain basic organizational similarities. However, there are important differences. As Hunt and Mackous (1969) point out, the specific components differ greatly. A person has great input capability, an unlimited and efficient permanent memory, and a slow, inefficient short-term memory. A digital computer is essentially the opposite. Hunt and Mackous argue that this is because of the great difference in human and computer task environments. Computers receive discrete and independent jobs in rapid succession, which require perfect accuracy. Human tasks change relatively slowly over time, context effects from other jobs are crucial, and approximations are the rule rather than the exception.

CONSUMER CHOICE TASKS AND MEMORY

As noted in earlier chapters, the range of choice tasks performed by consumers is very broad, with decisions being made not only at many levels (save vs. spend, criteria, store, brand, and so on) but also in very different task environments, ranging from reading *Consumer Reports* to watching television commercials to ordering from a catalog to searching through a supermarket. There may also be great differences across tasks in the availability of external memories (e.g., store displays) and their usage. Such factors complicate the examination of memory research, since in general the results of memory research are specific to the type of task performed. Therefore, to gain an understanding of what parts of the memory literature are most relevant for understanding consumer choice requires some notion of what consumer tasks are to be considered. In general, this notion of *task analysis* is an important one, as noted in Chapters 2 and 3. Newell and Simon (1972) argue that a thorough task analysis yields a great deal of knowledge about how behavior must be structured to adapt to that environment. Particular tasks impose particular constraints on the processing needed to perform those tasks. Hence, a limited and brief view of some important consumer tasks is presented below, with particular emphasis on the areas of memory research implicated. This task analysis is limited to the major types of tasks performed outside of the store and the major types of tasks performed in the store.

Tasks performed outside the store

We consider three main types of tasks that may be carried on outside of the store: receipt and processing of information, formation of rules or strategies for combining criteria, and choice of an alternative.

The consumer receives information outside of the store from many sources: commercials on television, advertisements, word of mouth, and so on. This information may be presented to the consumer or may be sought. Important questions relative to the memory component are whether or not the information is stored, and if so, what is stored. Whether or not information can be stored may be in large part a function not only of the consumer's interest in the information but also of how easy the information is to process. Factors impacting ease of processing include the organization of the information being processed, the sheer amount of information presented, and whether any competing activities are being carried out while the information is being presented (e.g., a consumer is talking while a television commercial is being shown). Competing activities may have less impact for print ads or for conversations in which the consumer has some control over the rate of processing required, than for media such as television or radio over which such control is lacking. Finally, the modality of presentation of the information, visual versus auditory, and the amount of repetition of the information may impact degree of retention, since these factors also affect ease of processing.

What information is stored may depend in large part on the use to which the consumer intends to put the information, if any. Consumers may wish to use the information to remind themselves of something when in the store, say a brand, which implies that recognition of that brand on the shelf may suffice. On the other hand, consumers may want to decide before arriving at the store, so that recall may be required. An individual difference variable, the degrees to which prior planning outside of the store and in-store decision making are used, may greatly influence the type of memory needed, whether for recognition or for recall.

A second out-of-store task considered is the formation of rules or strategies for combining criteria. Formation of such rules requires information on criteria and trade-offs among them. Information relevant for developing strategies may be obtained from ads, family members, product testing magazines, friends, and so on. However, rules for combining criteria seem to require recall more than recognition, since the rules per se are not usually found explicitly stated in the shopping environment. Thus recall of evaluative and belief information from memory may be necessary, and particularly recall of the rules for combining that information.

Finally, a third type of out-of-store task is choice of an alternative. As discussed above, the degree to which this occurs out of the store may be an individual difference variable. Choice in the store also occurs, probably more frequently. However, if choice outside the store is carried out, it may involve recall in matching brands against criteria, particularly if the matching is done incrementally, as ads or other pieces of information are received, rather than all at once. Such an incremental process may require at the very least a recall of the current stage of the process or the operations necessary to reconstruct that stage. In addition, how attribute and evaluative information is stored in memory can be important, since this can affect how alternatives are compared (i.e., whether information is recalled by attribute, across brands; or by brand, across attributes). Finally, external memory can be a factor for choices outside of the store if a display of information such as that in a table in *Consumer Reports* is available, for example. Such displays might ease the need for recall of properties of the alternatives, but might still require recall of factors relevant to weighting criteria.

Thus several factors relevant to memory have been identified: the distinction between recognition and recall, memory for rules and operations for combining criteria, form of storage for objects in memory, effects of processing load, effects of the organization of input information, modality effects, and effects of repetition.

Tasks performed inside the store

One basic feature that characterizes the in-store environment as a task environment is the external memory it provides. Brands are available for inspection, values for various attributes (e.g., price, nutritional values) can be obtained from the package, in-store displays may be available and so on. Within this in-store environment, two basic tasks are considered: formation of rules or strategies for combining criteria, and choice of an alternative.

As noted above, formation or usage of rules for combining criteria seems to involve mainly recall, since such rules are not normally directly available in the external memory to be recognized. There can be some recognition component in that examination of packages may remind the consumer of criteria to be used, but recall seems to be a major memory mechanism involved.

A second major in-store task is to choose an alternative by processing alternatives relative to the criteria. Here the level of prior experience may be important. In a simple habitual response situation, the consumer need only recognize what was bought previously, and may very well recall it. At the other extreme is extensive problem solving (Howard and Sheth 1969; Howard 1977) in which criteria and alternatives are being developed and processed in some detail. The discussion that follows is not as relevant for the habitual response case, but rather is more suited to decisions in which there is some problem solving.

Processing alternatives in the store may involve memory only to the extent of recognition of those brands to be processed further from some larger set of brands. However, some recall is probably involved. The particular product class being processed will also have an influence on use of recall versus recognition, since the completeness of the attribute information on the package varies over product classes. If little information is available from the external memory, recall may be more heavily implicated. The type of decision being made, whether a choice between product classes, or brands within a product class, may also influence use of recognition versus use of recall. For a choice between product classes, the physical setup of the store (e.g., the product classes are probably physically separated) implies that the external memory cannot be relied upon exclusively. Also, more abstract criteria may need to be developed and applied for choice among product classes than for choice among brands within a product class (Howard 1977). Thus recall may become relatively more important than recognition in choice among product classes. Finally, the context of the original learning about the brand is important in that recognition or recall may be affected if the context in the store differs from the original learning context.

Thus the major factors affecting memory involved in in-store tasks were the distinction between recognition and recall and the effects of differences in context between the receipt and attempted retrieval of information. This brief and simplified analysis of typical consumer choice tasks shows the complexity that rapidly arises in attempting to characterize task properties. It also points up the need for a systematic classification or taxonomy of consumer choice tasks, rather than the ad hoc scheme used here.[4] This is an impor-

---

4. The concept of a task analysis seems somewhat different from the recent work on situational factors in consumer choice (Belk 1975). Belk (1975 p. 158) defines situational factors to be roughly those factors which are not inherent properties of the individuals or stimuli of interest. Within the context of this definition, task analyses are in some respects narrower and in some ways broader than research on situational factors. The task analysis notion is narrower in the types of situational factors considered, with particular emphasis being placed upon those situational factors that will influence the type of information processing carried out. Thus the situational factors considered in task analyses are a relatively circumscribed area within the broad range of factors one might consider. In addition, some factors important in performing task analyses may be properties of stimuli (e.g., how many attributes there are for brands in a product class, or the medium through which a particular piece of information is propagated), and hence would not be considered situational factors by Belk's definition. Thus task analyses are broader in this sense than research on situational impacts alone.

tant area for future research. Despite the limitations, several areas of research on memory that seem particularly relevant for consumer choice were identified. In summary

> *Proposition 6.5:* Analysis of the properties of consumer choice tasks is very important for understanding the types of processing carried out in such tasks. In particular, the following areas of memory research seem relevant for consumer choice applications:
> a) Factors differentially affecting recognition and recall
> b) Organization of information when received by the consumer
> c) Effects of a difference in context between the receipt of and attempted retrieval of information
> d) Form of coding and storage for objects in memory
> e) Effects of total processing load on the individual
> f) Memory for rules and operations
> g) Effects of the modality of information presentation
> h) Effects of repetition of information

In the discussion above, it was also obvious that the presence or absence of an external memory was important in determining how various consumer choice tasks might be carried out. Thus, we state

> *Proposition 6.6:* One important characteristic of consumer choice tasks is the presence and extent of external memory.

Discussion of each of these areas of memory research is relatively lengthy, so it is deferred to the more detailed sections below. For another discussion of some memory factors influencing consumer choice, see Olson (1978).

SUMMARY

Memory processes are involved in all phases of the processing and interpretation of information. Information which is currently stored in memory is used to interpret new information inputs, and new information inputs can also become stored in memory if processed sufficiently. The basic internal memory system consists of a set of very short-lived sensory stores, a short-term memory where current processing is carried out, a long-term memory where items of information are stored, and the various control processes or strategies used by individuals for getting information into and out of memory. An external memory may also exist in the shopping environment. Short-term memory is of limited capacity, and time is required to transfer a piece of information from short-term to long-term memory. Long-term memory is a repository of semantic, visual, and auditory information. Finally, consumer choice tasks differ, and the aspects of memory required for these tasks are affected by these task differences.

LINKAGES TO OTHER COMPONENTS OF THE THEORY

As noted above, memory is linked to the other components of the theory in that they of necessity use memory. Motivation is tied to memory in that the goal hierarchies developed may be stored in long-term memory and are processed in short-term memory while being implemented. We noted in Chapter 4 the close link between memory and perception. Prior knowledge in memory plays a crucial role in interpreting the meaning of incoming stimuli. Also, learning about the environment can lead to storage of information in memory.

Information acquisition and evaluation processes require memory. Internal search directly examines the contents of memory to see if relevant and useful information can be retrieved, and memory is continually being used during external search to interpret and perhaps store the information found.

Choice processes both use and feed into memory. Rules and criteria for choice, alternatives to be considered, previous choices, and so on may be stored in memory and used. If such data are not currently in memory, then the making of a choice may lead to new information's being stored. Feedback based on the outcomes of consumption also can lead to storage of new information.

Finally, memory is closely linked to processing capacity. The very idea of short-term memory is defined in terms of limited processing capacity. Competing tasks which require processing capacity detract from memory processes. Kerr (1973) reports more detailed findings: memory look up for familiar stimuli appears to require very little or no processing capacity; responding in recall (including retrieval) requires more capacity than rehearsal; and transformation tasks, which require "computations" on items to develop a response, also require more capacity than rehearsal.

MORE DETAILED ASPECTS OF THE MEMORY COMPONENT

The major facets of the memory component were presented above. In that discussion, memory factors which might be important in consumer choice were outlined in Proposition 6.5. The factors given there are considered in turn below, followed by a consideration of individual differences in the memory component. Before turning to these discussions, however, some perspective on the implications of this research should be given. The problems studied in memory research are often simplistic and narrowly focused, using digits, letters, nonsense syllables, or words as stimuli. As Wright (1974a) notes, this research is deficient as far as being directly applicable to consumer research problems in the simplicity of the stimuli and the fact that the responses studied are not evaluative in nature. Reitman (1970) also points out that human beings outside the laboratory do not often deliberately rehearse and attempt to memorize items, and that laboratory tasks attempt (with limited success) to decouple the study of memory from the strategies people typically use to remember things. These strategies, of course, are of great interest for understanding how consumers make real-life decisions. Thus the results to be presented below should be taken as *indications* of how various processes operate, and should raise issues to be considered in the consumer research context. Actual applications of the results might require new research examining the relevant issues in more realistic consumer choice settings.

FACTORS DIFFERENTIALLY AFFECTING RECOGNITION AND RECALL

In the following, the focus is upon differences between recognition and recall. It has been noted above that in general recognition performance is higher than that for recall; that is, recognition is in some sense "easier" than recall. Also, the tasks of recognition and recall differ in terms of the basic type of processing that leads to effective performance. To recognize a stimulus from among a set of other distracting stimuli, information allowing one to *differentiate* or *discriminate* the previously encountered stimulus is necessary. To recall, however, information allowing one to *reconstruct* the stimulus is required, since the stimulus itself is not present. This distinction between discrimination and reconstruction is implicated again and again in the findings discussed below. As a guide to the following discussion, we state

> *Proposition 6.5.i:* Factors differentially affecting recognition and recall are
>
> a) Frequency of occurrence of stimuli
> b) Plans for learning generated by subjects
> c) Rehearsal and transfer times
> d) Arousal levels

Frequency of occurrence of stimuli

The first set of findings showing differences between recognition and recall is that words with low frequency of occurrence in normal text seem to be recognized better than words of high frequency, whereas the reverse is true for recall (Kintsch 1970; Shepard 1967). Low frequency words are easier to discriminate, whereas high frequency words seem to lead to more associations of the type needed to reconstruct the word for recall. This could have implications for the types of brands chosen, depending upon whether choice is guided by recognition (say in-store) or recall (say by planning outside of the store). A less frequently seen brand, even if attractive when seen, might be chosen less frequently in the out-of-store situation (recall) relative to the in-store situation (recognition), with the reverse true for more frequently seen brands.

Plans for learning in recognition and recall

The *plans for learning,* or how subjects go about the task, appear to differ between recognition and recall. Given the difference in the tasks themselves, with discrimination required for recognition and reconstruction for recall, this difference in plans should be expected if human beings adapt to the task environment (Newell and Simon 1972).

Eagle and Leiter (1964) studied the effects of different plans for learning in an incidental learning experiment.[5] They told one group of subjects that they would hear a list of 36 words that would later be recalled (intentional). A second group was told that the words were to be recalled, but that in addition each word was to be classified as a noun or verb as it occurred (intentional with orienting task). Finally, a third group was not told about the recall task, but simply classified the words as nouns or verbs (incidental). The findings showed that intentional groups recalled more than incidental groups, but that the incidental and intentional with orienting task groups actually recognized more. Eagle and Leiter explain these results by postulating that the important variable is the plan for learning subjects use, how they process the list, not the intentional or incidental manipulation per se. They argue that an effective strategy for recall is to *select* some words for maximal attention (e.g., by grouping, or forming associations). For recognition, however, a strategy that results in a spread of attention over the words on the list should be better. The task of classifying words by types of speech was seen as spreading attention, whereas the intentional group, without this task and with recall instructions, was seen as focusing attention. Eagle and Leiter (1964, p. 62) conclude that "intention plays an important role in learning only to the extent that it leads to a plan that is effective for guiding learning." Although the specific finding that recognition was higher for incidental groups than for intentional groups may be questioned (Postman 1975), the major point is that Eagle and Leiter introduced the idea of differential plans for learning.

Barbara Tversky (1973) argued that subjects may actually encode information differently, depending on the type of test expected, recall or recognition. In her experiments, subjects were given recall or recognition test expectations before processing the lists to be memorized, and then both recall and recognition tests after processing. Hence, each group performed on one test they did not expect. Subjects performed better on the memory test which they were led to expect. The task expected may lead to a form of encoding which the subject believes will be useful for that task. In particular, Tversky

---

5. As noted in Chapter 4, the customary distinction between intentional and incidental learning is that learning is intentional when subjects have instructions to learn the relevant material and incidental when there are no instructions to learn.

(1973, p. 285) argues that "recognition is enhanced by integration of the details of each item, while recall is enhanced by interrelating items within a list." Frost (1972) reports results similar to those of Tversky. Subjects set to expect a recognition task for a set of pictures appeared to use visual codes as well as verbal codes, but subjects set for a free recall task seemed to use mainly verbal codes. The conclusion is that encoding and storage processes may be goal-oriented, adapted to the particular tasks expected.

Thus the learning plans of the subject may be a function of expected task requirements, and effective plans may *differ* for recall and recognition. The consumer, in encoding incoming information, may encode with some task in mind. This may imply that in some cases the expectation of using recall or recognition procedures in shopping is set *a priori*, that consumers make this decision at the time of encoding. Since the learning plans may differ depending upon these task expectations and the plans may influence how effectively information is processed, empirical study of this assumption of prior task expectations is desirable. Of course, an alternative hypothesis to setting expectations about use of recognition or recall *a priori* would be that the task itself determines whether recall or recognition is used, particularly the degree of difficulty involved. Simple tasks may stimulate more use of recall, and more complex tasks may lead to greater use of recognition. The reactions of consumers to ads presenting a great deal of information (e.g., nutritional information) might thus be to use recognition, since coding for recognition might be easier than coding for recall under such a heavy information load.

Rehearsal and transfer times

Rehearsal may effect recognition and recall differently, although the results to date are mixed. As noted above, rehearsal can vary from rote repetition to semantic elaboration. Woodward, Bjork, and Jongeward (1973) found that rote repetition rehearsal could improve recognition, but had no effect on recall. However, Chabot, Miller, and Juola (1976) and Nelson (1977) found improvements for recall as well. Finally, as noted above, the time required for transfer of a chunk of information to long-term memory differs for recognition (two to five seconds) and recall (five to ten seconds). Thus communications to consumers, particularly television or radio commercials for which the consumer cannot control the rate of information presentation, may have very different effects depending on whether recognition or recall is attempted by the consumer.

Effects of arousal level

A final factor which may differentially affect recognition and recall is the level of arousal at the time the desired information is to be retrieved from memory (M. Eysenck 1976). This factor can be important for consumer choice in that arousal (defined by Eysenck [1976, p. 389] as "some elevated state of bodily function") may be characteristic of high time pressure or high conflict choice situations. Eysenck hypothesizes that under high arousal, search processes are biased toward more accessible stored information, more so than under low arousal. Thus high arousal may lessen the difficulty of retrieving readily accessible information, but increase the difficulty of retrieving less accessible information. Eysenck then argues that a recognition task, by providing the subject with the item that then must be judged 'old' (recognized) or 'new' (not recognized), involves in general more accessible information than a recall task. Research results are summarized that show, as predicted, that under high arousal recognition response speeds are facilitated, but recall response speeds are hindered. These findings could be important for consumer choice, since consumers who tend to use recall may be less able to operate effectively under time pressure or conflict than those consumers who tend to use recognition. Perhaps, on the other hand, consumers in fact choose to rely on either recall or recognition adaptively, choosing to rely on recognition more in situations in which they feel time pressure, conflict, or some other source of arousal, and choosing to rely on recall more for less demanding choice tasks.

ORGANIZATION OF INFORMATION INPUT

In tasks for which recall is the focus, subjects have been consistently shown to use strategies for remembering that concentrate on organizing, associating, and grouping together the items to be learned (Bower 1970, 1972). If groupings are already present in the materials that are the inputs to be learned, then this can greatly facilitate recall. For example, Bower, Clark, Lesgold, and Winzenz (1969) show that lists presented in hierarchical groupings are recalled to a much greater extent than lists of the same words organized randomly. They attribute the result to the ability to develop effective plans for retrieval with little processing effort for the grouped lists. Buschke (1976) also notes the prevalence of grouping behavior during memory tasks.

However, the effects of organization in the input may be beneficial only if this organization *corresponds* to the rules subjects might normally use to group the data. If the groupings or chunks in the input do not match those usually used by subjects in organizing their own memories, the input groupings may hinder performance. Bower and Springston (1970) showed, using the location of pauses in the input to segment groups, that there are optimal groupings, in effect, that correspond to subjects' natural grouping patterns. For example, optimal pauses in letter sequences may be to make nonsense syllables "pronounceable" (DAT BEQ JAX versus DA TBE QJA, etc.) or "meaningful" (FBI PHD TWA IBM versus FB IPH DTW AIBM). Bower (1970, p. 35) also reports experiments that have similar findings and notes that "free recall suffers if the person is forced to change his prior groupings of the material." Finally, evidence in studies of chess perception shows that chess masters have greater difficulty in recalling configurations of pieces from nonmaster games:

the positions seem unreasonable, because they do not match the structure of configurations or groupings the chess master has learned to see in master games (Chase and Simon 1973).

Thus grouping in the input data can aid later recall, but only if this organization matches subjects' normal groupings or grouping tendencies. The implication is that if an advertisement is to present information which is already "chunked" or "grouped" for the consumer, whether that structuring is helpful to the consumer or not will depend on how consumers group or would tend to group the information.

EFFECTS OF CONTEXT

In prior chapters, context played an important role in the formation of expectations about future events and in perception. The role of context has been investigated in memory studies as well. One series of studies of context is research on encoding specificity. The encoding specificity hypothesis states that no context, even if strongly associated with a particular item or event, can be effective in aiding retrieval for that item or event *unless* the item or event was originally encoded in terms of that context (Thomson and Tulving 1970). In most of the studies performed on the encoding specificity hypothesis, "context" refers to a word paired at input with the word later tested, and effects of the strength of association of the context word with the tested word are examined, as well as effects of deleting the context word when testing, changing the context word, or adding context. Many studies have shown, for both recognition and recall, that changes in context are associated with poorer performance (e.g., Thomson 1972; Thomson and Tulving 1970; Tulving and Thomson 1971). Although information may be *available* (in memory), in the wrong context it can be *inaccessible*.

Such effects of the relationship of the context at memory input to that when memory is to be accessed have not been specifically studied in consumer research. However, advertisements present information in a particular context, which very often does not match the in-store context. Perhaps information usage, usage of particular attributes as criteria, or even recognition of brands is influenced by the degree to which the context posed by the ad is present in the actual choice situation. Thus if in-store recognition is desired, the package should be shown in the advertisement. In one case, a cereal manufacturer with a very powerful commercial ingeniously put a scene from the commercial on the front of the package, thus bringing the context of the commercial into the store.

FORM OF CODING AND STORAGE OF OBJECTS IN MEMORY

A series of research studies has examined whether encoding and memorization of properties of objects are easier if all the attribute values of one object are presented (object coding), or if all the values on a particular attribute for the set of objects under study are presented at one time (dimension coding). Haber (1964) used a brief presentation (1/10 second) of cards portraying stimuli which varied along three dimensions, one of which was emphasized to the subjects as being important. Some subjects were instructed to use an object coding method, while others were instructed to use dimension coding. Haber found that dimension coders were slower and less accurate in recalling unemphasized dimensions. Lappin (1967) used different stimuli, again with three dimensions, and did not instruct his subjects on coding schemes. Rather, he tested recall by objects and by dimensions. He found better recall for the three dimensions of each object than for the same dimension over three objects. Montague and Lappin (1966) found, in a replication of Haber's (1964) results, that object coding was faster than dimension coding. However, they did not find differences in accuracy, contrary to Haber's results. Johnson and Russo (1978) found that subjects tended to store information in the form it was presented to them, whether by object or by dimension. However, they did not find differences in time or accuracy depending on the organization of the input.

Thus there is mixed support for the notion that when inputting data, coding by objects may be more effective for later recall. In Chapter 5 we found that processing by attribute seemed to be preferred by some subjects when comparing alternatives. The implications of these two findings will be discussed further in Chapter 7.

EFFECTS OF PROCESSING LOAD

Studies cited earlier in this chapter have shown that the effective capacity of short-term memory is a function of the total processing load on the individual. If processing capacity is required for some activity that competes with a memory task, less capacity is available for memory processing. In addition, there may be task effects on memory processing; that is, the information input rate characteristic of a task or the processing rate required in performing that task may affect memory. Seibel, Christ, and Teichner (1965) assert that the rate of incoming information itself is not the critical factor, but rather the rate of *internal processing* the task requires in analyzing and transferring the information into memory, in interaction with this presentation rate. This is completely congruent with a capacity allocation theory of memory. In this capacity allocation view, it is not the presentation rate per se that requires capacity, but the task to be performed. Thus the more processing required by the task in a limited time period, the greater the effects on memory performance. If the tasks of monitoring and processing the incoming data are not demanding, high input rates may be tolerable.

Since the tasks involved in consumer choice differ greatly across situations, the considerations above may be quite important for consumer choice. If advertisements presenting a great deal of information per unit time are shown to consumers, memory performance may depend upon what is required of consumers in processing the ad. For example, whether recall or recognition is used could be important. Recognition might be less affected by presentation rate than recall, since forming associations and other strategies for recall may require more effort than analyzing a single item for later recognition. Also, if a consumer is processing an ad by looking to see if certain elements are above a threshold (e.g., "Does this product have at least 25 percent of the U.S. Recommended Daily Allowance of vitamin C?"), this may be much easier than attempting to comprehend and learn actual parameters (e.g., 32 percent of the U.S. RDA for vitamin C). Thus prior existence of aids to processing, such as cutoffs, thresholds, and standards, may affect the impact of information rate. Also, as discussed above, the structure and existence of chunkings or groupings of information in the input can affect the impact of input rate.

MEMORY FOR RULES AND OPERATIONS

In judging alternatives, consumers may combine evaluations on various criteria. The rules for combining criteria are thus important aspects of the choice process. There are very few studies that examine memory for such rules. Dosher and Russo (1976) and Russo and Wisher (1976) show that in mental arithmetic tasks, memory for sequences of operations and intermediate processing details is better than memory for the actual original numbers comprising the arithmetic task. For example, intermediate subtotals in an adding and subtracting task are recognized, but the original numbers are not. However, Dosher and Russo (1976) also found that changing operators (e.g., from subtract then multiply to divide then add) did not affect recognition rates. Thus the processing sequence used is apparently recognized, but not the operators used to generate the sequence. However, this finding may hold only for well-learned, almost automatic operators like the arithmetic operators used by Dosher and Russo. One piece of evidence for this conception is that Kolers (1973) showed that subjects *do* seem to remember more complex operations they perform in acquiring information. Subjects later recognized sentences that had originally been presented in inverted and reversed forms better than sentences which had been presented normally. Kolers (1975) later showed that subjects with high levels of practice reading such sentences did not display higher memory levels; the operations were presumably no longer unusual after the extended practice.

This literature on memory for the rules and operations used in processing data is not very conclusive. Either the sequence of operations followed or the rules used to generate the sequence may be recognized under varying circumstances. Also, these studies use recognition, not recall. If, as argued above, use of rules for combining criteria is based more on recall, these studies may not be applicable. However, Johnson (1978), in an initial test of the impact of decision processes on consumer memory, did use recall response times to study similar issues. His results resembled those noted above: final choice out-comes and intermediate processing results were recalled faster than the origi-nal data on the alternatives used. It is clear that more research is needed before any confident statements about consumer memory for rules and opera-tions can be made, however.

EFFECTS OF INPUT MODALITY

There is a great deal of research on differences in memory as a func-tion of the sensory modality of the input (e.g., visual versus auditory). The findings have shown that for simple stimuli such as series of digits or numerals, there are modality effects on short-term memory, but *not* on long-term memory. Penney (1975) reviews this research in some detail. The findings show that there has consistently been better short-term recall of auditory input, in particular for the most recently presented items. For lists in which auditory and visual presentations are mixed, recall tends to be organized by modality of the input, and auditory recall is better. Recall performance is best when the initial presentation and the test are in the same modality, and when auditory and visual tasks compete, the auditory task seems to have priority (Penney 1975). These findings, although based upon a great deal of research, may not be too applicable to consumer choice because of the emphasis on simple stimuli and short-term memory phenomena. However, some ads may use simple digit stimuli (e.g., nutritional ratings) and the findings can serve as a source of hypotheses to be examined in a consumer context. For example, the notion that competing audio and visual portions of an ad will lead to down-graded recall of the visual information could be quite important for under-standing the effects of proposals for presenting visual nutritional information in ads with competing audio portions (Bettman 1975b). Also, the notion that the modes at presentation and at test should coincide may imply that points should be made visually that relate to in-store aspects of choice.

Although the findings above can serve as a source of hypotheses, they differ drastically from research involving more complex stimuli. Several authors have noted the powerful beneficial effects on memory of forming visual images involving the input stimuli (Bower and Winzenz 1970; Paivio 1971). Lutz and Lutz (1977) have demonstrated such effects of visual imagery using advertisements as stimuli. In addition, Shepard (1967) and Standing (1973) have demonstrated human beings' remarkable recognition memory for pictures. Shepard, for example, used many ads for stimuli and found that sub-jects recognized, from a series of about 600 pictures, 96.7 percent, 99.7 percent, 92 percent, 87 percent, and 57.7 percent at test delays of zero, two hours, three days, seven days, and 120 days, respectively. Finally, Rossiter (1976) shows that visual memory of the package may be quite important in children's cereal choices, and may also be for adults. He found that cereal preferences assessed visually by using a drawing task differed from preferences assessed verbally.[6] Paivio (1975) argues that in general there is a dual coding system in memory, with an imagery system that deals with nonverbal information, and a verbal system that deals with semantic concepts. Other theorists disagree with this view; see Kieras (1978) for a review and model of imagery effects. The nonverbal imagery system needs more research to determine its impact on consumer choice processes, as most research has concentrated on the verbal concept system.

The implications from these sets of findings are that modality effects may be important and that past research should be used only as a broad guide. Further studies in the consumer context seem essential given the differences in stimuli and tasks used.

EFFECTS OF REPETITION

One of the oldest notions in the literature on memory is that repeated exposure to a stimulus enhances future recall or recognition for that stimulus. Most of the work on the effects of repetition has involved a passive view of human learning, with repetition serving to "stamp in" an item, to increase the strength of that item's memory trace. This research will be briefly reviewed, and then the implications of viewing the human being as a more "active" learner are discussed.

Sawyer (1974) presents a good summary of the effects of repetition as related to marketing phenomena. The basic findings are that recall and recognition increase as a function of presentation frequency, and that there are decreasing increments in memory performance as repetition increases (i.e., later exposures appear to add less and less to performance).[7] Ray and Sawyer (1971) present a thorough study of repetition effects which documents an increase in recall from approximately 27 percent to about 74 percent for one to six repetitions, respectively. Even rote repetition, without more elaborative processing, may improve recognition or recall (Chabot, Miller, and Juola 1976; Nelson 1977). Finally, for single series of stimuli, it has been shown that recall performance is better when a given number of repetitions is spaced or distributed rather than massed at once (Postman 1975, pp. 316–318). Zielske (1959), in a classic study in marketing, showed that for final level of recall, distributed presentation was better than massed presentation, but noted that the amount of final retention may not be the relevant criterion for the marketer. If maximum temporary response is desired, massed presentation may be better; if

---

6. Rossiter (1975) also found that musical imagery (jingles, songs in ads) was important for children. Standing (1973) found that recognition for music was at about the same level as recognition for words in his study.

7. Also, if grouping is involved in the inputs, changes in grouping over the course of the repetitions will hinder recall, even though the underlying individual items are the same (Bower and Winzenz 1969).

maximum exposure is desired, distributed presentation was better in Zielske's study.

This view of repetition ignores the notion of the human being as an active processor governed by plans and goals. In several studies cited above, it was noted that memory performance may depend upon the learning plans formed by the consumer. Krugman (1972) points this out, and rejects the notion that the effects of learning must be through "practice" alone. He asserts that the important aspect is that interest or involvement be present, that the consumer has some plan or need for using the information in the ad. He then claims that three repetitions are enough: the first is a "What is it?" response, with a preliminary decision about whether the ad is of any use or interest; the second repetition generates more detailed evaluative responses and planning for future actions if the preliminary decision in the first exposure was favorable; and the third exposure becomes the reminder to carry out any plan formed in the second exposure. Most people may screen out ads at the first exposure; however, if later an interest in the product category or brand is present, the person may see an ad which in reality is their 23rd exposure; but it might be processed as if it were the *second* exposure at that point (Krugman 1972, p. 13). Thus for group data, different levels of interest in a product over time could lead to gradually increasing curves of response to repetition (because with increased repetition the odds that someone who is interested would have had the first "What is it?" exposure would increase), even though for the individual the response was in some sense more rapid.[8] Goldberg and Gorn (1974) offer evidence consistent with Krugman's notion, in that exposure to one commercial affects children's attitudes toward a toy and their persistence at a task to obtain the toy. However, an increase to three exposures did not change either attitude or persistence beyond the initial effect of the first exposure.

While the specific mechanisms and numbers of exposures proposed by Krugman may be debated, there may be a strong component of active planning and assessment in human learning. If an ad is seen to be of use, based upon interests, future choice tasks expected, or other factors, then consumers may use the information in the ad to generate partial plans for choice (e.g., "Check this brand," "Look at this new attribute in my decision," and so forth).[9] The important question then becomes whether sheer repetition has an effect on this process of forming plans, or whether repetition functions solely to make sure information is available at the relevant time when it is needed.

---

8. This discussion parallels the debate over "one-trial" or "all-or-none" learning versus incremental or gradual learning. Restle (1965) has shown that a strict distinction is not meaningful, since the one-trial case is a special case of gradual learning.

9. Of course, even if the consumer is trying actively to learn the information contained in an ad, if there is a great deal of information, a number of repetitions may be necessary before the consumer can learn that information. Thus the number of repetitions necessary for the consumer to carry out plans for learning may vary as a function of the information load in the ad.

At this point the evidence seems to be that both processes operate. As Krugman (1965) himself notes, low involvement and high involvement learning may be governed by different processes. For low involvement learning, sheer repetition may have effects, particularly if recognition is involved rather than recall (Woodward, Bjork, and Jongeward 1973; Chabot, Juola, and Miller 1976; Nelson 1977; Postman 1975, p. 303; Robertson 1976). For learning under higher involvement, more elaborate and focused processing may ensue.

INDIVIDUAL DIFFERENCES IN THE MEMORY COMPONENT

The following proposition enumerates several individual difference variables involved in the memory component:

> *Proposition 6.7:* Individual differences can affect aspects of the memory component. Significant individual difference variables may be:
> a) The amount of product-related information held in memory
> b) The organization of that information in memory, particularly the "vocabulary" of familiar patterns or chunks held
> c) The memory control processes used for input and retrieval of information
> d) The degree to which in-store processing is used rather than out-of-store processing
> e) The degree of use of external memory
> f) The degree to which recognition or recall is used in implementing choices
> g) The degree to which passive versus active learning strategies are used

SUMMARY OF THE PROPOSITIONS

The following propositions summarize the points made above.

Proposition 6.1: The internal memory system consists of a set of sensory stores, a short-term memory, and a long-term memory. Each of these memories has different properties and functions.

> *Proposition 6.1.i:* Short-term and long-term memory are not necessarily physiologically separate memory stores. Rather, a single memory is postulated, with a limitation on how much of that memory can be simultaneously activated.

> *Proposition 6.1.ii:* In addition to the internal memory system, consumers may have access to an external memory, comprised of package information, written shopping lists, buying

guides, and so on. The availability of external memory devices may vary over choice situations.

Proposition 6.2: Memory control processes are the strategies used by individuals for controlling the flow of information into and out of memory. Important control processes are

a) Rehearsal   b) Coding

c) Transfer   d) Placement

e) Retrieval   f) Response generation

Proposition 6.3: Short-term memory is characterized by the following properties:

a) A limited capacity of about seven chunks, with capacity falling to two or three chunks if tasks other than the memory task are simultaneously imposed.

b) Times for transferring one chunk from short-term to long-term memory of five to ten seconds if recall of the information being transferred is required and of two to five seconds if recognition is required. If information is not rehearsed, it is lost from STM in about thirty seconds or less.

c) Items are coded both acoustically and semantically in STM.

Proposition 6.4: Long-term memory is a permanent and essentially unlimited store, characterized by the following properties:

a) Semantic concepts, associations among concepts, visual images, and auditory events may be stored.

b) The form of storage for the semantic concepts can be viewed as a network, with nodes representing concepts and links representing the associations between concepts.

Proposition 6.5: Analysis of the properties of consumer choice tasks is very important for understanding the types of processing carried out in such tasks. In particular, the following areas of memory research seem relevant for consumer choice applications:

a) Factors differentially affecting recognition and recall

b) Organization of information when received by the consumer

c) Effects of a difference in context between the receipt of and attempted retrieval of information

d) Form of coding and storage for objects in memory

e) Effects of total processing load on the individual

f) Memory for rules and operations

g) Effects of the modality of information presentation

h) Effects of repetition of information

Proposition 6.5.i: Factors differentially affecting recognition and recall are

a) Frequency of occurrence of stimuli

Plans for learning generated by subjects

c) Rehearsal and transfer times

d) Arousal levels

Proposition 6.6: One important characteristic of consumer choice tasks is the presence and extent of external memory.

Proposition 6.7: Individual differences can affect aspects of the memory component. Significant individual difference variables may be:

a) The amount of product-related information held in memory

b) The organization of that information in memory, particularly the "vocabulary" of familiar patterns or chunks held

c) The memory control processes used for input and retrieval of information

d) The degree to which in-store processing is used rather than out-of-store processing

e) The degree of use of external memory

f) The degree to which recognition or recall is used in implementing choices

g) The degree to which passive versus active learning strategies are used

NEEDED RESEARCH

Several research questions relevant to the propositions above are now discussed. Basic research on internal memory structure in psychology seems to be adequate for the present (Propositions 6.1, 6.1.i). However, one aspect of the overall memory system that does need research is external memory (Propositions 6.1.ii, 6.6). In particular, various types of external memories need to be identified, their availability in various choice situations needs to be characterized, and consumer usage of external memory aids should be studied.

Little is known about how consumers use memory control processes (Proposition 6.2). In particular, coding processes seem fruitful for study, how the consumer associates items relevant for choices. Also, retrieval strategies could be studied (e.g., do consumers retrieve information from memory by brand or by attribute).

One major area for research is in developing more detailed analyses of consumer choice tasks (Proposition 6.5). To do this properly, a scheme for classifying or developing a taxonomy of tasks is needed. The factors used in such a scheme should relate to the way information is processed, to factors which influence that processing. Such factors might include the type of external memory available (Proposition 6.6), time pressure, the types of information available to the consumer and how they are presented (e.g., are only television commercials used, or only print advertisements), and so on.

Research into the specific memory areas outlined in Propositions 6.5 and 6.5.i is needed, particularly by examining the findings presented above using stimuli and experimental situations more relevant to consumer choice. Research in recognition versus recall, organization of information, and form of storage of information is considered below. The other memory research areas cited above are not dealt with in detail.

One important aspect of memory research relevant for consumer choice is the clarification of what kind of memory is most relevant in a task — recognition or recall. Of course, it may turn out that an individual difference variable (Proposition 6.7), the degree to which prior out-of-store planning is used as opposed to in-store processing, is more important than the influence of the task. However, factors leading to recall or recognition should be studied. The plans for learning of consumers in task situations also need study. Do consumers decide a priori whether to encode for later recognition or recall, or is this a function of the task itself rather than a conscious decision? For example, if an ad presents a high information load per unit time, recognition encoding may be used because that is all that is possible.

Organization of information in memory is also an important area for study. In particular, the grouping and chunking rules used by consumers need empirical study. First, the typical chunks and groupings used by consumers should be described. (See Friendly [1977] or Sternberg and Tulving [1977] for proposed methods for studying such groupings.) Second, effects of structuring communications to be consistent or inconsistent with these groupings should be examined. This can have important implications for whether information should be prechunked before being presented to consumers to try to facilitate usage of that information, as in public policy applications. Finally, the effects of repetition on grouping patterns should be examined to see how repeated exposures are processed in developing chunks of information.

Another potential research area, mentioned in Chapter 5, concerns the form of storage of brand and attribute information and the effects this may have on information search and information combination (Payne 1976b). A particular form of storage (by brand or by attribute) may be more or less compatible with various acquisition and processing strategies. Clustering in free recall protocols might be used to examine form of storage (Buschke 1976), although this clustering confounds storage and retrieval strategies. Reaction time experiments could also be used to examine structure, but the same confounding appears to be present (Collins and Quillian 1969). Posner (1973) notes that one standard approach to attempting to remove this confounding influence is to use a speeded task in which the subject is told to process as quickly as possible while maintaining a certain accuracy level. Johnson and Russo (1978) and Johnson (1978) report applications of reaction time data to studying form of storage in a consumer setting.

Finally, individual difference variables needing research (Proposition 6.7) are organization of information in memory, the degree of in-store versus out-of-store processing, the degree of use of recognition versus recall, and the degree to which external memory is used.

CHAPTER 7

Decision Processes: Choice among Alternatives

In earlier chapters the processes of setting goals and obtaining information helpful in attaining those goals have been considered. The actual selection of an alternative has not yet been examined. Now we look at the detailed decision processes used to compare and ultimately choose among alternatives, utilizing the information which has been gathered. The various pieces of information that have been obtained must be combined and integrated so that the consumer can make a choice. Questions such as how particular pieces of information are combined, what heuristics are used to compare alternatives, and what factors influence the consumer's utilization of specific heuristics must be addressed. Therefore, in this chapter and in Chapter 8 a detailed analysis of the alternative selection process is presented.

Before proceeding with this analysis, however, several comments are in order. First, the study of the question above, how consumers choose among alternatives, has been the focus of much consumer research. However, most of this research has considered only the actual phase of comparing alternatives. Questions relating to goals, attention and perception, acquisition of information, and use of memory have not been considered as an integral part of most studies. Thus the present theory, while also analyzing the comparison process in detail, considers other elements necessary to understand choice.

Second, for the sake of clarity the discussion above has presented a simplified view of the overall choice process. The notion of a sequence from goals through obtaining information implies that comparison of alternatives occurs only after all information has been gathered, for example. However, as noted in earlier chapters, it seems clear that consumers are engaged in comparison of alternatives while they are still in the process of gathering information. As information is gathered, a partial comparison may be made that may lead to more search, and so on. Thus search and comparison processes may be simultaneous rather than sequential in many cases.

OVERVIEW OF THE DECISION PROCESSES COMPONENT

In the simplest case of choice among alternatives, as outlined above, the consumer has formed some goals, acquired and evaluated some information, and must ultimately choose some alternative. Consumers make many different kinds of choices, so the types of alternatives being considered can vary: types of information, brands within a product class, different product classes, and so on. What is invariant, however, is that the alternatives are somehow compared and a choice is made.

In general, consumers do not have the resources or the abilities necessary to process the total amount of information which might potentially be available for making any particular choice. As we have noted many times in previous chapters, consumers have limited processing capacity. Hence, comparisons among alternatives may usually be made by using some simple rules of thumb, or heuristics.[1] Such heuristics are a way of simplifying the choice task and adapting to limitations in processing capacity. Many types of heuristics have been proposed to describe how consumers compare alternatives. Several of these possible heuristics are considered below. In addition, different rules of thumb may be used by different individuals or by the same individual in different situations. Thus there are important impacts of individual differences and choice situation factors on how alternatives are compared.

In addition to characterizing the specific heuristics used, one can also examine how a heuristic is implemented; that is, any given heuristic can be applied using different methods. This concept of methods for implementing heuristics can perhaps best be clarified by giving an example. In Chapter 2 the distinction was made between two ways in which choice processes might be implemented. One characterization was that the consumer may have a set of strategies or rules stored in memory, and that these rules are called forth in their entirety when needed and directly applied. This might be called a *stored rule* method for implementing choice. A second conception, a *constructive* method, is that rules of thumb are developed at the time of choice using fragments or elements of rules stored in memory. These fragments or elements may be beliefs about alternatives; evaluations; simple rules of thumb involving subsets of beliefs (e.g., "Compare these products on attribute A to see if they differ very much"); rules for integrating beliefs (e.g., "Count how many attributes alternative X is best on" or "Average those ratings"); rules for assigning weights (e.g., "If performance is comparable across brands, weight price heavily"); or perhaps even computational rules. Presumably the elements used will be a function of what is available in the particular choice situation and how easy various pieces of information are to process (e.g., a "Compare prices" element may not be used if unit prices are not given and different

---

1. In this chapter the terms rule, decision rule, heuristic, choice heuristic, strategy, rule of thumb, model, and so on are used interchangeably. All refer to the comparison processes used by consumers.

brands have different-sized packages). The basic idea behind the distinction between stored rule and constructive notions is that in some cases completed heuristics or rules do not exist in memory, but must be built up from subparts. The consumer may have only a general plan to guide the construction of a heuristic in a particular situation. Thus choice heuristics might vary from one situation to the next if a constructive method is used, depending on how the elements available were put together.[2] Stored rules will tend to be used in situations in which there is a good deal of prior experience, and constructive processes in situations in which there is little prior knowledge.

The distinction above is only one that could be considered relating to how choice heuristics are implemented. Others are proposed below. It should be noted, however, that the specific way a heuristic is carried out may depend on many factors, particularly on the degree of prior experience and knowledge relevant for the choice at hand. For example, three situations that might be distinguished are those in which (1) elements are available in memory for producing a heuristic and are deemed sufficient for the situation; (2) elements are available in memory but are not sufficient; and (3) elements are not available in memory. In the first case in which elements are available and sufficient, the choice heuristic can be constructed from these elements, or simply recalled and applied, if enough experience has accrued. In the latter two cases, the consumer must modify or develop elements to make a choice. Details of these situations and other impacts on implementation of choice heuristics are given below.

Finally, interrupts can occur in the process of comparing alternatives and making choices. Criteria for comparing alternatives may conflict, information may be lacking, and so on. Reactions to interrupts will depend on the consumer's interpretation of the significance of the interrupts. Such reactions have been discussed in detail in earlier chapters and will not be considered again in this chapter.

Thus the consumer is depicted as using heuristics to compare alternatives and make choices. Such heuristics allow consumers, with their processing limitations, to adapt to potentially complex decision problems. Various heuristics are possible, and which ones are used may depend on individual and situational factors. Consumers can carry out these heuristics in various ways,

---

2. The notion of limited short-term memory capacity discussed in Chapter 6 has implications for each method discussed above. The limited capacity could be seen as implying a constructive method, since only a few elements at a time could be activated in short-term memory. However, the "completed rule" concept behind the stored rule method could still be used if one assumes that the completed rule is called into short-term memory and "interpreted" in sequential pieces. Thus in both cases only portions of a rule are active at one point in time. The crucial distinction is whether the flow of processing is dictated by the preexisting complete rule or by the active construction process. (See also Kosslyn and Shwartz [1977] for a similar discussion and some evidence which favors the constructive method.)

depending on the choice situation and their degree of previous experience and knowledge. Interrupts can also occur that can lead to changes in goals. Figure 7.1 summarizes the relevant portions of the theory for the decision processes component.

The basic aspects of the decision processes component are now examined in more detail: choice heuristics; implementation of choice heuristics; methods for studying choice heuristics; and consumer usage of choice heuristics. Following these discussions, linkages to other components of the theory are considered, then more detailed aspects of decision processes.

MAJOR ASPECTS OF THE DECISION PROCESSES COMPONENT[3]

CHOICE HEURISTICS

Consumers are subject to limitations in processing capacity. This means that detailed and complex calculations or comparisons among alternatives may be the exception rather than the rule. Consumers may often use simple heuristics to make comparisons. These heuristics allow adaptation to the potentially complex choices consumers must make. This can be stated as

> *Proposition 7.1:* Consumers are subject to limitations in processing capacity. Heuristics or rules of thumb may be used to make comparisons among alternatives in most cases, rather than complex calculations.

Other impacts of limitations in processing capacity on consumer judgments are considered in the more detailed sections.

The various types of heuristics consumers use to compare alternatives are now considered below. In this chapter fairly well-structured and formally defined heuristics are the focus. Chapter 8 presents a more detailed discussion of decision nets, a way of representing more idiosyncratic heuristics. In the following discussion, major aspects characterizing choice heuristics are first considered, followed by presentation of various alternative rules of thumb.

Aspects of choice heuristics

Wright (1975) proposes that a choice heuristic should specify two aspects of the process of choice among alternatives: (1) the process by which an alternative is evaluated, i.e., the specification of how some indicator of value is assigned to an alternative. This aspect of a choice heuristic can be

---

3. The terminology used in the literature on choice varies greatly. In the psychological literature the terms object and dimension are often used, whereas in consumer research the terms brand and attribute are common. In this chapter, for convenience the terms are used interchangeably, particularly dimenson and attribute, although some researchers have argued that this is inappropriate (Wright 1973b).

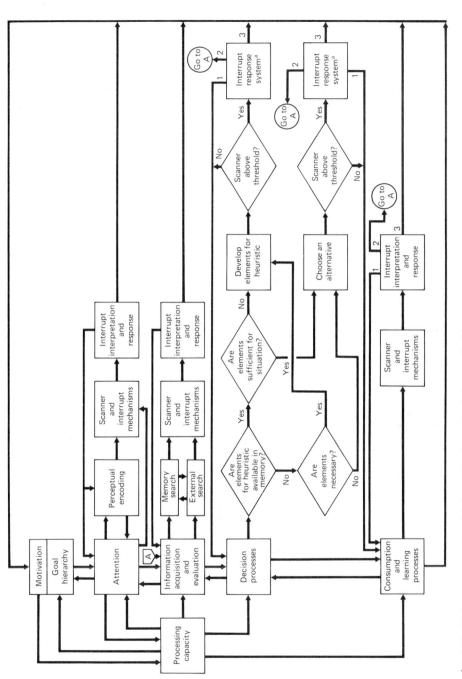

[a]For details of the interrupt response system and the interpretation of the numbered responses, see Fig. 2.4.

Fig. 7.1 Decision processes segment of the theory.

viewed as taking information about alternatives as inputs and arriving at an *attitude* as an output. According to this view, then, an attitude is seen as the degree of affect toward or against the alternative, and as a direct component of the process of choice.[4] As we shall indicate below, this view may not be entirely accurate. (2) A decision rule must also specify the choice criterion, or the process by which one alternative is chosen from among the set of alternatives that have been evaluated. This choice criterion then adds intention to the evaluation. Wright (1975) notes that choice criteria could be "Choose the best," "Choose the first alternative that is satisfactory," and so on.

The two aspects above do not appear to be sufficient to fully characterize choice processes. Wright omits a crucial third aspect, namely (3) the form of processing used in examining alternatives while making a choice. Two basic processing forms were outlined in Chapter 5. In one case, each alternative is processed and evaluated as a whole, and then a choice is made on the basis of these overall evaluations using the choice criterion. This may be called Choice by Processing Brands (CPB). The second basic form of processing involves comparison of all alternatives on a single attribute, followed by comparisons on a second attribute, and so on. This may be denoted Choice by Processing Attributes (CPA).

This distinction about form of processing may affect the validity of the two aspects proposed by Wright. If CPA is used, a heuristic may not yield a direct overall evaluation for each alternative as Wright proposes. For example, in some heuristics where processing by attribute is used, some alternatives may be eliminated from further consideration after the first attribute has been examined. This group of alternatives which is eliminated may form one evaluation class, with further classes formed in a similar fashion as the process of comparing brands across a sequence of attributes continues. Thus instead of a *direct* evaluation of each alternative, there is only an indirect indication of evaluation, an evaluation derived arbitrarily from the results of the processing. It is not clear that such a *derived* evaluation would have any meaning to the consumer, however. More detailed examples of such derived evaluations are given below when each heuristic is considered. However, the major point is that the notions of an evaluation process and of an attitude seem to be based on the view of brand processing, where each alternative is evaluated as a whole and then evaluations are compared across alternatives. As shown below, many choice rules do not fit into this mold. Thus Wright's characterization of heuristics as necessarily having a direct evaluation aspect is rejected. Instead, one must consider whether a heuristic yields a direct evaluation or only an arbitrarily derived one. We consider the relationship between attitudes and choice processes in more detail in a later section.

---

4. Although attitudes are often viewed as having cognitive, affective, and conative components, for the present we are concerned only with the affective component. Some researchers (e.g., Fishbein and Ajzen 1975) argue that attitude is only this affective component.

Most discussions of decision rules in consumer research fail to fully specify the exact nature of the choice criterion or the form of processing. The choice criterion is usually left implicit or it is assumed that the best alternative will be chosen. This latter assumption ignores the magnitude of the difference between the first and second alternatives, however. This difference could be important, as the degree of conflict experienced by the consumer may be affected (see Proposition 4.4) and perhaps the response to that conflict (e.g., if the two top alternatives are close enough, one may wish to seek more information before choosing). The form of processing has usually been left totally unspecified, which is highly unfortunate given the interaction between form of processing and the other aspects. The above discussion can be summarized as

Proposition 7.2: Choice heuristics can be characterized by three aspects:

a) How an *evaluation* for each alternative is developed, either directly as a result of the heuristic, or by being derived arbitrarily

b) The *choice criterion* used to choose among the alternatives

c) The *form of processing* (e.g., by brand or by attribute) implied. The form of processing interacts with the other aspects, particularly the evaluation aspect

Alternative choice heuristics [5]
In the following sections, various proposed choice heuristics are considered. For each, the type of evaluation developed, the choice rule specified, and the form of processing implied are considered.

Affect referral. Perhaps the simplest rule was proposed by Wright (1975), the affect referral heuristic. In affect referral, a consumer does not examine attributes or beliefs about alternatives, but simply elicits from memory a previously formed overall evaluation for each alternative. Thus the evaluation process is wholistic. The most highly evaluated alternative is then chosen. Thus a "Choose the best" choice criterion is used. Finally, form of processing cannot be specified, since for only one "attribute" (evaluation), the two basic forms of processing cannot be distinguished. Note that this rule presumably is most applicable for choices where a great deal of previous experience has accrued. For example, affect referral may eventually be used after the consumer has initially processed and made choices using other heuristics. Over time the consumer may learn overall evaluations and simply use these. In addition, affect referral might be used for choices in low involvement product classes, where the consumer does not wish to engage in any detailed processing.

---

5. Note in the following discussion that the focus is on the *structure* of the rules presented rather than the *content*, or the specific attributes used.

Linear compensatory. A general class of heuristics is the *linear compensatory* type. Alternatives may be described in terms of multiple attributes. For any particular alternative, let v_i be an evaluation of the *i*th attribute (of *n*) and w_i be a weight associated with the *i*th attribute. Then the *linear additive* model postulates that the evaluation *E* for an alternative is given directly by the heuristic as

$$E = \sum_{i=1}^{n} w_i v_i. \tag{7.1}$$

This type of model is very common in consumer research, particularly as used in the multiple-attribute attitude model literature (Wilkie and Pessemier 1973).

An alternative rule is the *linear averaging* rule, with the evaluation given by

$$E = \sum_{i=1}^{n} w_i^* v_i \quad \text{where} \quad \sum_{i=1}^{n} w_i^* = 1. \tag{7.2}$$

One can distinguish between equal or differential attribute weights for either case. These linear models are called compensatory because positive and negative data on several attributes can balance, offset, or compensate one another. The choice criterion usually assumed for linear compensatory models is to "Choose the best," and these models clearly assume processing by brand.

General information integration. A generalization of the linear compensatory rule is a heuristic where attribute weights and evaluations are combined to obtain an overall evaluation for an alternative using some general function, not necessarily a linear function. For example, multiplicative or general polynomial models can be used to derive an evaluation for each alternative. Researchers in information integration theory in psychology (e.g., Anderson 1974a) and in conjoint measurement theory (e.g., Green and Wind 1973) have considered both linear and other types of combination rules. The choice criterion is again implicitly "Choose the best," and processing by brand is implied.

Conjunctive. Another type of heuristic is the conjunctive rule. In using this heuristic, the consumer is assumed to set up minimum cutoffs for each dimension. If an alternative does not pass all of the cutoffs, it is rejected. Hence, this heuristic weights negative data more heavily (Wright 1974b). The evaluation is a derived one, with an alternative classed as either acceptable or nonacceptable. A direct evaluation for each alternative is not provided, therefore, beyond this binary classification. Finer derived evaluations could perhaps be developed by applying the process recursively with changing cutoff levels, but this does not seem to be relevant to what consumers appear to do. The choice criterion has typically not been well specified for this heuristic, which is unfortunate, since the conjunctive rule may yield more than one acceptable alternative. Some researchers have specified a rule of "Choose the first satisfactory alternative" (a conjunctive satisficing model); others have used the conjunctive heuristic as the first stage (an elimination phase) in a two-stage procedure (this is discussed below under phased processes). Finally, the form of processing implied is processing by brand. Note that the conjunctive heuristic is noncompensatory; that is, high values on one attribute *cannot* compensate for a below cutoff value on another attribute.

Disjunctive. A fifth heuristic is the disjunctive heuristic. The consumer is assumed to develop acceptable standards for each dimension (which may be higher than the minimum cutoff levels for the conjunctive heuristic). Then if an alternative passes a standard for any attribute, it is accepted. Again, the evaluation process yields groups of acceptable and nonacceptable alternatives and hence the evaluation is derived rather than direct. The choice criterion is poorly specified, with "Choose the first satisfactory alternative" or phased strategies possible. The form of processing is by brand. In the disjunctive rule, positive data is weighted more heavily (Wright 1974b). Finally, this heuristic is also noncompensatory.

Lexicographic. The lexicographic choice heuristic assumes that attributes can be ordered in terms of importance. Alternatives are then first compared with respect to the most important attribute. If one alternative is preferred over all others for this attribute, that alternative is chosen, regardless of the values the alternatives have on the other attributes. If some set of alternatives are tied and preferred over all others on this first attribute, the second most important attribute is considered, and so on. A "Buy the cheapest" rule is a lexicographic rule with price as the most important attribute. The lexicographic rule can be used to yield derived evaluations of alternatives. For example, those alternatives eliminated after the first attribute has been examined might form one class, with other evaluation classes formed as further attributes are examined. Alternatively, the evaluation for each alternative might be a rating on the most important attribute. This proposal has problems with ties on this attribute, however, as it is not clear how ratings on the attribute examined next to break the tie should be integrated with the ratings on the most important attribute to yield an evaluation. Thus it again appears that such derived evaluations may not really be meaningful. The choice criterion is unspecified; the assumption appears to be that one alternative will eventually win out. The case of ties still remaining after all attributes have been examined is not considered. Finally, the lexicographic heuristic implies processing by attribute, and is noncompensatory.

Sequential elimination. A general sequential elimination heuristic can be outlined. The consumer, as in the conjunctive heuristic, is assumed to have minimum cutoffs for each attribute. Then, an attribute is selected and all alternatives not passing the cutoff on that attribute are eliminated. Then another attribute is selected, and so forth. There is no rule for specifying the sequence in which attributes are examined in this general case. A specific version of the sequential elimination rule is presented below. Note that the evaluation is again derived rather than direct, as the groups of alternatives eliminated at each stage can be considered to be an evaluation class. Also, the choice criterion is unclear; presumably the assumption is implicitly made that eventually one alternative will be left. Processing by attribute is assumed.

Elimination by aspects. Tversky (1972) proposed a special case of the general sequential elimination rule, the elimination by aspects heuristic. Attributes are assumed to have differing weights. Then an aspect, or attribute, is selected with probability proportional to its weight. All alternatives not having satisfactory values for the selected aspect are eliminated. A second attribute is then selected with probability proportional to its weight, and the process continues. Again equivalence classes of alternatives can be used to obtain derived evaluations. The choice criterion appears to assume that one alternative will eventually be selected. Processing is by attribute. Note that this model is a special case of the general sequential elimination model in which a probabilistic rule for ordering the selection of dimensions has been adopted.

Lexicographic semiorder. The lexicographic semiorder heuristic (Tversky 1969; Pollay 1970b; Russ 1971) is closely related to the lexicographic heuristic. In a lexicographic semiorder rule, a second attribute is considered not only in cases where values for several alternatives on the most important attribute are equal but also for cases where the differences between the values on the most important attribute are not significant or noticeable. This same process may then be used for further attributes if more than one alternative still remains. Thus a consideration of whether differences are significant is imposed upon a lexicographic ordering. Again evaluation is not direct, but can be derived from consideration of sets of alternatives eliminated at the same time. The choice criterion is "Choose the best" (assuming that one alternative will eventually "win"). Processing is by attribute. Tversky (1969) and Pollay (1970b) show how this rule can lead to intransitive choices in which A is chosen over B, B over C, and C over A. An example is shown in Table 7.1 for three hypothetical cereals described by protein content and price per pound. Assume that protein content is the more important dimension, but that differences of two or less percent are viewed as not significant. Also, assume that differences in price per pound of $.05 or less are viewed as not significant. Then A will be preferred to B (since the protein difference is not significant but the price per pound difference is), B to C, but C to A (since the protein difference is now significant). Tversky (1969) also cites an example in which the cost of each added accessory to a car may not be significant enough to reject, but the cost of the total package of accessories may.

TABLE 7.1
Alternative cereals to illustrate the lexicographic semiorder rule

ALTERNATIVE	PROTEIN CONTENT (PERCENTAGE OF RECOMMENDED DAILY ALLOWANCE)	PRICE PER POUND
A	6	$ .90
B	8	1.00
C	10	1.10

Additive difference. Tversky (1969) proposed a decision heuristic called the *additive difference* rule which also allows for intransitivity. As formulated, the heuristic considers binary choice, between two alternatives, say X and Y. The decision maker first considers differences between the subjective values for X and Y on each dimension. Let $U_i(X_i)$ and $U_i(Y_i)$ be the subjective values (utilities) for X and Y on dimension i. Then quantities of the form $U_i(X_i) - U_i(Y_i)$ are considered, differences in the evaluations on dimension i. Each of these differences is then "weighted" by applying an increasing continuous difference function φ_i, which specifies the contribution of the subjective differences for dimension i to the total relative evaluation of X and Y. Then X is preferred or indifferent to Y if and only if

$$\sum_{i=1}^{n} \varphi_i \, [U_i(X_i) - U_i(Y_i)] \geq 0. \tag{7.3}$$

Note that this heuristic yields only *relative* evaluations of alternatives, or a measure of the difference in evaluation between alternatives, rather than evaluations for each alternative individually. If the evaluation for one alternative is set arbitrarily, of course, then an evaluation for the other would follow directly from the difference measure. The choice criterion is given explicitly in Eq. (7.3). Processing is initially by attribute, although combining relative evaluations across attributes is also required. In general the additive difference heuristic is a compensatory rule. Finally, although the additive difference rule is formulated for binary choice, it may be extended to choice among more than two alternatives by sequentially comparing pairs of alternatives, retaining the winner each time for use in the next comparison (Payne 1976b).

This heuristic can be related to some of the others outlined above. First, Tversky (1969) shows that the additive and the additive difference heuristics imply the same choices under certain restrictions on the form of the difference functions φ_i. He notes, however, that the form of processing would still differ: by brand for the additive and by attribute for the additive difference heuristic. Also, Tversky (1969, p. 42) notes that the lexicographic semiorder heuristic can be viewed as a special case of the additive difference rule. Finally, transitivity holds for the additive difference rule with more than two attributes if and only if the difference functions φ_i are multiplicative constants.

If any difference function is nonlinear, or departs from the multiplicative constant form, intransitivity results.

Phased strategies. A final general type of heuristic is phased strategies (Wright 1974e; Wright and Barbour 1977; Russ 1971). These are hybrid heuristics in which a first phase is used to eliminate some alternatives from consideration and a second phase is used to make comparisons among the smaller set of those alternatives remaining. For example, a conjunctive rule might be used as a first phase, with those acceptable alternatives remaining evaluated by using a linear compensatory heuristic. As another example, Russ (1971) used a conjunctive satisficing rule as the first phase with lexicographic and lexicographic semiorder heuristics in the second phase. Phased strategies can be very useful heuristics in that one effective way to simplify a complex choice may be to reduce the set of alternatives considered in detail to a small set. Howard and Sheth (1969) specifically included the concept of a limited evoked set of alternatives in their theory to capture this idea. However, they do not directly consider phased strategies.

TABLE 7.2
Choice heuristics and their properties

HEURISTIC	EVALUATION PROCESS	CHOICE CRITERION	FORM OF PROCESSING
Affect referral	Wholistic	Choose the best	Indeterminate
Linear compensatory	Weighted sum	Choose the best	Brand
General information integration	General function	Choose the best	Brand
Conjunctive	Derived[a]	Unspecified	Brand
Disjunctive	Derived[a]	Unspecified	Brand
Lexicographic	Derived[a]	Unspecified	Attribute
Sequential elimination	Derived[a]	Unspecified	Attribute
Elimination by aspects	Derived[a]	Unspecified	Attribute
Lexicographic semiorder	Derived[a]	Unspecified	Attribute
Additive difference	Relative	Choose the best	Attribute

[a] Overall evaluations for an alternative may be derived, but are not directly obtained or used by the rule.

The ten heuristics (excluding the hybrid phased strategies) presented above are summarized in Table 7.2, with their associated specifications for the evaluation process, choice criterion, and form of processing. Most of the rules depicted here do not provide a direct evaluation, only a derived one, and attribute processing may not be conducive to forming such direct evaluations.[6] As noted above, we thus reject Wright's (1975, p. 60) notion that a choice model must "define a process by which single multiple-attribute options are evaluated." This emphasis on evaluation of single alternatives appears to derive from a heavy reliance in the past on the linear compensatory rule, and a failure to distinguish brand versus attribute processing. Thus the notion of choice rules as yielding *attitudes* appears to be inadequate, at least as far as the idea that choice rules provide an attitude measure as a direct output. Further consideration of the role of attitudes in choice process is deferred to the detailed sections below. The discussions above are summarized as

> *Proposition 7.3:* Many different choice heuristics can be identified. Among the important heuristics are affect referral, linear compensatory, general information integration, conjunctive, disjunctive, lexicographic, sequential elimination, elimination by aspects, lexicographic semiorder, additive difference, and phased strategies. Most of these heuristics yield derived rather than direct evaluations for each alternative. This calls into question the view that attitudes are a necessary component of choice processes.

IMPLEMENTING CHOICE HEURISTICS

As noted above, in most studies of consumer choice, the concern has been with overall descriptions of choice heuristics, not with any of the specific details of how these heuristics are carried out. For example, choice heuristic research usually describes some combination rule for product data that is then used to predict choice, without specifying how in fact the consumer implements such a heuristic, how the processing implied by the heuristic is done. As another example, Howard and Sheth (1969) describe extensive problem solving, limited problem solving, and routinized response behavior as three general types of choice process. However, they do not specify, for example, how consumers engage in extensive problem solving, what methods are used. Howard (1977) describes these three types in much more detail, particularly extensive problem solving, but does not discuss the mechanisms outlined below.

One particular pair of methods for implementing choice heuristics was discussed above, the *stored rule* method and the *constructive* method. Two other distinctions made in earlier chapters seem to be relevant for characterizing implementation of heuristics: the extent to which decision making is carried out in the store versus out of the store, and the use made of memory, particularly use of recognition versus use of recall.

---

6. For an example of a model which does attempt to form a direct evaluation based on attribute comparisons, see Nakanishi, Cooper, and Kassarjian (1974).

In-store versus out-of-store processing

In some cases, processing of alternatives may be carried out prior to arrival in the store environment. Thus the decision may be made using only what is available in advertisements, memory, or other out-of-store sources. This may be called a *prior* method. The *in-store* method refers to cases where the consumer waits until actually in the store to make the choice. In this case the in-store display may serve as an external memory, removing some memory burden from the consumer. Also, the alternatives and attributes considered might tend to be those easily available in the shelf display, which may differ from those which might be available if the prior method were used (e.g., if a *Consumer Reports* article were read at home and the decision made then). Finally, situational influences may be of different types under the two methods, since the in-store and out-of-store situations differ. For example, decisions made in-store might be more sensitive to variations in display, deals, and so forth, and decisions made at the consumer's home, say, might be more sensitive to which family members the consumer talked to, what television ads happened to be seen recently, and so forth.

Use of memory in implementing choice heuristics

As noted in Chapter 6, consumers may use memory differently in comparing alternatives. One major distinction is between a *recognition* or a *recall* method. At some times consumers may rely on recognizing a package design when seen, for example, or recognizing a particular attribute listed on the package that they wish to consider. In other instances, recall may be used, with the consumer able to retain in memory and retrieve when necessary the brand desired, the attributes to be considered, etc. It was hypothesized in Chapter 6 that individuals may actually process information differently, use different strategies and even different ways of coding the information, depending on how they believe they will be using that information (Eagle and Leiter 1964; Tversky 1973). The consumer may process incoming information with some task in mind, with expectations about whether recall or recognition will be used. For example, recognition strategies may be used under heavy information loads, for advertisements presenting a great deal of information, since coding for recognition is presumably easier than attempting to code for recall. Thus there are three sets of methods considered for implementing choice heuristics, specifying how heuristics may be formed (stored rules vs. constructive); where processing occurs (in-store or prior); and how memory is used (recognition vs. recall).

Relationships among the methods

These three methods seem interrelated, not independent. The constructive, in-store, and recognition methods seem to fit together, as do the stored rule, prior, and recall methods. For example, if the consumer has rules stored in their entirety in memory, then recall will likely be used to retrieve these rules, as effective recognition cues for rules are probably not available.

Also, if a predetermined rule exists, choice may be made prior to arriving at the store. Of course, this need not be true—rules could be recalled and implemented in the store (e.g., a "Buy the cheapest" rule)—but the tendency might be for rules to be used more *a priori*.

In a similar manner, constructive activity seems to be related to use of the in-store environment to provide information for building the rule at the time of choice, and use of recognition while in that in-store environment. The use of the in-store display as an external memory aid would imply that use of recognition would be encouraged. Again, constructive activity could be carried out outside of the store, if external memory aids were found there (e.g., print ads or *Consumer Reports* tables), or could be accompanied by use of recall, but the main tendency might be that described above. Such relationships may be contingent on particular choice environment properties. For example, constructive activity may be carried out wherever the best external memory is available, either in-store or out-of-store (see the washing machine scenario of Chapter 2, for example, in which the availability of information in a *Consumer Reports* table leads to constructive activity outside of the store). The notions above, while perhaps plausible, are in great need of research to determine their applicability. The above discussions above can be summarized as

> *Proposition 7.4:* Consumers may use various methods for implementing choice heuristics. Three important sets of methods are
>
> a) Constructive versus stored rule methods
>
> b) In-store versus prior methods
>
> c) Recognition versus recall methods
>
> Stored rule, prior, and recall methods may tend to be associated, as may constructive, in-store and recognition.

Factors influencing usage of various methods

In the discussions above, it may seem that the implication is that some consumers are characterized by use of certain methods, and some by others. This individual difference notion may be true to some extent. However, it seems more likely that each consumer uses all of these methods, with the extent of use of each perhaps determined by the consumer's product class experience and by the specific nature of the choice the consumer is making.

In general, it seems that with little experience, consumer processing may be initially constructive, and characterized by in-store information acquisition and use of recognition. This choice of methods not only allows for adaptation to a choice environment about which the consumer knows little, but also is probably less strain on memory in a situation in which the consumer has little organization to his or her beliefs about the product class (Howard 1977). The less this organization, the harder it would be to recall a great deal of information relevant to the choice (Bower 1970). In effect, construction, in-store, and recognition methods may be used in choice situations where building and recalling an overall rule would be too difficult. As experience with a product class grows, the consumer may organize the elements used to construct heuristics into some overall rule, with such a rule eventually becoming a learned unit. Recall becomes easier as more knowledge is acquired and organized, and in-store processing becomes less necessary. Thus, in general, stored rule, prior, and recall may be used more the greater the degree of prior experience and knowledge relevant to the choice at hand.[7]

This notion of the relationship between usage of methods and prior experience can be examined in more detail. This more detailed analysis is carried out only for the constructive and stored rule methods. Parallel analyses could be done for the other methods. We again consider three situations discussed earlier in this chapter: cases in which elements of a heuristic are not available in memory; cases in which elements are available in memory and not sufficient; and cases in which elements are available in memory and sufficient. These three situations may correspond to increasing amounts of relevant prior knowledge and experience.

Even if elements of a heuristic are not available in memory, this does not necessarily mean that information search and constructive processes will be used. If there is only one alternative, and the purchase must be made, then the choice is trivial. Also, the choice may be so trivial to the consumer (e.g., choice of two brands of toothpicks) that one alternative is simply taken, although possibly a heuristic could have been constructed upon closer examination (e.g., looking at number of toothpicks in the package, price, and so on). However, in general lack of prior experience may lead to constructive processes. There are several ways a choice heuristic might be constructed. For example, alternatives include the use of elements developed for other product classes (e.g., buy the cheapest); search for information and development of elements for the specific product class under consideration; or simply trying a brand to learn from the consumption experience what elements for constructing a heuristic might be. The way information is presented in the situation can affect the elements used. If information is not easily processable it may not be used, even if available and deemed important by the consumer (Russo 1975; Slovic 1972a). Finally, several authors have noted that the specific elements or fragments developed and used may be a function of the situation, or the particular "state of mind" of the individual, and hence can differ from one choice to the next (Tversky 1972; Nakanishi 1974; Wright 1974b; Shepard 1964). This

---

7. One could argue that simple rules used in other types of choice situations might be used, rather than construction, in very difficult choice situations in which construction might also be too hard. Thus we might expect use of stored rules in simple or very complex choice tasks, and use of construction in moderately complex tasks. The simpler hypothesis that use of stored rules may increase with degree of experience is retained for the present, however.

may be particularly true if processing is carried out in the store, as postulated above in Proposition 7.4. Then the properties of the available set of alternatives can impact the elements used.

Consumers may usually have some information in memory relevant to a choice. In many cases, some of the elements needed to construct a heuristic may be available, but they may not be sufficient. This insufficiency may be a result of lack of some information, bad experience with a previous choice, changes in the situation (e.g., changed availability of brands), or new information acquired by the consumer. Haines (1974a) explicitly postulates that the function of information is to cause reexamination of the adequacy of existing choice rules. If existing elements are inadequate, a new heuristic may be constructed with modified or new elements. However, note that in this situation the consumer will presumably be experiencing conflict, so that the actual response will depend on conflict handling strategies and the specific situation. It is possible, for example, that under high time pressure a consumer may use the existing elements even if he or she feels they are inadequate. In this case the goals for developing elements depicted in Fig. 7.1 may be of the form "Use these elements now, but change them next time when I have more time to devote to it," if the choice is one which recurs frequently.

Finally, the consumer may have all the elements needed for a particular heuristic in memory, with no departures from expectations or other interrupts occurring. The choice heuristic may then be constructed from the existing elements, or recalled and applied (the stored rule mechanism) if the elements have been chunked over time into a learned strategy. One would hypothesize that over time this case would lead to increased use of the stored rule method.

The sections above characterize hypothesized relationships between degree of experience and knowledge and usage of various processing methods. It should be noted that these proposed relationships are highly speculative, and are in great need of research before they can be applied with any confidence. The points made can be presented as

> *Proposition 7.5:* Usage of the various methods for implementing choice heuristics may be influenced by degree of prior knowledge and experience relevant to the choice in question. With little experience, constructive, recognition, and in-store methods may be used; with more experience, increased usage of stored rule, recall, and prior methods might be expected.

This conception of how choice heuristics are implemented can be contrasted with the view implicit in most consumer research on choice heuristics. In this previous research, memory is often treated as a fixed, given data array, in many cases a brands by attributes matrix. Processes of encoding and acquisition of information are ignored. The information is simply seen as available to be utilized, without search or retrieval efforts. Retrieval is assumed to be automatic and error free. In addition, the rule being studied is also assumed to exist in complete form in memory, and the computations required by the rule are assumed to be made in an error-free fashion. Thus the present theory attempts to expand the view of how choice is actually implemented. Consumers may use recall or recognition, and have fallible memories. Rules may not exist, but may need to be built. Consumers may make mistakes in trying to apply a rule (e.g., they may not find the cheapest brand, even if that is their rule). Where the consumer processes, inside or outside of the store, may be important. The process of comparing alternatives cannot be studied in isolation from the other components of choice, and how heuristics are implemented should not be ignored.

METHODS FOR STUDYING CHOICE HEURISTICS AND THEIR IMPLEMENTATION

In the sections above we have considered alternative choice heuristics that might be used and different methods consumers might use to implement such heuristics. Before considering what factors affect the usage of various heuristics, we must first examine how one can study choice processes; that is, before characterizing under what conditions various heuristics are used, we must look at how one can ascertain which heuristics consumers in fact appear to be using. Several types of methods are considered: correlational approaches, information integration methods, protocol analysis, information monitoring, eye movement analyses, and response time analysis.

Correlational methods

There are two basic types of correlational approaches to studying choice rules (Scott and Wright 1976). In the first type, called a known brand belief survey, respondents may be asked to provide scale values for their beliefs or evaluations for each attribute for a set of known brands, and perhaps scale values for the weight for each attribute. The respondents also provide an overall preference measure for each alternative. The reseacher then uses some mathematical or other manipulation (corresponding to the choice heuristic[s] of interest) on the attribute rating data to obtain a predicted preference measure. For example, for the linear compensatory model a summation over attributes of weights times evaluations would be computed; for the lexicographic model, the rating on the most important attribute might be used. Note that this procedure essentially forces every heuristic into a brand processing mold, as an evaluation for each alternative must be developed. As shown above and summarized in Table 7.2, many rules do not provide a direct evaluation, so the researcher must arbitrarily define a derived one. The researcher can then correlate the predicted and actual evaluations, with the choice heuristic yielding the highest such correlation held to be supported.

Such correlations may be computed across individuals, or within individuals if several alternatives are judged by each individual.

A second type of correlational approach uses an active evaluation task. Subjects are given hypothetical alternatives, with each alternative being characterized by a given set of scale values. The subject is asked to provide an overall rating for each alternative and perhaps weights for the attributes. Then the known scale values characterizing each alternative are used to compute evaluations according to the various heuristic(s) being studied, as before, and correlations are computed. There are other variations, but these are the two major approaches.

There are several problems with the known brand belief survey that make the active evaluation approach more desirable (Scott and Wright 1976). The foremost among these is that in the known brand belief survey one may not even be studying any combination or processing of information. One may be studying only the *results* of processing information, as ratings may be retrieved from memory if the alternatives are familiar to the subject. Thus memory structure is perhaps being studied, but not choice heuristics. In the active evaluation approach, in which subjects are presented with data and asked to combine it, processing is to some extent available for study.

In addition to the problem with forcing brand processing notions onto all heuristics, cited above, there are several problems with correlational approaches in general that limit the usefulness of these methods for studying details of decision processes. One essential problem is that no direct evidence about process is gathered, as only some notion of "degree of fit" is available for each proposed heuristic. As Hoffman (1960) first noted, a rule is only a paramorphic representation; that is, a good degree of fit does not necessarily tell us anything about the actual processes used by the subject. Two different heuristics may provide equally good fits, or different heuristics may suggest nearly equivalent algebraic models.

Two other factors related to this paramorphic problem plague the use of the correlational approach. First, as has been demonstrated in study after study, the linear compensatory rule is so robust that it will usually fit most data quite well. Thus the linear model almost always does at least as well as any nonlinear model (Dawes and Corrigan 1974; Goldberg 1968; Green 1968). Dawes and Corrigan (1974) discuss why linear models fit well, and conclude that there are several major reasons: (1) in most applications, the relationship of each variable taken individually to the criterion is monotone; (2) error in measurement of independent variables tends to make optimal functions more linear (in fact, Lord 1962 shows that even when a conjunctive multiple cutoff function is appropriate under errorless measurement, if error is high enough a linear approximation is appropriate); (3) deviations from optimal weights on the variables do not make much difference. Dawes and Corrigan (1974) then argue that these conditions are characteristic of many decision situations investigated, so that a task analysis would imply that linear models should provide good paramorphic representations, even if other heuristics are being used. This unfortunately makes it difficult to study choice heuristics using correlational methods, since one can rarely find cases in which the linear model does not fit well, even if subjects claim they are not using a linear compensatory approach. Since the linear model will fit even simulated data generated by nonlinear rules well (Dawes and Corrigan 1974, p. 98), it is difficult to determine whether subjects are using approximately linear rules or whether the linear model just fits well but subjects are in fact using other heuristics.

A second problem is that correlations between the rules and data are often not very different over various rules, yet subjects are often classified as following a particular heuristic if the correlation for that rule is highest for their data. This may be very unreliable if differences in correlations are small. One should test for significant differences between correlations before classifying subjects. Einhorn (1971) tested for differences in his study and found that only 21 of 78 tests for one experiment and 23 of 60 tests for the second experiment showed significant differences using an alpha level of .10. Goldberg's (1971) data also show small differences. Finally, in a consumer research context, Bruno and Wildt (1975) report intercorrelations of .86 or higher among the predictions of linear, maximax (like disjunctive), and lexicographic rules for their data.

Thus different heuristics often provide degrees of fit which are virtually identical. Consumers should *not* be classified without close examination of the performance of the second best heuristic, third best heuristic, and so on. Small differences may be due to random error alone. Bruno and Wildt (1975) argue that choice of a single rule in a situation in which several rules predict nearly equally well is misleading and throws away potentially valuable information. They reason that one way to gain insight in situations in which there are small differences between heuristics is to examine the overlaps in predictions directly, rather than choosing the "best" rule for each individual based on some marginal predictive differential. For example, they show that 30.6 percent of their sample have first and second preferences that are identically predicted by the linear, lexicographic and maximax rules. For these three heuristics all to predict the same, Bruno and Wildt argue that those brand attributes that have the highest ratings must also be among the most important. Examination of other overlapping sets yields additional conclusions. The idea is that examination of such overlaps provides added information, more than obtained by examining a single rule alone. The fact that each heuristic places some restrictions on what kinds of stimuli will be preferred means that overlaps can provide narrower limits on what type of processing was carried out. This complementarity analysis seems to be a valuable tool for examining data for which rules tend to make similar predictions, and avoids the pitfalls of choosing a single rule for each subject.

Another set of criticisms of correlational approaches focuses on the problem of using correlation as an index of fit. First, the scale values subjects provide (in known brand belief surveys) or that are provided to subjects as part of a profile (in active evaluation tasks) are normally at most interval data. For nonlinear rules, however, interval scales are not sufficient to ensure invariant correlational results. Ratio scales must be used (Goldberg 1971). Otherwise, degree of fit can change depending on the particular interval scaling chosen (Schmidt 1973; Schmidt and Wilson 1975). A second problem is the interpretation of degree of fit itself. Anderson (1974a) argues that use of degree of fit is inappropriate for judgments of rule validity. Rather, what is needed is an approach where one *directly* tests a theoretical model, and more importantly, tests for *significant deviations* from the model. This testing of deviations avoids the ambiguities inherent in determining whether a high level of correlation "supports" a particular rule, and can potentially allow *rejection* of an incorrect model (Platt 1964). For example, Anderson and Shanteau (1977) present data from four experiments where correlations between a linear rule and the data are at least .98, but serious systematic deviations from linearity are evident in each case.

Finally, correlational approaches are ill-suited to the study of individual differences in use of choice heuristics. One must devise an algebraic model to represent each possible combination rule that might occur, and assume that the model with the highest correlation is most appropriate. Birnbaum (1973) shows how this approach can yield erroneous results, particularly when there are scaling problems of the sort discussed above (see Alf and Abrahams 1974 and Rorer 1974 for critiques of Birnbaum's position). In addition, one must conceive of the possible decision rules *a priori*. Inductive approaches are not aided by correlational analyses. Thus correlational approaches seem to be beset by many problems which limit their usefulness for the study of consumer choice heuristics, although ingenious applications of correlational approaches combined with other types of data can yield insights (Weitz and Wright 1978).

Information integration approaches

A typical information integration study begins with the specification of some pieces of information that the consumer can combine to form some judgment. For example, Bettman, Capon, and Lutz (1975a,c) examine integration of two pieces of information, a belief and an evaluation, to form an attitude. Bettman (1975a) studied integration of information on uncertainty and consequences in consumer judgments of perceived risk. Each piece of information is conceived to be a factor in an analysis of variance (ANOVA), with several levels (e.g., several degrees of belief, from very unlikely to very likely). Given the specification of the pieces of information, consumers are presented with profiles of data for which the number of items in each profile corresponds to the number of pieces of information to be integrated, and each element in the profile is a particular value for one of the pieces of information. For example, Bettman, Capon, and Lutz (1975a) presented subjects with two item profiles, one item being a specific belief level, and the second being a specific evaluation level for that belief. Note that the subject is thus presented with information that must then be integrated, an active evaluation task. The subject is *not* queried about his or her own beliefs. The subject makes some response (e.g., a rating of attitude in Bettman, Capon, and Lutz, or a rating of amount of risk in Bettman) to each profile, and usually receives the set of profiles corresponding to a complete factorial design, often with several replications. For example, in Bettman, Capon and Lutz (1975a), the belief and evaluation factors each had five levels, and the subjects received two replications of the resulting 5×5 factorial design, or 50 profiles in all. Anderson (1971, 1974a) has been the major proponent and developer of this information integration approach.

Given the profile rating data, methods of analysis need to be used which can allow one to study the combination rules apparently used by subjects. Fortunately, Anderson (1971, 1974a) has developed a relatively complete set of methods, based upon detailed examination of the results of analysis of variance applied to each subject's individual data. Methods for distinguishing adding, averaging, and multiplying models have been developed. Also, more complex models in which the weight given to a piece of information depends on the extremity of the information can be applied.

This information integration methodology has several advantages. First, *a priori* scaling assumptions for the independent variables are *not* required to analyze the ANOVA data. Rather, scales can be developed by using Anderson's functional measurement procedure (Anderson 1974a). Thus the problem with variation in the level of correlation if interval scaled independent variables are used in nonlinear models, discussed above for correlational approaches, does not apply. Second, the information integration approach does study combination of information, since subjects are presented with data they must combine to render a judgment. Third, the ANOVA analyses developed by Anderson (1974a) allow one to test for *deviations* from specific models (Anderson and Shanteau 1977; Platt 1964). Finally, the information integration approach allows one to inductively examine the data. Differing patterns of results in the ANOVA may suggest previously unconsidered decision rules (e.g., Bettman, Capon, and Lutz 1975a,c).

Although the information integration approach has these advantages, it also has several severe problems. First, the factorial task structure and profiles presented may be too simplistic and unreal, lacking in external validity. The relatively transparent task structure may force the results. Second, the information integration approach is still subject to the paramorphic problem of correlational approaches. Subjects may appear to add, average, or multiply, but may in fact be using simpler heuristics (e.g., if both scales are high, give a high rating; if both are low, give a low rating; if both are medium, give an average rating; and so on). Finally, the nature of the task given to subjects makes study of some kinds of heuristics difficult. For example, sequential elimination strategies would be hard to examine using this approach. Also, giving subjects a profile, which must then be evaluated, forces subjects to process by brand.

Hence, rules implying processing by attribute are not handled well by these methods.

Protocol methods

Protocol analysis has been used in several consumer research studies (e.g., Wind, in Robinson, Faris, and Wind 1967; Alexis, Haines, and Simon 1968; Bettman 1970; Russ 1971; Payne 1976a,b). In using this method, the subject is instructed to think out loud as he or she is actually performing the task of interest, say shopping or choosing among alternatives. This verbal record is termed a protocol. It may be distinguished from introspection or retrospective report in that the subject is theoretically verbalizing thoughts as they occur in the course of problem solving. The protocol data are then used to gain insights into the processes being used. The major advantage of the method is that a great deal of data on internal events may be made available for inspection. Without these data available, details of the heuristics may be lost. Protocol data are then used to develop a model of the processes used by consumers in making judgments. In most of the research to date, these models have taken the form of decision nets (Bettman 1974a) in which attributes are arrayed in a branching structure that specifies the specific rules to be applied in judging alternatives (see Chapter 8 for details of these studies).

Many new analysis methodologies have been specifically developed for protocol data and the resulting consumer processing models. Newell and Simon (1972) have pioneered the development of structured methods for analyzing protocols and developing models from them, and Payne (1976a) has been the first to apply these methods in consumer research. Bettman (1971a, 1974c) has done extensive work in developing measures which allow the researcher to compare and analyze processing models expressed as decision nets. In particular, measures of net structure and measures of similarity for pairs of nets are developed, and issues of fit and model generality are discussed. Recently Takeuchi (1975) has proposed a new measure for the weight of a particular attribute in a decision net.

There are also disadvantages to protocol analysis, however. The collection of protocol data in the volume necessary for model inference is extremely time-consuming. Thus only very small samples have been used (e.g., two consumers were modeled in Bettman 1970). In addition, the quality of the data has been questioned. Subjects' protocols may not reflect what they are actually doing. This could reflect biases or self-censoring of protocols as they are being reported, or simply that subjects are unable to verbalize internal processes (Wright 1974d; Nisbett and Wilson 1977; Weitz and Wright 1978). It is particularly difficult to obtain verbalization of currently occurring thoughts, rather than retrospective rationales, when protocols are taken during shopping trips for items about which the subject has some prior knowledge and experience. Also, protocol output is not obtained for all processing performed. There may not be output corresponding to all internal states (Lindsay and Norman

1972, pp. 517–520). Subjects may select which processing to verbalize based upon what they believe is important, and not verbalize precisely that data most valuable to the researcher (Frijda 1967).

The process of providing protocols may also affect the choice processing being carried out. Dansereau and Gregg (1966) hypothesized from their data on mental multiplication that verbalization added a brief external memory at the expense of processing speed, and these two effects seemed to roughly cancel out. Flaherty (1975) found, in a study of algebra problem solving, that subjects who relied on the verbal information in the problem to guide solution were adversely affected by giving protocols (more errors), but subjects who used physical representations of the problems were not affected. Protocol production may compete for processing capacity and hence interfere with the main problem solving task (although the Flaherty [1975] results suggest that the interference may be structural, with only other verbally oriented tasks affected).

Given a set of protocol data, developing a model from those data has been both time-consuming and informal. It is not clear exactly how the models were obtained from the protocols in most applications, other than some rough "eyeballing" technique. Haines (1974b) has demonstrated that giving the same protocol to different modelers yields widely different results. Some progress has been made in protocol analysis, however. Waterman and Newell (1971) have examined automated approaches, and Swinth (1976), Gaumnitz, Swinth, and Tollefson (1971), and Swinth, Gaumnitz, and Rodriguez (1975) have examined procedures for having subjects develop their own decision models.

Thus in summary there are many problems with protocol analysis, and this brief treatment does not cover more detailed criticism. (See Bettman 1974a; Baker 1967; Dennett 1968; Frijda 1967; or Payne and Ragsdale 1978 for more details.) However, protocols can also provide many potentially useful data.[8]

Information monitoring approaches

As discussed briefly in Chapter 5, information monitoring methods have recently been used to study consumer processing. Jacoby (Jacoby 1975; Jacoby, Chestnut, Weigl, and Fisher 1976; Bettman and Jacoby 1976; Jacoby 1977) has been a main proponent of this approach, with independent work in parallel done by Payne (1976a,b). The typical approach has been to present information to subjects on an information display board, essentially a matrix array (with, say, brands as rows and attributes as columns). Information cards are available in each cell of the matrix, giving the value for the particular attri-

---

8. Wright's (1973a, 1974c) cognitive response method is related to protocol analysis, with several of the same advantages and disadvantages. One further caution in cognitive response methods is that the thought gathering process is somewhat more retrospective, rather than being done immediately during processing. Thus more concern with rationalizing in the responses may be necessary.

bute and brand appearing in that row and column (e.g., the price for Brand X). The subject is asked to choose a brand after selecting as many information cards as desired, one at a time. The sequence of cards selected becomes the major data yielded by the method. Thus a detailed record of the sequence of information examined is made available by directly controlling the selection process for information.

The major disadvantages of the information monitoring approach concern the nature of the task. First, it is a relatively obtrusive process, with subjects perhaps biasing their information seeking behavior since it is so obviously under observation. Second, internal processing is not studied directly, but only external information seeking responses (i.e., which cards are selected). Internal processing of alternatives by decision rules may not be revealed explicitly in the information seeking sequence. Third, several of the studies (e.g., Jacoby, Chestnut, Weigl, and Fisher 1976; Bettman and Jacoby 1976; Bettman and Kakkar 1977) have used actual brands, with the brand names available to the subject. Any prior knowledge the consumer may have can bias the search patterns observed. There is no observation of the internal memory search operations (if any) going on in parallel with the explicit search through the matrix. Fourth, it is not known whether consumers examine only information they do not already know in the matrix or whether they check up on the information they think they know. Fifth, only goal-directed selection of information will tend to be observed; that is, the consumer must choose to take a card. Accidental exposure to some information while looking for something else may not be found, since the values on the cards are hidden unless they are actually chosen. Finally, the matrix structure of the information presentation makes it equally easy for a consumer to process by brand or by attribute. This is not like many actual consumer tasks in which information is often organized by brand (e.g., supermarket shelves, commercials), hindering attribute processing. This is discussed further below. For a more detailed discussion of this method, see Arch, Bettman, and Kakkar (1978).

Eye movement analysis

Analysis of eye movements has also been recently applied to study of consumer choice rules (Russo and Rosen 1975; Russo and Dosher 1975; Van Raaij 1976b). In using this method, the choice objects are displayed either on a screen in front of the subject, in tabular format (Russo and Dosher 1975, Russo and Rosen 1975), or perhaps as separate packages (Van Raaij, 1976b). The sequence of eye movements used by the subject in examining the choice objects is then recorded using some form of sensing apparatus. To allow the sensing apparatus to give accurate measures, subjects' heads must often be immobilized to prevent large head movements. Finally, to guard against ambiguous interpretations due to subjects' use of peripheral vision, there must be relatively large separations between items in the visual display. The resulting eye movement data can then be examined to look for patterns in the sequence of fixations. The main advantage of eye movement data is that a detailed trace of the information examination process is provided, and eye movements may be relatively more difficult for subjects to censor than verbal protocols. In addition, eye movement data may be more useful than data such as protocols for examining processes which occur rapidly, since the eye movements can be sampled with a rapidity more congruent with that of the process being considered. Newell and Simon (1972) report an application of eye movement data by Winikoff (1967) to a problem-solving situation, and found that the eye movement data corresponded quite well to protocol data, but also added some important information.

Russo (1978a) argues that eye movement analysis may be more adequate for studying information acquisition processes than information monitoring approaches. Russo notes that the card selection responses typical of information monitoring studies may require (relatively) a good deal of effort, and hence use of any information already stored in memory about the alternatives is encouraged. Such information acquisition from memory is then not observed by the researcher. Eye movements, on the other hand, are relatively effortless, and hence direct acquisition may be encouraged, rather than use of memory. More of the actual acquisition process could then be directly observed, perhaps. Therefore, Russo claims, sequences of eye movements may yield more extensive and complete records of information acquisition behaviors than sequences of cards selected in an information monitoring task.

Several new methods have been developed for analyzing eye movement data. One of the major issues is developing measures that allow the researcher to make inferences from the eye movement sequences. Russo and Rosen (1975) develop measures for indicating when a subject is making a comparison between a pair of alternatives. Russo and Dosher (1975) also examine measures for attribute and brand processing. Finally, Russo and Rosen and Russo and Dosher used a combined methodology that seemed to be quite effective. In addition to the eye movement data, prompted protocols were obtained, prompted by a replay of the sequence of eye movements to the subject after his or her choice was made. This type of multimethod approach seems quite valuable, as the various methods have different strengths and weaknesses and can often complement each other with inferences made that would not be possible with a single method.

Eye movement data also have unresolved problems. First, collection of such data is very time-consuming and sample sizes are usually small. Also, the apparatus often used is quite obtrusive, since head movement must be restricted and subjects are obviously quite aware that their eye movements are being monitored (some newer eye movement systems do not require this restriction of the head). The apparatus is also quite complex and expensive to construct. The choice stimuli used in eye movement studies have often been simplistic arrays because of the desire to be able to localize eye movements. More detailed and complex visual stimuli might cause problems, although standard product shelf displays and videotaping procedures could be used if only aggregate characteristics of the looking behavior need to be observed (Russo 1978b). Finally, the fixations are information seeking responses, and do not necessarily reveal the details of internal processing. Rules for interpreting sequences of movements are developed that purportedly relate to internal processing, but the link is indirect. Just and Carpenter (1976) and Rayner (1978), however, discuss evidence which supports the notion that there is a linkage between eye movements and processing. For a detailed discussion of eye movement methods in consumer settings, see Russo (1978b).

Response time analysis

Analysis of response times, although a technique long used in psychology, has been used only recently to study consumer choice processes (e.g., Johnson and Russo 1978; Gardner, Mitchell, and Russo 1978; Wright 1977; Jacoby, Speller, and Kohn 1974a,b). The basic data collected in using this approach are the times taken to complete a response, usually measured as the time between the presentation of a stimulus and the response to that stimulus. Measurement of such times can be carried out with varying degrees of sophistication, ranging from use of tachistoscopes to use of stop watches (Russo 1978b). The assumption is usually made that this time directly reflects the amount of processing effort used in completing the task. By comparing the mean response times over different experimental conditions, it is hoped that one can learn about the information processing characterizing such tasks.

Various types of insights can be obtained from analysis of response times. Several authors have used such analyses to study the structure of memory (e.g., Collins and Quillian 1969; Johnson and Russo 1978; Hayes-Roth 1977). Other applications have included analyzing models of processing stages in memory search tasks (S. Sternberg 1969) and testing models of reasoning processes (R. Sternberg 1977). In these latter applications, the times characterizing component processes of some overall process are often of interest, and various models of these components can be tested. Finally, response times can also be used to determine what factors affect processing effort, such as the degree of congruence between information format and the choice heuristic being used (Bettman and Zins 1978), or the degree of involvement with the task (Gardner, Mitchell, and Russo 1978).

A major advantage of response time analysis is that it can be used to study covert, rapid processes such as memory search. Other methods do not seem as generally powerful in exposing such memory phenomena. Some have argued that although response time measures are very useful for studying such brief processes, they may be less useful for longer tasks (Russo 1978b). The longer the duration of the task, the greater chance that factors not manipulated by the experimenter may affect response times.

Response time analysis also has certain disadvantages. Perhaps the most problematical is the trade-off between speed and accuracy. In almost all tasks, subjects can choose to sacrifice accuracy to attain greater speed, or they may take more time in order to improve accuracy. A discussion and an example of the problems created by the speed–accuracy trade-off are cogently presented by Pachella (1974). The usual technique for dealing with this trade-off is to attempt to have subjects perform at the same accuracy level in all experimental conditions. This is often accomplished by instructing subjects to take the time necessary to maintain some low error rate in performing their experimental tasks. This strategy may be difficult to implement in consumer research settings in which there may often be no objectively correct response against which subjects' responses can be compared (Gardner, Mitchell, and Russo 1978).

A second disadvantage is that response time measures are very aggregate measures, and as such may be difficult to interpret; that is, knowing only how long a process took does not directly lead to insights about components of the process. Initial theorizing about the process is essential for designing experiments using response time analysis if there is to be some hope of obtaining insights (Gardner, Mitchell, and Russo 1978).

Finally, response time analysis is an obtrusive method, with subjects usually aware that their response times are being measured. This is particularly true for cases where speed-accuracy trade-off instructions are used. One can, of course, measure response times unobtrusively if such instructions are not given, but this may compromise the validity of the data. For further details on response time analysis see Johnson and Russo 1978; Gardner, Mitchell, and Russo 1978; Wright 1977; Pachella 1974; or Chase 1978.

This completes our discussion of methods for studying choice heuristics. Overall, correlational methods seem less adequate than the other approaches. However, each method has its own biases and disadvantages. (See Russo [1978b] for a comparison of these methods.) Thus multimethod approaches should be used (Wright 1974d; Russo 1978b) in which several approaches are used in the same study. Since the various methods have different strengths and weaknesses, they can often complement each other.

One additional point should also be made. The theory presented in this book emphasizes processes that should be observed at the individual level. Individual differences are expected, rather than seen as undesirable sources of error variance. Thus analysis of process data should be undertaken at the level of the individual. General mechanisms or processes are sought only within this framework of individual analysis. As Simon (1975, p. 288) so aptly states, "we must avoid blending together in a statistical stew quite diverse problem solving behaviors whose real significance is lost in the averaging process."

Proposition 7.6: Several methods for studying choice heuristics have been proposed:

a) Correlational methods

b) Information integration approaches

c) Protocol methods

d) Information monitoring approaches

e) Eye movement analysis

f) Response time analysis

Correlational methods seem less adequate than other approaches. Use of multiple methods in a study is desirable. Individual level analyses should be used.

CONSUMER USAGE OF CHOICE HEURISTICS

Now let us consider how choice heuristics are used by consumers. One important function of choice heuristics is to allow consumers to adapt to complex choice tasks without exceeding the limited processing capacity available to them. This implies that choice heuristics can be characterized both by how difficult they are to execute, and by their potential for leading to "good" choices (Wright 1975). Theoretically, some rules should be more difficult to carry out than others. For example, the compensatory heuristics (e.g., linear compensatory, additive difference) seem to require a good deal of computation and to place heavy loads on short-term memory capacity, since the computations must be performed in short-term memory and the result of the computations to date must also be stored in short-term memory. On the other hand, sequential elimination strategies may be easy to perform, since one is continually reducing the set of alternatives, and only cutoffs are used. Also, some heuristics seem a priori to be likely to yield better choice outcomes than others. For example, those heuristics which require consideration of all attributes for all alternatives (e.g., linear compensatory, conjunctive) would seem to allow more potential for good choices than those heuristics which do not (e.g., lexicographic or sequential elimination).

Thus one can make a priori arguments about the difficulty and potential for optimality of choice heuristics. However, these theoretical notions may not correspond to how consumers judge these heuristics. Wright (1975) studied how consumers view choice strategies. He based his analysis on the idea that consumers are continually trading off optimality and simplicity in deciding how to process data. If a rule which would lead to good choices is hard to apply, some degree of optimality may be sacrificed to obtain a simpler process. As noted in more detail below, Dawes (1976) argues that this premise may be misleading. People may not make trade-offs, but may be operating at the highest level allowed by their built-in cognitive processing limitations.

Wright presented four rules to subjects and had each subject use one of those rules to make choices for fourteen sets of alternatives. The four rules were equal weight averaging, differential weight averaging, conjunctive, and lexicographic. In addition, three numbers of alternatives to process in each set were used, two, six, and ten. This factor was crossed with the rules factor to yield a 3 × 4 design. After using the rules, subjects' accuracy in applying the rules to the choice sets could be derived, and questions were asked to measure subjects' perceptions of ease of use of the strategy and optimizing potential of the strategy.

The results showed that accuracy of use decreased as the number of options increased. Also, the lexicographic strategy tended to be used more accurately. Perceived difficulty of executing the strategy increased with number of options. Compensatory strategies were not seen as difficult, nor was the lexicographic rule for less than ten options. The conjunctive rule was seen as reasonably difficult to apply. The subjects perceived the conjunctive strategy to offer the most optimizing potential. Thus contrary to the *a priori* notions above, subjects perceived a conjunctive strategy as both more difficult and as having more optimizing potential than compensatory models. These conclusions must be tempered by the fact that subjects were memorizing and applying rules constructed by the experimenter, for well structured sets of alternatives. In more realistic situations, subjects' perceptions might differ. Also, in general the difficulty of a heuristic should depend a great deal upon the structure of the task being performed (e.g., how information is presented), a factor not investigated by Wright.

> *Proposition 7.7:* Choice heuristics differ in difficulty of execution and in their potential for leading to good choices. Subjects' perceptions of difficulty and optimizing potential do not agree with theoretical analyses. Difficulty and optimizing potential may be affected by properties of the choice environment.

We have now examined how consumers perceive properties of choice heuristics. Next the factors that influence which heuristics seem to be used by consumers are considered. In general, there are two major classes of influences. First, different individuals may, as a result of prior experience, have different preferred strategies. Second, there may be strong impacts of task or situational factors on use of heuristics, so that the same individual may use different heuristics in different choice situations. Discussion of research on usage of choice heuristics is presented in the detailed sections below. For now, we state

> *Proposition 7.8:* Consumers' usage of choice heuristics may be affected by
> a) Individual differences
> b) Task and situational factors

SUMMARY

The consumer, subject to processing limitations, uses heuristics to make choices. Many alternative heuristics have been proposed, and usage depends upon individual differences and task factors. Consumers may implement choice heuristics in several ways, depending upon degree of prior knowledge and experience and upon the particular choice situation. Several methods are available for studying decision processes, each with its own strengths and weaknesses.

LINKAGES TO OTHER COMPONENTS OF THE THEORY

Decision processes are interwoven with the other constructs in the theory. First, processing capacity has profound impacts on the types of choice heuristics developed by consumers. Limitations on processing capacity imply that complex rules requiring great amounts of computation may rarely be used. Rather, heuristics which allow simpler processing will be developed.

Motivation is tied to decision processes in several ways. First, as noted in earlier chapters, choices are made to accomplish goals, and thus the goals held by the consumer will influence the process of comparing alternatives. In fact, one can view this comparison process as simply a detailed level of the goal hierarchy. Choices can also influence motivation, in that interrupts from a choice process can lead to changes in goals. Finally, choices are continually being made about what goals to pursue.

Attention, perception, and information acquisition and evaluation are also linked to choice processes. As noted earlier in this chapter, comparison of alternatives may in general be carried out simultaneously with the input of information; that is, as information is being gathered on alternatives, those alternatives are also being compared. In general, the attention, perception, and acquisition processes provide the information needed for choice. The particular choice heuristic used can also influence which information is attended to and sought. If a "Buy the cheapest" rule is used, then price information will be the focus, for example. Finally, decisions are involved in all of these other components—what to attend to, which information to search for, and so on.

Memory is connected to the process of comparing alternatives in several ways. The limitations on short-term memory influence the kinds of heuristics used, and heuristics both use data from and input data to long-term memory.

MORE DETAILED ASPECTS OF THE DECISION PROCESSES COMPONENT

SPECIFIC PROCESSING LIMITATIONS

In the sections above the use of heuristics as a way of making choices given limited processing capacity was discussed. In this section, more detailed studies of particular processing limitations are considered. In particular, we consider two broad categories: limitations on computational abilities and capacity, and limitations in judgments of uncertain events.

Computational and capacity limitations

Limitations on short-term memory capacity were discussed in detail in Chapter 6. In consumer choice, short-term memory is often augmented by an extensive external memory, the in-store display. Information is available from packages and in-store promotional material. However, even with this added memory aid, problems may arise. Several authors have claimed that even with the appropriate information available, consumers are limited in their ability to perform manipulations or necessary computations. There is evidence for this assertion in studies of consumers' abilities to use price data. Friedman (1966) instructed his subjects, 33 young married women, to select the most economical package for each of 20 products on sale at their local supermarket. He found that 43 percent of their selections were incorrect, and that the errors added an average of 9.14 percent to the cost of the products. Branscombe (1975) reported results of a national study which showed large deficiencies in consumers' abilities to make the calculations needed in the marketplace. Ross (1974) reviews other studies with similar results. Russo, Krieser, and Miyashita (1975) and Russo (1977) argue that even if data on price per unit are already available, they are not necessarily *processable*. If shelf tags with unit prices are presented in the standard fashion, underneath each product, consumers may have a difficult time comparing all of these tags. Russo, Krieser, and Miyashita and Russo changed the display of unit price information from these separate tags to a single organized list, displaying unit price data for all brands and sizes. They showed that in an actual in-store test, the new format was associated with lower prices paid per unit. Thus the mere existence of information may not be sufficient; consumers may utilize information only if they are able to process it.[9]

Several studies have examined prechunking or preorganization of data as a means of improving processability. Chervany and Dickson (1974), in a production game context, found that presenting subjects with statistical summaries rather than raw data led to improved results (lower production costs). Winter (1975) manipulated the form of price information presented to consumers, with one group receiving price indices for nine product categories at each of four stores and the second group receiving unprocessed price information for over 160 items at each of the four stores. The dependent measure was the ability to recall the lowest priced store for each of 25 items. The results showed that the group receiving the unprocessed information was more accurate in choosing the lowest priced store. However, this result was shown to be due to inaccuracies in the index used, in the sense that aggregation caused information about specific items to be lost (e.g., store A may have been less

---

9. Anderson (1978) presents a similar argument, noting that provision of a summary fact sheet to judges might help those judges make bail setting decisions more in accord with their own ideals of justice (see Ebbesen and Koněcni [1975] for the substantive findings underlying Anderson's arguments).

expensive than store B on an overall index for a particular category, but more expensive than store B for some particular items in that category). If stores were in fact ordered on items the same as they were for indices, performance would have been better for the indices. Thus the congruence of the chunks with what is required must be carefully examined in an attempt to prechunk data (see Chapter 6). In particular, the compatibility of the chunk with the type of response to be performed should be examined (e.g., in Winter's [1975] study, a general index was used for a task requiring specific item responses. One suspects that if general category responses were requested, the index would have been superior).

One final set of studies dealing with computational and processing abilities is the series of information overload studies reported by Jacoby, Speller, and Kohn (1974a,b). Jacoby, Speller, and Kohn presented subjects with descriptions of hypothetical brands of laundry detergent (1974a) or rice and prepared dinners (1974b). They varied the amount of information presented to consumers by manipulating the number of brands (4, 8, or 12 in the 1974a study; 4, 8, 12, or 16 in the 1974b study) and number of pieces of information per brand (2, 4, or 6 items in the 1974a study; 4, 8, 12, or 16 items in the 1974b study). Subjects were asked to choose a brand. The "accuracy" of their choice was measured by obtaining ratings on the importance of each possible piece of information to them in making a choice, and their ideal rating for each piece of information. Using these data, a weighted deviation score from the ideal could be calculated for each consumer for each alternative given to that consumer. The alternative with the smallest deviation from the ideal was the "optimal" choice for that consumer, and could be compared with the consumer's actual choice. Also, in the 1974b study, the entire rank order of a consumer's actual preferences was compared with the rank order predicted from the rating data.

In analyzing their data, Jacoby, Speller, and Kohn (1974a,b) multiplied number of alternatives times number of pieces of information per alternative to form what they called information load. They then presented results which showed that accuracy increased up to an information load of approximately 24 items (1974a) or approximately 48 to 64 items (1974b) and decreased or remained constant thereafter. The conclusion drawn was that consumers may actually make poorer decisions with more information—there may be an "information overload."

Several authors have disputed this conclusion (Russo 1974; Wilkie 1974; Summers 1974). In addition to criticisms of the basic study design, two issues in the analysis and interpretation of the data were raised. First, the critics noted that multiplying number of alternatives times number of pieces of information to arrive at an index of load may not make sense psychologically (e.g., is the 4 alternative, 12 pieces of information situation the same as the 12 alternative, 4 pieces of information one?). They then note that the number of pieces of information per alternative may be a more meaningful dimension, as only this dimension is under control of the public policymaker or marketer. When the data are examined along this dimension, choice accuracy *increases* as more information is added. The decrease in accuracy seems to be found only when the number of alternatives is increased. The second major criticism relates to this latter point. The criterion measure used is based upon subjects' ratings and hence is subject to error. There is a greater probability of error from random factors alone as the number of alternatives increases. The results of the Jacoby, Speller, and Kohn studies are not conclusive, therefore. Whether increased information availability aids or hinders the consumer is still an open issue. As noted in Chapter 6, the issue may not be one of availability, but one of degree of internal processing required (Seibel, Christ, and Teichner 1965). In general, consumers can try to protect themselves from overload by selection of some subset of the information presented.

The above discussion can be summarized as

> *Proposition 7.1.i:* Consumers have limited computational skills and processing capacities. In particular,
>
> a) Consumers perform unit price and other consumer mathematics computations poorly
>
> b) Preorganization of data can aid processing, but only if the organization is congruent with the consumer's organization in memory and the requirements of the task
>
> c) Whether information overload occurs and hinders consumer choices is still an open issue

Limitations in judgments of uncertain events

In the following, several types of limitations in judgments of uncertain events are considered. In particular, judgments of probability, use of associations, and judgments of contingency are considered. Most of these limitations have been demonstrated at a conceptual level, but not in consumer choice situations (Slovic, Fischhoff, and Lichtenstein 1977).

Tversky and Kahneman have performed extensive research on limitations in judgments of probability. Two heuristics which appear to be used extensively in judging probability are availability and representativeness. Availability refers to the ease with which relevant instances of an event can be imagined. The more instances which can be easily imagined, the more likely the event is judged to be. Tversky and Kahneman (1973) present several studies showing the particular biases which result. Classes of items where instances are more easily recalled are judged to be more frequent than classes of items of the same size where the instances are less easy to recall. This could lead to biases in consumer choices. For example, negative outcomes may be remembered better (be more available) than positive outcomes, so the judged relative frequency of negative outcomes might be biased upward. This could impact surveys of consumer satisfaction. Also, in cases in which a consumer is considering a product that he or she may or may not actually use (e.g., an encyclopedia set), usage situations may be more easily available than nonusage situations. Only after purchase does it become apparent to the purchaser that he or she overestimated the usage frequency. Finally, consumers' *a priori* estimates of the relative frequencies of various choice outcomes may depend on which outcomes have been explicitly presented to them via ads, word-of-mouth, etc. Outcomes that have been mentioned may tend to be more available and hence judged more frequent (Fischhoff, Slovic, and Lichtenstein 1978). This effect may impact later evaluations of actual usage experience for products where performance is difficult to assess.

A second heuristic is representativeness (Kahneman and Tversky 1972; 1973). "A person who follows this heuristic evaluates the probability of an uncertain event, or a sample, by the degree to which it is: (i) similar in essential properties to its parent population; and (ii) reflects the salient features of the process by which it is generated." (Kahneman and Tversky 1972, p. 431) For example, in judgments of the randomness of a sequence, reliance on irregularity and belief in local representativeness (a small segment will have properties like the whole) are found. Subjects asked to produce random sequences have far too many short runs, and reject sequences which appear to have long runs. Kahneman and Tversky (1972) also note that since representativeness is not affected by sample size, judgments of probability will not be affected by sample size manipulations. They report data that support this contention, and suggest that subjects do not have the conception that sampling variance decreases as sample size increases. A related phenomenon is what Tversky and Kahneman (1971) refer to as a belief in the law of small numbers, a belief that the law of large numbers also applies to small numbers. They note that psychologists, in planning their experiments, may seriously overestimate the replicability of results based on small samples.

Use of availability or representativeness may be affected by the task given. In particular, representativeness seems to be used if general properties and population parameters are stressed in the task, but availability tends to be used if particular instances are presented (Tversky and Kahneman 1973). Both heuristics, although apparently used in different circumstances, are similar in that degree of mental effort is used to judge probability (Kahneman and Tversky 1972). The harder events are to imagine, the less probable they are considered to be. Representative outcomes are easier to imagine, and availability is clearly based on mental effort.

Other investigators have shown that biases exist which are based upon interpretation and use of associations (as was the availability heuristic). In particular, intuitive judgments of correlations and causality may be suspect. Chapman and Chapman (1967, 1969) demonstrate a phenomenon they call illusory correlation in a striking set of experiments. Using a clinical judgment task, Chapman and Chapman show that when subjects have strong intuitive associations between two events (say a particular type of Rorschach response and a particular clinical symptom), they report strong correlations between those events even if the data they have just seen have no or even strong negative correlations, and they fail to see any actual associations there may be in the data. Only when the invalid associated event is actually removed from the data are the actual associations perceived. "One of the most striking findings of these studies is the persistence of illusory correlation in the face of contradictory reality . . . illusory correlates blind the observer to the presence of valid correlates of the symptom." (Chapman and Chapman 1969, p. 280) People appear to see what they intuitively expect, even when it is not there. That is one of the inherent biases in a constructive perceptual process guided by expectations. This may explain why consumers perceive relationships between price and quality, for example, even if data may not support the relationship (Friedman 1967).

Ward and Jenkins (1965; Jenkins and Ward 1965) have examined subjects' judgments of the degree of contingency between two events. They find that subjects judge contingency by the frequency with which two events occur simultaneously, ignoring cases where one event occurs without the other. This effect is accentuated by presentation of data about the occurrence or nonoccurrence of each of the two events in a trial by trial fashion. If a tabular summary of the data is presented, subjects form more appropriate estimates of the degree of relationship between two events *only* if no trial by trial information was also given. Thus the organization of experience is crucial.[10]

These notions lead to the following:

> *Proposition 7.1.ii:* Humans may be subject to several limitations in judgments of uncertain events.
>
> a) Heuristics such as availability and representativeness can lead to biases in probability judgments
>
> b) Intuitive or conceptual associations between events can lead to inaccurate perceptions of actual empirical relationships between the events
>
> c) Judgments of contingency may in general be inaccurate

Dawes (1976) makes one final point on human beings' processing limitations. He notes that many authors ascribe faulty decisions to motivational factors—that if it were not for self-seeking motives, appropriate decisions would be made. Dawes claims that this view is cognitive conceit, that human beings may greatly overestimate their processing abilities. Individuals may not make as many conscious trade-offs of optimality versus simplicity in

---

10. Feldman's (1963) study, in which subjects presented with a random sequence of events perceive patterns and causality, also supports this notion of human beings as having biases in assessing contingency.

processing as supposed; in implementing simple rules, individuals may be doing all they are cognitively capable of. Dawes (1976, p. 11) summarizes by stating, "Conscious judgment — as opposed to automatic processing based on vast experience — is feeble. Yet it is precisely this sort of feeble conscious processing on which most people rely when attempting to solve most interpersonal and intrapersonal problems. This feebleness alone — without the help of motivational factors — may account for many of our disasters."

THE ROLE OF ATTITUDES IN CHOICE PROCESSES

As discussed above, many choice heuristics do not develop direct evaluations for each alternative. A choice can be made with these heuristics without forming such an overall evaluation (e.g., lexicographic or sequential elimination heuristics). This raises a major issue, whether an attitude, an overall evaluation of each alternative, is a necessary or even useful component of choice processes. The heavy emphasis on the concept of attitude in current theories of consumer choice (e.g., Howard and Sheth 1969; Howard 1977; Hansen 1972; Engel, Blackwell, and Kollat 1978) may be related to the reliance in research on choice on linear models, which do develop a direct evaluation, and the past reliance on correlational methods, which also are biased toward direct evaluations and brand processing, as noted above. The important questions are whether the attitude construct too narrowly limits the types of choice processes congruent with it, and whether an evaluation of each alternative is needed to depict many choice processes.

Before discussing this issue, a brief digression on the nature of attitudes is undertaken. Anderson (1976, p. 72) views the formation of attitudes as a constructive process: "an attitudinal judgment is typically the product of some momentary constructive process. If an issue is familiar, then the attitude may be stored directly as given data. In general, however, the person cannot have stored responses ready for each new contingency but must construct them as they become needed. Even for familiar issues, the overt attitudinal judgment will inevitably reflect momentary situational factors. It may be misleading, therefore, to say that the person 'has' an attitude. Rather, he has the materials for constructing a variety of attitudinal judgments. . . . In a very real sense, therefore, the person not only does not know his own mind but is continually making it up." (See also Anderson 1978.)

This view, then, implies that *constructing attitudes and constructing and implementing choice heuristics may in general be two different tasks that need not be interrelated*. For example, if a consumer is asked how he or she liked product X (perhaps after X has been chosen) by a researcher or another consumer, an attitude may be constructed. If the consumer is familiar with product X, he or she may have an already constructed evaluation, which has been stored. However, this does not imply that the evaluation is *used* when a choice is made.

Of course there may be situations in which attitudes are directly used in making choices (e.g., see the affect referral rule described above). One might hypothesize that with little experience with a given choice, choice rules with no direct link to attitudes may be used (e.g., conjunctive, lexicographic). After experience has been gained, perhaps attitudes are used more directly as a component of choice.

The viewpoint taken here, therefore, is that attitude need not be directly related to choice processes. Rather, formation of attitudes and choice may be separate phenomena, which may go on in parallel with each other. The relationship of attitudes to choice may vary depending upon degree of experience with a choice. Thus attitude need not be a necessary component of all choice processes. This view, obviously quite speculative and greatly in need of research, can be expressed as

> *Proposition 7.3.i:* Attitudes and choice can be separate phenomena, which may go on in parallel with each other. Attitudes need not be a necessary component of all choice processes. The relationship of attitudes to choice processes may vary with degree of experience with the choice.

We now turn to examination of consumer usage of choice heuristics. Two basic areas of research on choice heuristics are examined: research focusing on how alternatives are evaluated, and research focusing directly on the processes used to compare alternatives.

STUDIES OF EVALUATION OF ALTERNATIVES

Much of the initial work on choice heuristics was carried out using correlational methods to assess the predictive accuracy of various possible heuristics. As noted above, this method in effect assumes brand processing and forces the experimenter to develop evaluations for each alternative, even for heuristics for which such evaluations may be arbitrary. Thus the results of these studies should be regarded with caution. There are two sets of findings discussed below: studies of the predictive accuracy of various heuristics, and studies of task and individual difference factors.

Predictive accuracy studies

There have been many studies of the predictive accuracy, or the degree of fit, of particular choice rules to data. One large set of results has considered the adequacy of linear compensatory rules. As noted above, research on clinical judgments has consistently shown linear rules to predict better than nonlinear rules (Goldberg 1968; Green 1968; Dawes and Corrigan 1974). In consumer research, a major stream of research on the multiattribute attitude model (Wilkie and Pessemier 1973; Lutz and Bettman 1977) has examined the accuracy of the linear compensatory model. Using mostly known brand belief surveys, correlations of the order of .3 to .6 have been obtained between predicted and directly measured attitudes. Bettman, Capon, and Lutz (1975a,b,c), using an information integration approach, also find support for a linear compensatory model of attitudes. However, their work supports an averaging as opposed to adding model. There has been substantial disagreement in previous research in this area (e.g., Anderson 1971, 1974b; Fishbein and Hunter 1964), so the issue is not yet settled. Finally, research using conjoint measurement approaches (Green and Wind 1973) has generally found linear models of consumer evaluations to be adequate.

There also have been many studies which compared the accuracy of linear compensatory and other rules. Einhorn (1970, 1971) was one of the first to take such an approach. He developed algebraic approximations to conjunctive and disjunctive rules. If there are n predictor variables X_i for some dependent variable Y, then a multiplicative model

$$Y = \prod_{i=1}^{n} X_i^{b_i}, \qquad \text{estimated as } \log Y = \sum_{i=1}^{n} b_i \log X_i, \qquad (7.4)$$

is an approximation to a conjunctive rule. All predictors must be high for the dependent variable to be high. For the disjunctive rule, an approximation is given by

$$Y = \prod_{i=1}^{n} (a_i - X_i)^{-b_i}, \qquad \text{estimated as } \log Y = -\sum_{i=1}^{n} b_i \log (a_i - X_i). \qquad (7.5)$$

Here the constant a_i is chosen so that $\log (a_i - X_i)$ is defined for all values of X_i. For this approximation, any high X_i tends to make Y high. These approximations have severe problems, however (Wright 1974b). Both of these approximations are still additive and compensatory when logarithms are taken, and both are nonlinear, so interval scale measures of X_i will not yield invariant correlations. Thus the results of using these models may not strictly be evidence for or against conjunctive and disjunctive models, especially since theoretically the conjunctive and disjunctive models do not yield direct evaluations, only derived ones.

Einhorn (1971) applied these models in a correlational study using an active evaluation task to predictions of job preference and selection of graduate students. For the job preference task, the conjunctive approximation seemed to perform better than the linear model, whereas the linear model performed well in the student selection task. Nystedt and Magnusson (1975) and Goldberg (1971), also using active evaluation tasks, both found that the linear model performed better than the conjunctive approximation, which was in turn better than the disjunctive approximation for clinical judgments tasks (judgments of patients). Heeler, Kearney, and Mehaffey (1973), examining selection of products by supermarket buyers, also found that the linear rule was better than the conjunctive and disjunctive approximations. Montgomery (1975), however, also studying the supermarket product selection task, found that the linear rule was less accurate than a rule based on a branching network, essentially a noncompensatory model.

Thus, in general, the linear compensatory heuristic does well in these accuracy studies. However, this may be due to biases in the methods used as well as to the power of the linear model. As noted above, correlational methods must develop some predicted evaluation for each alternative, and hence effectively assume brand processing for all rules. Also, in most studies, information on alternatives has been *presented by brand*, e.g., with information on each alternative displayed on a separate card. Thus these results would be *biased toward* use of models that are characterized by brand processing (e.g., linear, conjunctive) and *biased against* models characterized by attribute processing (e.g., lexicographic, elimination by aspects). The above results are expressed as

> *Proposition 7.8.i:* Correlational studies of the predictive accuracy of various choice heuristics have found that the linear compensatory rule does better than other heuristics. This result may be due both to robustness of the linear statistical model and biases in the methods used in addition to any actual use of linear models.

Effects of task factors and individual differences

Many of the studies cited above have implicitly assumed that a single choice heuristic is "best" and have tried to find that heuristic. Other researchers have denied that a single "best" heuristic exists, and have argued that in fact the use of any given rule will be affected by the task; that is, heuristic usage may be *contingent* upon properties of the task situation. Wright (1974b,e; Wright and Weitz 1977) has examined these task effects in a series of studies. In the first study, Wright (1974b), using an active evaluation task, used Einhorn's approximations, but did *not* interpret them as disjunctive and conjunctive heuristics. Rather, he argued that the conjunctive approximation overweights negative data, and the disjunctive approximation overweights positive data. Other research (Kanouse and Hanson 1971; Feldman 1974; Hass, Bagley, and Rogers 1975) has shown overweighting of negative data. However, task effects had not been considered. Wright examined both time pressure and distraction conditions (in an independent study for each) and predicted that under time pressure or distraction individuals would overweight negative information more than under more leisurely conditions. Time pressure did tend to increase reliance on negative data (i.e., the conjunctive approximation fit better), and distraction showed a tendency toward the hypothesized effect.

In a related study, Wright and Weitz (1977) studied the effects of time horizons on product evaluation strategies. They found that subjects evaluate possible negative outcomes more severely when these outcomes are expected sooner rather than later, and also evaluate these outcomes more severely when greater commitment to an alternative is required. Finally, Wright and Weitz suggest that under time pressure, subjects tend to dichotomize dimensions into accept and reject regions, with severe downward rating of moderately negative outcomes.

In a third study of task effects, Wright (1974e), using an active evaluation task, examined the effects of incomplete data, noncomparable scalings across alternatives, extraneous data, and effects that occur when an initial strategy fails to discriminate a single alternative as "best." As incomparable scalings and extraneous data were added, subjects tended to decrease use of basically compensatory strategies and increase use of basically lexicographic rules. Finally, in a treatment in which a linear compensatory heuristic led to ties in evaluations, even in a relatively simple environment with no incomparable scalings or extraneous data, a lexicographic strategy was used. Thus if a heuristic doesn't work in a particular task environment, another may be used. Slovic (1975) found a similar result.

Slovic and MacPhillamy (1974) and Wright (1974e) also both studied the effects of incomplete information. In both studies, two alternatives, with two pieces of information for each, were presented on a trial; there was one dimension for which data were available for both alternatives. The second piece of information for each alternative was on different dimensions for each alternative. Slovic and MacPhillamy (1974) found that the common dimension was given more weight, even when subjects were warned not to do so in the instruction. They argue that this bias may result because it eliminates the need to weight dimensions; only the question of which alternative is better on the common dimension need be answered. Wright (1974e) found opposing results, that rules using the common dimension to predict choice did poorly when compared with other rules. The reason for the differences in results is not clear (see also Yates, Jagacinski, and Faber 1978).

In another study of task effects, Slovic (1972b) shows that subjects' responses change as a function of the task in that for some pairs of gambles subjects prefer gamble A to gamble B if asked to set prices for the bets to indicate the worth of the bet to them, but prefer gamble B to gamble A if simply asked to choose between the two. Thus the rules used for weighting attributes of the bets (probabilities and payoffs) appeared to differ for the two tasks. The compatibility between a dimension and the required response appears to affect the weight given to the dimension.

The results of the above studies thus show a great diversity of task effects on usage of heuristics. Many of these effects provide evidence for what Slovic (1972a, p. 14; see also Simon and Hayes 1976) calls the principle of con-

creteness. "Concreteness represents the general notion that a judge or decision maker tends to use only the information that is explicitly displayed in the
stimulus object and will use it only in the form in which it is displayed. Information that has to be stored in memory, inferred from the explicit display, or
transformed tends to be discounted or ignored."

Very little work is available on individual difference factors as related
to usage of different choice heuristics. In one of the few studies, Park and
Sheth (1975), using a known brand belief survey, examined individual-task
interactions as they affect use of heuristics. They measured degree of prior
familiarity with the product classes studied. They found that the best degree
of fit for a weighted linear compensatory rule was under high familiarity, but
the best fit for disjunctive and conjunctive models was under moderate
familiarity. This may support the idea of a preliminary elimination phase in
situations in which one is not highly familiar with the alternatives. Also, Park
(1976) discusses further effects of familiarity and product complexity on
degree of fit for various heuristics.

The discussions above of the effects of task and individual difference
factors are summarized in the following propositions:

> *Proposition 7.8.ii:* Studies of the predictive accuracy of
> choice heuristics have found task effects and individual differ-
> ence effects on the accuracy of various heuristics. Familiarity
> with the brands to be studied was the major individual differ-
> ence factor. Important task factors include:
>
> a) Time pressure and the perceived time horizon for the
>   choice
> b) Distraction
> c) Noncomparable scale formats and extraneous data
> d) Incomplete data
> e) Type of response required
>
> *Proposition 7.8.iii:* Consumers tend to use information as it is
> displayed. Information that has to be transformed or pro-
> cessed a great deal may tend to be discounted or ignored.

STUDIES OF ALTERNATIVE COMPARISON PROCESSES

In addition to the studies of the assumed evaluation process described
above, a good deal of recent research has attempted to examine directly the
processes by which alternatives are compared. In most cases these studies
have used methodologies which allow aspects of processing to be observed.
Two basic areas of research are now considered: studies of phased strategies,
and studies of form of processing (by brand or by attribute).

Studies of phased strategies

Many studies find evidence for phased strategies. A phased strategy is one in which an initial phase of eliminating unacceptable alternatives is followed by a secondary choice phase comparing the remaining alternatives in more detail. Svenson (1974) and Lussier and Olshavsky (1974) report protocol data supporting this notion, particularly when the initial set of alternative brands was large (6 to 12). Lussier and Olshavsky (1974) report that subjects' protocols indicate that attributes are also eliminated in the first phase before detailed evaluations are made if the number of attributes is large. Van Raaij (1976b), using eye movement data, also found elimination of attributes.

Sheridan, Richards, and Slocum (1975), using questionnaire data, found evidence for an initial screening of job alternatives followed by a more detailed choice phase. Lehtinen (1974), also using questionnaire data, found evidence for an elimination phase in automobile choices. Russ (1971), using protocol data and model fitting techniques, found that the models that fit best over several indices were a satisficing first phase combined with lexicographic semiorder or adding models as a second phase, thus suggesting a first stage elimination process. Pras and Summers (1975), using rank-order correlational techniques, found that a conjunctive model performed better when all alternatives were included, and a linear rule was slightly better when only acceptable alternatives were included in the analysis. This pattern of findings may support the notion of a conjunctive elimination phase followed by a compensatory choice phase. Thus many studies find elimination phases.

Some studies have not found evidence for phased strategies. Russo and Rosen (1975), using eye movement data and prompted protocols, found no elimination phase in a choice among six alternatives. They hypothesize, however, that such a phase may occur for larger sets of alternatives. Finally, Bettman and Jacoby (1976), using an information monitoring approach, did not find evidence of an elimination phase. This may be explainable in that Bettman and Jacoby used real brands as alternatives, whereas many of the other studies used hypothetical alternatives. Hence, in the Bettman and Jacoby study the elimination phase may have already been performed by subjects before they came to the experiment, and is carried out by the subjects by looking at brand name alone, without being reflected in the sequence of cards selected. Thus, we conclude

> *Proposition 7.8.iv:* Phased strategies, with an elimination phase and a choice phase, may be found when the number of alternatives is large.

Wright and Barbour (1977) have performed one of the few studies on the detailed nature of subjects' rule usage in the second phase of a phased strategy, after the elimination phase has been completed. Wright and Barbour had subjects complete an elimination phase. They then examined what occurred if no alternative passed all cutoffs. They found, as hypothesized, that most subjects considered the group of options that survived the next-to-last cutoff. Also, they found that lexicographic and compensatory rules were used most often to choose an alternative in the second phase.

Studies of form of processing

Form of processing, by brand or by attribute, is an important aspect characterizing choice heuristics. As shown in Table 7.2, several of the choice heuristics proposed (lexicographic, sequential elimination, elimination by aspects, lexicographic semiorder, and additive difference) imply processing by attribute, and several (linear compensatory, general information integration, conjunctive, and disjunctive) imply processing by brand. This suggests that one way to analyze what choice heuristics consumers are using is to examine the form of processing, therefore.

There are some theoretical arguments related to what form of processing might be expected. In Chapter 6, research was summarized which provided mixed support for the notion that for inputting data on alternatives, processing by brand (object) was more effective for later memory performance. However, for choice processing, processing by attribute may be easier for subjects; that is, it may be easier to compare alternatives on one attribute, then move to the next attribute and so forth. Tversky (1969) argues that intradimensional evaluations (processing by attribute) are easier than interdimensional ones (processing by brand), because the alternatives can be compared using the same units (since the same dimension is utilized). Tversky then argues that evaluating each of two alternatives one at a time and comparing these overall evaluations is more difficult than evaluating both alternatives on a dimension and eventually combining over dimensions, since processing by dimensions (attributes) requires only half as many interdimensional comparisons as processing by alternatives. Tversky (1969) also states that processing by dimensions can lead to dropping dimensions from the analysis if all alternatives are seen as equivalent for those dimensions. Finally, Tversky notes that dominance relations among alternatives (e.g., alternative A is better than or equal to alternative B on all dimensions) are much easier to handle using processing by attributes.[11]

There is some empirical evidence for processing by attribute. Russ (1971), using protocol methods, found that of 80 information acquisition sequences, 57 were by attribute, 15 by brand, and 8 had some other structure.

---

11. This is not meant to imply that processing by brand strategies do not have advantages. Such strategies permit the use of interrelations between dimensions when dimensions are not independent, and such strategies may also lead to transitive choices (Russo and Dosher 1975). See Montgomery and Svenson (1976) for further discussion.

Bettman and Jacoby (1976) found roughly equal amounts of brand and attribute processing. Capon and Burke (1977) found 71 percent attribute processing. Russo and Rosen (1975) used eye movement and prompted protocol data to study choice among six alternative used cars described by three attributes. They found that the eye-fixations consisted mainly of paired comparisons among alternatives (essentially processing by attribute rather than by brand).

The most extensive set of studies suggesting attribute processing is presented by Russo and Dosher (1975). They consider choice situations in which only two alternatives are present, and use eye movements (stimuli were presented to subjects as arrays on cathode ray tubes) and prompted protocols to collect data on the choice process. In a first study, involving choice among scholarship applicants described by three attributes, input (reading) of data was consistently by alternative, but processing was by attribute. Fifty-seven percent of postreading time was spent in processing by attribute, 14 percent on processing by object, and 29 percent was unclassified. Subjects using an attribute strategy could develop three attribute differences for a particular choice. Russo and Dosher also examined the heuristics subjects appeared to use to combine these differences into an overall evaluation. One simple heuristic for three dimensions is dimensional reduction (DR), dropping of one dimension. Then an ordinal judgment of which of the two remaining dimensional differences is more crucial is sufficient to choose an alternative. A second heuristic is the majority of confirming dimensions (MCD) heuristic in which only the direction of the difference is considered. For this heuristic the alternative favored by the most dimensions is chosen. Half of the subjects appeared to use each heuristic. Protocols showed that subjects were aware of both heuristics but tended to choose one predominantly. In a second study, Russo and Dosher again used choices between scholarship applicants, but expanded the number of dimensions considered to range from two to five dimensions per alternative. Again, processing by attributes was the dominant strategy (65 percent of fixations compared to 19 percent for processing by object). Also, as the number of dimensions increased, more use was made of the majority of confirming dimensions heuristic.[12]

Russo and Dosher (1975) postulate a choice heuristic based on these findings. The model is a simplified version of Tversky's (1969) additive difference model. If X_i and Y_i are the ratings for alternatives X and Y on the ith dimension, and U a subjective utility function, then subjects appear to follow these steps: (1) compute $X_i - Y_i$; (2) estimate the utility of this difference, $U(X_i - Y_i)$; (3) use a heuristic such as DR or MCD to make a choice; (4) revise this choice, if

---

12. Wright and Barbour (1977) also found this heuristic in their data, and called it "attribute dominance." May (1954) likewise found this rule used in an experiment on choices of hypothetical marriage partners.

needed, according to the specific values of the dimensional differences. This model may be compared with the additive difference model discussed above. First, the additive difference model assumes subjects compute utilities of X_i and Y_i and *then* take the difference; $U_i(X_i) - U_i(Y_i)$. Subjects appear to compute the difference and then compute utilities. Second, subjects simplify the combination process across dimensions compared with the process assumed by the additive difference model. Finally, subjects seem to discriminate only a few levels of utility differences in their protocols.

In two final studies, Russo and Dosher (1975) examine the generality of their processing by attribute results. One study used gambles as stimuli, since processing by alternative should be encouraged due to the relationship between dimensions (i.e., payoffs and probabilities). Based on eye movements, half of the subjects appeared to follow attribute processing and half alternative processing. However, the protocols showed that subjects almost always calculated dimensional differences and used these in their choice process. Thus even when processing by alternative should perhaps be favored, attribute processing may be observed.[13] In a final study, using descriptions of used cars, the dimensional ratings were *not* numerical, as they had been in all the previous studies, but verbal. In this study, more processing by alternative was observed than processing by attribute. Thus if dimensional differences are hard to calculate, dimensional (attribute) strategies may be less likely. As long as dimensional differences can be calculated, subjects may tend to use them, even if the dimensions are interrelated.

The support for a heuristic version of the additive difference model cited above seems to depend on the number of alternatives as well as the ease of computing dimensional differences. Russo and Dosher (1975) examined only binary choices. Payne (1976b) suggested that the additive difference notion can be extended to the multialternative case by using a standard revision strategy: compare A with B, compare the winner of A and B with C, and so on. However, standard revision strategies do not appear to be found often: Svenson (1974) found that one of his six subjects and Russo and Rosen (1975) found that two of their twelve subjects used standard revision. Payne (1976b) found evidence consistent with an additive difference model for two alternatives, but not for six or twelve, where conjunctive or elimination by aspects models were supported. Wright and Barbour (1977) found evidence for the simplified additive difference model with three to five alternatives. Park (1978) also reports use of a similar model. Finally, the phased processing studies cited above suggest use of some kind of brand processing heuristic (e.g., a conjunc-

---

13. Rosen and Rosenkoetter (1976), also using eye movements, found more processing by alternative for gambles and hypothetical vacation trips for which the dimensions were also interrelated, however,

tive rule) in the *elimination* phase, with increased use of attribute processing heuristics (e.g., heuristic additive difference or lexicographic) in the *choice* phase when there are fewer alternatives remaining.[14] Thus, in general, the heuristic additive difference model or other forms of attribute processing heuristics tend to be found with small numbers of alternatives. Brand processing rules may be used to reduce the original number of alternatives to a small enough set that attribute comparisons can be made.

The results above support the heuristic version of the additive difference model, with caveats relating to number of alternatives, phase of the comparison process, and type of data (i.e., whether differences are easy to calculate). Task analyses and the results of other studies, however, suggest that further restrictions should be placed on the generality of these findings. These restrictions concern the format of the information presentation and the degree of experience of the subjects.

Tversky (1969) argues that the format of presentation of the data has important effects. If alternatives are displayed sequentially (as in advertisements for example), processing by objects may be encouraged. If information on dimensions of several alternatives is available simultaneously, people may show strong tendencies to process by attribute. Johnson and Russo (1978) show similar effects of format on storage in memory. They analyze recall response times and show that information seems to be stored in the way it is presented. If presented by brand, it tends to be stored by brand; if presented by attribute, it tends to be stored by attribute.

Potential format effects in processing can also be demonstrated by doing task analyses for the studies discussed earlier in this section. The information displays used (mostly matrices or visual arrays) make brand or attribute processing equally easy in terms of the effort required to carry them out. Some studies, however, do not have such matrix displays, and the effects of format can be seen. For example, Svenson (1974) presented subjects with descriptions of seven houses, with each description presented in detail in a separate booklet. He found, using protocols, more processing by alternative early in the protocols, with more attribute processing later. Presumably the use of individual booklets made processing by alternative easier and processing by attribute more difficult, at least when there were several booklets being considered. Van Raaij (1976b) presented data to housewives on actual and simulated packages. Eye movement data showed 50 percent of the eye transitions were by brand and only 17 percent by attribute. The package for-

---

14. There may in some cases be three phases during the comparison process: an elimination phase, a choice phase, and a checking phase in which the consumer "checks over" the alternative tentatively selected to get an overall picture of it. Then there might be brand processing in the elimination phase, attribute processing in the choice phase, and brand processing again in the checking phase.

mat again appeared to make brand processing easier.[15] Finally, Bettman and Kakkar (1977), in a direct study of format effects detailed in Chapter 5, found strong format effects on the type of acquisition strategy used, with the form of processing used being that which was easiest given the display.

Degree of experience (prior knowledge) held by consumers also appears to impact the form of processing results. Supermarket shelves are often organized by brand, as are most commercials. Hence over time a brand name will come to summarize a great deal of information. To the extent that consumers use brand name as a summary construct in this way, processing by brand is facilitated (Bettman and Jacoby 1976; Jacoby, Szybillo, and Busato-Schach 1977). Processing by brand may be used in supermarkets to a large extent, since this is easiest given the format of the available information. Thus experienced shoppers may tend to have used brand processing a great deal. Bettman and Kakkar (1977) found that their subjects, all experienced shoppers, tended to use more brand processing in a matrix display task in which actual brands were used. In the studies finding attribute processing in a matrix display task, either artificial alternatives, alternatives about which subjects would have little prior knowledge, or inexperienced subjects (e.g., Russ 1971; Bettman and Jacoby 1976) were used. In addition, Jacoby, Chestnut, Weigl, and Fisher (1976) found that brand processing was associated with high consumption frequency, and processing by attributes with low consumption frequency.

Finally, note that most of the studies above used artificial stimuli and/or laboratory settings. Hence, the simplified additive difference model may be used because it is an easy way for subjects to complete an uninvolving task. Whether such a strategy would be used for choices important to the subjects is a significant question for future research.

> *Proposition 7.8.v:* There seem to be important task and individual difference effects on form of processing. The major factors are
>
> a) Number of alternatives
>
> b) Phase of the alternative comparison process
>
> c) Ease of computing dimensional differences

---

15. In another study, Van Raaij (1976a) found that consumers acquired much more information from these packages than the same consumers acquired from an information display board. This once again demonstrates that different methods present different processing tasks to consumers. Display board tasks appear to require more effort to actually select and examine the information cards desired from the matrix than is required in looking at some package label. Thus the processing used in display board tasks may depart in significant ways from processing in some typical consumer information acquisition tasks.

d) Format of the information display

e) Degree of knowledge about the alternatives

Attribute processing will tend to be found when there are few alternatives, when in the choice phase rather than in the elimination phase of the comparison process, when dimensional differences are easy to compute, when the format allows attribute processing, and when there is little knowledge about the alternatives. Brand processing will tend to be found when these conditions are not met. These conditions may in general not be met in most consumer choice environments.

Proposition 7.8.vi: Studies of alternative comparison processes suggest the following results:

a) If the number of alternatives is small (roughly five or less), and other factors do not discourage attribute processing, heuristic forms of the additive difference model may be used

b) If the number of alternatives is large (roughly six or more), there may be an elimination phase, perhaps using brand processing, followed by a choice phase

Thus there are several conclusions from studies of consumer usage of choice heuristics. The conclusions from correlational studies tend to conflict with those using process methods. As noted above, this may be a function of the biases inherent in the methods themselves. This suggests that one important area for future work is use of task analyses to analyze the *research tasks* given to consumers, as well as use of task analyses to consider actual consumer choice tasks. In the above, task analyses were used to suggest biases in correlational methods and format effects in studies of form of processing.[16]

What generalizations can be drawn from the above about how consumers select which heuristics to use? One basic and very important factor seems to be the structure of the task being engaged in by the consumer. Some heuristics will be easier to apply than others (e.g., see the discussion on format effects above), or will "work" better than others in a particular choice environment (e.g., see the discussion of Wright's [1974e] and Slovic's [1975] results above). Such heuristics will tend to be chosen.

---

16. Interestingly, even within the framework of the multiattribute attitude model, which assumes processing by brands, processing by attribute phenomena may occur. Wilkie, McCann, and Reibstein (1974) show that varying the method of measuring belief scores from a processing by brand form to a processing by attribute form affects the dispersion of these belief ratings; the degree of fit of the model; and the number of statistically significant attributes.

Proposition 7.8.vii: Consumers will tend to choose those choice heuristics which are easy to apply and work well in a particular choice environment. The structure of this choice environment thus can play a powerful role in determining usage of choice heuristics.

STUDIES OF IMPLEMENTATION METHODS

Consumers may implement choice heuristics in many ways, several of which were outlined above in Propositions 7.4 and 7.5. There has been only a limited amount of research on such implementation processes. Some theoretical and some empirical work has been attempted.

In the major example of theoretical work, Waterman (1970) developed an artificial intelligence program for playing draw poker. His program used detailed rules as elements to build heuristics. The program modifies existing elements if they are unsatisfactory and creates new elements if needed.

Empirical research on consumer implementation methods is sparse. Bettman and Zins (1977) attempted to study constructive and other types of processing by using consumer protocol data as an input to a panel of judges. The panel attempted to judge whether each of many choice "episodes" was constructive or nonconstructive in nature. The protocol data proved to be extremely ambiguous and difficult to judge. Of those items on which the judges agreed at a reasonable level (about 44 percent of the items), roughly 25 percent of the episodes were judged as being constructive in nature, and 75 percent nonconstructive. Another finding was that the protocol data themselves are subject to many biases and limitations for making inferences about the nature of processing carried out by consumers. In particular, for choices where the consumers had prior experience, retrospective rationales for why the brand now purchased was originally chosen were often given in the protocols. In addition, even the detailed protocol data proved very ambiguous, with not enough detail. Bettman and Zins suggest experimental approaches to studying constructive processes.

Bettman and Kakkar (1976) attempted to test consumer usage of various methods for implementing choice heuristics, the interrelationships among these methods, and the relationship of usage of these methods to degree of prior experience. Subjects were given scales describing the methods given in Proposition 7.4, and were asked to rate how descriptive each was for their choice process for cereals. Stored rules, prior, and recall methods were said to be more descriptive. In addition, correlations were taken among the methods which suggested that constructive, in-store, and recognition were associated, as were stored rules, prior, and recall, although these correlations were biased upward by measurement problems. Finally, it was found, using multiple regression, that constructive, in-store, and recognition methods seem to be associated with little prior purchase experience. In particular, difficulty in comparing alternatives, use of a satisfactory rather than optimizing goal, and consideration of many brands were associated with these methods. The opposite was true for stored rule, prior, and recall methods.

These results simply support Propositions 7.4 and 7.5. Hence, no new generalizations are given. However, given the measurement problems inherent in these studies and the elusiveness of the phenomena, the conclusions above are best viewed as very tentative speculation. Much more research is needed.

INDIVIDUAL DIFFERENCES IN THE DECISION PROCESSES COMPONENT

Those individual difference variables most relevant for the decision process component are outlined in the following:

Proposition 7.9: Individual differences can affect aspects of the decision processes component. Significant individual difference variables may be:

a) The particular heuristics or rules of thumb known by the individual

b) Processing abilities (e.g., intelligence, speed of processing)

c) Perceptions of the degree of difficulty and the potential for leading to good choices of various choice heuristics

d) The amount and organization of product-related information in memory

e) The degree to which various methods are used for implementing choices (i.e., stored rules vs. constructive, prior vs. in-store, recall vs. recognition)

SUMMARY OF THE PROPOSITIONS

Proposition 7.1: Consumers are subject to limitations in processing capacity. Heuristics or rules of thumb may be used to make comparisons among alternatives in most cases, rather than complex calculations.

> *Proposition 7.1.i:* Consumers have limited computational skills and processing capacities. In particular,
>
> a) Consumers perform unit price and other consumer mathematics computations poorly
>
> b) Preorganization of data can aid processing, but only if the organization is congruent with the consumer's organization in memory and the requirements of the task
>
> c) Whether information overload occurs and hinders consumer choices is still an open issue

Proposition 7.1.ii: Humans may be subject to several limitations in judgments of uncertain events.

a) Heuristics such as availability and representativeness can lead to biases in probability judgments

b) Intuitive or conceptual associations between events can lead to inaccurate perceptions of actual empirical relationships between the events

c) Judgments of contingency may in general be inaccurate

Proposition 7.2: Choice heuristics can be characterized by three aspects:

a) How an *evaluation* for each alternative is developed, either directly as a result of the heuristic, or by being derived arbitrarily

b) The *choice criterion* used to choose among the alternatives

c) The *form of processing* (e.g., by brand or by attribute) implied

The form of processing interacts with the other aspects, particularly the evaluation aspect

Proposition 7.3: Many different choice heuristics can be identified. Among the important heuristics are affect referral, linear compensatory, general information integration, conjunctive, disjunctive, lexicographic, sequential elimination, elimination by aspects, lexicographic semiorder, additive difference, and phased strategies. Most of these heuristics yield derived rather than direct evaluations for each alternative. This calls into question the view that attitudes are a necessary component of choice processes.

Proposition 7.3.i: Attitudes and choice can be separate phenomena, which may go on in parallel with each other. Attitudes need not be a necessary component of all choice processes. The relationship of attitudes to choice processes may vary with degree of experience with the choice.

Proposition 7.4: Consumers may use various methods for implementing choice heuristics. Three important sets of methods are

a) Constructive versus stored rule methods

b) In-store versus prior methods

c) Recognition versus recall methods

Stored rule, prior, and recall methods may tend to be associated, as may constructive, in-store and recognition.

Proposition 7.5: Usage of the various methods for implementing choice heuristics may be influenced by degree of prior knowledge and experience relevant to the choice in question. With little experience, constructive, recognition, and in-store methods may be used; with more experience, increased usage of stored rule, recall, and prior methods might be expected.

Proposition 7.6: Several methods for studying choice heuristics have been proposed:

a) Correlational methods
b) Information integration approaches
c) Protocol methods
d) Information monitoring approaches
e) Eye movement analysis
f) Response time analysis

Correlational methods seem less adequate than other approaches. Use of multiple methods in a study is desirable. Individual level analyses should be used.

Proposition 7.7: Choice heuristics differ in difficulty of execution and in their potential for leading to good choices. Subjects' perceptions of difficulty and optimizing potential do not agree with theoretical analyses. Difficulty and optimizing potential may be affected by properties of the choice environment.

Proposition 7.8: Consumers' usage of choice heuristics may be affected by

a) Individual differences
b) Task and situational factors

> *Proposition 7.8.i:* Correlational studies of the predictive accuracy of various choice heuristics have found that the linear compensatory rule does better than other heuristics. This result may be due both to robustness of the linear statistical model and biases in the methods used in addition to any actual use of linear models.

> *Proposition 7.8.ii:* Studies of the predictive accuracy of choice heuristics have found task effects and individual difference effects on the accuracy of various heuristics. Familiarity with the brands to be studied was the major individual difference factor. Important task factors include:

> a) Time pressure and the perceived time horizon for the choice
> b) Distraction
> c) Noncomparable scale formats and extraneous data
> d) Incomplete data
> e) Type of response required

Proposition 7.8.iii: Consumers tend to use information as it is displayed. Information that has to be transformed or processed a great deal may tend to be discounted or ignored.

Proposition 7.8.iv: Phased strategies, with an elimination phase and a choice phase, may be found when the number of alternatives is large.

Proposition 7.8.v: There seem to be important task and individual difference effects on form of processing. The major factors are

a) Number of alternatives

b) Phase of the alternative comparison process

c) Ease of computing dimensional differences

d) Format of the information display

e) Degree of knowledge about the alternatives

Attribute processing will tend to be found when there are few alternatives, when in the choice phase rather than in the elimination phase of the comparison process, when dimensional differences are easy to compute, when the format allows attribute processing, and when there is little knowledge about the alternatives. Brand processing will tend to be found when these conditions are not met. These conditions may in general not be met in most consumer choice environments.

Proposition 7.8.vi: Studies of alternative comparison processes suggest the following results:

a) If the number of alternatives is small (roughly five or less), and other factors do not discourage attribute processing, heuristic forms of the additive difference model may be used

b) If the number of alternatives is large (roughly six or more), there may be an elimination phase, perhaps using brand processing, followed by a choice phase

Proposition 7.8.vii: Consumers will tend to choose those choice heuristics which are easy to apply and work well in a particular choice environment. The structure of this choice environment thus can play a powerful role in determining usage of choice heuristics.

Proposition 7.9: Individual differences can affect aspects of the decision processes component. Significant individual difference variables may be:

a) The particular heuristics or rules of thumb known by the individual

b) Processing abilities (e.g., intelligence, speed of processing)

c) Perceptions of the degree of difficulty and the potential for leading to good choices of various choice heuristics

d) The amount and organization of product-related information in memory

e) The degree to which various methods are used for implementing choices (i.e., stored rules vs. constructive, prior vs. in-store, recall vs. recognition)

NEEDED RESEARCH

Significant areas for research related to the propositions presented above are now considered. Propositions 7.1, 7.1.i, and 7.1.ii deal with consumers' processing abilities and limitations. Research which is directed at ascertaining what processing abilities consumers possess would be valuable. Also, research on information overload is needed, since current research is not conclusive. Finally, another area for research is characterization of the limitations shown in judgments of uncertain events. The notions of availability and representativeness as heuristics for judging probability have not been applied in consumer choice contexts. Also, the phenomenon of illusory correlation as applied to the price–quality relationship seems worthy of study. If price–quality relations and other variables' relations with quality are manipulated in data presented to subjects, will the actual relationships be perceived, or do consumers have strong expectations about a price–quality relationship that will lead them to ignore the data?

Studies are also needed to assess the array of choice heuristics possessed by individual consumers (Propositions 7.2, 7.3). The types of heuristics available may influence how well the consumer can adapt to various choice environments, and knowledge of which heuristics are most commonly available might be valuable for consumer education efforts. Methods which actually examine processing (protocol, eye movement, response time analysis, information monitoring) seem potentially most useful. Research is also needed into how attitudes and choice processes are related (Proposition 7.3.i). Again process methods seem most useful.

Propositions 7.4 and 7.5 consider methods for implementing consumer choice heuristics. Very little is known in this area, particularly with respect to use of constructive processes. Virtually nothing is known about the nature of the elements or fragments used to construct heuristics: are small segments of a choice rule stored, are content (belief and evaluation) data stored separately from structure (combination rule) data, and so on. Factors that influence the proposed relationships between the various implementation methods and that influence the usage of each method also need study. For example, one might propose that the type of external memory present will influence the relationships between the methods. One could argue that wherever the better external memory exists, in-store (displays) or out-of-store (*Consumer Reports* articles, for example), will be the situation in which constructive methods may tend to be used. Since external memory is better in the store in many cases, this might support the hypothesized relationship between constructive and in-store methods.

An extremely important area for research is development and improvement of methods for observing and analyzing process data (Proposition 7.6). As discussed above, the information integration, protocol, information monitoring, eye movement, and response time approaches all have substantial problems which remain unresolved. Easier and faster methods for obtaining process data and for analyzing that data once obtained are most important goals for future research.

Finally, Propositions 7.7 and 7.8 and its subpropositions emphasize the major need for studies of task properties in consumer choice. Analyses of both actual consumer choice tasks and the properties of experimental tasks given to consumers are needed. Task impacts on the heuristics used by consumers appear to be very powerful, so characterizing those task factors that are most influential is a crucial need. This need for task analyses occurs again and again throughout this book, and is a major future research need.

CHAPTER 8

Decision Nets and
Choice Processes

In Chapter 7 the basic concepts underlying the decision processes component of the theory were considered and several alternative depictions of choice heuristics were proposed (e.g., linear compensatory, conjunctive, lexicographic, and so on). In the present chapter, decision nets are presented as another alternative for modeling choice heuristics. Decision net research is discussed in a separate chapter for several reasons. First, there is a good deal of research on decision nets. Second, and more importantly, decision nets represent a slightly different way of modeling choice heuristics from the rules outlined in Chapter 7. The heuristics presented in Chapter 7 were all relatively simple and well structured; that is, each heuristic could be defined by a fairly simple statement of the operations implied (e.g., for a conjunctive rule, all attributes for a given alternative need to surpass cutoff levels for the alternative to be acceptable). As will become apparent below, decision net models can be more idiosyncratic to the particular individuals modeled, and the resulting rules hence can be more complex and less easily described by some simple structure. Thus in some sense decision nets represent less structured heuristics than those presented in Chapter 7.

As noted above, decision nets are simply another way of representing choice heuristics. Since the basic outline of the decision processes component, the role of choice heuristics, and the linkages between the decision processes component and other components of the theory have already been presented in Chapter 7, the organization of the present chapter departs from those of previous chapters. We begin with a discussion of the concept of a decision net, defining the phenomenon considered. The second section of the chapter reviews previous research on decision nets. Limitations of the decision net approach are discussed in a third section, followed by a section on the methods for analyzing decision nets. Finally, needed areas for research are presented.

THE CONCEPT OF A DECISION NET

The decision net approach to studying information processing has been characterized by the viewpoint that a good way to understand decision processes is to start with individual subjects, and build detailed models of the choice heuristics used by these particular individuals in specific choice situations; that is, an individual may have certain rules or heuristics for combining and manipulating information in making choices, and a model of these decision processes would actually depict all of the detailed heuristics used. In psychology this work was started by Newell and Simon (1958, 1972), and there have been studies of this type carried out in many fields. Of particular interest for the present, of course, are those studies carried out in consumer choice. Thus, in general, decision net research concentrates on models of particular buyers' actual choice heuristics.

The method usually used in decision net research is to have an individual actually perform the consumer choice behavior of interest, and to have the consumer think out loud as he or she is doing so. This verbal record is called a protocol, and should be distinguished from retrospective questioning of the consumer about the decision. Advantages and disadvantages of this protocol method were discussed in Chapter 7. Given these protocol data, a model of how the consumer makes choices is developed. Such a model usually specifies the attributes of the choice objects or situation that seemed to come into play, and the sequence and method of combination used for these attributes or cues. The particular type of choice heuristic model used in these studies is a *decision net*; that is, the attributes or cues are arrayed in a branching structure, as shown by two hypothetical examples for toothpaste in Fig. 8.1. The order in which attributes are examined is modeled by the path structure of the net. The branches out of each point in the net have often been found to be based merely on whether or not the level of an attribute is satisfactory (e.g., "Is it satisfactorily economical to use?"), or whether or not a certain condition is present (e.g., "Is it available [in stock] at the store?"). In essence, then, a decision net is a flowchart of how consumers appear to combine attribute and situational information.

Net A in Fig. 8.1 shows the typical structure of these decision net models. The consumer first examines whether the particular brand of toothpaste being considered satisfactorily prevents cavities. If it does not, the alternative under consideration is rejected. If it does, whether or not it is satisfactorily economical to use is examined next, and so on. Note that influences of other family members and situational factors such as availability are considered. In this net the in-stock question represents a test for the presence of a condition, whereas the other three questions test whether levels of attributes are satisfactory.

Note that specifications for the three aspects of choice heuristics presented in Proposition 7.2 are implied in the description above. First, the *evalua-*

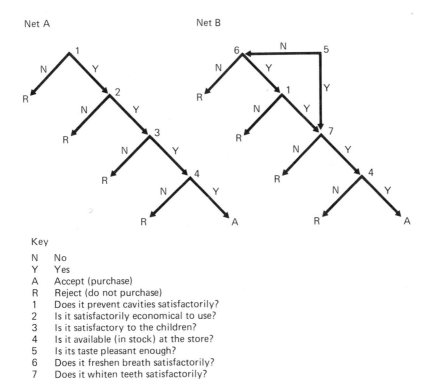

Net A   Net B

Key

N	No
Y	Yes
A	Accept (purchase)
R	Reject (do not purchase)
1	Does it prevent cavities satisfactorily?
2	Is it satisfactorily economical to use?
3	Is it satisfactory to the children?
4	Is it available (in stock) at the store?
5	Is its taste pleasant enough?
6	Does it freshen breath satisfactorily?
7	Does it whiten teeth satisfactorily?

Fig. 8.1 Hypothetical decision nets for toothpaste.

tion developed for each alternative is a *derived* evaluation, with a grouping into acceptable and nonacceptable alternatives. Second, the *choice criterion* has not typically been well specified, which causes some problems, since a decision net may yield more than one acceptable alternative. Some researchers have specified a "Choose the first satisfactory alternative" rule. Finally, the *form of processing* implicitly assumed in almost all applications is brand processing; that is, the nets are used to process one brand alternative at a time, with the alternatives being either chosen or rejected. By applying the net to several brands, one can then predict which brand or brands should be chosen and which should be rejected, and then compare these predictions with the individual's actual choices. In summary, we propose

> *Proposition 8.1.:* Decision nets are another alternative for representing consumer choice heuristics. Decision nets are branching structures using attribute and situational factors to predict acceptance or rejection of an alternative. The three aspects characterizing choice heuristics are specified as follows for decision nets:

a) The evaluation process is derived, not direct.

b) The choice criterion is unspecified in most cases.

c) Form of processing is by brand.

RESEARCH ON DECISION NETS

If consumer choice is conceived broadly, Clarkson (1962) developed the first decision net models of consumer choice behavior. He modeled the rules used by a particular trust investment officer to select stock portfolios. Protocols were used to gather the data, and the process of trust investment was modeled in three parts: selection of a list of stocks suitable for investment, formulation of an investment policy, and selection of a portfolio. The most interesting aspects of the models are the two latter stages. The stage of formulating an investment policy takes information about the client as input, and develops goals for the portfolio as a result (Clarkson 1962, p. 47). Thus the formation of general goals is modeled, one of the rare instances in the literature in which this has been done. Then, depending upon the outputs of the policy formulation stage, *different* decision nets are developed for each general goal. Nets for two of these goals, yield and growth, are shown in Figs. 8.2 and 8.3. Thus Clarkson (1962) explicitly recognizes that different general goals lead to differing choice rules. The model was tested by using it to predict the stocks selected for four accounts the trust investment officer had processed (but after the model had been developed). The model matched 24 of 29 stock selections overall, and was shown to do significantly better than a model that randomly selected from the list of stocks suitable for investment, and also better than several other naive models. Clarkson (1962, pp. 77–90) also presented excerpts from the protocols and compared them to the processes implied by the net. This form of support for net models has since been used by most investigators. Swinth, Gaumnitz, and Rodriguez (1975) report decision net models for stock selection decisions that also perform well.

A series of models of women's clothing choices was presented by Haines and his associates (Alexis, Haines, and Simon 1968; Haines 1974a, b). In these studies, subjects were told they could make three shopping trips, with $25 to spend on the first two and $75 on the third. All clothing purchased could be kept. The women were accompanied on their shopping trips by "interviewers" who carried portable tape recorders, and the subjects were instructed to think out loud during the selection process. Protocols were rejected which were "characterized by long periods of silence, brief descriptions of 'why I am doing this,' and the absence of slang and the redundancy common to ordinary speech" (Haines 1974b, p. 91). The resulting models for selection of dresses (Fig. 8.4) and raincoats (Fig. 8.5) are shown (the women's suits models are shown in Haines 1974b). No results are reported on the match of model choices with actual choices, and it is not clear that multiple choices

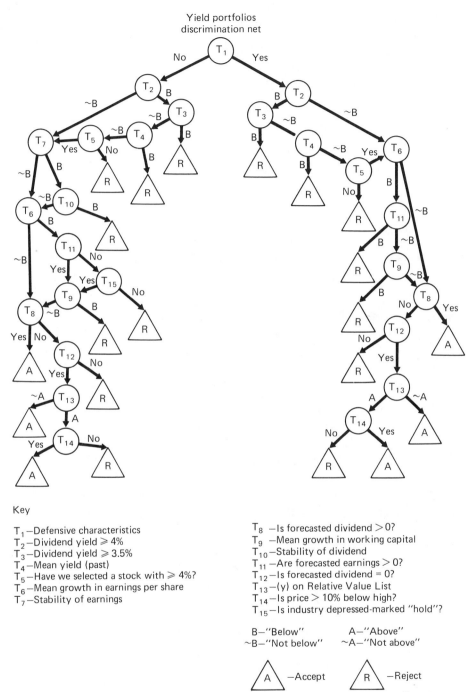

Key

T₁—Defensive characteristics
T_1—Defensive characteristics
T_2—Dividend yield $\geqslant$ 4%
T_3—Dividend yield $\geqslant$ 3.5%
T_4—Mean yield (past)
T_5—Have we selected a stock with $\geqslant$ 4%?
T_6—Mean growth in earnings per share
T_7—Stability of earnings

T_8 —Is forecasted dividend $>$ 0?
T_9 —Mean growth in working capital
T_{10}—Stability of dividend
T_{11}—Are forecasted earnings $>$ 0?
T_{12}—Is forecasted dividend = 0?
T_{13}—(y) on Relative Value List
T_{14}—Is price $>$ 10% below high?
T_{15}—Is industry depressed-marked "hold"?

B—"Below"   A—"Above"
~B—"Not below"   ~A—"Not above"

A —Accept   R —Reject

Fig. 8.2 Clarkson's yield portfolio stock selection model. (Taken from Geoffrey P.E. Clarkson 1962, *Portfolio Selection: A Simulation of Trust Investment,* Prentice-Hall, p. 110.)

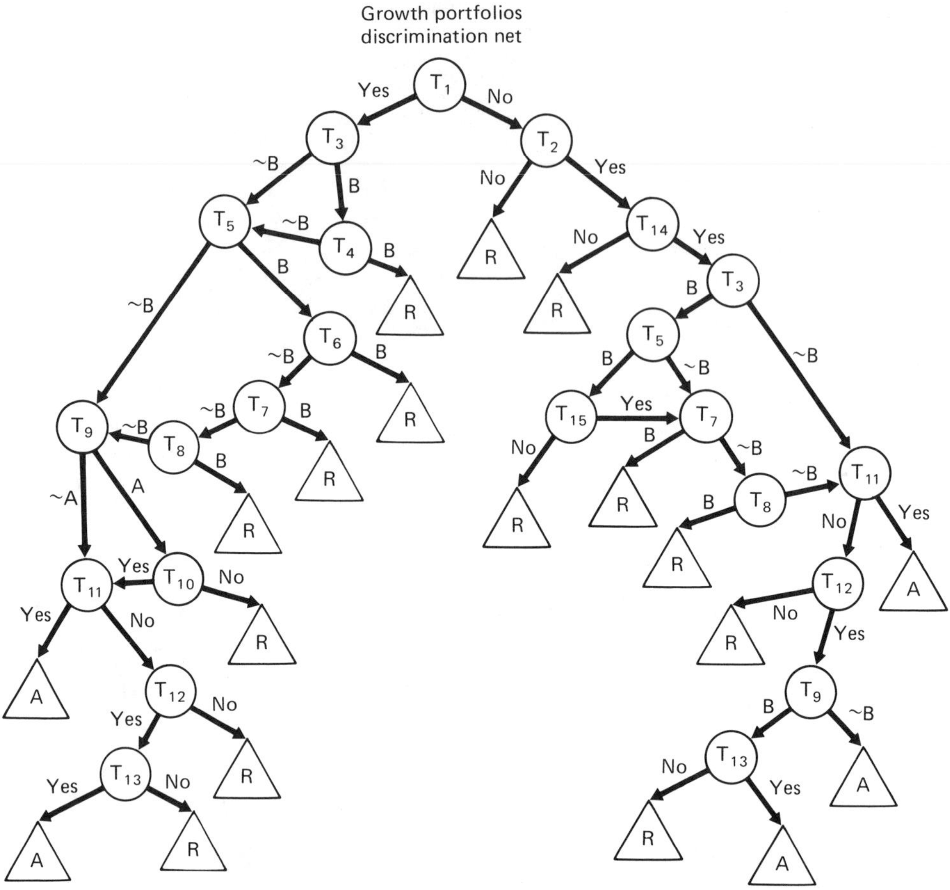

Fig. 8.3 Clarkson's growth portfolio stock selection model. (Taken from Geoffrey P.E. Clarkson 1962, *Portfolio Selection: A Simulation of Trust Investment*, Prentice-Hall, p. 111.)

were in fact made. However, the models seem to mirror the protocols presented.

A general decision net framework for examining buyer choices for grocery products was developed by King (1969). This framework, based on protocol data, used very general "processing units" (e.g., "apply shopper's brand knowledge and decide to buy or not to buy"). No detailed models for these individual "processing units" have been reported, however, and no data were processed through the model.

Detailed models of two consumers' grocery product choices were reported by Bettman (1970). Two housewives were modeled, and protocols were collected from them with a tape recorder each time they shopped over a six- to eight-week period. Instructions to think aloud as they shopped were given. The models developed for each consumer were seemingly quite different. The decisions for one consumer (labeled C_1 and depicted in Fig. 8.6) were based largely upon price. For the other consumer, decisions were made based upon preferences of her husband and others, and desires for convenience and freshness (this model is shown in Bettman 1970). The models are much more detailed than the framework proposed by King (1969), but still leave many branches in the net at a very general level, providing a lower level of explanation than might be desired. For example, such cues as "Do children or husband have a preference?", "Does this class have health (hygiene) factors?", or "Is the cheapest brand good enough?" need to have more detailed explanatory models. The Alexis, Haines, and Simon (1968; Haines 1974a,b) models suffer from the same problem. One of the important cues in the Bettman models that was specifically measured was perceived risk, with different parts of the nets being used depending on the degree of risk present. However, degree of conflict may have been the actual underlying factor, rather than perceived risk, as argued in earlier chapters.

The net models developed by Bettman were used to process one alternative at a time, either accepting or rejecting it. A sample of alternatives was processed through the models, consisting of both choice alternatives from the shopping trips used to develop the model and choice alternatives from validation shopping trips taken four months later. Approximately 87 per cent of the overall choices were correctly matched. This figure may be biased upward due to the general nature of the branches and the subjective coding decisions required for many of these cues in processing the data. However, the results still appear quite good. Also, excerpts from the protocols seemed to support the form of models.

Two final comments about the Bettman models are necessary. First, the models are more complex than those presented by Haines et al. (Alexis, Haines, and Simon 1968; Haines 1974a,b) and Clarkson (1962). This may be because the Bettman models cover many product classes, whereas these other models are more narrowly focused. In this sense, the increased complexity is

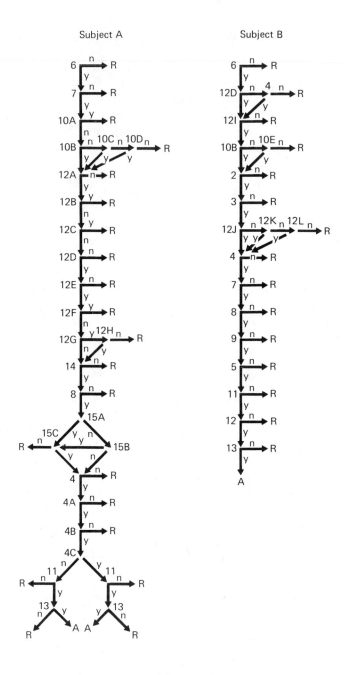

Key

A   Accept
R   Reject
n   No
y   Yes
2.   Do I need this type of item?
3.   Do I have this type of item, color included, already in my wardrobe?
4.   Is the item practical—in style, in fabric—i.e., will it be comfortable to wear and easy to care for?
   a)   Is it a dress I could not make?
   b)   Is it well made?
   c)   Can I wear it in many situations?
5.   Is the item on sale?
6.   Is my size available?
7.   Is the item within the price range I can afford?
8.   Does the item fit in hips, thighs, rear, and at the waist?
9.   Does the item fit at the neckline, shoulders, and bustline?
10.   Color
   a)   Is it black?
   b)   Is it yellow or blue?
   c)   Is it red with white flowers?
   d)   Are the colors not too bright?
   e)   Green, cranberry, or butterscotch print?
11.   Is the item worth the price?
12.   Do I like the item in general?
   a)   Does it have large, rounded, glossy buttons?
   b)   Does it have short cap sleeves?
   c)   Is it a shirtwaist, or does it accent the waist?
   d)   Does it have long sleeves?
   e)   Is it youthful and/or innocent and demure?
   f)   Is the skirt straight?
   g)   Is the skirt pleated?
   h)   Is it not polka dot or clashing patterns?
   i)   Round or roll (cowl) collar?
   j)   Cotton or synthetic mixture?
   k)   Cotton pique?
   l)   Arnel knit?
13.   Do I like it better than other dresses considered?
14.   Is it a known and favored brand?
15.   Length
   a   Is it too long?
   b   Is it too short?
   c   Can the length be easily adjusted?

Fig. 8.4 Women's dress shopping decision models. (Adapted from Alexis, Haines, and Simon, 1968, pp. 201–204.)

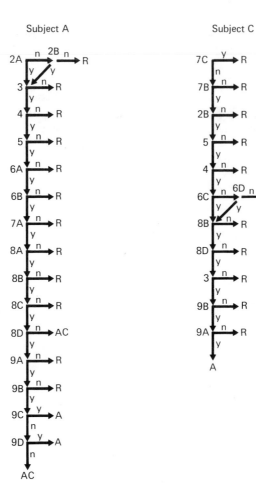

Key

A   Accept
R   Reject
AC   Accept conditionally
n   No
y   Yes

2.   Is it desired brand:
       a)   London Fog?
       b)   Misty Harbor?
3.   Is it lined?
4.   Is my size available?
5.   Is it within the desired price range?
6.   Style:
       a)   Does it not have "football" shoulders?
       b)   Is it A-line or straight?
       c)   Turndown collar?
       d)   Mandarin collar?
7.   Color:
       a)   Is it dark blue, black, or beige?
       b)   Is it blue or peacock (blue with some green in it)?
       c)   Is it orange?
8.   Fit:
       a)   Is it not tight underarms and without pull across back?
       b)   Are sleeves right length?
       c)   Does it fit correctly without the lining?
       d)   Is the length correct?
9.   Practicality:
       a)   Is it easy to care for?
       b)   Can it be worn with most of my clothes?
       c)   Is a less expensive lining unavailable?
       d)   Is the more expensive lining worth the difference?

Fig. 8.5 Raincoat shopping decision models. (Adapted from Haines, 1974a, pp. 111–114.)

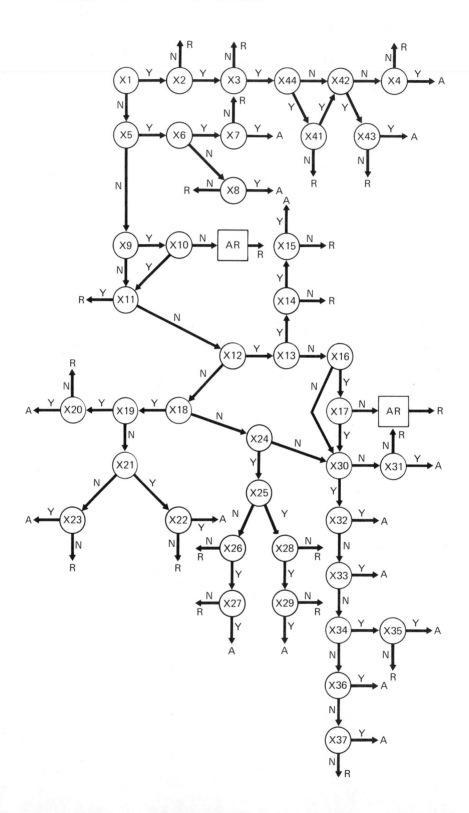

Key

A: Accept
R: Reject
AR: Associate risk (bad experience) with this
      product
Y: Yes
N: No

X1:   Is this meat or produce?
X2:   Is price below justified level?
X3:   Is color okay?
X4:   Is this the biggest "okay" one?
X5:   Are these eggs?
X6:   Is the price of extra large over five cents more than the price of large?
X7:   Is this large size?
X8:   Is this extra large size?
X9:   Was this product bought last time for this product type?
X10:   Was experience with it okay?
X11:   Is risk associated with this product (bad experience)?
X12:   Is this product class high risk?
X13:   Do children or husband have a specific preference?
X14:   Is this their preference?
X15:   Is it the cheapest size?
X16:   Does this class have health (hygiene, diet) factors?
X17:   Is this okay on these factors?
X18:   Is this for company?
X19:   Is the cheapest brand good enough?
X20:   Is this the cheapest?
X21:   Had a good experience with any brands in this class?
X22:   Is this that brand?
X23:   Is this the cheapest national brand?
X24:   Are children the main users?
X25:   Did they state a preference this week?
X26:   Have they used this up in the last two weeks?
X27:   Is this cheapest size?
X28:   Is this that one?
X29:   Is this the cheapest size?
X30:   Are several "okay" brands cheapest (that they have in stock)?
X31:   Is this the cheapest (that they have in stock)?
X32:   Have a coupon for this one?
X33:   Is this one biggest?
X34:   Is there a single national brand?
X35:   Is this it?
X36:   Have I used this before?
X37:   Is this the closest?
X41:   Does this feel okay?
X42:   Is this for a specific use?
X43:   Is this size okay for that?
X44:   Is this produce?

Fig. 8.6 The model for consumer C_1. (Reprinted from James R. Bettman, 1970, Information processing models of consumer behavior. *Journal of Marketing Research* 7 (August): 371. Published by the American Marketing Association.)

merely a reflection of the increased complexity of the task environment modeled (Newell and Simon 1972; Simon 1969). Second, several authors (e.g., Wright and Barbour 1975; Pras and Summers 1975) have characterized the Bettman and Haines *et al.* models as lexicographic. This is clearly not correct, for several reasons. First, these decision net models postulate processing by *brand*, rather than the processing by attribute assumed by the lexicographic model. The underlying choice process depicted was thus quite different from a lexicographic process. Second, nets that do not have a simple single-branch structure do not mirror the structure required for the lexicographic rule, in addition to the differences in form of processing.

Russ (1971) examined buyer brand evaluations in another area, small household appliances (frying pans, electric coffee makers, irons, portable radios, and table and clock radios). Protocols were taken at two different points in time for each individual, but in an experimental rather than in an actual shopping setting. Russ examined predictions of various types of choice rules to choose a "best" model. He found that a model which combined an initial conjunctive satisfying phase with a lexicographic semiorder choice phase was most accurate. Although Russ did not directly do so himself, nets can be developed from his protocol data. Examples of such nets developed by the present author are shown in Fig. 8.7.

Finally, two recent papers have studied the processes used by supermarket officials in making product-related choices. Rados (1972) developed a flowchart model of the heuristics used by an executive to make the weekly advertising decision (i.e., what products to include in the weekly newspaper ad) for a division of a large supermarket chain. The form of the model was related to propositions made by Cyert and March (1963) in their behavioral theory of the firm, but the model was not used to process data and match predicted choices with actual choices in the article. Montgomery (1975) developed what he termed a "gatekeeping" model of supermarket buying committee accept–reject decisions for new products. He used a heuristic procedure to develop a net structure, rather than protocols, after determining appropriate cues for these nets by observing buying committee decisions and by interviewing those involved in the decision. The resulting net correctly matched 115 of 124 decisions, or 93 percent. A linear discriminant analysis model matched 107 of the 124 decisions, or 86 percent.

The studies above have several general characteristics in common. First, research using decision nets has concentrated on a deterministic approach to modeling choice, with stochastic elements not playing a role in these models. Instead of subsuming the effects of different situations or individual differences in a stochastic error term, these factors are included in the model directly as much as possible. Second, the models have been developed for particular individuals, and the results show the idiosyncratic nature of consumers' choice heuristics. In those cases above in which several consumers were modeled, the models are in general quite different. This idiosyncratic na-

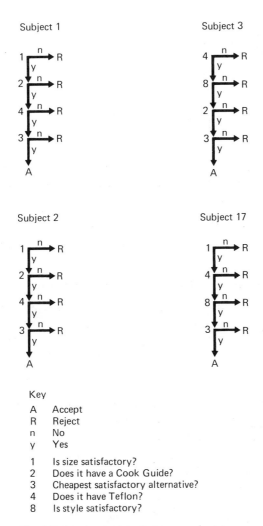

Key

A   Accept
R   Reject
n   No
y   Yes

1   Is size satisfactory?
2   Does it have a Cook Guide?
3   Cheapest satisfactory alternative?
4   Does it have Teflon?
8   Is style satisfactory?

Fig. 8.7 Russ's electric frying pan decision models. (Reprinted from James R. Bettman, 1971. A graph theory approach to comparing consumer information processing models. *Management Science* **18** (December, Part II): P-127.

ture of the models supports the point made above that decision nets are a slightly different way of depicting choice heuristics from the heuristics in Chapter 7. These earlier heuristics (e.g., conjunctive, lexicographic) assume a constant *general structure,* but idiosyncratic parameters. For example, the conjunctive rule always assumes that attribute levels must surpass cutoffs, but allows the particular attributes to be included and the particular cutoffs used to vary. Decision net models, on the other hand, make no assumptions about constant general structure, except in the very broadest sense that a branching net of some sort is used. As noted above, decision nets are thus in some ways a representation of less structured heuristics than those developed in Chapter 7.[1] This idiosyncratic nature of decision net models can cause problems in generalizing the results found. This problem is discussed further below. Finally, the research on decision nets has emphasized the importance of situational factors and properties of choice tasks. In summary,

> *Proposition 8.2:* Decision nets have been successfully applied to modeling consumer choices. This research has been characterized by
>
> a) A deterministic approach to modeling choice
>
> b) Idiosyncratic models of particular individuals
>
> c) An emphasis on situational and choice environment factors

LIMITATIONS OF THE DECISION NET APPROACH

Although decision net research has been relatively successful in modeling consumer choices, there are several areas in which limitations of the previous research are apparent. The two major areas are the depiction of the way decision nets are implemented, and notions related to form of processing and the range of choice heuristics which can be depicted by decision nets. This is stated as

> *Proposition 8.3:* Two major areas in which limitations are found in decision net research are in the characterization of
>
> a) The implementation methods used
>
> b) The form of processing used and the range of choice heuristics depicted

IMPLEMENTATION OF DECISION NETS

In Chapter 7 the notion of implementation of a choice heuristic was discussed, and several alternative implementation methods were considered. One of the most cogent critiques of decision net research (Nakanishi 1974) concerns the implementation methods implicitly assumed in this research:

---

1. Howard (1977) argues that decision nets are used in the most structured choice situations (routinized response behavior) and that linear compensatory approaches are used in less structured situations. This view seems contrary to consumers' processing limitations, however, and Park (1976) suggests that weighted linear models are more appropriate under conditions of high familiarity. The binary cutoffs used in net models may be all the consumer can use initially, since little knowledge is present. Thus nets may be used in either very complex or very simple situations, with other rules requiring more detailed knowledge being used in intermediate situations.

that a net was a fixed program, recalled in its entirety from memory and rigidly followed by the subject during a decision. Thus use of stored rule and recall methods was assumed.

Nakanishi notes that several of the net models developed are complex, and "since memorizing the exact sequence of more than a dozen cues would be extremely difficult, it is hard to believe that subjects in previous studies executed those information-processing rules in a predetermined sequence" (Nakanishi 1974, p. 77). In addition, as noted above, many cues are modeled at a very general level. Thus Nakanishi (1974 p. 77) states that "decision net models so far published tend to be too complex for a subject to memorize in their entirety, but are still too oversimplified to explain all of the mental activities accompanying a purchase decision." Finally, Nakanishi argues that such a fixed sequence of cue processing ignores environmental or task influences and temporary "states of mind" of the individual. More realistically, the sequence of cues may be affected by the environment, particularly to the extent that the environment is variable and to the extent that the individual tends to process in the actual shopping environment rather than doing a *priori* planning.

These arguments imply that use of recall and stored rules may not be likely in many complex consumer choice situations. Of course, if a decision is made repetitively in a stable environment, over time a fixed learned sequence of processing may occur. However, this may only be a special case. Nakanishi's arguments imply that other implementation methods, such as constructive, recognition, and in-store processing, are likely in other circumstances, particularly situations in which there is little prior experience (see Proposition 7.5). The findings of Bettman and Zins (1977), reported in Chapter 7, support this argument. They found, using the protocol data collected by Bettman (1970), that there was evidence for the use of constructive processes in these data (about 25 percent of the choice episodes which could be classified by judges were deemed constructive in nature).[2] Thus the rigid implementation notions of the previous decision net studies seem clearly incorrect.

This rejection of the stored rule and recall implementation notions of previous decision net research causes some problems in interpreting the results of this prior research. In particular, if constructive methods were used by consumers in these studies, it is not clear what the resulting decision nets depict. In the simplest case, if the consumer was studied in an environment that remained stable throughout the data collection process, a decision net could represent the choice heuristic "as constructed," with the realization that the actual implementation method was a constructive process. However, in

---

2. Nakanishi (1974) proposed a specific constructive process, a contiguous retrieval model, that is based upon retrieval of elements that are closely associated with one another in memory. Such associative retrieval is one form a constructive process may take, but it is not the only one. As noted earlier, little research has been carried out on constructive mechanisms.

general, one would expect the choice environment to vary, and hence might expect some changes in the choice heuristic from one situation to the next. In such a case, the interpretation of the net developed in the research is not clear. Perhaps such a net represents the "average" outcome of the constructive process over the situations studied. Although the answer to this problem is not evident, the view of decision nets as implemented by constructive or other methods is a significant departure from the assumptions underlying previous research on decision nets. In summary, we state

> *Proposition 8.3.i:* Decision nets can be implemented using a range of implementation methods. Prior conceptions of the use of stored rule and recall methods alone are too rigid. Constructive and other methods may also be used. Use of constructive methods causes problems in interpreting the decision nets found in previous research.

FORM OF PROCESSING AND THE RANGE
OF CHOICE HEURISTICS DEPICTED IN DECISION NETS

A second challenge to past research on decision net models has come from the recent studies on choice processes reviewed in Chapter 7. These studies found that in many cases processing by attribute rather than by brand was prevalent. This finding about form of processing is directly contradictory to the use in decision net research of processing by brand—one brand at a time is processed through the net and either accepted or rejected. This may not be as contradictory as it appears, however. The decision net results are based for the most part on in-store protocols. Store displays are typically arranged by brand. Thus brand processing may in fact be used to a great extent in such a situation. The studies finding attribute processing typically used tasks where attribute processing could be performed easily. Thus the difference in findings may be due to task differences (Svenson 1974; Van Raaij 1976b; Bettman and Kakker 1977). Also, if nonnumerical attribute values (e.g., semantic ratings from memory) are used, more processing by brand may result, since differences would be hard to compute for the attributes (Russo and Dosher 1975). Finally, consumers with greater experience may be accustomed to use of brand processing (Bettman and Kakker 1977).

However, it is likely that processing by brand is not the only form of processing used in decision nets. Processing form, as intimated above, is undoubtedly flexible and adaptive to the particular task environment. Even previous decision net models have indirectly introduced attribute processing, by examining such cues as "Is this the cheapest?", or "Is this one biggest?" Thus processing by attribute should be allowed as a plausible alternative form of processing for decision nets. The question then becomes whether decision nets, with both attribute and brand processing considered, are able to depict the range of choice heuristics potentially used by consumers. One way of examining this question is to see whether the various types of heuristics depicted in Chapter 7 can be represented. It should be noted that processing by attribute or by brand is a specification that is *independent* of the *structure* of the net. For example, consider a single branch net such as the hypothetical Net A in Fig. 8.1.[3] If processing by brand is assumed, that net represents a conjunctive model. If processing by attribute is assumed, with elimination of non-satisfactory alternatives at each step, a form of sequential elimination model is obtained. In fact, Tversky (1972) states that the elimination by aspects model can be interpreted as having such a net in any *given* situation, but having the sequencing of cues in the net vary over situations. Disjunctive models can also be depicted, assuming brand processing in the net, by a single branch net of the form where a "positive" answer to any of the tests leads to acceptance. Finally, compensatory aspects can also be modeled by decision nets with brand processing. For example, in Net B of Fig 8.1, if taste is not pleasant, this can be compensated for by satisfactory ability to freshen breath and prevent cavities.

   Although decision nets can represent a wide variety of heuristics, therefore, even respecification of form of processing will not suffice to allow nets to depict some other choice heuristics. For several of these heuristics, *comparisons across alternatives* are needed, rather than the *comparisons to a standard* assumed in decision nets. For the lexicographic model, for example, the most important attribute must be determined, and then the best brand for that attribute determined. This could be modeled in a net by a standard revision strategy, with a test of the form "Is this better than the previous best?", but this seems very contrived. For the heuristic version of the additive difference model, differences on attributes are calculated, and then perhaps the number of attributes on which each alternative is best is calculated. These processes again require extensions to the binary tests used in decision nets. Finally, phased processes require some process to keep track of which alternatives have been eliminated and which remain.

   Thus the answer to our question raised above is that nets of binary tests alone *cannot* represent the potential range of heuristics used in choice processes. The analysis above has shown that other heuristic mechanisms are needed. One might then ask what *is* the role of decision nets using binary tests in depicting choice processes? Are more general flowcharts or process models always required? These questions cannot be answered precisely at this point. However, several statements can be made. First, decision nets with binary tests and processing by brand may be used in situations where processing by attribute is difficult. For example, Svenson's (1974) protocol data support this notion. He found that in his protocols 71 percent of all comparison references

---

3. Approximately single branch nets have been found when choices for single product categories have been studied (Alexis, Haines, and Simon 1968; Haines 1974a,b). Nets with multiple branches tend to be found when decisions for several product classes are modeled (e.g., Bettman 1970).

were comparisons to a standard, and 29 percent were comparisons between alternatives.[4] He also found that the standard seemed to stay relatively constant over the course of a choice process. Since Svenson's stimuli were detailed booklets for each alternative, attribute processing should have been discouraged. Second, decision nets, since they class alternatives into acceptable and nonacceptable groups, might be used for the *elimination phase* of a phased process, perhaps using brand processing. Then another heuristic might be used to make a final choice among the set of acceptable alternatives. In this case, study of nets as the implementation of the elimination phase would be warranted.

Thus decision net representations using binary tests alone may still be quite useful. However, in general, more extended processing notions will need to be used, such as across alternative comparisons, calculations performed across alternatives and dimensions, and so on. Perhaps these could be expressed in decision nets by careful delineation of the form of processing for alternatives and clever definition of binary tests, but more general models seem to be required, using decision net notions as only one part. Decision net models have implicitly assumed some of these more general processes rather than incorporating them (e.g., the "Is this the cheapest?" test noted above). Other problems in decision net research related to data collection, modeling methodology, and change and learning in net models are discussed in Bettman (1974a). In conclusion, we state

> *Proposition 8.3.ii:* Prior characterizations of decision nets as using only brand processing may be true in some situations but, in general, attribute processing is also possible. Even if attribute processing is allowed, decision nets can still not depict certain types of choice heuristics. Decision nets must be augmented with other types of processing heuristics.

ANALYSIS METHODS FOR DECISION NETS[5]

In the section above describing prior decision net research, depictions of the models as branching structures were simply presented. Further characterizations of the models were not attempted. However, to gain more insights into decision net models, methods for analyzing such models are needed. Such methods are reported in this section. Following a brief digression on typical research methods used to study consumer choice, a graph theory framework for studying decision nets is developed. Then several applications to analyz-

---

4. Wright (1974d, p. 274) notes that this type of finding may be due to biases in protocol data. Subjects may report only cutoffs, not the processing which produced them, or they may present only thoughts related to "final solutions" or "crucial cues."

5. This section is largely taken from Bettman (1971a and 1974c).

ing decision nets are proposed: measures of decision net structure; measures of information processing efficiency; measures of similarity and grouping of individuals; measures of reliability in developing decision nets; and measures of attribute weights. Techniques are developed and then applied to both the actual models discussed in earlier sections and to hypothetical decision net data. Finally, limitations of these techniques, particularly in light of the problems with prior decision net research discussed above, are considered. Thus we may state

> *Proposition 8.4:* Analysis methods are needed for further characterizing decision net models. Graph theory techniques are useful in developing such methods. In particular, methods are available for providing
>
> a) Measures of decision net structure
> b) Measures of information processing efficiency
> c) Measures of similarity and grouping of individuals
> d) Measures of reliability in developing decision net models
> e) Measures of attribute weights

The analytical methods used in consumer research have usually been of two sorts. In one type of study, theoretical notions, previous studies, or intuition are used to postulate certain hypotheses. An appropriate experiment is designed to test these hypotheses that includes a specification of which measurements will be examined. These measures are then analyzed by using statistical methods and the hypotheses accepted or rejected. The second sort of analysis takes as its starting point some situation of interest. This situation is then observed, and the observations are codified into some number of measurements describing the situation. These measures are then explored using statistical tools to see if any interesting regularities occur. The hope, of course, is that this will lead to further studies of the first type.

Consumer decision net research has not really followed either of these traditions. In decision net studies, the approach, as shown above, has been to observe consumers, codify these observations into a decision net, and possibly examine the descriptive and predictive validity of the net. This takes the same point of view as the exploratory research outlined above, but stops short of attempting to explore for regularities. This has led to shortcomings in consumer decision net research. The findings of different researchers have been difficult to interrelate; the models all seem idiosyncratic, as generalization has been difficult due to model complexity; and few stable content-oriented findings have been reported.

One major factor leading to these difficulties is the lack of a theory of "statistics" for decision nets. In cases where the measurements are numbers, many well-defined and well-known procedures exist for combination and analysis. However, the decision net approach yields complex nets as its data points. The problem is that there are no techniques for combining or analyzing this type of datum. This section presents several types of analytical procedures that can be used to examine decision nets. By using such tools, it is hoped that regularities and patterns in consumer choice processes can emerge from future decision net studies, rather than simply complex diagrams.

A GRAPH THEORY FRAMEWORK

To provide a terminology for the analysis, rudiments of graph theoretic notation are given. It has been noted that consumer decision nets for purchasing or not purchasing products can be fruitfully looked at as graphs (Bettman 1969, 1971a, 1974c). A graph consists of a set of points, or nodes, with lines (arcs) connecting pairs of nodes. In the graphs considered here, the arcs are specifically directed from one node to another. Consumer decision nets can then be represented as follows: each node represents a test of a particular attribute or condition (e.g., "Is price high?"). The arcs out of each node depict the sequence of processing taken, depending upon the outcome of the test; that is, the arcs lead to whichever condition should be checked next, given the outcome at the present node. Eventually a purchase or no purchase decision is made. For example, Fig. 8.8 is a simple hypothetical decision net with five attributes. Processing would proceed as follows: if attribute 1 is not present, reject; if it is, check attribute 2, and so on.

Several concepts and some notation from graph theory will be necessary in the development to follow. A path from some node *i* to some other node *j* is a sequence of arcs leading from node *i* to node *j* which takes arc direction into account. In Fig. 8.8 there is a path from node 1 to node 4, but no path from node 5 *to* node 2, because arc directions are not correct. Given a graph, one can enumerate all the paths through that graph. In the graph of

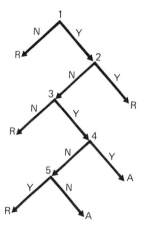

Fig. 8.8 Hypothetical decision net with five attributes. Each node represents a test of whether or not the attribute is present in an alternative. N = No; Y = Yes; A = Accept the alternative; R = Reject the alternative. (Reprinted from James R. Bettman, 1974, Toward a statistics for consumer decision net models. *Journal of Consumer Research* **1** (June): 73.)

Fig. 8.8 there are six paths which start at node 1: 1 to R; 1 to 2 to R; 1 to 2 to 3 to R; 1 to 2 to 3 to 4 to A; 1 to 2 to 3 to 4 to 5 to A; and 1 to 2 to 3 to 4 to 5 to R. Of these six paths, two lead to acceptance or purchase, and will be called *acceptable paths*. If we have a set of data representing a particular consumer's choices to which the net has been applied, relative frequencies for traversing each arc can be calculated. Hypothetical frequencies for the graph of Fig. 8.8, based on a set of alternatives processed over some time period by a particular consumer, are given in Table 8.1. Given such data, the relative frequency with which that consumer went down a particular path can be obtained by multiplying the relative frequencies corresponding to arcs on the path. For example, for the path from 1 to 2 to 3 to 4 to A, the probability is $(.80)(.375)(.70)(.20) = .042$.

TABLE 8.1
Hypothetical arc traversal frequencies for Fig. 8.8[a]

FROM	TO	FREQUENCY
1	R	.20
1	2	.80
2	R	.625
2	3	.375
3	R	.30
3	4	.70
4	A	.20
4	5	.80
5	A	.50
5	R	.50

[a] Reprinted from James R. Bettman, Toward a statistics for consumer decision net models, *Journal of Consumer Research* **1** (June 1974): 73.

Finally, the length of a path is simply the number of arcs it contains. Then the distance from node i to node j is given by the length of the shortest path from node i to node j, and is denoted by d_{ij}. If there is no path, the distance is considered to be infinite. Given this graph theory vocabulary, methods for analysis can now be outlined.

MEASURES OF DECISION NET STRUCTURE

Even in the absence of any evidence about how a decision net performs for some actual set of data, measures that depend purely upon the structure of the graph representing the decision net can be developed. These measures may say something about how information is combined, or the relationships among attributes.

One set of measures of this type is the length of the longest and of the shortest acceptable path in a decision net. These measures represent upper and lower limits to the amount of information (i.e., number of attributes) that must be processed to arrive at an acceptable alternative, and hence give some indications about the potential information demands in a decision net. These measures were computed for the following examples of consumer decision nets in the literature: Haines' women's suit nets (Haines 1974b); Haines' raincoat nets (Haines 1974a and Fig. 8.5); Alexis, Haines, and Simon's women's dress nets (Alexis, Haines, and Simon 1968 and Fig. 8.4); and Clarkson's yield and growth portfolio selection models (Clarkson 1962 and Fig. 8.2 and 8.3). The results are shown in Table 8.2. The average length for an acceptable path is also given. Note that Haines' models as a group depict a much tighter range of processing than do the Clarkson models. That mirrors the model structures—if processing by brand is assumed, Haines' models are very nearly conjunctive models (i.e., all attributes must be at a satisfactory level) containing one long path (in fact Consumer 2 for women's suits has exactly this type of net). The Clarkson models have more branching. That is, there are many paths for making accept–reject decisions in the Clarkson models, rather than just one.

A second type of measure relates to how deep a node is in the decision net (i.e., in what order the attributes are processed). The deeper the node is in the net, the later the attribute is considered in the decision process. If there is only one path from the first node in the net to a particular node, then the distance from the first node to that node represents an unambiguous measure of depth.[6] For example, for Fig. 8.8, node 2 is of depth 1, node 3 of depth 2, and so on. If there is more than one such path, the average length of these paths can be taken to be the depth of the node.[7] In the example of Fig. 8.8, the depth of node 4 is 3. If there had been another path from node 1 to node 4 of length 4, the depth would then be 3.5. Call the depth of node i D_i. These individual D_i measures give an indication of the order in which an attribute is considered. Hence, they can be used in conjunction with other data to examine which factors explain attribute sequence in the decision process.

In addition, an overall measure of the length of processing the net requires is given by the average of the D_i measures for all nodes. If there are p nodes in total, this would be given by $\sum_{i=1}^{p} D_i/p$. If a net has several short paths, this measure would be small, since no path would be very long. If the net has one long path, the measure would be larger. In fact, for a net consisting of a single path with p nodes, the measure is exactly $(p-1)/2$. In a sense this measure depicts the depth versus breadth properties of the net. This measure is also

---

6. For characterizations of graphs where this is possible, see Harary, Norman, and Cartwright (1965), pp. 267–280, 287–288.

7. Multiple occurrences of an attribute in a net could complicate this procedure. For such cases in this section, the simple alternative of averaging the lengths of all paths to the attribute, regardless of how many places in the net the attribute appears, was taken.

TABLE 8.2
Measures of decision net structure[a]

MODEL	NODES	LENGTH OF SHORTEST ACCEPTABLE PATH	AVERAGE LENGTH OF ACCEPTABLE PATH	LENGTH OF LONGEST ACCEPTABLE PATH	AVERAGE DEPTH OF NODES
Haines' Women's Suit, 1[b]	22	16	19.00	22	9.02
Haines' Women's Suit, 2	12	12	12.00	12	5.50
Haines' Raincoat, A	16	14	15.17	16	7.03
Haines' Raincoat, C	12	11	11.50	12	5.13
Haines' Clothing, A	25	21	22.67	25	10.84
Haines' Clothing, B	18	15	17.00	19	8.15
Clarkson's Yield	15	4	9.79	15	5.11
Clarkson's Growth	15	5	8.68	12	4.27

[a] Reprinted from James R. Bettman, Toward a statistics for consumer decision net models, *Journal of Consumer Research* **1** (June 1974): 74.
[b] The numbers and letters are the identifications given to subjects in these studies.

shown in Table 8.2. Again the measure mirrors the shorter paths in the Clarkson models, although the nets themselves look more complicated. There are many short processing paths in these models, and not in the Haines models.

A final measure of decision net structure requires additional input from the subject. This measure was proposed by Swinth (1976). Swinth proposed taking the set of acceptable paths and having the subject rank these paths in order of preference; that is, a path defines a set of attribute values. Although several combinations of attribute values may be acceptable, some combinations may be preferred to others. Thus Swinth was attempting to develop a finer metric for alternatives than the simple binary accept–reject notion. Swinth applied this preference technique to prediction of graduate business students' job choices with moderate success (Swinth 1976, p. 15). The technique was less successful in ranking selections of stocks for investment (Swinth, Gaumnitz, and Rodriguez 1975).

MEASURES OF INFORMATION PROCESSING EFFICIENCY

Bettman (1971b) and Haines (1974b) have suggested that in certain situations subjects may "collapse" their decision nets to simpler structures (i.e., they examine fewer attributes) if there are patterns of attributes in the environment that the subject has learned to expect. On the basis of such results, Haines formulated what he termed the principle of information processing parsimony: "Consumers seek to process as little data as is necessary in order to make rational decisions" (Haines 1974b, p. 96). Testing the implications of such a notion may require, among other things, a measure of the information processing efficiency of a decision net.

Efficiency is measured here only relative to some given set of data which has been processed through the net. From such data, relative frequencies of arc traversal such as those shown in Table 8.1 can be calculated. As shown above, the probability of traversing a given path can then be determined. If we define

P = set of all paths through the net

π_j = probability of traversing path j for data set X

L_j = length of path j (number of arcs in path j)

$E(X)$ = information processing efficiency for data set X,

then a measure of information processing efficiency can be defined by

$$E(X) = \sum_{j \in P} \pi_j L_j. \tag{8.1}$$

This gives the expected number of arcs traversed (or expected number of attributes considered) for application of the net to an alternative, which may measure the average amount of information that needs to be examined for any particular alternative. Thus smaller values of $E(X)$ may correspond to more efficient nets. This measure is always specific to a given data set (or given environment where the data set was collected, therefore) because of its dependence on π_j. Figure 8.9 shows three hypothetical nets with three attributes and relative frequencies for a given data set. Note that the graphs are identical except for the order of the attributes. The measures of efficiency for the three graphs are 1.95, 2.35, and 1.80, respectively. Net 1 has four paths: a path from node 1 of length one with probability .5; a path from node 1 through node 2 of length two with probability (.5)(.1) = .05; a path from node 1 through nodes 2 and 3 of length three with probability (.5)(.9)(.4) = .18; and a path from node 1 through nodes 2 and 3 of length three with probability (.5)(.9)(.6) = .27. Thus a sample computation (for graph 1) is $E = .5(1) + .05(2) + .27(3) + .18(3)$, or $E = 1.95$. This set of examples in Fig. 8.9 shows how it is more efficient (in terms of examining fewer attributes on the average) to have those nodes which will lead to quick judgments (e.g., shorter paths) for relatively more alternatives placed earlier in the net. The measure cannot be applied to the models used in earlier sections because the underlying data for the models, needed to develop the arc traversal relative frequencies, are not presented in the published accounts.

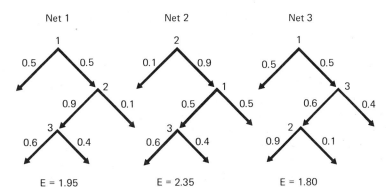

Fig. 8.9 Example decision nets for efficiency computations. Numbers on the nodes label the attribute the node represents. The numbers on the arcs represent the relative frequency of arc traversal. (Reprinted from James R. Bettman, 1974, Toward a statistics for consumer decision net models. *Journal of Consumer Research* **1** (June): 75.)

The efficiency measure above assumes that each attribute requires the same amount of cognitive effort to process, since all arcs are counted equally in obtaining the length of a path. This could be generalized by defining the cost of path j, C_j, as being the amount of the cognitive effort required to process all the arcs in that path. This allows arcs to have different weights. Then the efficiency measure could be modified by simply substituting C_j for L_j in Eq. (8.1). Also, one possible problem with the efficiency measure as proposed is that it is not normalized; that is, it does not take into account the number of nodes in the graph. Graphs with greater numbers of nodes will tend to have larger values for E(X). However, it is not clear, without seeing how the measure behaves in actual cases, whether normalization is desirable or not. If desirable, then one method for accomplishing it would be to divide E(X) by the total number of nodes in the graph.

The efficiency measure could be used to research such questions as the proposed principle of information processing parsimony. Suppose frequency of arc traversal in the subjects' decision processes could be manipulated by the experimenter by changing the types of alternatives presented. Then, since the probabilities for traversing paths would change, the most efficient order for examining nodes might change. If this were the case, then the subjects should change the order in which they examine attributes as they perceive the change in arc traversal frequency. This prediction of the rule of information processing parsimony could thus be examined more rigorously by using the E(X) measure. This use of the measure illustrates how E(X) might be used to examine changes over time in a decision net involving a fixed number of attributes. Note that E(X) does *not* directly deal with net collapsing.

MEASURES OF SIMILARITY AND GROUPING OF INDIVIDUALS

Definition of a similarity measure for decision nets

This section outlines the development of a coefficient to measure how similar two decision net models are to one another. The major motivation for this work was to develop a methodology for deriving generalities from examination of several decision nets by seeing whether groups of consumers with similar heuristics could be found. The definition of this coefficient depends upon the graph theoretic notion of reachability. A node i reaches another node j if there is a path from i to j. By taking the length of the path from i to j into account, we may define $r_{ij}^n(G) = 1$ if there is a path in graph G from node i to node j of length n or less, and $r_{ij}^n(G) = 0$ otherwise. Also, the reachability structure of a pair of graphs may be further characterized by the largest distance measure d_{ij} between a pair of nodes i and j in either of the two graphs. Call this length ℓ. Now the path coefficient and its rationale can be given.

As argued earlier in this chapter, decision process models can be thought of as representing choice heuristics. The essence of a choice heuristic is the particular rules implied for processing information. Therefore, one should compare decision nets in terms of the order in which information is processed and the interrelationships of various types of information as implied by the structure of the nets; that is, if decision nets are represented as graphs, the order and sequence of particular nodes should be examined. Since the nodes in a decision net represent attributes or situational factors, two decision net models may be similar in the way they process information if corresponding nodes are processed in roughly the same sequence and have similar interrelations in the two models. We will refer to attribute and situational factors by the general term "cue" for simplicity in the discussion to follow.

Thus, one way of defining similarity is by examining path and reachability structure. If for some given node i there is a path to node j of length n or less in one model, then if such a path also exists in the second model, this should add to a measure of similarity between the two graphs. Note that it is therefore necessary to label all of the nodes and retain these labels, since the identity of cues is important in making comparisons. Both models will not necessarily use the same sets of cues, so this must also be taken into account.

Suppose we have two graphs representing decision processes which we wish to compare, G_1 and G_2. Let N_1 and N_2 be the sets of nodes for G_1 and G_2, respectively. Consider the binary variables, p_{ij1}^n and p_{ij2}^n, based on reachability structure, for the graphs G_1 and G_2, respectively:

$$p_{ijk}^n = r_{ij}^n(G_k) \qquad \text{if both } i, j \text{ in } N_k$$

$$p_{ijk}^n = 0 \qquad \text{if } i \text{ or } j \text{ or both are not in } N_k,$$

for $i,j = 1,2, \ldots, t$ and $k = 1,2$. The total number of different cues used by both graphs is denoted by t. Thus p_{ijk}^n just describes reachability for nodes which both appear in process k, but is zero if either node i or node j or both are not used in process k. Then a path structure similarity coefficient, $S_p(G_1, G_2)$, which can be used as a basis for comparing information processing models, is given by

$$S_p(G_1, G_2) = \frac{\sum_{n=0}^{\ell} \sum_{i=1}^{t} \sum_{j=1}^{t} p_{ij1}^n p_{ij2}^n}{\sum_{n=0}^{\ell} \sum_{i=1}^{t} \sum_{j=1}^{t} \left(p_{ij1}^n + p_{ij2}^n - p_{ij1}^n p_{ij2}^n \right)} . \qquad (8.2)$$

This coefficient mirrors the following ideas discussed above: if both graphs have a path from node i to node j of length n or less, this increases both the numerator and denominator, and hence similarity. If there is a path in only one graph, only the denominator increases. Also, nodes which are used only in one graph, not in both, can increase only the denominator, not the numerator, because of the way p_{ijk}^n is defined. Thus the greater the set of common cues used by both of the two decision processes, the greater the degree of similarity can be. Finally note that if a node i is in N_k, $p_{iik}^n = 1$ for all n. Bettman (1971a) develops upper and lower bounds for the S_p coefficient for the case of two general graphs. In addition, a detailed computational scheme is presented and exemplified. The coefficient is now applied to analyzing several decision net models presented in the literature.

Applications of the similarity measure

Alexis, Haines, and Simon's models of two consumers' shopping rules for raincoats (Haines 1974a) and of two consumers' shopping rules for women's dresses (Alexis, Haines, and Simon 1968) are given in Figs. 8.5 and 8.4, respectively. Three analyses were run on these nets (Bettman 1971a). One analysis was run to see whether those cues used by both the individuals modeled had similar path structure relations when the cues idiosyncratic to each individual were ignored. For example, for the raincoat decision, both Subjects A and C used cues 2B, 3, 4, 5, 8B, 8D, 9A, and 9B. In a second analysis, nodes such as 8A, 8B, 8C, and 8D were collapsed in the raincoat models into one node, 8, having to do with proper fit. The processes resulting from this node collapsing were then compared (for example, the order of nodes in the collapsed raincoat process for subject C is 7, 2, 5, 4, 6, 8, 3, 9). Finally, in a third analysis, the entire processes, with all nodes included, were compared. The results are shown in Table 8.3. Haines (1974b) also reported results for the entire process and some nodes cases for women's suit models. These results are also included in Table 8.3.

TABLE 8.3
Similarity coefficient results for Alexis, Haines, and Simon and Clarkson models[a]

| | ALEXIS, HAINES, SIMON | | | |
	RAINCOAT DECISION	CLOTHING DECISION	SUIT DECISION	CLARKSON
Same nodes	.554	.537	.584	.828
Collapsed process	.473	.210	NA[b]	—[c]
Entire process	.150	.060	.143	.158
Lower bound for entire process	.024	.010	.019	.024
Upper bound for entire process	.834	.711	.863	.715

[a] Each figure represents the similarity coefficient between the nets (or subsets of nets) for the two individuals modeled (in the Alexis, Haines, and Simon studies) or between the two types of investment policies modeled (Clarkson).

[b] Not available

[c] Not applicable to the Clarkson nets

Since it is unclear how one should interpret the similarity coefficient in absolute terms, relative comparisons are made. Note that the commonly used cues are used in much the same manner in the raincoat, dress, and suit models. Also, in all three cases, the entire process similarities are low, mainly because different cues are used. Comparing the results for the collapsed processes with those for the entire processes yields interesting insights. For the raincoat decision, these results imply that much of the dissimilarity in process may be due to details in the general cue categories, but that the general structure of the processes is reasonably similar for the two individuals; that is, details in color or style preference vary, but the general cues of color and style are used similarly. For the clothing decision, this is much less true. The raincoat models seem to be more similar than the two clothing decision models. It is the above type of microanalysis of information processing model structure that the path similarity coefficient makes possible.

Clarkson's (1962) yield portfolio and growth portfolio trust investment models are given in Fig. 8.2 and 8.3. These models were compared in the following manner. Since each model had two branches, one negative and one positive regarding a stock, and since cues could be used on both branches, cues were labeled to denote their branch location. Thus, for example, there were two cues T_6 used for the yield model analysis: T_6^N and T_6^P for the negative and positive branches. The corresponding cues for the growth model were T_3^N and T_3^P. The reason for labeling was so that comparisons for cues used by both models would be well defined for these multiple cue occurrences. In the entire process comparison, because of the size of the model, only the negative branches were compared. The results are given in Table 8.3. Again, the cues used by both models are used extremely similarly. The entire process similarity is low because different cues are used.

The models analyzed above were for single pairs of individuals only, modeled at one point in time. Russ (1971) developed models for 20 subjects in an experimental choice situation for small durable goods (frying pans, electric coffeemakers, irons, portable radios, and table and clock radios) at two points in time. Thus the Russ data provided an opportunity to look at stability of the process over time for the same individuals. The similarity coefficient was computed between the nets for choices of the same appliance by the same individual at the two different time points. Then these coefficients were averaged over individuals. These results are given in Table 8.4.

TABLE 8.4
Stability results for Russ models[a]

	AVERAGE SIMILARITY COEFFICIENTS
Frying pans	.300
Electric coffeemakers	.600
Irons	.469
Portable radios	.557
Table and clock radios	.421
Mean similarity coefficient over all subjects and appliance choices:	.466

[a] Reprinted from James R. Bettman, A graph theory approach to comparing consumer information processing models, *Management Science* **18** (December 1971, Part II): P-126.

These stability results should be interpreted with caution, because the set of alternatives available differed somewhat between experimental sessions. In spite of this difference, the coefficients remain reasonably high. However, the models are fairly simple models, so there can be no firm conclusion drawn about choice process invariance. The present method offers an intriguing research tool in this area, however. If subjects are modeled over time using the same alternative sets, similarity coefficients can be computed. Then the subjects could be given different alternative sets, and changes in the similarity coefficients due to variations in the alternative sets could be studied.

The applications above give some idea of the basic types of analyses that can be performed using the similarity coefficient defined above. Further applications, particularly some detailed analytical results on values of the similarity coefficient for single branch decision nets, are given in Bettman (1974c). Now we consider applications of the similarity coefficient for grouping consumers.

Applications to grouping of individuals

Given the similarity coefficient as defined above, if one has nets for a group of consumers, one can develop a matrix of similarity coefficients for pairs of consumers. One approach to determining whether there are generalizable properties of decision nets would then be to use this matrix of similarity coefficients as input to a cluster analysis. If groups of consumers with similar nets emerged, then generalizations might be possible. Data for carrying out such an analysis were available in the Russ (1971) data discussed above. Russ had 20 subjects judge several small appliances during two choice sessions. However, all 20 of his subjects did not participate in judging each appliance. At most nine subjects were modeled for any one appliance. For those subjects who judged the same appliance, pairwise similarity coefficients were computed for the second choice session. Table 8.5 shows typical results, for electric frying pans and table and clock radios. The average across-subject coefficients for these matrices are small compared to the average same subject, across-time coefficients (shown in Table 8.4), as would be expected.

The results developed for the Russ models show both the problems and prospects of using a path structure coefficient to aid in building process-oriented typologies. The matrix of interindividual similarity coefficients can be used as input to a cluster analysis to define groups. As shown in Table 8.5 there appear to be great idiosyncrasies in process. Thus the resulting clusters are not tremendously homogeneous. However, some reasonable results appear for electric frying pans. Subjects 1, 2, 3, and 17 have similar processes. Their nets are shown in Fig. 8.7. There are several general findings even for this small group of simple nets. First, the four consumers use similar cues, with all four considering price and if the frying pan has Teflon; three considering size and cook guide; and two considering style. Second, the sequencing of cues is similar. For example, Teflon is always considered before style, size is always considered first when it is used, and price is always considered last. Thus, although

TABLE 8.5
Russ models: similarity coefficient values for across-subject comparisons[a]

ELECTRIC FRYING PANS

	1[b]	2	3	7	8	11	13	17
1	1	1	.33	0	.071	.108	0	.395
2		1	.33	0	.071	.108	0	.395
3			1	0	.2	.108	0	.429
7				1	.133	0	0	0
8					1	.108	.2	.2
11						1	.25	.108
13							1	0
17								1

Mean similarity coefficient = .155

TABLE AND CLOCK RADIOS

	1	6	8	9	10	11	12	15	19
1	1	.12	.33	.12	.12	.087	.12	.091	.22
6		1	.12	.33	.33	.087	.4	.091	.087
8			1	.12	.4	.087	.33	.091	.087
9				1	.33	.22	.12	.241	.087
10					1	.087	.33	.091	.087
11						1	.087	.091	.224
12							1	.906	.087
15								1	.216
19									1

Mean similarity coefficient = .189

a Reprinted from James R. Bettman, A graph theory approach to comparing consumer information processing models, *Management Science* **18** (December 1971, Part II): P-126.

b These numbers are subject identification numbers.

the nets are very simple, some insights are possible. It is hoped that the approach of computing similarity coefficients and then clustering could yield generalizable results for larger samples of consumers. The ultimate goal is to discover systematic individual differences and infer more general information processing models from the idiosyncratic individual models used as data points. Other work on grouping and making inferences from these groupings is presented in Bettman (1974c).

MEASURES OF RELIABILITY IN DEVELOPING DECISION NET MODELS

One significant issue in protocol analysis concerns the degree to which different modelers, operating from the same protocols, would produce similar results. Haines (1974b) gave protocols for one women's suit decision to four students in a class on artificial intelligence. The resulting models were compared using the similarity measures discussed above. These comparisons among models supposedly representing the same process were then examined relative to the comparison reported in Table 8.3 above between the processes for subjects one and two. The striking results were that half of the similarity coefficients among the models developed by the students from the same protocol data were less than the coefficient between subjects, both for the entire process and same-nodes calculations. As Haines (1974b, p. 98) states, "Half the time different people working from the same protocol appear to get more similar results than the same person producing a decision tree from two different protocols." Thus the reliability in protocol modeling appears to be quite low. This argues for more attention to standard and reproducible methods for analyzing protocols (Waterman and Newell 1971; Payne 1976a,b).

MEASURES OF ATTRIBUTE WEIGHTS

One disadvantage of decision net models is that there has been no clear way to define the weight for a particular attribute, how "important" that attribute is for explaining behavior. There is no easy corresponding notion to that of a beta weight for a regression model, for example. Bettman (1974c) discussed several measures of attribute weight, but all seemed quite ad hoc. Takeuchi (1975) proposes a measure of attribute weight that seems useful. This notion, described below, applies only to nets in which processing by brand is assumed. In nets in which processing is by attribute, the order of processing of attributes may provide a natural ordinal measure of weight or importance (as in a lexicographic model) and the Takeuchi measure does not seem to apply.

To develop the framework for this measure, Takeuchi (1975) develops a function he terms the reliability function for a decision net. This concept, related to the characteristic function notion developed by Bettman (1969; see also Chapter 9), is based on the fact that if the binary yes–no decisions for nodes in a net are independent, the probability of going down any particular path is the product of the probabilities for going down each branch of that path. An example of this type of calculation was performed above for the net and hypothetical data shown in Fig. 8.8 and Table 8.1. The reliability function is then defined as the sum of the probabilities for traversing all of the *acceptable paths* for a net. Thus the function provides the probability that an alternative selected at random will be acceptable. For the specific probabilities given in Table 8.1, the function, denoted by R, for the net of Fig. 8.8 is

$$R = (.8)(.375)(.7)(.2) + (.8)(.375)(.7)(.8)(.5) =$$

$$.042 + .084 = .126. \tag{8.3}$$

In more general terms, if p_i is the probability of following the "yes" branch out of node i (and $1 - p_i$ is therefore the probability of going down the "no" branch), then the function for the net of Fig. 8.8 is

$$R = p_1(1 - p_2)p_3 p_4 + p_1(1 - p_2)p_3(1 - p_4)(1 - p_5). \tag{8.4}$$

Given such a function, one measure of the weight for node i might be $\partial R/\partial p_i$, the partial derivative of R with respect to the probability of following the "yes" branch out of node i (Takeuchi 1975). For the net of Fig. 8.8, the calculations of $\partial R/\partial p_i$ for each node yield (using the frequencies of Table 8.1 as probabilities) .158 for node 1, $-.336$ for node 2, .180 for node 3, .105 for node 4, and $-.168$ for node 5. The minus values imply that increases in the probabilities of going down the "yes" branch for that node lead to decreases in probability of acceptance. For each change of amount Δp_i in the probability for node i, probability of acceptance will change by $\Delta p_i \ \partial R/\partial p_i$. For example, if p_4 were increased from .2 to .3 in the above example, overall probability of acceptance would increase by .1(.105) = .0105. Note that this figure is derived from data *across* alternatives (the p_i data), and it is not clear if it can be applied directly to recommendations aimed at changing degree of belief that a *particular* brand should be processed down the "yes" branch for some attribute.

Takeuchi (1975) applied this notion to Bettman's (1970) legitimization model for Subject C_4. Takeuchi assumed probability figures for "yes" responses of .4(X48), .8 (X40), .9(X41), .7(X42), .2(X43), .6(X44), .6(X45), .7(X46), and .7(X47). The resulting importance measures are .700(X48), .001(X40), .002(X41), .0007(X42), .0003(X43), .0005(X44), .0002(X45), .0002(X46), and $-.599$ (X47). For these probabilities, therefore, exposure to television advertising (X45, X46) had little influence compared with prior experience (X48 and X47).

Finally, for nets with special structure, some generalizations can be made. For example, for a single branch conjunctive net of the form shown in Net A of Fig. 8.1, there is a single acceptable branch, and if there are n nodes in the net, $R = \pi_{i=1}^{n} p_i$. Thus, $\partial R/\partial p_i = \pi_{j \neq i} p_j$. This implies that node i is "important" if the probabilities of successfully passing tests at other nodes are high. Relative to other nodes, then, node i will be more important if p_i is small and the other p_j's are large. Analyses of this sort could also be carried out for single branch disjunctive nets and other special types of nets.[8]

LIMITATIONS OF THESE ANALYSES

The analysis methods proposed above have some limitations, particularly in light of the discussions earlier in this chapter about general problems with decision net research. First, all of these methods examine the net as a complete unit. However, the view of problem solving and choice as a constructive process makes the interpretation of such units difficult, as discussed above, although depiction of nets as units may still be meaningful for many situations. Second, if a net constructed for a particular situation varies as a result of that situation (e.g., for the Russ 1971 data as discussed above), then measures of net similarity confound situational and other effects on process structure (Nakanishi 1974). Third, all of the techniques above are implicitly based on notions of processing by brand. Processing by attribute may occur, however, as shown above. The distinction between these two forms of processing can impact the interpretation of the analysis techniques, as shown above for the case of developing importance measures. Thus although these methods appear promising, more work is needed in interpreting the results of such methods.

SUMMARY OF THE PROPOSITIONS

The propositions summarizing the major statements made in the chapter are now presented below.

Proposition 8.1: Decision nets are another alternative for representing consumer choice heuristics. Decision nets are branching structures using attribute and situational factors to predict acceptance or rejection of an alternative. The three aspects characterizing choice heuristics are specified as follows for decision nets:

a) The evaluation process is derived, not direct

b) The choice criterion is unspecified in most cases

c) Form of processing is by brand

Proposition 8.2: Decision nets have been successfully applied to modeling consumer choices. This research has been characterized by

---

8. This section presents some ideas based on the use of a probabilistic view of decision nets. Perhaps these notions could also be applied to using decision nets to predict probability of purchase rather than individual choices.

a) A deterministic approach to modeling choice

b) Idiosyncratic models of particular individuals

c) An emphasis on situational and choice environment factors

Proposition 8.3: Two major areas in which limitations are found in decision net research are in the characterization of

a) The implementation methods used

b) The form of processing used and the range of choice heuristics depicted

> *Proposition 8.3.i:* Decision nets can be implemented using a range of implementation methods. Prior conceptions of the use of stored rule and recall methods alone are too rigid. Constructive and other methods may also be used. Use of constructive methods causes problems in interpreting the decision nets found in previous research.

> *Proposition 8.3.ii:* Prior characterizations of decision nets as using only brand processing may be true in some situations, but in general attribute processing is also possible. Even if attribute processing is allowed, decision nets can still not depict certain types of choice heuristics. Decision nets must be augmented with other types of processing heuristics.

Proposition 8.4: Analysis methods are needed for further characterizing decision net models. Graph theory techniques are useful in developing such methods. In particular, methods are available for providing

a) Measures of decision net structure

b) Measures of information processing efficiency

c) Measures of similarity and grouping of individuals

d) Measures of reliability in developing decision net models

e) Measures of attribute weights

NEEDED RESEARCH

Areas in which research seems especially needed are now presented, organized in terms of the propositions presented above. One area of need is for more decision net models to be developed (Propositions 8.1 and 8.2). If the resulting decision net models of individuals are idiosyncratic, then to be able to infer any generalities in processing which may be present one needs to have a fairly large number of such models available. However, very few decision net models have been developed, due to the time-consuming nature of the data collection and analysis methods used. Thus faster methods for collecting process data and developing decision nets from those data are needed.

Also, decision net research can be applied to different areas from those to which it was previously applied. For example, one could examine how consumers partition product classes (e.g., are choices of coffee first made by brand, then between instant, regular, and so on; or is the reverse true) by developing decision nets for choices in that class and examining the branches which occur.

Research is also needed in the areas in which past research has shown limitations (Propositions 8.3, 8.3.i, 8.3.ii). In particular (Proposition 8.3.i), the nature of the constructive process and the meaning of decision nets as depictions of the outcome of such a process are both important areas that have seen little research to date. How one could interpret a decision net if constructive processes are used was discussed above. Several possible interpretations were presented, but research is needed to examine the validity of these views. Possible outcomes of such research might range from saying only the *elements* used to construct a net are meaningful units of study to findings that the entire net may in fact provide insights into the overall process.

In addition, echoing a theme that has occurred repeatedly in earlier chapters, analysis of specific tasks and their effects on choice process form is essential (Proposition 8.3.ii). Studies of how task structure affects processing form, by brand or attribute, are particularly required. At this point the conflict between the notions of processing by brand, used in most decision net studies, and processing by attributes, found in many other studies, has at least two possible interpretations: one is that decision net modelers have ignored micro-level processing concerns and have misrepresented the form of processing used by consumers; a second is that the differences are strictly reflections of task effects. Studies using process tracing methods (such as protocols) in which task structure is manipulated to reflect environments of varying degrees of congeniality to attribute or brand processing (and also examining which manipulations correspond to actual consumer choice environments) may help to resolve the differing interpretations.

Studies of those heuristics that need to be used to augment decision net models to obtain more general processing models are also needed (Proposition 8.3.ii). As noted above, the simple binary decisions used in decision nets often merely summarize a good deal of underlying processing. Direct analyses and characterizations of these underlying processes would be useful.

Finally, analysis methods for general process models should be developed, analogous to those outlined above for decision net models (Proposition 8.4). In particular, measures for models in which processing by attribute is used need to be developed.

CHAPTER 9

Consumption and Learning Processes: Changes in Choice Heuristics

The focus of this chapter is on the dynamic, over time aspects of choice. In particular, the effect of feedback from the outcomes of some choice on future choices is considered. As the consumer utilizes or consumes those alternatives previously chosen, the outcomes of these earlier choices are realized. These outcomes may provide the consumer with knowledge about the adequacy of the choice heuristic used. Thus the concern is with the consumer's reactions to feedback from outcomes as one form of learning. For the most part, we will concentrate on potential changes in choice heuristics—what aspects of these heuristics may be changed, how they may be changed, and what factors may influence such changes. Some other learning phenomena have been presented in earlier chapters (e.g., memory, latent learning, low involvement learning), and these discussions are not repeated in this chapter.

OVERVIEW OF THE CONSUMPTION
AND LEARNING PROCESSES COMPONENT

In the course of developing and implementing choice heuristics, consumers may gather and process information. On the basis of this information, assumptions and hypotheses about the potential outcomes of choosing particular alternatives may be made. After a choice is made and the alternative chosen is consumed, the outcomes actually realized can serve as a source of information, as evidence for the consumer relevant to the assumptions and hypotheses made earlier.

In general, then, outcomes from choice may provide new information to the consumer. The point of view taken in this chapter is that the impact of any particular outcome depends upon *how that outcome is interpreted*, on the *inferences* made about the outcome; that is, different inferences about the cause of an outcome can lead to different actions on the part of the consumer. For example, if the consumer has a poor usage experience with a particular brand, whatever actions are taken might depend upon the inferences made about the cause of the poor performance: a poor product in general; failure to follow usage instructions; using the product in an inappropriate situation; and so on.

Several types of actions might be taken by the consumer after an outcome has been interpreted, depending upon both the interpretation of the outcome and upon the goals held by the consumer. These actions may range from doing nothing to undertaking a good deal of processing, information search, and so on. In many cases, however, an outcome may lead to some plans for changing choice heuristics. These changes may be made at the actual time of experiencing the outcome, or might be deferred until the next choice occasion (e.g., the consumer may decide to "Remember to reconsider this choice next time"). The changes made could be in any of the elements underlying a choice heuristic: the actual rule used to compare alternatives, the sets of alternatives or attributes considered, the beliefs or evaluations held, and so on. The change might be either in the direction of simplifying the choice heuristic used (usually if outcomes are as expected) or in the direction of elaborating the heuristic (usually if the outcomes departed from expectations). Further discussion of specific types of changes is provided below. The general notion, however, is that learning is not solely acquisition of habits, but may lead to new cognitive organizations.

Events other than the outcomes of choice can also lead to changes in choice processes. Two particularly important sources are information from advertisements and other media sources, and information obtained during interpersonal interactions.

Finally, interrupts play a role in changes in choice heuristics. First, if outcomes depart from expectations, an interrupt may be likely, leading to an assessment of the adequacy of the choice heuristics used. Second, there may be interrupts during the actual process of changing choice heuristics. Information may be lacking, the outcomes realized may lead to conflicts among criteria, and so forth. The general reactions to interrupts have been discussed in earlier chapters and are not considered further below.

In summary, the consumer experiences outcomes from choices. These outcomes can provide information relevant for assessing the adequacy of the choice heuristics used. This information may be processed and interpreted, leading to inferences about the causes for the outcomes. Based upon these inferences and current goals, plans to change the choice heuristics used may be formed. These plans may be implemented at the time or deferred. Interrupts may occur while carrying out these plans.

The discussion above summarizes the processes involved in learning from the outcomes of choice. The relevant portions of the theory are shown in Fig. 9.1. In the next section the major aspects of the consumption and learning

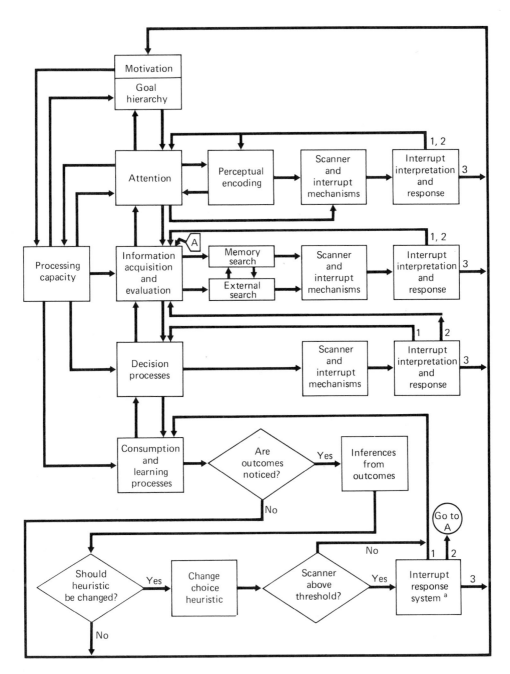

[a]For details of the Interrupt response system and the interpretation of the numbered response, see Fig. 2.4.

Fig. 9.1 Consumption and learning processes segment of the theory.

processes component are considered. Following a discussion comparing standard stimulus–response approaches with the cognitive approach to learning espoused in this book, sections on inferences from outcomes, effects of inferences from outcomes, and other sources of changes in choice heuristics are presented. Then, the linkages of the consumption and learning processes component to other components in the theory are examined, and more detailed aspects of consumption and learning processes are considered.

MAJOR ASPECTS OF THE CONSUMPTION AND LEARNING PROCESSES COMPONENT

MECHANISTIC VERSUS COGNITIVE APPROACHES TO LEARNING

Hilgard and Bower (1966) distinguish two basic approaches to the study of learning—the stimulus–response and cognitive approaches. These are each characterized briefly below.

Stimulus–response approaches

There are many theories of learning which focus on the relationship between a stimulus and some resulting response, without considering intervening thought processes. For example, in classical conditioning, an unconditioned stimulus (say food) which is known to elicit an automatic unconditioned response (salivation) is presented simultaneously with some neutral stimulus (say a light or bell). Eventually, presentation of the neutral stimulus alone (the conditioned stimulus) will elicit salivation (the conditioned response). In a second standard learning paradigm, instrumental conditioning, the frequency of a response is held to be a function of the frequency of rewards and punishments given to that response. In such theories, there are common underlying assumptions. First, the individual is seen as inactive —energy is provided by the stimulus. Second, the linkages between stimuli and responses are characterized as being formed virtually automatically through repetition, and reinforcement is seen as being an essentially automatic process if a reward is given.[1] Outcomes are generally viewed as being directly and automatically linked to reinforcement; that is, if a positive

---

1. This automatic view of associations and reinforcement is seen clearly in the linear learning model of consumer choice (Massy, Montgomery, and Morrison 1970). In this model, purchase of Brand X at time t results in an automatic increment to its probability of purchase at time $t + 1$. Hence, a positive outcome and reinforcement are assumed. If a different brand is bought at time t, the probability of purchase of Brand X at time $t + 1$ is decreased, even if the other brand was bought because Brand X was out of stock or for some other reason unrelated to dissatisfaction with Brand X. Thus outcomes are not even directly considered in this model. Rather, an act is seen as automatically linked to a particular outcome, and this outcome then leads to specific changes in probability of response.

outcome is experienced, that strengthens the tendency to repeat the same response to a particular stimulus. If a negative outcome occurs, for whatever reason, that is seen as decreasing the tendency to emit the response which led to the outcome. Thus the meaning of an outcome is not interpreted or assessed. In general, what is learned are habits and responses (Hilgard and Bower 1966).

Cognitive approaches

The mechanical notions presented above are not sufficient to characterize learning during choice. There are, of course, instances where passive and more automatic learning processes occur (see, for example, the discussion in Chapter 4). However, active learning is also important. In cognitive approaches, learning is generally viewed as being a process of active interaction with the environment, not a passive stamping-in of stimulus–response connections. The consumer is viewed as having hypotheses about the nature of the choice environment (Feldman 1963; Bower 1975). Given such hypotheses about alternatives and their potential outcomes, individuals may gather information to check these hypotheses. This information gathering process can be indirect, attempting to infer how an alternative will perform before trying it, or direct, by trying an alternative to see how it actually performs. When an alternative is chosen and consumed, and outcomes occur, the effect of those outcomes on future choices may not be automatic. Rather, the consumer may interpret these outcomes, and the inferences made about the causes for the outcomes can be important. The meaning of an outcome can be *generated* by the consumer; it is not automatically inherent in the outcome. The outcome provides information which can then be processed and used to form inferences. For example, a negative outcome will not necessarily lead to a decreased likelihood of repurchasing an alternative. If the negative outcome is deemed to be due to failure to follow package directions, for example, the alternative may very well be repurchased.

Thus, rather than automatic notions of association or reinforcement, the cognitive approach stresses the active process of forming inferences from outcomes. Consumers do not simply acquire habits and responses but also information and cognitive structures (Hilgard and Bower 1966, p. 10). Thus the notions of association and reinforcement can be seen from a cognitive perspective as part of a general inference process (McKeachie 1976). In the following section we examine this process of inference from outcomes. We summarize the above as

Proposition 9.1: Mechanistic approaches to learning are inadequate. Consumers can actively interact with the choice environment. The outcomes of choices are a source of information to the consumer, and may be processed and interpreted to provide inputs for future choices.

INFERENCES FROM OUTCOMES

In general, we have argued that outcomes from choices will be interpreted, and that inferences will be made about the causes of outcomes. Before examining this notion further we should note that consumers will not necessarily notice or attend to all outcomes and go through the process of assessing the meaning of these outcomes. One might expect the consumer to pay attention to an outcome if it departs from expectations and an interrupt occurs, or if there was a specific goal to examine the results of the choice (e.g., an instruction·to oneself to "Be sure to see how this choice works out"). Having this type of goal for noticing the outcome of a choice might depend on such factors as degree of knowledge about the set of choice alternatives (with little knowledge perhaps leading to more concern with outcomes); degree of conflict felt in making the decision (with higher conflict leading to more concern); or degree of personal involvement in the consumption process by the consumer (with higher involvement potentially leading to more noticing). Day (1977) proposes other factors that might be involved, such as advice to be cautious from one's friends.

> *Proposition 9.2:* Consumers do not necessarily attend to all outcomes. Outcomes may be assessed if they depart from expectations or if there was an *a priori* goal for noticing the outcomes. Such goals may depend on such factors as the degree of prior knowledge, the degree of conflict felt in making the choice, the degree of involvement felt by the consumer, or advice from friends.

If outcomes are attended to, then the process of forming inferences about the causes of these outcomes can be crucial. As noted above, the impact of an outcome on future choices may depend heavily upon what the consumer infers the meaning of the outcome to be. This process of forming inferences about causes for events has been studied a great deal in social psychology under the rubric of attribution theory (Kelley 1967). The attributions or inferences made for a purchase outcome can be varied. If the outcome was satisfactory, the individual may simply say, "That was good, I'll get it again." That is not necessarily an increment to some probability of response, as postulated in many stimulus–response approaches, but rather a simple self-instruction for a future situation. If the outcome was even more satisfactory than expected, the consumer may try to persuade others to buy the item, or may decide "that was so good I won't consider anything else next time." Finally, if an outcome was unsatisfactory, many inferences about the causes are possible: the alternative itself is poor, the usage directions were not followed, the product was not appropriate for the particular usage situation but would be for others, the particular item was a lemon but others are good, and so on. In general, these attributions or inferences about outcomes might be classified as directly related to the alternative (i.e., the cause is something about the product itself) or as related to the situation or other factors (i.e., the cause is some factor not inherent to the product alone, such as the consumer's not following directions or using the product in an inappropriate situation).

Attribution theorists have considered several factors which may influence these assessments of causality. The statement of Kelley (1967) provides an example of this thinking. In Kelley's view (1967, p. 197), an outcome would be attributed to a certain cause if four criteria were present: (1) *Distinctiveness:* the outcome is attributed to the cause if the outcome uniquely occurs when the cause is present and does not occur in its absence; (2) *Consistency over time:* each time the cause is present, the outcome should be the same or nearly so; (3) *Consistency over modality:* the outcome should occur if the cause is present, even if other aspects of the mode of using the product vary; and (4) *Consensus:* the attribution is made in the same way by other observers. For example, suppose a consumer serves food X for breakfast and finds that no one likes it. If the food had been served several times before for dinner and people had liked it; if other times the food had been served for breakfast it had not been liked; if the people served and other parts of the meal had differed over these occasions; and if upon voicing an opinion that "people just don't like X for breakfast" others had agreed, the consumer may infer that the cause of the unfavorable outcome was not the product itself, but that people don't like to eat X for breakfast. Note that the notions above seem most valid for decisions in which the consumer has a good deal of prior usage experience (e.g., for assessing consistency over time and modality), or for cases in which the consumer has had multiple observations of some event.

For decisions for which the consumer has more limited usage experience or only a single observation of some event, more simplistic inference processes may occur. In particular, Kelley (1971) proposes that individuals use simple expected causal patterns, or causal schemata, in such situations. The particular pattern or schema evoked would depend both on individual differences and the nature of the situation. Markus (1977) develops a similar construct, self-schemata, for explaining how self-perception is structured, how individuals perceive their own behavior. Note the similarity of these notions to the role played in perception by expectations, scripts, chunks, and schematas, as discussed in Chapter 4 (e.g., see Propositions 4.2, 4.2.i, and 4.10).

There is also some evidence that simpler heuristics, such as availability (see Chapter 7) may be used to make inferences in many situations in general. Pryor and Kriss (1977) note that information about an event which is made more salient, and hence more available, may be seen as more closely related to the cause of that event. (See also Carroll, Payne, Frieze, and Girard [1975] and Fischhoff [1976] for other examples of the use of simpler heuristics in making causal inferences.) Thus inferences may be based upon the relative salience or availability of information about potential causes, as well as upon the very rational analyses described above. For example, if the guests in our example above had been bemoaning their hangovers from a particularly boisterous party the previous night, the consumer might view this as the cause for their not liking food X, because this cause is salient and highly available in the situation.

As the discussion above implies, there can be a great deal of complexity in understanding the attributions made by consumers about outcomes. However, such inference processes may underlie a good deal of consumer learning from outcomes. A general theory of learning based upon the types of inferences or attributions formed about outcomes would be very useful (see also Valle and Wallendorf 1977). We state

> *Proposition 9.3:* The process of forming inferences or attributions about the causes of outcomes may be a vital component of the learning process.

Now the effects of such inferences on future choices are considered.

EFFECTS OF INFERENCES FROM OUTCOMES

There may be a range of effects of inferences from outcomes on future choices. There could be no effect at all, for example. If an outcome is satisfactory, one may simply use the same heuristic again. Also, if the consumer is under time pressure in making a choice, inferences made from previous outcomes may not be implemented, but a previous choice may simply be repeated. In general, however, the attributions made about causes for outcomes can lead to plans to change the choice heuristics used.

General plans and self-instructions for changing the choice process may be developed from an analysis of the outcome. For example, the consumer may generate self-instructions for the next purchase occasion ("Be sure to remember to check attribute X," or "Let's try this one more time because I made the recipe wrong."). A general notion of the future actions to be taken as a result of the interpretation of the outcome might be developed. The nature of such plans and self-instructions is very poorly understood at this time, and this seems to be an important area for research. These general plans are also presumably based upon the *goals* of the consumer; that is, the response to an outcome may depend on what the consumer wants to do. For example, the consumer's goal may be to save face if a purchase turns out badly, or to obtain better performance. If the goal is to save face, perhaps the outcome will be reinterpreted as not being bad after all, as might be predicted from dissonance notions. If the goal is to better performance, and inherent factors of the alternative are seen as the cause of the poor performance, other alternatives might be considered, perhaps using information gathered as a result of experience to modify the heuristics used. Cohen and Goldberg (1970) tested the dissonance prediction versus the learning prediction and found support for learning.

These general plans to change the choice heuristics used may include plans to change any of the elements underlying the construction and use of choice heuristics: beliefs, evaluations, the heuristics used to compare alternatives, the set of attributes or alternatives considered, and so on. (See Chapter 7 for further discussion.)

Consumer research on the impacts of outcomes has typically focused on summary measures of these effects, rather than on details of the underlying processes. For example, several researchers have studied the effect of expectations about product performance and the effect of whether or not these performance expectations were confirmed or disconfirmed on some postexposure evaluation of the product (Cardozo 1965; Olshavsky and Miller 1972; Anderson 1973; Oliver 1977). These studies have typically found that higher initial expectations lead to higher evaluations if performance is held constant, unless expectations are extremely high relative to performance (Anderson, 1973); and that higher levels of performance lead to higher evaluations if expectations are held constant. (See Oliver [1977] for a review.) Such research can provide general insights into the impacts of outcomes, but has not yet directly examined the processes proposed above for forming inferences and using such inferences in changing choice heuristics. Detailed analyses of this sort might be a fruitful next step for such research. For example, one might examine whether the specific inferences made from outcomes are a function of the degree of departure of performance from expectations; what conditions might affect such a relationship (e.g., whether the basis for the expectations is advertising, word of mouth, or accumulated usage experience); and how such inferences are related to future choices.

Consumer researchers have thus generally not explicitly considered inferences from outcomes and their effects. However, some recent work in attribution theory appears relevant for examining these phenomena. Weiner (1972, 1974) has developed a framework for classifying the causes of success and failure in achievement situations which may be useful in understanding factors related to the specific types of choice heuristic changes which might be made. Weiner notes that ability, effort, task difficulty, and luck appear to be major causes underlying performance on achievement tasks. These factors can be classified by using two dichotomous dimensions: internal vs. external locus of control, and stable vs. unstable. Thus Weiner proposes that ability is internal and stable, effort internal and unstable, task difficulty external and stable (for a given task), and luck external and unstable. He cites evidence that suggests that the stability dimension is related to changes in expectations (i.e., beliefs about likelihood) of success or failure. In particular, attributions about stable causes may lead to expectancies that outcomes will tend to be the same in the future, but attributions to unstable causes may lead to expectancies that different outcomes might occur. The evidence also suggests that the internal vs. external dimension is related to evaluative responses, that internal attributions may lead to greater evaluative reactions than do external attributions. Thus his model predicts conditions under which certain types of attributions may lead to certain types of changes. (See Frieze [1976] and Valle and Frieze [1976] for further work using this approach.)

This framework might be very useful if it could be adapted to choice situations, rather than achievement situations alone. For example, one might hypothesize that attributions made directly to the product itself might lead to changes in beliefs, in the choice rules used, or in the set of alternatives considered. Attributions to factors not directly related to the product might lead to changes in consumption processes or changes in the contingencies used in choice heuristics (e.g., for which situations a product is suitable). Valle and Wallendorf (1977) make a promising initial attempt to use the Weiner approach in studying consumer behavior, but much more research appears necessary.

This discussion may seem to imply that if changes in choice heuristics are to be made, if general plans or self-instructions are developed, that this will be done immediately, at the time of the outcome. This need not be true. Individuals may not make such changes until prompted to do so by the next choice for that item. To summarize the discussion thus far, we state

> *Proposition 9.4:* Consumers may develop general plans for changing choice heuristics, based upon their inferences about causes of the outcomes experienced. These plans may range from no change to changes in any of the elements underlying the choice heuristic. The changes may be made at the time of the outcome or only when prompted by the next purchase occasion.

Thus far we have not characterized in any detail the types of changes which might be made in choice heuristics. Two major types of changes are simplification and elaboration of choice heuristics. Each of these is now discussed briefly and in more detail in later sections.

Simplification of choice heuristics

One common result of choice may be simplification of the choice heuristic used. In some cases, the consumer may engage in some moderately complex choice heuristic and choose Brand X. If the outcome of using Brand X is extreme satisfaction and this is attributed to properties of Brand X, then the choice heuristic may be simplified to "Buy Brand X."

In more general terms, simplification of choice heuristics may result from chunking of information, in which case some summary notion can be checked by the consumer (such as brand name in the example above) rather than examining values for each individual attribute. If one believes high price means quality, one need check only price, not other properties of the alternatives. If one feels brands offered by Company Y are always good values, then one may check only who makes the product (the standard generalization learning notion). In each of these examples, a chunk has been formed in which one piece of information serves as a summary for the specific attribute values that are assumed to be associated with that one piece of information. The process to study becomes the inference process leading to the chunking, therefore (e.g., how one infers from prior outcomes that high price means quality or that Company Y's products are good values). This simplification process is examined in the more detailed sections below.

Simplification will presumably occur most often when outcomes are as expected. In such cases, the consumer can form summary chunks most easily, since expected patterns of attributes are recurring. However, one may also find simplification if outcomes are not as expected. For example, one may drop complications from a choice heuristic if the outcome of using an alternative is better than expected. If a choice rule of buying the store brand for family use and buying another brand for guests had been developed, high satisfaction with the store brand might lead to dropping the contingency on usage situation, for example.

Elaboration of choice heuristics

Elaboration of choice heuristics, the addition of complications, may result from departures from expectations in the outcomes obtained. One may learn to discriminate among alternatives more finely if an outcome is not deemed satisfactory. New attributes may be added for consideration, beliefs may be modified, and so forth. For example, one may decide that Brand X is not adequate because of Attribute Y, which had not been considered previously, and may decide to look at Attribute Y the next time. Alternatively, one may decide that Brand X suffices for some uses, but not others. These usage contingencies could lead to elaboration of the choice heuristic.

Elaboration can also result in cases in which one expects that the outcome might be unsatisfactory (because of having to choose a brand quickly under time pressure, for example), but does not know what the source of dissatisfaction might be. The results of using the brand can then provide information about how to elaborate the choice heuristic for future occasions. Finally, elaboration can result from desires for variety or novelty seeking (Howard and Sheth, 1969; Bettman, 1971b). In summary, we state

Proposition 9.5: Two major types of changes in choice heuristics are

a) Simplification

b) Elaboration

OTHER SOURCES OF CHANGES IN CHOICE HEURISTICS

In general the focus of this chapter is on changes in choice heuristics stemming from the inferences made about the outcomes of choice. There can be other sources of changes, however, and we will briefly consider two here: information from advertisements and other media sources and interpersonal interactions.

The information available to the consumer from advertisements, consumer rating publications, and so on can lead to changes in choice heuristics. Haines (1974a) states that one function of information is to cause the consumer to examine his or her choice process to see if that process is adequate. Such an examination might result more from information which led to an interrupt, i.e., was surprising or somehow departed from expectations. Information which was in line with expectations should have less effect on choice process changes. Haines' view is very compatible with Krugman's (1972) view, presented in Chapter 6, in which consumers assess the implications of information and then decide what to do about it (i.e., form a general plan).

Another potential source of changes is the effect of interpersonal interactions. The influence of others on the choice processes of an individual has been alluded to only briefly in previous chapters. Cues relating to preferences of others were used in decision net models, for example, but the process of influence has not been discussed in the book thus far. The influence of others can be viewed in general as potentially leading to changes in the elements underlying choice heuristics. Only a few studies have been carried out which look at influence effects on choice processes. Clarkson (1968) modeled dyad (two person) choice behavior using decision nets, with explicit rules for influence. The general influence notion used was that if there were consistent choice differences, new choice elements were added to the net of the less dominant member of the dyad. How one models such dominance *a priori* was not solved.

Olshavsky (1973) examined protocols (tape recordings) of sales person–customer interactions. He found that the sales person can greatly change choice processes, or even take them over in some cases. The sales person could influence the order and number of alternatives considered, the salience of attributes, and the decision as to whether or not an attribute level was satisfactory for hard to judge attributes. Further discussion of sales person–customer interactions from an information processing viewpoint is presented in Olshavsky (1976).

More generally, Cohen and Golden (1972) and Burnkrant and Cousineau (1975) argue that the observed behaviors and evaluations of others regarding a product may be used as information about the actual performance of that product. Rather than the responses of other consumers serving as norms to which the consumer complies, they may serve as information inputs the consumer uses as one element in constructing a choice process. This view of the communications from and the behavior of other consumers as information inputs which must be interpreted seems to be a good approach to interpersonal influence. This information processing view of influence is suggestive, but very little work has been done using such an approach. This would seem to be a valuable area for future research.

> *Proposition 9.6:* Potential sources of changes in choice heuristics in addition to choice outcomes are
>
> a) Information from media sources
>
> b) Interpersonal interactions

SUMMARY

The consumer experiences outcomes from previous choices. If these outcomes are noticed, they can provide information about the adequacy of the heuristics used to make the choice. The consumer may actively interpret these outcomes, and may form inferences or attributions about the reasons for them. These inferences may lead to changes in choice heuristics. The types of changes made will depend upon the exact inferences made and current goals. Major types of changes are simplification and elaboration of choice heuristics. Other sources of changes in choice heuristics are information from media sources and interpersonal interactions.

LINKAGES TO OTHER COMPONENTS OF THE THEORY

Consumption and learning processes and the changes in choice heuristics which may result are linked to the other theory components. As noted above, what is done as a result of the inferences made from outcomes (and even the inferences made) will depend upon what one's goals are. This is not a one-way link, however. The inferences made can also lead to changes in goals. For example, one may decide not to go through with plans to try other alternatives if the alternative tried was found to be extremely satisfactory, or one may form goals for more information search. Thus the motivation component is tied to learning from outcomes.

Attention and perception are also linked to consumption and learning. The consumer must attend to outcomes before inferences are made, and the inferences made will depend on how the outcome and other aspects of the environment are perceived. In addition, the expectations held by consumers, the ways in which information is chunked, play an integral role in simplification processes for choice heuristics. Consumption outcomes can lead to changes in the chunks held by the consumer, and hence changes in these choice heuristics. Consumption and learning processes are also related to information acquisition and search. First, the information available at the time may greatly influence how the outcomes of a choice are interpreted. Second, occurrence of interrupts in interpreting these outcomes or in making changes in heuristics can lead to increased search.

Memory is implicated with the processes of learning in at least two ways. First, if choice heuristics are changed, then these changes presumably impact the elements of choice heuristics stored in memory. The plans or self-instructions formed need to be retained. Second, memory is clearly used in the process of interpreting outcomes and drawing inferences. For example, the factors proposed by Kelley (1967), discussed above, require a good deal of memory for past choice occasions and the associated outcomes.

Decision processes are intertwined with the consumption and learning component in that the choices made lead to outcomes, which then lead potentially to learning. Also, the consumer must often choose among alternative inferences for an outcome. Finally, processing capacity impacts the change process as well. As noted above, changes may not be made, even if desired, if capacity is not sufficient (e.g., if the consumer is under time pressure).

MORE DETAILED ASPECTS OF THE CONSUMPTION AND LEARNING PROCESSES COMPONENT

Research on simplification and elaboration processes for choice heuristics is considered below. This research has been done mainly within the context of decision net models of choice heuristics. Thus the discussion of necessity focuses on decision nets below although the general concepts should apply to other forms of choice heuristics.

SIMPLIFICATION IN CHOICE PROCESSES

Basic notions about simplifications in choice processes were considered above. Very little work has been done in actually depicting mechanisms for carrying out such simplification. Bettman (1971b) performed one of the only detailed studies of such a mechanism. In earlier work, Howard and Sheth (1969) had noted that consumers seemed to progress from complex, extended choice processes to more simple, habitual decision rules as they gained more experience for a particular purchasing task. Bettman (1971b) noted this result and a related result: simple models often perform well in matching choices even if a more complex model is developed from protocol data or other process observations. Howard and Sheth (1969) had not presented a detailed mechanism for this simplification process, but Bettman attempted to develop such a mechanism. In the discussion below, this mechanism is presented. The discussion is presented in the following sequence: first, a comparison of the predictions of simple and more complex models of the same consumers' choices is undertaken and the implications of this comparison are developed; then the general processes underlying choice heuristic simplification are considered; finally, more detailed mechanisms are examined.

Comparing predictions of simple and complex choice models

In attempting to obtain some initial insights into choice heuristic simplification, Bettman (1971b) developed simple models for the grocery product choices made by two consumers modeled in more detail in Bettman (1970). One of these detailed models, for Consumer C_1, was shown as Fig. 8.6. Bettman found that simpler models of consumer C_1, shown as Fig. 9.2, and the other consumer, C_4, performed quite well. In fact, the simpler models matched 82.4 percent of the choices for C_1 and 70.8 percent for C_4, compared with matches of 87.2 percent and 87.5 percent, respectively, for the complex models. Thus the much simpler models do very well in comparison with the more complex models derived from the protocols.

In attempting to explain these results, Bettman (1969, 1971b) developed the notion of a *conditional decision process*. The decision net models considered are conceived to be graphs (see Chapter 8), with the nodes of the graphs representing tests on particular cues and the arcs depicting the processing sequence taken. Now, suppose a configuration or pattern of some set of cues were given, with the cues assuming certain *given* values (e.g., low risk and cheapest price). For that particular set of cues, since the arcs to be taken out of the nodes representing those cues would then be known, the graph conditional on that knowledge will be simpler than the original graph.

As an example, consider a decision process with just two outcomes, Accept and Reject. Also, let X_i represent a "yes" response to the test on cue i, and $\overline{X}_i$ a "no" response. Then Fig. 9.3 is an abstract decision process graph with five cues. Suppose we know that "yes" responses hold for cues 2 and 4, and hence that the arcs labeled X_2 and X_4 are to be followed. Then, the graph of Fig. 9.3 can be collapsed to the simpler graph in Fig. 9.4, because of the certainty of following the arcs corresponding to X_2 and X_4. Note that we can think of the fact that cues 2 and 4 will have "yes" responses as specifying a particular *pattern* or *configuration* for the set of cues 2 and 4. Thus, a simpler model can be obtained from a more complex one by looking at the complex model *conditional* on some pattern or configuration of cues.[2]

---

2. A formal mathematical technique has been developed for carrying out this type of collapsing for any particular given pattern or configuration of cues, involving the notion of a characteristic function representing any decision net with binary branches (Bettman 1969). This characteristic function, as noted in Chapter 8, is obtained by multiplying the variables corresponding to the branches of each acceptable path in the net, and then adding up over all acceptable paths. For example, the characteristic function of the net in Fig. 9.3 is given by: $C = X_1X_2 + X_1X_2X_3X_4 + X_1X_2X_3\overline{X}_4\overline{X}_5$, where $\overline{X}_i = 1 - X_i$. If the cue configuration $\{X_2 = 1, X_4 = 1\}$ is given, then the characteristic function conditioned on this configuration is obtained by substituting $X_2 = 1$ and $X_4 = 1$ into C above and simplifying: C given $\{X_2 = 1, X_4 = 1\} = X_1X_3$. This is the characteristic function for the net of Fig. 9.4.

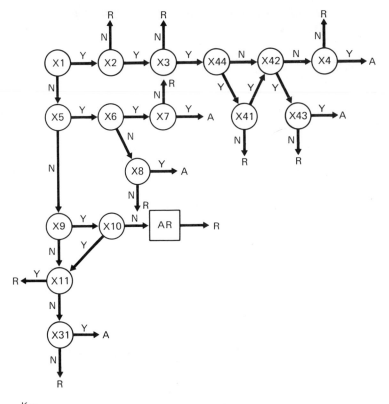

Key

A: Accept
R: Reject
AR: Associate risk (bad experience) with this product
Y: Yes
N: No

X1: Is this meat or produce?
X2: Is price below "justified level"?
X3: Is color satisfactory?
X4: Is this the biggest "okay" one?
X5: Are these eggs?
X6: Is the price of extra large more than five cents more than the price of large?
X7: Is this the large size?
X8: Is this the extra large size?
X9: Was this product (brand) bought the last time a purchase in this class was made?
X10: Was experience with it okay?
X11: Is risk associated with this product (bad experience)?
X31: Is this cheapest (that they have in stock)?
X41: Does this feel okay?
X42: Is this for a specific use?
X43: Is this size okay for that?
X44: Is this produce?

Fig. 9.2 A simple model for consumer C_1. (Reprinted from James R. Bettman, 1971, The structure of consumer choice processes. *Journal of Marketing Research* **8** (November): 466. Published by the American Marketing Association.)

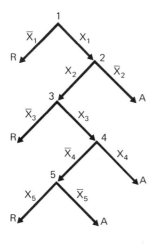

Key   A   Accept
      R   Reject

Fig. 9.3   Abstract decision process graph.

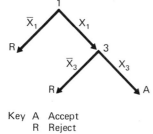

Key   A   Accept
      R   Reject

Fig. 9.4 Simpler conditional decision process graph obtained from the graph in Fig. 9.3 by conditioning on the pattern of "yes" responses to both cues 2 and 4 (i.e., following arcs X_2 and X_4).

This notion of a decision net conditional on some pattern of cues provides an idea for explaining why simple nets can predict well in many instances. It was shown (Bettman 1969) that *both* of the simple models used for consumers C_1 and C_4 could be obtained from the more complex models by conditioning those complex models on certain patterns of cues, or cue configurations. In addition, these patterns of cues were very plausible for the persons modeled.[3] Again, we reemphasize this point that a simpler model can be viewed as a complex model conditioned by a given pattern or configuration of cues.

_____

3. For C_1, these configurations represented product types that were seen as being of low risk, not for company or children; or products that were of high risk with no particular family preference or health factors. Note that several different configurations can lead to the same simple process. For C_4, the simple process resulted from configurations in which the product class was seen as high risk, in which there was a brand that had been tried before with good results, and in which no new brands had recently appeared. In both cases, these configurations seemed very typical for each consumer.

Now we can consider why these simple models predict well. We have argued in earlier chapters that individuals often perceive the world in terms of cue patterns, or configurations, rather than in terms of separate cues. In Chapter 4 the important role of expectations and expected patterns in perception was shown. Suppose that the perceptual structure of the consumer's choice environment is such that it is often characterized by certain *given configurations* of cues, or certain expectations about patterns of cue values. Then a simple conditional model using only a small set of cues may be invoked a large part of the time; that is, the conditional decision process given the particular frequently perceived cue pattern or configuration may be *simple,* and used often. Thus, for example, perceptions that most alternatives are acceptable to one's family and are characterized by little risk might lead to a simple "Buy the cheapest" rule rather than actually checking family member preferences, assessing risk levels, or considering other attributes.

Now we define consistency of cues in terms of expectations. Those cue patterns that are as expected and are encoded as configurations are seen as consistent; those that depart from expectations, which lead to an interrupt, are seen as inconsistent. Then, as shown above, if cues are consistent, simpler decision rules (conditioned on the configuration) may be used. Since consistent combinations tend to occur frequently (one tends to see the world as one expects to), simpler rules may then account for many decisions. If cues are not consistent, more complex processes may be used. This two-step process of assessment of matches with expectations and then applying either simple or complex processing has also received support from other theories (Hunt 1971; Kelley 1971; Orvis, Cunningham, and Kelley 1975; Hoffman 1968; Howard and Sheth 1969; Newell and Simon 1972). Thus simple models may predict well because consumers perceive patterns of cues, and those patterns perceived frequently may lead to simple conditional nets. In summary,

> *Proposition 9.5.i:* Simple choice heuristics can be viewed as more complex heuristics that have been conditioned on patterns or configurations of cues. If such patterns of cues occur frequently, these simple heuristics may predict well.

Processes underlying choice heuristic simplification

This explanation above for why simple processes may predict well also provides a possible mechanism for simplification of choice processes. Since nets conditioned upon configurations or patterns of cues become simpler nets, the *process of forming more extensive expected configurations* is one mechanism for simplification. The process of forming larger configurations is just the process of chunking, however, developing larger and larger patterns which characterize the task environment. Starting with individual cue values, larger and larger chunks may be formed over time. Lindsay and Lindsay (1966) note that frequently occurring patterns are eventually processed as a complete unit. (See also Hayes-Roth 1977.) This chunking process would thus imply a progressive simplification in choice heuristics as the conditioning configuration (chunk) becomes larger. In purchasing behavior, therefore, chunking may serve the function of building stable expectations for the shopping environment; these expectations then allow the use of simple rules. Heuristics may become simpler over time because these chunks become larger.

Formation of chunks over time is a process that is not well understood. However, we might hypothesize that during the course of developing inferences about the causes of outcomes consumers may develop new cognitive organizations and may actively form associations among attributes as outcomes are interpreted. These inference processes thus could lead to the restructuring involved in developing new chunks. For other hypotheses about how new chunks are developed, see Rumelhart and Norman (1978) and Hayes-Roth (1977). We state, therefore,

> *Proposition 9.5.ii:* The process of developing inferences from outcomes may lead to the chunking of cues into larger and larger patterns or configurations. The choice heuristic conditional upon these patterns therefore becomes simpler. Thus chunking may be a basic mechanism for choice heuristic simplification.

Detailed mechanisms for choice heuristic simplification

Although this process of chunking in the perceptions of the choice environment has been proposed above as a mechanism for simplification in choice heuristics, the details of this mechanism are not understood. For example, no work has been done on what is actually changed in a choice process as chunks are formed. It is not known how the "collapsing" or conditioning of a complex net is carried out. Are elements eliminated from consideration entirely? One possibility is that more general rules are used in the process of developing a choice heuristic when this process is viewed as a hierarchy; that is, there may be general rules governing which elements to use in constructing more detailed heuristics (e.g., "Ignore elements related to Attribute X."). These general rules for what factors to include may then be used to reduce the sets of alternatives or attributes under consideration (Lussier and Olshavsky 1974).

This discussion implies that even simple rules require a good deal of conscious processing, with decisions made about what factors to consider, and so on. This view seems clearly inadequate to describe the habitual, relatively nonconscious aspects which appear to govern a great deal of choice behavior. In addition to hypothesizing that heuristics may be simplified, therefore, some consideration must be given to simplification of the operation or implementation of such heuristics. One assumption might be that the general rules used to develop heuristics, discussed above, can also be chunked into patterns. Thus the consumer would initially develop these general rules, then chunk these rules together. This process might eventually lead to response patterns, with a set of responses performed as a unit, and requiring little detailed effort (what Schneider and Shiffrin [1977] call automatic processes, requiring no active attention). As a simple example, the process of driving to the store can often be thought of as executed as a unit without much conscious effort. Other aspects of choice responses can be simplified this way as well. March and Simon (1958) outline the notion of a performance program or strategy, which is a well-learned response pattern. At any one point in time, the consumer presumably has some repertoire of such simple performance programs.

Finally, one might ask what will happen if expectations are not met. Is the complex process from which the consumer started still available for use? This depends on the assumptions made about the nature of the collapsing process. (See Hayes-Roth 1977.) If elements are simply dropped, then these elements will need to be reconstructed. If more general rules are used to decide what to include, then these rules can be changed, and the previous elements used to·construct a more complex process. Such reconstruction of a complex rule may be aided by memory of earlier processing sequences (Russo and Wisher 1976). However, it is obvious that all of the notions above are highly speculative, and that research is needed. In summary, we state

> *Proposition 9.5.iii:* Detailed mechanisms for simplification in choice heuristics need to be specified. Important questions are
>
> a) How the conditioning of a net is carried out
>
> b) How simple, habitual responses are developed
>
> c) How a complex heuristic is reconstructed if needed

ELABORATION OF CHOICE PROCESSES

Heuristics can change not only by being simplified over time but also by being elaborated. The major type of elaboration studied thus far has been discrimination processes, or additions made to a heuristic because the heuristic did not discriminate among alternatives well enough in previous choices. One detailed model of mechanisms for accomplishing discrimination learning is the Elementary Perceiver and Memorizer (EPAM) model of Feigenbaum (1963; Simon and Feigenbaum 1964). The notions underlying this model are now applied to consumer choice heuristics.

Suppose a consumer has a decision net, which sorts alternatives into accept and reject categories. Suppose a brand was sorted to an "accept" decision by the net, but upon usage was deemed unsatisfactory. Suppose also that the consumer did not want to "accept" that brand again. Then Feigenbaum's model would *add a new test* to the net. This test would be added at the end of the previous path leading to acceptance. The added test would be one that would now properly reject the brand, based upon some feature which was deemed in the interpretation of the outcome to be associated with the poor performance. For example, suppose a consumer started with a simple decision net for toothpaste purchases shown in Fig. 9.5a. Suppose further that a brand classed as acceptable by the net was deemed unsatisfactory because the children don't like the taste. Then a test about satisfying the children would be added at the previous accept node, as shown in Fig. 9.5b. Finally, suppose a toothpaste which the consumer did not consider economical is recommended strongly by the family dentist, and the consumer decides to try this brand. Then a test might be added at both the No branch of node 1 and the Yes branch of node 3, since both of the these branches would lead to an error at this point.[4] Now the net of Fig. 9.5c shows that the uneconomical brand will be accepted; however, if another brand were recommended by the dentist that was economical, the choice might change. If the children did not like the recommended brand, a further test might be added, and so forth. This example shows Feigenbaum's general notion. The idea is that one starts with a simple net, and elaborates only as much as is necessary to discriminate. Thus responses to usage outcomes can potentially add tests to nets if such tests were not made previously and are seen as being related to the outcome obtained (i.e., tests may be added by instructing oneself to "Be sure to check X").

There are several problems with the EPAM approach, however. First, the net building rules seem too rigid. Individuals probably reorganize their heuristics much more than is implied by the EPAM add-onto-the-end notion. Also, EPAM appears to assume a fixed net that is recalled and used in its entirety. As noted in Chapter 8, this conception seems to deny the notion of constructive choice processes. Finally, consumers may not only add tests but may also modify previous tests (standards, what is tested, etc.). The EPAM approach, even with these problems, is the main work depicting a mechanism for net elaboration, however.

> *Proposition 9.5.iv:* Discrimination processes are one major form of elaboration of choice heuristics. Discrimination learning has been modeled by the addition of tests to choice heuristics. More flexible models seem desirable.

The research cited above summarizes the main studies on simplification and elaboration of choice heuristics. In both cases, decision net representations of choice heuristics were used. Studies using other representations have not been longitudinal or focused on process change, in general. The entire notion of change in heuristics, perhaps because of the difficulty in re-

---

4. Note that we have added two tests at once in this example. Feigenbaum (1963) states that it seems more efficient to add many tests at a time if there are many differences between alternatives.

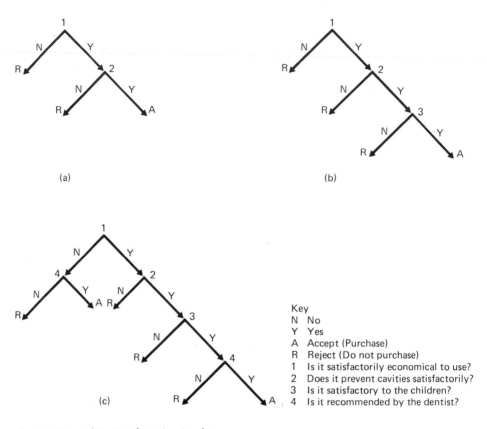

Fig. 9.5 Discrimination learning in choice processes.

searching it, has seen little work. Even the mechanisms described above by Bettman (1971b) and Feigenbaum (1963) are more hypothetical then empirically based. Some very interesting recent work on categorizing and modeling changes in strategies can be found in Neches (1977) and Neches and Hayes (1978).

INDIVIDUAL DIFFERENCES IN THE CONSUMPTION AND LEARNING PROCESSES COMPONENT

Several types of individual difference variables seem relevant to consumption and learning processes. One area that seems quite important is differences in abilities, particularly abilities for processing and analyzing information. Such abilities would be related to the degree to which the consumer *can* effectively interpret the causes of outcomes and develop changed heuristics based upon these interpretations. Mischel (1973) proposes several types of individual difference variables that seem relevant: (1) cognitive and behavior construction competencies; (2) encoding strategies and personal constructs; and (3) self-regulatory systems and plans.

Cognitive and behavior construction competencies refer to the abilities to generate varied patterns of behavior, conceptually or by observing and copying a model. These abilities seem closely related to the ability to construct new heuristics.

Encoding strategies and personal constructs refer to how an individual encodes and groups inputs. These factors are thus related to the "vocabulary" of chunks possessed by an individual, and chunks were shown above to play a crucial role in simplification processes.

Finally, self-regulatory systems play a significant role in the change processes outlined above, since one major effect of inferences from outcome may be to form general plans for change or to give oneself self-instructions. The abilities individuals have for carrying out such self-imposed plans then become important factors.

Another individual difference variable that should be considered is degree of prior experience with a choice, as this can influence the extent to which the consumer notices and attempts to interpret the outcomes of choice. Thus, we state

> *Proposition 9.7:* Individual differences can affect aspects of the consumption and learning processes component. Significant individual difference variables may be:
>
> a) Cognitive and behavior construction competencies
>
> b) Encoding strategies and personal constructs, including the vocabulary of familiar patterns or chunks possessed by an individual
>
> c) The self-regulatory systems used for carrying out plans
>
> d) The degree of prior experience with a choice

SUMMARY OF THE PROPOSITIONS

The propositions below provide an overview of the consumption and learning processes component.

> *Proposition 9.1:* Mechanistic approaches to learning are inadequate. Consumers can actively interact with the choice environment. The outcomes of choices are a source of information to the consumer, and may be processed and interpreted to provide inputs for future choices.

> *Proposition 9.2:* Consumers do not necessarily attend to all outcomes. Outcomes may be assessed if they depart from expectations or if there was an *a priori* goal for noticing the outcomes. Such goals may depend on such factors as the degree of prior knowledge, the degree of con-

flict felt in making the choice, the degree of involvement felt by the consumer, or advice from friends.

Proposition 9.3: The process of forming inferences or attributions about the causes of outcomes may be a vital component of the learning process.

Proposition 9.4: Consumers may develop general plans for changing choice heuristics, based upon their inferences about causes of the outcomes experienced. These plans may range from no change to changes in any of the elements underlying the choice heuristic. The changes may be made at the time of the outcome or only when prompted by the next purchase occasion.

Proposition 9.5: Two major types of changes in choice heuristics are

a) Simplification

b) Elaboration

> *Proposition 9.5.i:* Simple choice heuristics can be viewed as more complex heuristics that have been conditioned on patterns or configurations of cues. If such patterns of cues occur frequently, these simple heuristics may predict well.

> *Proposition 9.5.ii:* The process of developing inferences from outcomes may lead to the chunking of cues into larger and larger patterns or configurations. The choice heuristic conditional upon these patterns therefore becomes simpler. Thus chunking may be a basic mechanism for choice heuristic simplification.

> *Proposition 9.5.iii:* Detailed mechanisms for simplification in choice heuristics need to be specified. Important questions are

> a) How the conditioning of a net is carried out

> b) How simple, habitual responses are developed

> c) How a complex heuristic is reconstructed if needed

> *Proposition 9.5.iv:* Discrimination processes are one major form of elaboration of choice heuristics. Discrimination learning has been modeled by the addition of tests to choice heuristics. More flexible models seem desirable.

Proposition 9.6: Potential sources of changes in choice heuristics in addition to choice outcomes are

a) Information from media sources

b) Interpersonal interactions

Proposition 9.7: Individual differences can affect aspects of the consumption and learning processes component. Significant individual difference variables may be:

a) Cognitive and behavior construction competencies

b) Encoding strategies and personal constructs, including the vocabulary of familiar patterns or chunks possessed by an individual

c) The self-regulatory systems used for carrying out plans

d) The degree of prior experience with a choice

NEEDED RESEARCH

The general view of learning presented above has many implications for future research. Before discussing these, however, the problems involved in studying learning processes are considered. Focusing on the dynamic, long-term aspects of choice leads to several research problems. First, longitudinal studies, where data are collected for the same individuals over extended time periods, can lead to problems of sensitizing the individuals being studied, and hence changing their behavior. In addition, collection of data over time is in general more time-consuming and laborious than collecting data at one point in time. A second problem with studying consumer learning is that most consumers have already learned a great deal about their shopping environments. This inhibits the attempt to study learning by observing actual ongoing consumer choice processes. For example, Bettman and Zins (1977), as noted in Chapter 7, found that prior learning appeared to bias the protocols obtained from subjects. This implies that laboratory studies or studies of how consumers choose from product classes with which they are not at all familiar may be needed. Finally, the issues discussed in this chapter, in which detailed changes in choice heuristics are considered, pose even more problems. In Chapter 7 we noted the great difficulties inherent in determining what types of heuristics consumers use. Attempting to characterize *changes* in these heuristics thus magnifies these difficulties.

One of the major areas for research on learning processes concerns how inferences or attributions are derived from outcomes (Propositions 9.1, 9.3). Possible causes for satisfactory or nonsatisfactory performances need to be categorized and factors leading to the assignment of these causes to outcomes need to be considered. For example, the way persuasive communications about products are structured may influence the reasons attributed for failures. In general, development of an attributional theory of learning appears quite valuable. Carroll, Payne, Frieze, and Girard (1975) argue that use of information processing notions and methodologies for studying attribution processes might be quite helpful.

A second area of research suggested by the general view of learning presented above is a study of the factors associated with setting a specific *a priori* goal to analyze the outcome of a choice, rather than having such an analysis be instigated by departure from expectations (Proposition 9.2). Degree of experience with the choice set, degree of conflict experienced in the choice, involvement, and advice from friends were cited as potentially related factors.

Research on the association between the types of inferences made about outcomes and the types of changes in choice heuristics contemplated by the consumer is needed (Proposition 9.4). Are some types of attributions about causes for outcomes associated with certain types of changes? The framework developed by Weiner (1972, 1974) might be adapted for this purpose.

The specific mechanisms underlying choice heuristic changes are in great need of research (Propositions 9.5, 9.5.i, 9.5.ii, 9.5.iii, 9.5.iv). There are very few studies which examine mechanisms of process change, and these have been carried out within the decision net paradigm. Research on changes over time in other types of heuristics is needed. Also, the process of chunking needs study to further understand the mechanisms of simplification of choice processes. Chunking and the formation of expectations would undoubtedly be affected by the mode of presentation of information about a product class. These processes might be more rapid if information about several alternatives were displayed simultaneously, rather than showing alternatives one at a time. The more detailed mechanisms involved in simplification of choice heuristics (Proposition 9.5.iii) also need empirical research. Finally, discrimination processes need study, particularly whether tests are merely added to existing heuristics or whether new heuristics are developed in other ways.

Another potential research area is the influence of other individuals on choice heuristic changes for a given individual (Proposition 9.6). In particular, studies of how family member interactions change choice heuristics from those constructed separately by individual members seem potentially valuable. Finally Mischel's (1973) individual difference factors should be specified and applied in a consumer choice context (Proposition 9.7). In particular, construction competencies, encoding strategies, and self-regulatory systems need to be studied. The latter seems particularly useful, as self-instructions may be crucial in carrying out plans and possibly in carrying out changes in choice processes (i.e., instructions to oneself to change some aspect when the next choice is made). Very little is known about such plans and self-instructions, so this seems to be a very fruitful area for study.

This chapter completes the description of the components of the theory. In the next few chapters applications to public policy and marketing are discussed, followed by comparison of the theory to those proposed by other researchers.

CHAPTER 10

Implications for Public Policy Decisions

This chapter focuses on the dissemination of information to consumers by public agencies, and considers how insights from research on consumer information processing may help to improve the effectiveness of such programs for information provision. In general, questions relating to what information should be provided and how that information should be provided can be viewed as part of a broader issue, how to design information environments for consumers. An information environment is described by the characteristics of the array of product-related data available to the consumer. Some of these characteristics are type of information available, amount of information available, and how the information is presented and organized.

Wilkie (1975a) provides an excellent discussion and summary of the need for consumer information processing research relevant to public policy decisions. In particular, Wilkie (1975a, p. ix) focuses on two contributions research on consumer information processing can make toward developing an effective information environment for consumers: "(1) by assisting in the selection of information most needed by consumers, and (2) by improving the effectiveness with which that information is communicated to consumers." This chapter concentrates on the second of these areas, insights into effective modes of presentation of information. Before specifically considering these insights, the general nature of the public policy context is discussed. Next, a framework for examining the design of consumer information environments is presented. Then the characteristics of different ways in which public policymakers can present information to consumers are examined, followed by a discussion of how suitable these various information provision methods are for the various types of choice tasks faced by consumers. General implications for the design of consumer information environments are presented, and issues related to specific groups of consumers are examined.

THE NATURE OF THE PUBLIC POLICY CONTEXT

The general nature of the public policy context must be understood before examining the insights obtainable from consumer information processing research. Several aspects of this context are now discussed.

ASSUMPTIONS ABOUT THE CONSUMER AND CONSUMER INFORMATION PROCESSING MADE BY POLICYMAKERS

Policymakers tend to have a view of the consumer and consumer processing abilities that departs in many significant respects from that presented in previous chapters (Wilkie and Gardner 1974). First, the consumer is implicitly assumed to have a great deal of processing capacity and a great deal of time for processing. As we have noted above, however, consumers are better characterized as having relatively limited processing capacity. This capacity limitation leads consumers to use heuristics and other techniques for simplifying the choices they must make. Thus the public policy view would tend to overestimate the amount and complexity of processing which might be done.

Second, individual differences in consumers tend to be ignored in the view of policymakers. Most consumers are assumed to process available information in similar ways, regardless of prior choice experience or other factors. In particular, price is assumed to play an important role in most decisions. In contrast to this view, in previous chapters the prevalence of individual differences and the potentially large effects of prior experience on processing have been stressed.

Finally, policymakers have tended to assume that more information is always better for consumers and that information can be readily understood by consumers, without undue concern with how that information is presented. This also represents a substantial departure from the view of this book. We have seen that consumers often attempt to simplify difficult tasks. If too much information is available or if the information is too hard to understand, consumers may ignore a good deal of that information.

Thus there appear to be major differences between the implicit view of the consumer held by public policymakers and that implied by research on consumer information processing. Each of these viewpoints might also lead to different recommendations for how information should be provided to consumers. Recommendations based on the information processing view, discussed in later sections, will in general be more concerned with how to present information so that consumers can handle it, given their limited processing abilities; and with how to account for individual differences.

THE VIEW OF CONSUMER CHOICE TASKS HELD BY POLICYMAKERS

Public agencies often take a different view of consumer choice tasks from that which is taken in marketing applications. In particular, the policymaker might place relatively more emphasis on choice among *product classes,* or comparison of the performance of an entire product class with standards, and relatively less emphasis on choice among brands within a product class than would a marketer. For example, provision of nutritional information might be viewed as valuable for comparing several product types to see which is most nutritious, rather than only for comparing to see which brand is most nutritious within a product class (e.g., comparing cereal to eggs, rather than comparing different brands of cereal). Also, public agencies are mainly concerned with providing *objective* ratings on product attributes to consumers (e.g., nutrient content, mileage ratings), not with providing persuasive messages about various attributes which can be assessed only subjectively (e.g., style, prestige, taste). Such views of consumer choice tasks may not coincide with the views of consumers themselves. It is not known how consumers perceive the tasks they face, whether consumers see a significant number of choices as involving product–product comparisons with objective data, for example.

THE GOALS UNDERLYING PROVISION OF INFORMATION

A final facet of the public policy context is that there may often be an attempt to be neutral about brand choice in that information presented by a public agency should not discriminate against or be in favor of certain brands *a priori* (Wilkie 1975a, p. 8). However, the actual goals of public policy programs are often not clear. Goals can range from cognitive objectives (stress on knowledge and understanding of the information presented, and the ease with which that information can be processed) to desired behavioral outcomes (stress on the actual use of the information in making choices). For example, for a nutritional information program, one type of more cognitive goal might be to assure that consumers could readily determine which products were most nutritious *if* they so desired. Then whether or not the consumer actually chose more nutritious products would not be a concern with such a goal. The focus would be on facilitating processing. At the other extreme, a goal for such a program might be to persuade consumers to use and act upon the nutritional information presented, and actual shifts in consumption might be a major concern. Wilkie (1975a, pp. 9–10), Bettman (1975b, pp. 175–176) and Jacoby (1974) discuss issues relevant to the goals of information provision programs; the general conclusion is that it is crucial for goals to be determined *a priori,* whether cognitive or behavioral, since the goals selected can influence the form of the most effective design for the program.

Given this context of public policy programs, Wilkie (1975a) argues that much research on consumer information processing is inappropriate for application to public policy questions, and should be reoriented. Consumer processing research has concentrated almost exclusively on choice among brands and on persuasive rather than objective communications. This difference in focus should be borne in mind in the discussion of the factors influencing the design of information environments presented below. The emphasis on objective rather than persuasive communications by public agencies is perhaps the most relevant difference, since the brand choices made by consumers may clearly be affected by public agency information programs. The processes underlying brand choice are still important, even if specific aspects of brand competition may not be the focus.

A FRAMEWORK FOR EXAMINING THE DESIGN OF CONSUMER INFORMATION ENVIRONMENTS

The goal of many information provision programs seems to be to simply make information available to consumers. However, mere availability may not be sufficient to allow consumers to use the information if they so desire. Russo, Krieser, and Miyashita (1975) and Russo (1977) argue that one must distinguish between the *availability* and the *processability* of information. Processability refers to the ease with which consumers can understand and utilize a particular piece of information. Thus the greater the processing effort required to comprehend and use some piece of information, the less the processability of that information. Information must in general be *both* available and processable to potentially be utilized.[1] In the following we will focus on the processability of the information presented to the consumer.

In examining processability, we consider three factors: how information is presented, the types of processing used by consumers in comparing alternatives, and what types of choice tasks consumers face. In general, one can analyze processability only by considering the *interaction* of these three factors. We have argued in many places in this book that the properties of the particular choice task being undertaken may determine to a great extent what the most easily utilized heuristics and methods for implementing those heuristics will be. In other words, for any task, one can perhaps determine what kinds of processing are needed for or are characteristic of that task. Thus the ease with which a particular piece of information can be processed depends not only on how the piece of information is presented but also on how *congruent* that mode of presentation is with the kind of processing characteristic of the task of interest. For example, suppose consumer processing for some task is characterized by a heuristic that utilizes attribute processing, and by use of in-store rather than prior processing. Then presentation of information by brand in an out-of-store context would be quite incongruent with these requirements.

We will now attempt to examine this complex interaction among modes of presentation, the types of processing required, and different choice

1. Recall that depending on the goals of a program, usage may not be necessary; that is, it may be intended only that consumers should be aided in perceiving and processing the information, with no commitment to how or even if consumers use the information. Thus processability is still important whether usage is a goal or not.

tasks. We will proceed by first characterizing different modes the policymaker can use to present information to consumers. Then specific types of choice tasks are considered, and the types of processing hypothesized to characterize each task are discussed. Finally, those presentation methods which seem most congruent with those processing types are considered. It is felt that consideration of these factors may enable us to draw some general conclusions about information provision; particular programs are not considered. (See Bettman [1975b] for a discussion of a proposed nutritional information program, however.)

METHODS FOR PROVIDING INFORMATION TO CONSUMERS

Public policymakers can present information to consumers in many different ways: in television commercials, through radio and print advertisements, on packages, through in-store displays, and so on. The information presented might be for a single dimension (say automobile gas mileage ratings) or for many dimensions (say nutritional information) (Wilkie 1975b). Each major presentation method is briefly characterized below. The characterization of these methods focuses on those aspects that seem most relevant for understanding processability, or how well consumers could process information presented using each method if they desired. In particular, attention, memory factors, and organization of the information presented are considered for each method of presentation.

There are many other aspects related to the execution of information presentation campaigns by public agencies that could be considered. For example, one might wish to examine effects of the size or color of the display for visual presentations, or effects of different message approaches, such as use of humor. Alternatively, one could investigate impacts due to the source of a message (e.g., whether the message came from a firm or a public agency—see Dyer and Kuehl 1974; Hunt 1972; Kassarjian, Carlson, and Rosin 1975). However, the focus of the discussion below is on relatively detailed information processing factors. Other issues, such as those mentioned above, are beyond the scope of this chapter.

The following discussion is split into two major parts: methods of presenting information outside of the store, and methods of presenting information inside the store. The in-store and out-of-store methods appear to have different properties. In-store presentation will be temporally closer to the time of choice in many cases, and provides a readily available external memory source. Thus internal memory need not be as greatly involved for in-store presentations. On the other hand, out-of-store presentations might be seen more frequently by the consumer, since the consumer would typically see many television commercials during a week, for example, but might shop only once or twice. Other distinguishing characteristics of in-store and out-of-store methods are considered in the discussions below. For the present we simply re-emphasize that in-store and out-of-store presentations may have different characteristics, even if the same information is being provided.

PROVIDING INFORMATION OUTSIDE OF THE STORE

Three major methods for providing information to consumers outside of the store are considered: television commercials, radio advertising, and print advertising.

PROVIDING INFORMATION IN TELEVISION COMMERCIALS

Television, as a medium, has the properties that both visual and audio information can be presented, that there is limited time to process any particular commercial, and that the sequence and rate of presentation of information is not under the control of the viewer. Let us now consider various aspects related to consumers' abilities to process information required by the policymaker to be in television commercials. Thus we consider the case in which the information is presented in a manufacturer's commercial, although required by the public agency. The impacts discussed below might differ if the agency or some consumer group itself were presenting the information. Such differences are beyond the scope of this discussion, although parallel analyses could be carried out.

Attention

Although in some cases attention may not be required for learning to occur (see Chapter 4), in many cases the consumer must attend to the information presentation to be able to process and perhaps utilize the information provided. As outlined in Chapter 4, attention may be given to some piece of information based upon a consumer's goals (voluntary attention), or because of some property of the information itself (involuntary attention — e.g., novelty, incongruity).

The consumer's goals can play an important role in whether or not attention is given. The consumer may attend to and process the information placed in an advertisement by the policymaker if the effort necessary to process and assess the information is perceived to be worthwhile in terms of the goals held by that consumer. Thus the consumer is seen as weighing the costs and benefits of attending to and processing the information presented. The costs of processing the information are mainly related to the difficulty perceived by the consumer in performing the processing. The benefits from processing the information to the individual consumer may depend on whether or not a purchase of the product class or a related class is being contemplated, whether the consumer has a special interest in the kind of information provided (e.g., nutrition), or whether the ad itself attempts to stress the importance of the information presented. Krugman (1972) views the function of seeing an ad for the first time as allowing one to make this assessment of whether or not further processing is warranted. After seeing the ad for the first time, a decision may be made to not pay attention to subsequent repetitions if there is little of interest or value for the consumer in the ad.

Involuntary attention might be initially directed to ads providing information required by policymakers, because the type of information required may not have been seen in many previous advertisements. If most advertisements already had such information, however, such involuntary attention would not be as likely. Also, over time the novelty of the information would tend to decrease, as would the involuntary attention. Even if involuntary attention is achieved, the consumer still may undertake assessments like those described above to decide if further processing is to be done.

Memory factors

Four aspects of memory that seem most relevant for characterizing methods of information presentation are discussed below for television commercials; use of internal vs. external memory; use of recall vs. recognition; effects of processing capacity; and effects of repetition.

Use of internal vs. external memory. Television commercials seem to place a relatively heavy load on internal memory. Unless the consumer is able to write down the information presented, the information must be retained in the consumer's own memory to be used. There is no other readily apparent external memory device for information presented in television commercials.

Use of recall vs. recognition. Even if internal memory is used, the consumer may either attempt to recall or to recognize the information presented. As noted in Chapter 6, there is some uncertainty about whether consumers decide *a priori* whether to use either recall or recognition, or whether they merely do what is possible given the information presented. It is known that the plans for learning used by individuals differ depending on whether they expect a recognition or recall task (Eagle and Leiter 1964; Tversky 1973). One might expect consumers to use recognition only if they knew that the information were also available in the store to be recognized. However, one can also argue that since recognition is in general easier than recall, recognition may be all that is possible if difficult information is presented, with recall possible only if the information is relatively easier to process.

If recall is used, then the research on transfer speeds from short-term to long-term memory cited in Chapter 6 implies that roughly five to ten seconds of time are required to memorize one chunk of information for later recall. Thus the feasibility of processing the information presented and recalling it depends on the amount of information presented relative to the time available for processing, and the ability of the consumer to organize the infor mation into chunks. For example, if there are 15 seconds available for processing the information, and capacity is fully allocated to processing that information, perhaps two to three chunks could be recalled at a later time. For recognition, the transfer speeds are on the order of two to five seconds per chunk, so perhaps as many as eight chunks of information could be recognized later after a 15-second presentation.

Thus the amount of information that may be acquired during the limited time available in a television commercial depends on the ability of the consumer to chunk the information provided. The degree of chunking possible may depend largely upon the organization of the information in the ad and the degree of the consumer's prior knowledge and interest in the information. If information is prechunked for the consumer by the way the ad is designed *and* if these chunks are consistent with the way the consumer categorizes, then "larger" chunks and hence more information could be processed per unit time (Bower and Springston 1970). Also, if the individual has prior knowledge related to the information presented by the policymaker, so that the information can be integrated meaningfully with some existing knowledge, then more information in the ad can perhaps be chunked together and processed per unit time. The studies of chess perception cited in Chapter 4 (Chase and Simon 1973) show the great effect on memory of the size of an individual's "vocabulary" of patterns or chunks in memory. The greater the number of preexisting chunks or patterns, the faster information can be processed and the greater the amount of recall or recognition. Thus consumer education programs could be very useful in giving consumers the knowledge necessary to more rapidly assimilate incoming information.

Finally, the analysis above has assumed that consumers need to memorize the actual pieces of information presented and later recall or recognize them. However, consumers might process alternatives by using acceptable level cutoffs or standards for the types of information presented by the policymaker. Since remembering those alternatives which meet a standard (e.g., at least 50 percent of the U.S. RDA for Vitamin C, or a gas mileage of at least 20 miles per gallon) might be easier than trying to recall or recognize the value of the information itself, it is possible that more information could be processed per unit time if consumers did in fact use such standards.

Effects of processing capacity. The discussion above assumes that full capacity will be allocated to processing the information provided by the policymaker. However, studies cited in Chapter 6 demonstrate that distracting tasks and competing tasks can severely limit the processing capacity available for handling this information (Newell and Simon 1972; Olshavsky and Gregg 1970). Unfortunately, distractions and competition are likely to be the rule rather than the exception if the information is presented within manufacturers' television commercials. Suppose the public policy information is presented visually, for example, with the audio portion of the commercial being a standard persuasive message. Then competition between processing the policymakers information and possibly developing counterarguments and other responses to the persuasive message (Wright 1974c) could reduce the amount of the policymaker's information that could be processed and later recalled or recognized. Also, work in modality effects on memory suggests that if audio and visual information compete for attention, the audio information may have priority (Penney 1975). Thus for the best processability, there should be a total focus on the policymaker's information during the segment of the commercial when it is presented, with simultaneous audio and visual presentations.

Effects of repetition. The analyses just presented were for a single presentation. However, such commercials would presumably be repeated over time. The effects hypothesized to result from repetition depend upon the model of repetition effects used, as noted in Chapter 6. If one assumes a passive model in which the consumer passively has information "stamped in" with increasing strength as the number of repetitions increases, then perhaps repetition might increase the amount recalled or recognized. If one takes a more active view of repetition effects (Krugman 1972), then what the consumer decides to do on repeated exposures is crucial. If the consumer decided the ad is of interest, general plans for learning might be made (e.g., "I'll have to pay more attention to that part next time," or "I'll try to write it down" or perhaps even "I'll have to come up with a standard."). One decides if there is a need for the information or not, and then decides how to process further ads. The more information to be processed, the greater the number of added exposures needed to carry out one's plans. If the information is deemed to be of little interest, there may be little learning over time, although perhaps the salience of the dimensions presented by the policymaker might be increased through low involvement learning processes. (Krugman 1965).

Organization of the information presented

The presentation format for most commercials is by brand, since the commercial is being sponsored by some particular brand. Thus presenting information in manufacturers' television commercials will tend to favor processing by brand and hence the organization of knowledge in memory may also tend to be by brand (Johnson and Russo 1978). Some manipulations of commercial format might encourage attribute processing and storage. For example, comparative ads (Wilkie and Farris 1975), in which two or more specifically named brands in a product class are compared on a product attribute, could aid processing by attribute, particularly if the objective ratings provided by the policymaker were presented in such an ad.[2] Also, it might be possible to develop formats that provided information on a brand's standing on an attribute relative to other brands in a product class.

---

2. Wilkie and Farris (1975) argue that if comparative ads are used to present comparisons on nonobjective attributes, this could cause consumer confusion, as several manufacturers may make conflicting claims about how brands compare for a given attribute.

PROVIDING INFORMATION IN RADIO ADVERTISEMENTS

Radio has the properties that only audio information can be presented, that there is limited time to process any particular advertisement, and that the sequence and rate of presentation of information is not under the control of the listener. Again we limit discussion to the case in which the information is in a manufacturer's advertisement.

Attention

Again attention to an advertisement may be because of goals or involuntary factors. However, the possibilities for generating involuntary attention may be more limited than for television commercials since no visual displays are possible. Also, television may in general be more intrusive a medium than radio, and hence generate greater attention levels.

Memory factors

Use of internal vs. external memory. Radio commercials also seem to place a relatively heavy load on internal memory, with writing down what is said the major source of external memory.

Use of recall vs. recognition. The major recall and recognition factors discussed above for television presentations also hold for radio. However, there are additional facets which must be discussed. For example, it would seem that the information which could be presented via radio ads would be more limited than that given in television commercials. As shown in Chapter 6, memory for complex visual images is much better than that for verbal information (Shephard 1967). However, if the data are expressed as some small number of numerical ratings, then perhaps the finding that for simple stimuli audio presentation is more effective than visual presentation would apply (Penney 1975). If this were true, radio might be more effective than television in presenting numerical ratings *if* the ratings were presented only visually on television (note that use of both audio and visual was recommended above for television, however).

Effects of processing capacity. Distraction may be less extensive for radio advertising, since there would be no competing visual portions of the ad as with televison. However, if the consumer is listening to the radio while doing some other task (e.g., driving, doing housework), then there could be a great deal of distraction.

Effects of repetition. This seems to parallel the analysis for television commercials presented above.

Organization of the information presented

The presentation format is again mainly by brand and would thus tend to encourage use of brand processing and memory storage and discourage use of attribute processing and storage. Encouragement of attribute processing might be difficult for radio, since visual displays are not usable.

PROVIDING INFORMATION IN PRINT ADVERTISEMENTS

Print, as a medium, seems to impose fewer processing constraints on consumers than either television or radio (see Wright [1978] for a more extensive discussion). There is only visual information, but the consumer can control the length of exposure to the ad, and can also control to some extent the order in which information is examined. Again we consider information placed by the policymaker in manufacturers' ads.

Attention

The analyses above apply in general to the print advertising case. However, there are some differences. First, there may be many more ads potentially available per unit of time devoted to a magazine, for example, than there will be for the same amount of time devoted to radio or television (i.e., in the space of three or four magazine pages there may be ten to twenty ads). Thus each particular ad is probably less likely to gain the attention of the consumer. Second, as several authors have noted (Krugman 1968, 1971; McLuhan 1964), television is a more obtrusive medium than is print. One is *confronted* with a television commercial while watching, and both audio and visual information are possible.

Memory factors

Use of internal vs. external memory. Print ads provide much more external memory. One can more easily write things down, since exposure time is not necessarily limited, or the ad itself can even be used as an external memory aid if the consumer clips out the ad and saves it. Thus print ads in general may place fewer requirements on internal memory than television or radio presentations.

Use of recall vs. recognition. Since processing time is not necessarily limited by print ads, more complex information may be presented in print ads than in radio or television commercials. Arrays of objective data could be presented in print with some hope that the consumer could process these data (or clip them out), unlike what one might expect for radio or television presentation, given the processing times for recall and recognition noted above.

Effects of processing capacity. Since processing time is not inherently limited, the effects of distractions or competing tasks may not be as important as in the radio or television cases. However, if the consumer is under time pressure, then this self-imposed limitation on processing time could adversely affect the consumer's processing.

Effects of repetition. The extent and rate of repetition are more under the control of the consumer for print ads than they are for television or radio presentations that confront the consumer with the ad; that is, it is easier to ignore a print ad than to ignore a radio or television ad. Also, one can look at a print ad when one wants to, and as many times as one wants to. Thus the low involvement learning processes Krugman (1965) postulates might be less likely to operate for low interest print ads, since such ads could be ignored relatively easily. For ads in which the consumer was interested, however, fewer repetitions of print ads might be needed for the consumer to comprehend and use the information provided, since the consumer could devote more time to processing each exposure.

Organization of the information presented

The presentation format would still typically be by brand. However, since more complex arrays of information could be presented in print than could be presented on television or radio, one might be more readily able to present tables of information comparing brands to standards, or comparing properties of several alternatives.

PROVIDING INFORMATION INSIDE THE STORE

Two broad ways of providing information to consumers inside a store are considered: package information, and use of other in-store displays.

PROVIDING INFORMATION ON PACKAGES

Package information allows the consumer to control the length of exposure to the information, and also the sequence in which the information is examined. Only visual information is presented. The package information is also available at the time of actually obtaining the product.

Attention

The analyses above apply in general. However, there are usually many alternatives available in the store, and the consumer will limit attention to some subset of them. Package information is probably less obtrusive and more easily ignored than television or radio ads.

Memory factors

Use of internal vs. external memory. The package information provides a direct external memory source for the consumer.

Use of recall vs. recognition. Package information, since it is present in external memory, may aid the consumer in recall of other pieces of relevant information in internal memory. Also, since the package information is actually present in external memory, it need only be recognized or attended to, not recalled. Thus presentation of package information enables use of recognition by the consumer.

Effects of processing capacity. In general there may be a great many distractions in the store situation. However, the information is available in external memory and processing time may not be limited, so the impact of distraction may be minimal. Time pressure on the consumer could adversely impact processing the package information, however.

Effects of repetition. As with print advertisements, the extent and rate of repetition is more under the control of the consumer.

Organization of the information presented
The organization would clearly be by brand. Attribute processing might be relatively easy for those alternatives whose packages are near each other in the store display. For choices where there are few alternatives available, attribute processing could be possible. In addition, attribute processing might be greatly facilitated if a table comparing many brands could be placed on the package for each brand. Again, this would probably be feasible only in cases in which there are few brands available. Information remembered from packages would also tend to be stored in the format in which it was input (Johnson and Russo 1978).

PROVIDING INFORMATION IN IN-STORE DISPLAYS

Information could also be presented to consumers via special in-store displays. Such displays would allow the consumer to control length of exposure and the sequence of examining the information. The information would be visual, and could be available at the time of actually obtaining the product. Such displays could range from having booklets available with the store manager to having displays on the store shelves or counters (one such display is described in more detail below). Such displays might conceivably be sponsored by manufacturer or retailer associations or by the public agency itself.

Attention
The degree to which involuntary attention could be generated would depend on the type of display used. If booklets were available from the store manager, one would expect relatively low levels of involuntary attention. If a special display on or near the store shelves were used, a great deal of involuntary attention might result initially, as it might be a departure from the standard shelf or in-store displays.

Memory factors

Use of internal vs. external memory. This again depends on the type of display used. If the display is a booklet which can be used only at the manager's desk, then internal memory must be used. For a shelf display, an external memory is directly provided.

Use of recall vs. recognition. If a booklet available from the manager were used, recall might be required. With a shelf display, only recognition or attending to the display is needed, although the display might stimulate recall of other relevant information.

Effects of processing capacity. Effects of distractions would be greater for the booklet than they would be for the shelf display. Time pressure might also play an important role.

Effects of repetition. Repetition, extent and rate, is under the control of the consumer to a large extent.

Organization of the information presented

Information presented in a booklet could be arranged in tabular form, by attribute, or by brand. Shelf displays could also be arranged in various ways. One particular shelf display notion that could facilitate processing is outlined below.

This completes the characterization of several ways in which policy-makers could present information to consumers. Note that each of these different ways represents a different task to the consumer trying to process the information, with different properties. Each method can be characterized by the type of processing it implies, therefore. Different consumer choice tasks can also be described by the type of processing characterizing the performance of the task. Thus each method might be most effective for those choice tasks in which the *processing characteristics of the task are congruent with those implied by the presentation method.* Therefore, we now turn to a consideration of several types of tasks facing consumers, and examine what types of processing may be characteristic of those tasks, and hence which information provision strategies might be most appropriate.

ANALYSIS OF INFORMATION PROVISION
FOR SPECIFIC CONSUMER CHOICE TASKS

PROCESSING REQUIREMENTS OF VARIOUS CHOICE TASKS

Several conjectures concerning the types of processing required by or characteristic of various types of consumer choice tasks were presented in

Chapter 7. Those that are relevant for the analyses to be presented below are briefly reviewed here.

First, as noted in Proposition 7.8.v, one can characterize those choice tasks in which one would expect consumers to use heuristics requiring attribute processing, and those tasks in which brand processing might be used. Attribute processing will tend to be found when there are few alternatives, when dimensional differences are easy to compute, when the format of the information presented allows attribute processing, and when there is little knowledge about the alternatives. Heuristics using brand processing will tend to be found if these conditions are not met.

Also, there are several ways in which consumers may implement choice heuristics. Three major types of methods are how heuristics are formed (use of stored rules vs. constructive processes); where processing occurs (in-store or prior to shopping); and how memory is used (recognition vs. recall). Proposition 7.5 suggests conditions under which these methods might be used. With little experience, constructive, recognition, and in-store methods may be preferred; with more experience, increased usage of stored rules, recall, and prior processing may be found. Although these conditions are stated in terms of prior experience, one might argue that difficulty of the choice task is involved (presumably more experience might imply less difficulty with a task in many cases). Bettman and Kakkar (1976) found, for example, that use of constructive, recognition, and in-store mechanisms tended to be associated with difficulty in comparing alternatives and with examining many alternatives. Thus we will refer to both degree of experience and difficulty of the choice in the following.

We now consider specific choice tasks. In particular, we consider brand choice in which there is a good deal of prior experience, brand choice in which there is little experience, and product class choice. We will attempt to characterize the types of processing each task seems to require, and see how these requirements match with the types of processing implied by the various methods of information provision. Note that because of the general lack of research, these characterizations of both task processing requirements and of the matches that might be implied between tasks and presentation methods are highly speculative. Much more research would be necessary before any firm recommendations could be made. However, the analyses illustrate the kinds of thinking that might be applied if firmer research bases existed.

BRAND CHOICE WITH MUCH PRIOR EXPERIENCE

For choices involving comparison of brands within a product class with which the consumer has a good deal of experience, the consumer may tend to use brand processing, and use stored rule, recall, and prior methods. Such relatively easy choice tasks may be those where recall is *possible* for the consumer. Thus recall may tend to be used in those situations in which it can in fact be done. In such relatively easy choice situations, presentation of information outside of the store and organized by brand might be adequate. As Howard (1977) notes, information on price and availability is probably most relevant. Thus any of television, radio, and print advertising might be used. Since recall may tend to be used, the amount of information presented must be such that it can be processed in the time available for processing (e.g., for a television commercial during which available processing time is limited).

Note that there is a complication with the argument above. Although the consumer may have a good deal of prior experience with a product class, if the policymaker is presenting new information, it may complicate the task for the consumer. The greater the prior experience, presumably the more readily the consumer could chunk the new information, since an existing structure of knowledge about the brands may exist which could serve as a framework for comprehending the new data. Also, if print advertisements were used, more information may be processed since there is more time available for processing. Hence, even with new information the choice task may still be relatively easy. However, if the information presented were complex, or were presented in very large amounts relative to the time available, then the choice task might become fairly difficult. We now consider this case.

BRAND CHOICE WITH LITTLE PRIOR EXPERIENCE OR OTHER PROCESSING DIFFICULTIES

In cases in which there is little prior experience or in which there is some other processing difficulty (e.g., the information presented by the policymaker is complex or voluminous), the speculations above suggest that attribute processing, and constructive, in-store, and recognition methods may be preferred. Unfortunately, the typical ways in which information is presented to consumers are not compatible with these notions. For example, commercials and in-store displays are typically arranged by brand. Since the format of a display may determine to a great extent how the information in the display is processed (Bettman and Kakkar 1977), attribute processing may be discouraged. If recognition in the store is a preferred mechanism, store displays, typically arranged by brand, may also be incompatible with the preference for attribute processing. Finally, if information is presented outside the store that is not also available in the store, recognition may not be possible and recall may be necessary. Recall would also tend to be organized by brand if information were typically presented by brand (Johnson and Russo 1978).

This brief analysis implies that the typical information environment faced by consumers may contain elements incompatible with consumers' preferred heuristics and methods for difficult choice tasks. If attribute processing, in-store, and recognition methods are preferred, this has implications for how the public policymaker might present information. The presentation methods most congruent with the preferences above might be methods in which information is presented in the store, and is organized by attribute. In addition, since the choice task is difficult, any way in which the information provided could be simplified would be desirable. This might involve prechunking of the information, or summary ratings. Package information is typically organized by brand, so the preferred form of in-store presentation might be some kind of special shelf display organized by attribute.[3] Out-of-store methods may be less effective if they alone are used for such difficult choice tasks, since information is typically organized by brand and greater usage of internal memory may be required. Out-of-store methods might be very useful if *combined* with these in-store methods, however.

The implications of the above are that for difficult choice tasks, presentation of information by policymakers through some form of out-of-store advertising *alone* (television, radio, print) may present difficulties for consumers. Such methods seem incongruent with those heuristics and implementation methods that may characterize difficult choice tasks. There are several ways in which these difficulties might be surmounted. First, the public policymaker might use both out-of-store advertising and some special in-store display organized by attribute. This might facilitate use of recognition, as well as in-store processing by attribute. A second way, possibly more efficient, is to *not attempt* to present the actual information in the advertisement itself, particularly if that information is difficult to process. Instead, the ad might attempt to emphasize the benefits of processing the information and direct consumers to the special in-store display where the information would be available. Then the consumer would know where to find the information if he or she wanted to use it at a later date.

If the system above were to be used, i.e., having the ad merely directive and having a special in-store display, what form might the display take? The arguments above suggest that it should be structured to facilitate processing by attribute and to provide chunked or pre-processed information such as summary ratings. One display of this type was first proposed by Russo, Krieser, and Miyashita (1975) and later used by Russo (1977) for unit price ratings. The display might be mounted on the shelf for a product class, and would present, for that whole class, a listing of all brands and sizes, with the objective ratings of interest presented for each. This is very similar to Wilkie's (1975a) notion of presenting a brand by attributes matrix of ratings. An example of the actual type of display used for dishwashing liquid is shown in Fig. 10.1. Russo, Krieser, and Miyashita (1975) and Russo (1977) documented that this system seemed to

---

3. Processing by attribute can be done with the typical store display, certainly. However, the process of looking from one package to another becomes tedious, particularly for more than a few alternatives. A standard revision strategy of comparing two alternatives at a time and retaining the best for the next comparison could also be used (Russo and Rosen 1975), but this also seems as though it would entail a great deal of effort. Thus, as noted earlier, package information may be used for processing by attribute only if there were a few alternatives available.

Fig. 10.1
Example of an in-store display listing for unit price. Reprinted
from J. Edward Russo, 1977, The value of unit price information, *Journal of Marketing Research,* **14** (May): 194, published by
the American Marketing Association.

	LIST OF UNIT PRICES	
	Listed in Order of Increasing Price Per Quart	
Par 48 oz	54¢	36.0¢ per quart
Par 32 oz	38¢	38.0¢ per quart
Sweetheart 32 oz	55¢	55.0¢ per quart
Brocade 48 oz	85¢	56.7¢ per quart
Sweetheart 22 oz	39¢	56.7¢ per quart
Supurb 32 oz	59¢	59.0¢ per quart
White Magic 32 oz	59¢	59.0¢ per quart
Brocade 32 oz	63¢	63.0¢ per quart
Brocade 22 oz	45¢	65.5¢ per quart

work effectively for unit pricing. In their actual in-store study, consumers
saved about two percent, on average, over the case of a normal unit price display with separate tags for each item.

Russo (1975) suggests expanding the listing to include not only unit
price but also other ratings, perhaps including a summary quality rating. He
suggests that only two or three ratings per brand should be given, since consumers may have difficulty combining results from comparisons on many dimensions (Russo and Dosher 1975). Given this limitation, Russo (1975) argues
that summary attributes should be developed.

It is important to understand why such a system using an in-store display might work, so that the principles could be applied to designing other systems. The system appears to work because it handles many of the information
processing requirements considered above. First, the system removes some of
the memory demands from the limited time exposure commercial. The con-

LIST OF UNIT PRICES		
Listed in Order of Increasing Price Per Quart		
Supurb 22 oz	45¢	65.5¢ per quart
White Magic 32 oz	45¢	65.5¢ per quart
Brocade 12 oz	27¢	72.0¢ per quart
Supurb 12 oz	29¢	77.3¢ per quart
Ivory 32 oz	80¢	80.0¢ per quart
Dove 22 oz	56¢	81.5¢ per quart
Ivory 22 oz	56¢	81.5¢ per quart
Lux 22 oz	56¢	81.5¢ per quart
Palmolive 32 oz	85¢	85.0¢ per quart
Ivory 12 oz	32¢	85.3¢ per quart
Palmolive 22 oz	60¢	87.3¢ per quart
Palmolive 12 oz	34¢	90.7¢ per quart

sumer need only remember to look at the in-store display, not remember any detailed ratings. Second, since the list is available in the store, there may be no need to retain a lot in memory. Also, since the consumer may tend to process in the store for difficult choices, the list would be available where the processing occurs. Third, the format of the list display, perhaps arranged with columns for each attribute, could greatly facilitate processing by attribute. Fourth, by having summary attributes listed, the consumer may be aided in chunking the information for processing. Fifth, the centralized list perhaps makes more brands available for processing, and processing might be facilitated by the list, so that more alternatives might be examined without undue effort.

Although there are several possible advantages, there are also many potential problems with such a system. First, there may certainly be cases in which brand processing is desirable: when differences on dimensions are difficult to ascertain or compute, or when large numbers of brands are present and some must be eliminated, for example. However, if objective ratings are presented, differences should be easy to compute. Also, if the display is in essentially a matrix format, brand processing would be reasonably easy. Second, the person who tends to prefer out-of-store *a priori* processing to in-store shopping may be handicapped, although in general for difficult choices in-store processing might be preferred. The effect of individual differences in prior experience and hence in the choice task difficulty experienced is considered below. Third, there are potentially severe problems of implementing such a system (Bettman 1975b). A cost–benefit analysis would need to be conducted to determine if such a system would be worthwhile. Fourth, the public policymaker might need to provide ratings for all brands in a product class, so it is not clear how to handle brands not available in a particular store. Failure to provide information on these unavailable brands might hinder cross-store comparisons (e.g., for durable goods).

Fifth, the use of summary ratings or "prechunked" data is likely to be quite controversial. Day (1975) relates the criticisms that were encountered when a model that weighted dimensional ratings to provide an overall summary measure was suggested. Not all people have the same weights for dimension, and not all have the same ideal levels for ratings on a dimension. This problem, although still politically quite delicate, may not be insurmountable from a theoretical viewpoint. Dawes and Corrigan (1974) show that equal weight models (and even models in which weights are given the "right" signs but are otherwise randomly chosen) actually perform *better* than the models developed from ratings of human judges. This phenomenon implies that perhaps, statistically at least, summary indices using unit weights for each dimension could be quite good. As Dawes and Corrigan (1974, p. 105) conclude, "The whole trick is to decide what variables to look at and then know how to add." One way of meeting objections to summary ratings might be to have detailed information on dimensional ratings available in the store in a booklet for consumers who wish to examine these ratings in detail to supplement the summary indices. This may require more use of recall and more directed attention, however, as noted above.

A sixth problem with the overall system proposed above is that only ratings on objective dimensions would be provided. Ratings on more subjective dimensions would not be included, but subjective ratings on these dimensions might be quite important to the consumer. The consumer would have to somehow integrate knowledge of the subjective dimensions with the objective ratings contained in the in-store display. Finally, Chestnut (1976) has argued that the goal of increasing the ease with which processing can be carried out may lead to short-term benefits, but may actually decrease the extent to which there is any long-term retention of the information presented. Provision of an effective external memory aid might lead to less information's being actually stored in internal memory.

Thus although such a system might solve some problems related to the consumer's information processing abilities, other difficulties arise. The use of such a system is discussed further in a later section.

PRODUCT CLASS CHOICE

As discussed above, public policymakers view choice among product classes as one important type of task facing consumers. Such product class choices would appear to be difficult choice tasks for several reasons. First, the attributes available may differ across product classes. Second, not only will attributes differ but the values for even those attributes that are common to the product classes compared will tend to vary more across classes than they would within a single product class; that is, prices or nutritional content may vary more across alternative product classes than they would among the brands within one product class. Hence, more trade-offs may be required since there will be fewer attributes that can be eliminated from consideration because they have roughly equal values across alternatives. Third, there is little information available directly comparing product classes. Fourth, consumers may not see their task as one of comparing product classes against one another or against some standard. Most advertisements deal with brand choice within a product class, so it might be natural for consumers to see brand choice as their normal task. Finally, Howard (1977) notes that consumers may often compare product classes in the extensive problem solving phase of choice during which criteria are not yet formed. This lack of criteria, or in general a lack of a coherent framework for analyzing the alternatives, may make product class choices more complex.

For a difficult choice task, consumers may prefer attribute processing, and use of constructive, in-store, and recognition methods. However, these mechanisms tend to be *unavailable* for product class choices. Product classes to be compared are often physically separated in the store, so that use of recognition is hindered since the relevant alternative product classes are not simultaneously available. Hence recall may be required to a greater extent. If attributes are not common across product classes, attribute processing is also made more difficult. Even if information is presented in the store in a display that enhances attribute processing to the extent possible within a product class, the physical separation of product classes in the store can cause problems. Presentation of information through out-of-store sources like advertising may pose even more difficulties since such information is typically organized by brand and hence memory would tend to be organized by brand. Thus product class choices seem to be especially difficult to deal with.

Several methods might be tried for alleviating the difficulties associated with making product class choices. First, consumer education efforts might be made, encouraging consumer use of standards (e.g., does this alternative have sufficient protein?). As noted earlier, use of such standards may be less difficult than processing the actual ratings. Even if standards are employed, however, the results of applying the standards to the various brands in a product class must be recalled and perhaps compared to results of applying the standards to brands from other product classes. Second, booklets available from the store manager that attempt to present information useful for comparing product classes might be utilized. Television and other ads could be used to tell consumers to consult these booklets. As discussed above, such booklets may require more goal-directed voluntary attention and more use of recall than in-store shelf displays, however. A third option is the special in-store display described above for difficult brand choices. Even though such a list might be for only one product class, it may facilitate making evaluations of an entire product class relative to other product classes by making it clear how well all the brands in that class perform on the attributes provided. Evaluation of a product class from such a list may be much easier than attempting to examine each brand individually. Several alternative information provision strategies are available, therefore. However, none seems particularly compelling. Facilitating product class choice seems to be a very difficult undertaking.

GENERAL CONCLUSIONS REGARDING
INFORMATION PROVISION BY POLICYMAKERS

The analyses above lead to several general conclusions about information provision. These conclusions fall into the categories of processability; choice task difficulty; processing time and amount of information; effects of format; and individual differences and use of multiple methods. The general approach used above is worth repeating before examining these conclusions. The types of processing characterizing various methods of providing information were examined, as were the processing types characteristic of some different consumer choice tasks. Then an attempt was made to match the provision methods to the choice tasks in order to make the types of processing required by each as congruent as possible. Again, let us reemphasize that these analyses were very speculative, with much more research necessary before firm recommendations could be made.

Processability
In all of the analyses above, the less the processability, the less likely that consumers might attempt to process and assess the information. If the task appears very difficult, consumers may decide *a priori* it is hopeless and not even attempt to actually use the information. Even if consumers decide to try to process and use the information, the lower the processability, the less likely they can succeed. The sections above then attempt to detail the factors which may interact to determine processability—properties of choice tasks,

properties of the information provision methods, and properties of the heuristics used by consumers.

Choice task difficulty

The difficulty of the choice task faced by consumers may be an important factor influencing how information might be provided most effectively. For easy tasks, it is hypothesized that brand processing and stored rule, recall, and prior methods may be used. Those provision methods that are congruent with such processing types are television, radio, and print advertising. This assumes that the information to be presented is not so complex that the task becomes difficult if this information is presented.

For difficult choice tasks, it was speculated that attribute processing and constructive, in-store, and recognition methods may be preferred. The most congruent provision methods in such a case might be in-store displays that are organized to allow attribute processing, perhaps in conjunction with out-of-store provision methods. Provision of package information, while not necessarily facilitating attribute processing to the maximum extent, can also be useful in such choice situations. This is particularly true if there are few alternatives and if a table comparing these alternatives were put on each package. The discussion above points out the potential importance of influencing the consumer at the moment of decision in difficult choice situations and not relying solely on *a priori* information presentations. Thus the policymaker may want to present information in the choice environment in addition to or in place of using out-of-store media such as television advertising.

Processing time and amount of information

Whether recognition or recall is used, there are limits to the amount of information that can be processed within any given time period. This implies that the time allowed for processing should be a function of the amount of information presented. For television and radio commercials, in which processing time is limited, in some cases public policymakers have instead made the time available for processing a function of the length of the commercial (e.g., six seconds out of a 30-second commercial). This seems to be an inappropriate basis for determining processing time. If a great deal of information is to be presented, methods which do not necessarily limit processing time seem desirable: print advertisements and in-store presentation methods.

Effects of information format

The discussion above and studies presented in earlier chapters (e.g., Bettman and Kakkar 1977) suggest that the format in which information is presented may influence to a great extent the way information is acquired and processed. Thus if certain methods for processing information are easier to carry out or more effective for consumers than others, information should be presented in formats congruent with those methods of processing. For example, if processing by attribute is thought to be effective, then information should be organized by attribute to encourage such processing (e.g., Russo, Krieser, and Miyashita 1975; Russo 1977; Johnson and Russo 1978). Presentation of information by brand, as is typically done, may be effective only to the extent that heuristics congruent with brand processing are preferred. Format may be particularly important in extensive problem solving (Howard 1977). Thus one might determine which heuristics seem most effective for given choice tasks, and the design information displays that encourage the type of processing required. Some conjectures were made above for three types of tasks; other tasks would need separate analyses.

Individual differences and use of multiple methods

Individual differences among consumers may affect the analyses above. Consumers may vary in the amount of prior experience they have with various choices, and hence in the difficulty they experience for any particular choice task. Also, not all consumers will use in-store processing for difficult tasks, and so on. This implies that rather than concentrating on a single method of information provision, several methods which complement each other should perhaps be used. Television, radio, or print advertising might be used in combination with in-store methods such as package information or the special in-store display proposed. No one method is the total answer. Each method has certain advantages; providing information via several methods might allow consumers to obtain the information from that source which was easiest and most effective for them. As Wilkie (1975a, p. 11) states, "combinations of channels and formats will be required."

The analyses above relate to the broad problem of providing information to consumers. Consideration of specific programs (e.g., corrective advertising, nutritional labeling and advertising) is beyond the scope of this chapter. For applications of information processing notions to specific issues, see Wilkie (1975a, b), Ross (1974), Bettman (1975b), Day (1976), and Lambert (1977).

INFORMATION PROCESSING STUDIES
OF SPECIAL GROUPS OF CONSUMERS

For certain choices, particular groups of consumers are often viewed as being especially in need of information and/or protection, perhaps because they lack sufficient processing abilities or perhaps because poor choices might be potentially more harmful (Cohen 1972). Such populations might include children, the elderly, or the poor. For example, young children may be seen as not being able to understand commercials very well; elderly consumers or the poor may be seen as particularly in need of information on nutritional aspects of foods, since they have limited food budgets available. There has been work done on the information processing characteristics of children and of the elderly. Brief outlines of this work are given below. Then a general strategy for dealing with special groups of consumers is proposed.

CHILDREN'S CONSUMER INFORMATION PROCESSING

Prompted by concerns that perhaps children are not able to cope effectively with advertising for children's products, several studies have examined how children process and react to commercial messages. Calder, Robertson, and Rossiter (1975) suggest that children, especially younger ones, use isolated bits and pieces of information, with little overall integration, in making inferences and choices. Several studies report more detailed findings. Robertson and Rossiter (1974) examined the perceptions of commercials by first, third, and fifth graders. They showed that there is a steady increase with age in children's perceptions that commercials are intended to persuade. Increases with age in discrimination between programming and commercials, in recognition of the source of the message, in perception of the intended audience of the message, in awareness of the symbolic nature of commercials, and in perceptions of the possible discrepancies between the message and the product were also found. Robertson and Rossiter then attempted to relate increased perception of persuasive intent to decreased liking, decreased trust, and decreased intention to purchase the product advertised. However, the results are relatively weak and are subject to methodological problems (Ryans and Deutscher 1975).

Ward and Wackman (1973) have also studied children's processing of advertising. They found that understanding of the purpose of commercials increased with the cognitive level of the children (with cognitive level's being closely related to age), and perceived truthfulness of the commercials decreased with cognitive level. These and other results are used by Ward and Wackman to support their contention that younger children tend to focus on only a few dimensions, and especially on dimensions that are immediately perceived in the stimulus (e.g., color, size) rather than conceptual (e.g., ingredients, function). In a later monograph, Ward, Wackman, and Wartella (1977) replicated these earlier results. They also found that older children used more product attributes in total in comparing brands. Finally, they examined the impact of the family environment (e.g., use of budgeting, mother–child interaction patterns) on growth of children's consumer skills, and conclude that consumer education programs for children could be quite beneficial.

Rossiter (1976) suggests that in their focus on immediate perceptual input, children often use visual imagery. This reliance on visual imagery seems to be particularly characteristic of younger rather than older children, however (Cramer 1976). Rossiter studied perceptions of cereal, and found that children appear to have an extensive memory base of visual data, ranging from the

colors and design of the cereal boxes to the strong imagery found for any pre-
miums offered. This could enhance in-store choice behavior, as opposed to the
child's asking for a particular cereal out of the store; that is, the brand might
be recognized in the store, based on the visual imagery. Rossiter notes that this
could potentially pose problems for providing information to children if the
information to be provided is hard to convey visually. However, Rossiter also
finds that children recall jingles, so that perhaps jingles or ingenious visual displays could be used. In any case, Rossiter's work suggests that if one wishes to
provide information to children for product classes about which children
actually make attempts to influence what is purchased, such as cereal (Ward
and Wackman 1972), then visual imagery or perhaps jingles should be used.

The studies above, which reflect only a portion of the research on
children's reactions to advertising, do not provide strong evidence on the debate over whether commercials on children's television programs should be
regulated or not. Robertson and Rossiter (1974) point out that opposite conclusions regarding regulation could be drawn from their results depending on the
theoretical position of the decision maker. Thus further research is clearly
needed. However, these studies, as noted above, *do* provide inputs for how
information may be effectively presented to children if it were decided to
do so.

INFORMATION PROCESSING OF THE ELDERLY

Research on the information processing characteristics of the elderly
has tended to focus on memory abilities. Several studies have compared the
abilities of groups of differing ages on various mental tasks, and have found
that the groups of older subjects performed less well than the younger subjects. For example, Broadbent and Heron (1962) found that when presented
with a main task involving memory and a distracting task, older subjects tend
to do badly at one or the other, while younger subjects do reasonably well at
both. Clay (1954) found that complex problems with high information load
caused older subjects more difficulty than they caused younger subjects.
McGhie, Chapman, and Lawson (1965) found that older subjects tend to show
poorer short-term retention, but particularly for visually rather than aurally
presented data. Welford (1962, p. 337) notes (referring to memory search) that
"older subjects seem to find it relatively easy to search within a major class of
objects, but difficult to shift from one major class to another." Craik (1971)
found that recognition was not affected by aging to any great extent, but that
recall seemed worse for older subjects. All of these studies are congruent with
other work that in general shows poorer short-term memory functioning for
older subjects (Welford 1962). Finally, Anders, Fozard, and Lillyquist (1972) and
Anders and Fozard (1973) show that older subjects have slower search speeds
than have younger subjects in both short-term and long-term memory. Chiang
and Atkinson (1976) show that memory search speed is highly correlated with

visual search speed, so the results above may also imply the elderly would be slower in examining visual displays.

All these findings must be regarded with caution. Since cross-sectional (i.e, comparisons of subjects of different ages) rather than longitudinal (comparisons of subjects with themselves over time) designs were used, one cannot conclude that performance deteriorates with age. Factors related to the specific groups used (e.g., different age groups would have probably received different modes and amounts of formal education) might account for the results, rather than age itself. However, if the findings were correct, they may have implications for the choice processing of the elderly. First, the findings about difficulties in making shifts in search and difficulties in recall may imply that attempting to make choices between product classes by recall would be more difficult for the elderly. Second, tasks requiring rapid processing (e.g., viewing of television commercials that present a great deal of information) may be harder for older subjects due to their slower memory and visual search speeds. Finally, tasks in which distraction is likely to be present (e.g., viewing television commercials) would probably be difficult. These findings may suggest greater use of in-store displays or print ads in communicating to elderly consumers, since these methods do not limit processing time and may facilitate use of recognition memory rather than use of recall (see Phillips and Sternthal [1977] for similar arguments).

A STRATEGY FOR DEALING WITH SPECIAL GROUPS OF CONSUMERS

These research findings on special groups of consumers suggest a general strategy for the design of information environments. This strategy is to first determine any particular information processing abilities or limitations which characterize the group(s) of interest (e.g., the amount of knowledge about the choice, what kinds of heuristics are known, and specific processing capabilities and limitations [Hunt, Lunnenborg, and Lewis 1975]). Then one must also characterize the types of choice tasks these groups of consumers are engaged in. One can then attempt to provide information in ways that are as compatible as possible with the abilities and limitations of the group and the types of processing required by the choice tasks considered. Thus again we have a general approach of first determining the types of processing required by choice tasks, the types of processing encouraged by information displays, and consumer limitations; and then attempting to match the type of information display to these other requirements as well as possible.[4]

---

4. It may be that policymakers do not need to reach all groups to achieve some desired effects. If a large enough proportion of the marketplace acts on the information provided, marketplace forces may lead to "better" products even for those consumers unable or unwilling to process the information. What proportion is "large enough" is, of course, the crucial issue. For a theoretical treatment of this problem, see Wilde and Schwartz (1977).

NEEDED RESEARCH

The most general statement for research needs in the public policy area is for information processing studies of both designs of specific information provision programs and of more basic research areas such as memory (Wilkie 1975a). In both cases, however, a setting relevant to public policy concerns should be used. Information should be objective ratings, for example. Beyond these general statements, there are many specific areas in which research is needed.

Analysis of consumer tasks, a recurrent theme in this book, is one large potential research area. Much more research on characterizing the types of processing required by various types of choice tasks is necessary (e.g., are the speculations in Proposition 7.5 accurate?). Finally, different types of information displays also need to be examined with respect to the types of processing they encourage or discourage. Thus, in general, studies of the constraints various consumer tasks place on processing is essential.

A second general area of research concerns possible consumer education efforts. The simplifying heuristics actually known and used by consumers need to be determined. For example, if use of standards is helpful for making product class choices, do consumers actually use such standards? Could they be taught standards and how to use them? In general, a knowledge of what heuristics consumers use and how these might be improved is needed. Consumer education efforts could also be helped by studies of chunking of information. If policymakers knew how consumers chunk data, then messages could be designed that would be maximally congruent with what consumers already know, and hence might be more easily processed.

Other factors that could reduce processing burdens for consumers might also be studied. For example, the clinical judgment research cited above, showing the value of equal weight or even random weight models for making judgments (Dawes and Corrigan 1974), might be replicated using quality ratings or other possible summary ratings for products as dependent variables and attribute ratings of products as independent variables. The results of such research could then be examined to see whether using summary ratings derived from such models might be feasible. Wilkie (1975b, p. 227) also suggests other possible ways to reduce processing loads that could be researched. More studies of differences in processing abilities and limitations for special groups of consumers are also needed.

Finally, various combinations of modes of presentation need to be examined in field settings to test their effectiveness for various types of choices. For example, should one present information in both advertising and in-store displays, or should one only have the ad direct consumers to the in-store display? Another important issue is how special in-store displays like the one proposed above could be designed and implemented.

CHAPTER 11

Implications for
Marketing Decisions

The emphasis in this chapter is on the application of findings about consumer information processing to making marketing decisions. As was the case with the public policy implications discussed in Chapter 10, actual applications to marketing decisions are still in their formative stages, and in need of much more empirical research. Thus the topics considered below are in most cases interesting hypotheses, but have not been tested. Two major types of implications are considered: insights into gathering information from consumers; and applications of information processing principles to the formulation of marketing strategies (i.e., strategies for promotion, pricing, product, and distribution).

IMPLICATIONS FOR GATHERING INFORMATION FROM CONSUMERS

One major function of market research is to gather information from consumers, via questionnaires or some other form of measurement, that can be used to obtain insights into why consumers respond as they do to a firm's offerings or into which new offerings might be successful. The methods used to gather information pose an information processing task to the consumers who are being studied. Therefore, insights into consumer information processing are relevant for increasing our understanding of such methods. In the discussion below, two uses of consumer information processing notions are considered: methods for determining *what* to ask consumers, and questions relating to *how* to request information from consumers.

INSIGHTS INTO WHAT INFORMATION TO GATHER

Information processing notions have been used to determine what should be asked of consumers, and how the information obtained can be applied and interpreted. In particular, Palmer and Faivre (1973) discuss how research based on decision net models of consumer choice can be used. Palmer and Faivre use videotape replay of a consumer's shopping behavior to guide protocol collection (i.e., a subject watches himself or herself shop and then comments upon it). This "prompted protocol" method was also used by Russo and Rosen (1975) and Russo and Dosher (1975) in their eye movement studies of choice. The prompted protocols are gathered for choices of specific products, e.g., for deodorant choices, as reported in the Palmer and Faivre article. Then the protocols are used to develop decision nets.

Palmer and Faivre claim that nets of single individuals are not useful for making specific marketing decisions. However, they note that they have found empirically that if nets for a number of consumers are developed, similarities in process emerge that allow the development of a more general net. This general similarity may reflect the common structure of the "task environment" faced by the consumers for that particular product class. These generalized nets contain more abstract tests than individual nets (e.g., "Is anything about the brand not liked?" vs. "Does the brand have a bad smell?"). Other evidence for finding similarities in individual nets if general rather than specific tests are used was presented in Chapter 8. Haines' (1974a) two raincoat models were quite similar for the case in which specific nodes were collapsed into more general categories.

Given these generalized decision nets, one can use the insights from the net structure to develop a standard questionnaire. Thus the generalized net gives guidance for *what* should be measured. Continuing the example above, the questionnaire might attempt to elicit any features that were not liked about various brands. Thus the protocol method is just the first step in the process, followed by development of a general net, and then development of a questionnaire based on the general net that can be administered to a large sample. The general net can then be used to develop estimates of market response, given the data obtained from the questionnaires. In addition, proposed changes in marketing variables can be viewed as potential changes in the information consumers hold, which then have implications for the outcomes estimated by using the general net. Palmer and Faivre report that they have used this technique successfully in commercial applications in Britain for several years (see SCIMITAR V [1975] for a description of this system). Further results, applications, and advantages of the method are discussed in Palmer and Faivre (1973).

INSIGHTS INTO HOW TO GATHER INFORMATION FROM CONSUMERS

There are many different ways in which some particular type of information can be gathered from consumers. Each of these alternative methods may elicit different types of information processing from consumers, and hence different responses. Three types of information processing effects on the responses obtained using various questioning methods are discussed below: effects of form of processing (by brand or by attribute); effects of capacity limitations; and effects of the sense modality used to present the questions. In addition, general discussion of the effects of type of processing on obtained responses is presented.

Effects of form of processing on questionnaire response

In structuring a consumer questionnaire that requires some judgments about several attributes for each of several brands, there are two main options. One can ask the consumer about all attributes for a given brand, then move on to a second brand, and so on; or one can ask about all brands for a given attribute, then move on to a second attribute, and so forth. Thus questioning may be organized by brand or by attribute. As suggested in Chapters 5 and 7, this organization of the questionnaire may affect how consumers will process information from memory. Processing may be largely by brand if the questions are arranged by brand, and by attribute if the questions are organized by attribute. One might then suspect that the form of questioning, since it in essence imposes a form of processing, might affect consumer responses to the questions.

Wilkie, McCann, and Reibstein (1974) examined how measures of the degree to which each of several brands was felt to possess each of several attributes (measures of brand beliefs) were affected by the form of questioning, whether by brand or by attribute. They found that questioning by brand, as compared with questioning by attribute, was associated with less dispersion in the ratings across attributes for a given brand; higher levels of fit in the prediction of brand preferences; and fewer statistically significant attributes in the regression predicting preference. However, there were other aspects of the data for which no differences were found. Form of questioning thus affected some, but not all, properties of the data gathered. Wilkie, McCann, and Reibstein (1974) argue that which form is preferable depends on the purposes of the study, since questioning by brand seems to be associated with higher predictive power, but questioning by attribute with potentially greater diagnostic power, since more attributes were significant.

Myers (1977) describes a computerized questioning technique that has interesting potential applications in investigating these form of questioning issues. The computer can vary whether attribute or brand questioning is used, and can allow the subject to request the form desired. This flexibility might also allow for better handling of individual processing differences when obtaining brand belief ratings.

Effects of capacity limitations on questionnaire response

Hulbert (1975) studied one implication of consumers' limited information processing capacities for questionnaire response. Hulbert argued, based on Miller's (1956) notion of limits on the number of chunks (seven or so) which can be held in short-term memory, that consumers will use only a very small number of response values, even if given a scale with an essentially unlimited number of potential responses. Hulbert presented consumers with a magnitude estimation task in which stimuli were to be rated by assigning nonnegative numbers to them, with no further specifications on the scale. Thus respondents could discriminate among alternatives as finely as they wished. Respondents were asked to rate three sets of 70, 56, and 54 items. The number of distinct values used by respondents averaged less than nine for each of the three sets, suggesting that subjects did limit their discriminations. Hulbert then discussed how such limitation by subjects could cause problems if one wished to study responses to large sets of stimuli. Hulbert's results may be a function of the large number of ratings subjects had to make, however. If fewer items were to be rated, perhaps finer discriminations would have been made.

Such effects of limited processing capacity seem worthy of more study. In particular, how consumers respond to the degree of information load imposed by a questionnaire, possibly by changing the way they make their responses, is not known. Consumers may greatly simplify their responses the more complex the questionnaire, perhaps (as Hulbert found) by reducing the degree to which they discriminate among alternatives, or perhaps by using other simplifying strategies.

Effects of sense modality of the questions

A final area in which some research has been performed is comparison of the responses obtained from questioning based on different sense modalities. The main difference that has been studied is variation in response between verbal or visual modes of questioning. Rossiter (1976) found that children's preferences for cereal brands did not always match when assessed visually (by matching packages) or by a verbal scale. Visual and verbal choices of favorite brand matched for 42 percent of first graders, 53 percent of third graders, and 74 percent of fifth graders. Rossiter argues that symbolic transformations are required to switch mentally from a visual image of a preferred brand to the verbal label for that brand. Under conditions of high information load or required processing rate (e.g., in a long questionnaire), the transformation may be not performed or may be performed inaccurately. Thus if some significant proportion of consumers shop by using recognition based on visual images, assessment of preferences by verbal scales may be misleading.

MacKay and Olshavsky (1975) also show how visual and verbal assessments can differ. Subjects in their study were asked to draw a map of the relative locations of eight supermarkets in their town (a relatively visual task) and to respond to paired comparison judgments of interstore distances (a relatively verbal task). The paired comparisons were used to develop a map by multidimensional scaling. They found that the drawn maps corresponded more closely to the actual positions of the stores, but the distances in the maps derived from scaling were more closely related to consumers' verbal preference ratings for the stores.

Other information processing effects on responses

The discussions above have presented evidence that different forms of questioning, which may require different forms of processing, may elicit different responses. This point has been stressed in a slightly different form throughout the book. Different data collection methods can represent different information processing tasks for the consumer, and hence will present different processing demands. Task analyses are needed to ascertain the processing requirements imposed by various data collection methods, so that any potential biases engendered by these requirements can be examined. It would seem that the processing required by the questioning method should be maximally congruent with the processing used by consumers in the actual choice task one wishes to study. For example, one might conjecture that recognition measures of preference should be used for studying product classes in which choices are difficult or in which consumers have in general little experience, and that recall measures should be used for more familiar product categories (since recognition and recall processing methods may tend to be used by consumers in such environments [Proposition 7.5]). Krugman (1977) also hypothesizes that recognition measures may be more useful for low involvement choices. Also, one could argue that to the extent consumers use external memory and hence may not store information in their own memories, the responses to questionnaire items may be suspect. Finally, questioning methods that assume brand processing (e.g., asking for attitude ratings) may be inappropriate for investigating those consumer choice tasks characterized by attribute processing (perhaps tasks in which consumers have little experience or in which choices are difficult).

In general, therefore, research is needed to examine the processing characterizing various questioning tasks. For example, one might study the types of processing used in carrying out rating, ranking, or sorting tasks for comparing various alternatives; or the processing methods engendered by personal, telephone, or self-administered interview methods. Although studies have been done that show that various methods may differ in the responses elicited (e.g., Locander and Burton 1976; Whipple 1976; Henry and Stumpf 1975), what may be more important is to know the type of processing required by each method, that has usually not been examined. Then one might attempt to match the processing required by the data collection method to the type of processing characterizing the actual consumer choice task being studied.

IMPLICATIONS FOR MARKETING STRATEGY

The information processing view of consumer choice has implications for various aspects of marketing strategy. Implications for promotion, pricing, product and distribution decisions are considered below. In all of these cases, the viewpoint is that marketing strategies result in information's being presented to the consumer. This presentation may be direct, as through promotion, in which some pieces of information are directly disseminated to consumers. However, information is also presented to consumers indirectly. The price of a product, the brand name, the store in which it is sold, or the outcome of consuming that product all provide some information to the consumer. How the consumer interprets that information may then be crucial for understanding the consumer's responses. Thus factors influencing consumers' interpretations of and reactions to the information provided as a result of marketing strategy decisions are the focus below.

IMPLICATIONS FOR PROMOTION DECISIONS

The discussion in Chapter 10 provides a basic framework for questions relating to information provision to consumers. In that presentation the properties characterizing various modes of information provision were considered. In addition, the principle that the processing implied by the presentation method should be congruent with the processing required by or characteristic of the choice task being considered was enunciated. This matching of provision method to the consumer task is also an important factor in implications for promotional strategy. However, in addition to considering how to make processing easier for consumers we must also consider the persuasive goals of the marketer. In the discussion below, four broad sets of implications are examined: what types of information to provide, where information should be provided, how information might best be provided, and understanding consumers' reactions to the messages presented by the marketer.

Implications for what type of information to provide
Three basic influences on what types of information to provide are considered below: factors related to attention; congruence with the choice heuristics used by consumers; and other factors.

Factors related to attention. As emphasized in Chapter 4, consumers may direct attention to items of information for two basic reasons: because that information is needed to help attain current goals (voluntary attention); or because the information is novel, surprising, departs from expectations, and so on (involuntary attention).

To meet consumer needs for information in line with their goals, the marketer can study the search goals of consumers. As noted in Chapter 3, goals related to information processing needs have not been the typical focus of study in marketing research—broader motives or benefits have typically been the focus. However, to gain insights into what information should be provided, study of consumer goals for type of information sought may be helpful. This may be particularly true for product classes characterized by long interpurchase times or many changes over time, since consumers may then be more likely to search for new information rather than relying on memory.

A second method for gaining attention is through information that is novel, surprising, unexpected, and so on. Such information may then cause an interrupt, and hence be attended to. Evidence for this assertion is presented in Chapter 4. However, such attention due to an interrupt does not necessarily imply anything about how consumers will respond to the information. Attention may be implied, but no specific response. Finally, there is some interesting evidence that attempts to gain attention in this manner characterize some types of actual marketing decisions. Rados (1972) studied the weekly advertising decision for a large supermarket chain. He noted that one of the crucial elements in designing the weekly newspaper advertisement was to include several "hot" items that were certain to get attention.

Congruence of information with consumer choice heuristics. A second factor influencing what types of information should be presented to consumers is the array of choice heuristics used by consumers for the particular decision of interest. Assume that for the choice task being considered, certain types of heuristics are used by consumers, and also that certain beliefs are held by various consumer segments. Then Wright (1973c) argues that the content of the message, what is stressed, should vary as a function of these current beliefs and the choice heuristics used. He presents an example to support this argument. Suppose a consumer believes that a particular brand of toothpaste is (1) slightly below average in whitening power; (2) average in ability to freshen breath; (3) average in economy; and (4) slightly above average in prevention of decay. Then under various assumptions about the choice rule used by the consumer, the type of information that should be presented in the persuasive message would vary. For example, if the consumer used a compensatory rule with equal weights, then any aspect could potentially be promoted, since the effects of an equal change in beliefs on overall evaluation would be equal regardless of which belief were changed. If a conjunctive rule were used in which a brand had to be average or better on all attributes, then changing beliefs about whitening power would be necessary. Favorable changes in the beliefs about the other attributes would be irrelevant if the belief that whitening power is unacceptable remained unchanged. If a disjunctive heuristic were used that required at least one attribute to be very much above average, then changing whitening power to average as in the previous case would be irrelevant. Finally, if a lexicographic heuristic were used, with whitening power ranked as the most important attribute, favorable changes in other attributes would be ineffective unless the consumer could be convinced that whitening power was at least equal to that of other brands.

Thus the specific choice heuristic used and particular beliefs held may have implications for which promotional strategies would be most effective. To apply these notions, one would need to ascertain what proportions of the target market segments for a product used various heuristics and what beliefs were held for the particular product choice of interest. Given the current state of the art in determining the heuristics used by consumers, this is not an easy task. Correlational methods may be misleading, and process methods are expensive and time-consuming (see Chapter 7). Other methods for assessing heuristics appear necessary before the implications above could be applied, especially questionnaire-based methods that could be easily administered by the market researcher.

The examples above stress changing existing beliefs. If one wishes to present information on a new attribute (i.e., add a new belief), the effects also may differ depending on the type of choice heuristic assumed. One area in particular that has been studied for the case of presenting a new belief is whether an adding or averaging compensatory heuristic is used by consumers (Bettman, Capon, and Lutz 1975b, c). If an adding rule is used, presenting information leading to a new positively evaluated belief will increase the consumer's evaluation of the brand. However, if an averaging heuristic is used, the change in evaluation need not be positive, but depends on the evaluation of the new belief relative to the average evaluation of the old beliefs. If the average of the old beliefs is more favorable than the evaluation of the new belief, then the overall evaluation would actually *decrease* by adding the new belief, even if it were positive. If the average were less than the evaluation of the new belief, the overall evaluation would rise. Thus one needs once again to know both the heuristics used and the beliefs held by consumers.

Note that in all of the analyses presented above, the assumption was implicitly made that the heuristics used by consumers remain relatively stable for the choice of interest. This may be a reasonable assumption if some particular decision (e.g., choice of breakfast cereal) is being considered, since the structure of that specific choice task may determine to some extent the types of heuristics used. However, one might expect the heuristics used to vary over choice tasks, so that a marketer producing brands in several different product categories might have quite different strategies for the types of information to be presented for the various categories.

Other factors influencing what information to provide. Three other factors relevant to what information might be provided to consumers relate to influencing consumers' instructions to themselves, helping to structure consumers reactions to choice outcomes, and stage in the choice process. First, consumers have been depicted as generating plans or instructions for themselves about future actions they may take (Proposition 3.5). Marketers can provide information that suggests such future plans and reminds the consumer about them (e.g., "See our ad in the Sunday paper and be sure to take the ad with you when you go to the store" or "Be sure to remember the red and yellow package").

A second area in which consumers may be influenced is the interpretations they develop about causes for outcomes, discussed in Chapter 9. The marketer's message can try to influence these inferences if certain factors are felt to be important. For example, if the brand has complicated usage instructions, the marketer might stress that one must follow the directions, and might put "Did you follow directions?" in bold letters on the package. If the product should be used only in certain situations, this could be stressed. Such information may help to prestructure the kinds of inferences consumers may make about outcomes. In general, the marketer could study what inferences might be made for any particular product, and then attempt to structure which inferences will in fact be made by the messages presented.

Finally, as noted in Chapter 5, consumers may have demands for different types of information at different stages of the choice process. During extensive problem solving, information that defines the product and helps the consumer develop criteria may be most useful. During limited problem solving, comparative information on the relative performance of brands on various attributes is needed. During routinized response behavior, information on price and availability may be the focus (Howard 1977). Thus knowing the stage in the choice process characterizing various segments might be useful in determining what types of information to present.

Implications for where information should be provided

The discussion in Chapter 10 emphasized that presentation of information in the store (on the package or through various forms of point of purchase displays) and presentation of information outside of the store (through television, radio, print billboards, and so on) may have very different properties. In particular, the types of processing necessary for consumers to use the information may differ. Since the discussion in Chapter 10 was quite extensive, it will not be repeated here. Only the most salient points are presented.

Provision of information in the store. One of the most salient features of providing information in the store is that the information on packages or other displays can serve as an external memory for the consumer, available at the time the alternative is obtained; that is, the consumer can actually examine this information in the store, without needing to rely totally on his or her own memory. This presence of an external memory allows consumers to simply recognize various pieces of information, if they desire, rather than recall this information. (This is discussed further below.)

A second characteristic of in-store information provision is that there may be more situational impacts on the consumer that can influence how the information is interpreted (e.g., deals on various brands, differences in which brands are displayed near the marketer's brand, and so on). Finally, it may be somewhat easier for consumers to make comparisons among brands if information is provided in the in-store environment (by using package information) than to compare brands using memory for the information presented, for example, in television advertising.

Given these characteristics, under what conditions might the marketer wish to present information in the store? As noted in Chapter 7, consumers may tend to process in the store for decisions in which they have little previous experience or knowledge or in which the decision is difficult for some reason.[1] Thus a marketer in a product class characterized by low levels of consumer experience or by difficulty in the choice to be made might concentrate to a greater extent on in-store, point of purchase information displays or on greater amounts of package information. Even if consumers do have experience, the marketer may wish to encourage comparison of his or her product with others in the store, if the product is a new brand or is believed to have some differential advantage, for example. Such a desire might also argue for provision of information in the store, particularly on the package. Thus if the marketer feels consumers are processing in the store or wishes to encourage such processing, in-store information provision is needed.

Provision of information outside the store. Presenting information outside the store may require the consumer to rely on his or her own memory to a greater extent. Although print ads can provide an external memory device (by clipping the ad), television, radio, and billboards do not provide an external memory aid.

The conditions under which marketers might wish to concentrate on presenting information outside of the store would tend to be the opposite of those presented above for in-store presentation. In general, consumers may process outside the store for product classes in which the choice is easy and they have a good deal of experience. Thus a marketer with a brand in a product class in which consumers have a good deal of experience might concentrate more on out-of-store and less on in-store activity, since consumers may tend to decide outside of the store. Note that these prescriptions refer to the emphasis that might be appropriate for the marketer. It is not suggested that one or the other of in-store or out-of-store methods be used exclusively. Consumers will vary in their degree of prior experience, and the in-store and out-of-store methods have different properties, so some combination of approaches will in most cases be the best strategy, as noted in Chapter 10.

Implications for how information should be provided

Three major aspects of how information should be provided are discussed below: congruence with consumer choice heuristics; congruence with the methods used by consumers to carry out these choice heuristics; and approaches that attempt to change consumer processing.

---

1. Consumers might also process in the store for low involvement decisions, since it may be easier to process in the store than to think about the choice beforehand (Robertson 1976). In such cases, consumers may have little knowledge stored in memory, even though they may have made a choice many times.

Congruence with consumer choice heuristics. If consumers are known to use certain heuristics for a particular choice, then presenting information that is in the form required for using those heuristics may make the information easier to process by consumers and hence more attended to (See Proposition 7.8.iii). Wright and Barbour (1975) outline compatible forms of presentation of information for (among others) the affect referral heuristic (reference to overall worth of an alternative); compensatory rules (assertions about properties and the overall worth implied by these properties); the lexicographic heuristic (importance of attributes and comparisons of the brand advertised with other brands on that attribute); and the conjunctive heuristic (definition of cutoff levels, assertions about rejecting alternatives that do not meet cutoffs, and assertions about the advocated brand's meeting these cutoffs). Howard (1977) also discusses congruent forms of information for making comparisons and stresses that communications attempting to influence criteria need to be simple and as nonabstract as possible.

A survey of mass media advertising content carried out by Wright and Barbour showed that assertions about properties of alternatives, overall worth, and comparisons on specific dimensions were most often used, with assertions about properties being predominant. Thus advertisers seem to structure messages to be congruent with compensatory rules and brand processing. However, for situations in which consumers have little experience, attribute processing may be preferred. Thus one possible implication is that information that is congruent with heuristics using attribute processing might be provided for product classes with generally low levels of consumer experience. For example, for the heuristic version of the additive difference model, assertions about the differences between alternatives on various attributes and how one should trade off such differences would be appropriate.

Congruence with consumer implementation methods. Several methods used by consumers for implementing choice heuristics were discussed in Chapter 7—in-store vs. prior processing, use of recognition vs. recall, and use of constructive vs. stored rule approaches. It was hypothesized that these methods are related in that in-store, recognition, and constructive methods may tend to be used in situations in which little experience is present or in which choices are difficult; and prior, recall, and stored rule methods may tend to be utilized in easy and familiar choice situations. We have discussed the impact of the in-store vs. prior (out-of-store) distinction above. Now we focus on the use of recognition vs. recall. The implications of the constructive vs. stored rule distinction are considered in a later section.

Since consumers may attempt to use recognition more often in the store, the external memory provided by packages and in-store displays is a crucial consideration. Use of recognition presupposes some earlier presentation of information to the consumer, with later recognition of that information.

Therefore, in general there may be some out-of-store presentation, with recognition cued by the package or display in the store at some later time. This implies that the information on the package or display should be the same or nearly the same as that presented in the out-of-store advertising, so that it can be recognized. One typical method for ensuring this match is to show the package in the advertisement (if visual information can be presented, as for television and billboards). This need not be the only method, however. In one case, a cereal manufacturer with a very powerful advertisement ingeniously put a scene from that ad on the front of the cereal package, thus bringing the context of the commercial into the store. For radio commercials, either descriptions of the package ("Look for the red and yellow box.") or slogans that would be repeated on the package might be used. Finally, note that if the marketer wishes to have particular claims recognized, the claims should be presented in the store on the package or in a display, as well as in the advertisement. Although the information on the package may trigger recall of associated information from memory, there is no guarantee that any particular claim will be recalled in this fashion.

For the consumer to use recall of information, the information presented should be relatively simple and congruent with what consumers know. Recall will tend to be used for familiar choice situations, so the consumer will attempt to fit the new information into an existing set of beliefs about the product class. As noted in Chapter 6, different modes of presentation of information can affect the ease of recall of that information. For example, use of visual imagery is often a good way to enhance recall. Lutz and Lutz (1977) show that recall of brand names is higher for advertisements using certain types of visual imagery, for instance.

Whether consumers use recall or recognition, the ease with which the information presented can be processed will affect later usage. A general principle presented in Chapter 10 was that the amount of information that can be assimilated is a function of the time available for processing. For media in which the time available for processing is limited (television or radio), the amount of information that can be presented may also be limited. For cases in which the marketer wishes to present large amounts of information, or in which the information is complex, either media that do not limit the time available for processing should be used (print, in-store presentation), or the time given for processing should be expanded to meet the processing needs.

Approaches that attempt to change consumer processing. The approaches outlined above have all been reactive—taking various aspects (consumer heuristics, choice task structure, consumer processing methods) as *givens* and attempting to match the mode of information presentation to these givens. However, there are also approaches that attempt to accomplish the goals of the marketer by being proactive, by attempting to change the types of processing used.

An example of a proactive approach based on consumer information processing considerations is attempting to encourage certain types of processing. We have discussed above the impact the format of the information provided can have on consumer processing and memory (e.g., Proposition 5.3.iv). This impact of format can perhaps be utilized by the marketer. If the marketer wishes to encourage a particular type of processing, then the information presented to consumers can be organized in a way that does this. For example, for products sold in supermarkets it may be tedious to process by attribute, since the shelves are organized by brand. If a marketer feels there is a particular differential advantage on some attribute and wishes to encourage attribute processing, then a comparative advertisement or package information might be used. One manufacturer of paper towels has recently followed the latter strategy, putting a "comparison table" on their package, comparing their brand with five other brands on sheet count and square feet. If the information environment is not conducive to the processing desired in its current state, then the marketer can attempt to alter the information presentation format to produce the desired effect. In general, one might hypothesize that given an attribute advantage, the marketer should structure information so as to encourage processing by attribute; given an "image" advantage, processing by brand should be encouraged. Note that the strategy of encouraging processing by attribute might be easiest to implement using in-store presentations (package or other displays), although print advertising might also be used.

This discussion implies that one potential way to change the heuristics used by consumers is to change the format of the information presented. Thus if marketers felt that use of a certain heuristic would be favorable for their brand, information could be presented in ways congruent with that heuristic, as described in an earlier section, and the desired heuristic, might also be specifically advocated in the ad. For example, one could present differences between one's brand and another brand on several attributes, argue how these differences should be traded off, and stress this use of trade-offs if one wished to encourage an additive difference heuristic. Wright and Barbour note that they found no instances of attempting to change rules in their survey of media advertising. Tversky (1972, p. 297), however, presents an example of a television commercial outlining an elimination by aspects rule, and then argues that individuals may use rules that seem easy to state, defend, and apply. By providing such a rule, the advertiser may be able to influence the consumer to use that rule.

Note that the strategy presented here is the reverse of the strategy outlined earlier in which the choice rule is taken as given and the marketer attempts to structure messages appropriately. Usage of one strategy as opposed to the other might depend on the relative ease of changing those particular beliefs or other aspects necessary to achieve favorable choices for a given heuristic versus the ease in changing the heuristic to one that might result in more favorable choices given particular beliefs. The strategy of attempting to change heuristics might be easier in situations in which the consumer is using a constructive method, in which the heuristic used is being built during the choice process. This implies, given the hypotheses about methods and their usage presented above, that changing or suggesting heuristics may be most effective for difficult, less familiar choices, and that some form of in-store presentation should be used. Taking a heuristic as a given and structuring one's messages to fit that heuristic might be easier for familiar and easy choices, since stored rules would tend to be used, and out-of-store presentations would be appropriate.

One final example of actively attempting to change processing is to try to change the structure of the choice task itself. For example, choice among alternative product classes was hypothesized to be a very difficult choice task in Chapter 10. A marketer may wish to expand demand for his or her brand by competing with another product class, however. For example, a cereal emphasizing its nutritional content might wish to convince consumers that the cereal should be considered to be a good alternative to eggs for breakfast. One cereal manufacturer developed an ingenious approach to making this comparison easier for consumers. On the cereal package, a picture showed that one bowl of cereal was equal to an egg and one strip of bacon. This use of visual imagery attempted to make the comparison easier to process, and the use of in-store presentation is congruent with the methods (e.g. constructive, in-store recognition) that may tend to be used for difficult choices.

Understanding consumers' reactions to messages

One final way in which research on consumer information processing can be useful for promotional strategies is in gaining an understanding of consumers' reactions to specific promotional messages. Wright's (1973a, 1974a, c) thought-monitoring approach, discussed in Chapter 5, enables study of the specific inferences consumers draw from some message—positive and negative reactions, feelings about how believable the source of the message is, and so on. Although Wright examined only broad categories of responses to messages, Lutz and Swasy (1977) have proposed a more detailed approach that would examine the more specific inferences drawn from a message. Knowledge of these inferences could be useful in designing new messages and in diagnosing the impact of currently used messages.

IMPLICATIONS FOR PRICING DECISIONS

The pricing decision made by the marketer results in presenting the consumer with a piece of information about the product—its price. The important price is not the objective price figure. The *interpretation* of that price is what is important. A price may be interpreted as too high, too low, denoting quality or the lack of it, and so on. Jacoby and Olson (1977) provide an excellent discussion of consumer response to price from an information processing viewpoint (see also Olson 1977). Some of the major points made in that discussion are considered below. The areas considered include the acquisition of price; consumers' processing of price; interpretation of price changes; and models of actual pricing decisions.

Acquisition of price by consumers

One of the most basic questions relating to price information is whether consumers actually acquire that information. Jacoby and Olson (1977) review many studies examining acquisition of price, particularly those studies using information monitoring methods (see Chapter 7 for a description of these methods). The findings suggest that consumers often acquire price information, but not always. In addition, consumers tend to acquire price information more often if they are not familiar with the brands considered. If they are familiar with these brands, they are less likely to acquire price information, as the brand name may summarize for them the approximate cost of the product. For example, Jacoby, Szybillo, and Busato-Schach (1977) found that for a set of familiar brands, 57 percent of their subjects acquired price information when brand name was shown, but 83 percent acquired price when brand name was not shown.

If price is acquired, how consumers store price information in memory, if at all, has not been studied. Since price is available in external memory (on the package), it may not be stored in internal memory. If some information about price is stored, it could be an indication of the price range (expensive, average, cheap), an attempt to accurately remember the exact price, an approximation (around a dollar), and so on. Thus answers to surveys asking for recall of price may not have any obvious interpretations.

Processing of price by consumers

If price is acquired, the next question becomes how consumers process price information, how they use it. Three considerations are discussed: use of price ranges, price–quality inferences, and encouragement of price usage.

Use of price ranges. Jacoby and Olson (1977) cite several studies that show that consumers have acceptable ranges for the price they will pay, with a minimum and maximum acceptable price. Prices above the maximum are viewed as too expensive, and prices below the minimum are seen as perhaps indicating poor quality. Recall from Chapter 7 (Proposition 7.8.iv) that phased processes in general consist of a first phase in which some criteria are used to eliminate alternatives, and a second phase in which those alternatives remaining are compared in more detail. Price ranges may be used to eliminate alternatives in the first phase. Haines (1974b) finds evidence for such an elimination phase in his women's clothing studies. The women considered only those areas of the store in which clothing in the appropriate price range was displayed. Actual price levels may also be used in the second phase, to compare alternatives in detail, but the use of price ranges may be restricted to the first phase.

The implication of this use of price ranges for the marketer is obvious: the price of the product needs to be within the acceptable range to ensure detailed consideration of other aspects of the product. Even if a product has outstanding features, if its price is outside of the acceptable range, these features may never be examined. In such a case, the marketer would have to try to persuade consumers to look outside their normal acceptable range and give reasons for such a departure (e.g., "We know this is more than you usually pay, but here's why it's worth it").

Price–quality inferences. Jacoby and Olson (1977), Olson (1977), and Monroe (1973) summarize the research which has been done on whether consumers use the price of a product to infer its probable quality (e.g., high price means high quality). It appears that consumers may use price to judge quality in cases in which they are not familiar with the brands available, or in which the actual quality level is difficult to judge or discriminate (e.g., perfumes, liquors). Thus the marketer should probably not attempt to imply quality by a high price for a familiar brand, or for a product class where consumers could discriminate quality reasonably well. Price–quality inferences, once formed, may be very resistant to change, as shown by the illusory correlation studies cited earlier (Proposition 7.1.ii).

Encouraging consumer usage of price. If brands within a product class have different package sizes and different prices, consumers may not be able to use price in their choices because the calculations required to compare prices may be too difficult (Proposition 7.1.i). Even if unit prices are provided for consumers, standard unit price displays are also apparently hard to use (Russo, Krieser, and Miyashita 1975; Russo 1977). Thus if a marketer wishes to have consumers use price in making comparisons, some means might need to be found for making price information easier to process. This might involve matching the package size of a major competitor so that prices could be more easily compared, or presenting a price table comparing average prices for the product and its competitors on the package itself.

Interpretation of price changes

A change in price must also be interpreted by the consumer. The impact of any price change is thus not necessarily obvious. For example, suppose a price decrease occurs for some product. The standard prediction of economic theory would be that there should be an increase in demand for that product. However, there is a large number of possible consumer reactions to the decreased price (Jacoby and Olson 1977). For example, the consumer may not even notice the price change if external memory is relied upon and prices are not stored in internal memory; or if prices are remembered in broad categories. Even if the change is noticed, the consumer may decide the change is trivial; that it means another reduction is coming; that the product must be something no one wants so they have to lower the price; that the quality is low; and so on. Most of these reactions would *not* lead to increased demand.

The implication of the above is that before instituting a price change, the marketer should attempt to determine if it will be noticed, and how consumers will interpret the change. Assuming a decrease will lead to more sales can lead to a focus on issues such as "Will the sales increase offset the loss in revenue per unit?". These issues may be irrelevant if consumers' interpretations do not lead to an increase in sales at all.

Models of actual pricing decisions

Several researchers have built information processing models of the decision processes used by marketers in making pricing decisions (Howard and Morgenroth 1968; Cyert and March 1963; Capon and Hulbert 1972, 1975; Capon, Farley, and Hulbert 1975). For example, Howard and Morgenroth (1968) attempt to model the reactions of a firm to price changes instituted by a competitor. Cyert and March (1963, pp. 128–148) describe the heuristics used to set prices in a department store. In most of the cases, the researchers note that the managers involved believe that complex processes are being used. In fact the resulting models reveal simple heuristics, usually based upon past decisions and simple reactions to the moves of others. The apparent complexity appears to be in the business environment itself, but the responses are simple.

Such studies can be useful to marketers for several reasons. First, the models can show managers the simple heuristics actually being used, and this may yield insights into possible improvements in these pricing strategies. Second, the models can be used for training programs, to show trainees how pricing decisions are made in the company. Finally, Howard and Morgenroth (1968) suggest that such models could even be used in antitrust cases to show how pricing decisions were made.

IMPLICATIONS FOR PRODUCT DECISIONS

Two major types of implications are considered below: implications for product partitioning, and new product design.

Implications for product partitioning

Product partitioning refers to the way in which consumers partition a market. For example, for coffee, some consumers may first partition the market into instant and ground coffee. Then each of these categories may be divided into caffeinated and decaffeinated categories. Then various brands may be considered for each of the four resulting categories. This option is shown in Fig. 11.1a. A second option for partitioning the product class, shown

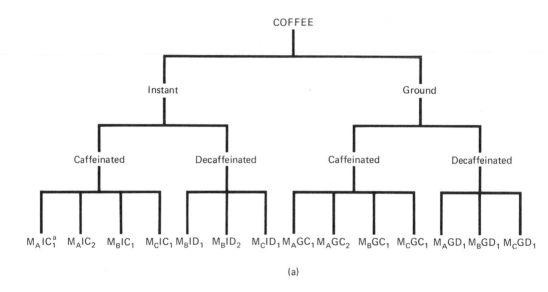

(a)

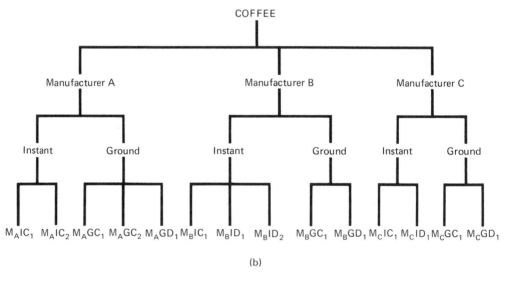

(b)

Key M_A = Manufacturer A   IC = instant, caffeinated   GD = ground, decaffeinated
      M_B = Manufacturer B   ID = instant, decaffeinated
      M_C = Manufacturer C   GC = ground, caffeinated

[a] Read as Manufacturer A, brand 1 of instant, caffeinated coffee.

Fig. 11.1 Alternative product partitionings.

in Fig. 11.1b, is that the consumer first divides the class by manufacturer (e.g., Maxwell House), then by instant versus ground, and does not consider the split of caffeinated versus decaffeinated. Many other partitionings are possible, of course, ranging from a one-level partition in which all separate alternatives are perceived to be distinct, to more complex hierarchical arrangements. Also, all consumers will not in general have the same partitioning. There may be segments of consumers using each of several types of partitions.

What are the managerial implications of such partitionings? Let us consider the example in Fig. 11.1. The assumption behind product partitioning notions is that consumers will tend to limit the alternatives they compare to those alternatives within the same set within the partition (e.g., to brands of instant, caffeinated coffees in Fig. 11.1a, or to instant coffees made by a specific manufacturer in Fig. 11.1b). Then the different forms the partitioning might take have different implications. For example, there will tend to be more loyalty to a given manufacturer's brands in the partitioning of Fig. 11.1b. Also, if Manufacturer A wanted to introduce a new instant decaffeinated coffee, it would cannibalize more sales from its other instant coffees if the partitioning of Fig. 11.1b were true than it would if the partitioning of Fig. 11.1a were true. In the Fig. 11.1a case, the new instant decaffeinated would compete with other instant decaffeinated coffees, not Manufacturer A's other instants.

In general, therefore, knowledge of how consumers partition product classes could be very helpful for formulating product line strategies — how to promote products in the line, which products to add to the line, and so on. The question then becomes how to determine how consumers do partition product classes. Typical approaches in the past have included analysis of brand switching data using mathematical models, such as in the Hendry approach (Kalwani and Morrison 1977); use of managerial judgment; and studies of consumer perceptions. The discussions in Chapter 7 suggest that approaches to studying consumer choice processes could be helpful. Methods such as protocol gathering, information monitoring, or eye movement studies could be used to determine how consumers search through and make comparisons among various alternatives. Such data could provide the information needed to determine how the product class was being partitioned. For example, a consumer could be presented with a matrix display depicting various alternative coffees, with information available for several attributes. Among these attributes might be caffeination, whether instant or ground, and manufacturer. Then, if the consumer acquired this information by examining instant versus ground first, then caffeination among those coffees that were instant, and finally compared several alternatives among those that were both instant and caffeinated, a partitioning like that in Fig. 11.1a would be supported.

Implications for new product design

Several implications of consumer information processing research for new product design are now briefly considered. First, suppose a new product is to be introduced into a product class in which consumers have little experience, or in which the choice among alternatives, given the introduction of the new product, would be difficult. Then consumers may tend to process by attribute, to the extent possible. This implies that the new brand should have some definite attribute advantage (rather than just a supposed "image" advantage), since consumers may be processing by attribute.

The argument above also implies that in *testing* this new product, those consumers sampled should be asked to make attributewise comparisons of the new product to those of competitors, since attribute processing may be used when the product is introduced. Thus seeing how the new product fares when attribute processing is used in the market testing stages may give better indications of how it will perform later.

Finally, the considerations above about how to present information to consumers may influence how the package is designed. If recognition is desired, or if comparative tables are to be placed on the package, for example, this may influence the specific package form chosen.

IMPLICATIONS FOR DISTRIBUTION DECISIONS

One obvious conclusion from the information processing viewpoint is that the marketer's choice of an outlet may provide information to the consumer about the marketer's product; that is, consumers may make inferences about products based upon the type of store selling the product. Cox (1967a) reports an interesting example of this phenomenon in his intensive study of risk perception in two consumers, a study in which one of his subjects reported that she used the image of the store to help reduce her feelings of risk. She felt that any product carried by a reliable store must be of acceptable quality. Roselius (1971) also found that consumers used store image to reduce risk. Thus, like the price–quality inferences discussed above, there may be store image–quality inferences made as well. Such inferences, as in the price–quality relationship case, would probably be made only for products about which the consumer had little knowledge and found it difficult to judge or discriminate the quality involved (e.g., clothing, in the Cox article). Stafford and Enis (1969) studied the effects of price and store image on quality judgments and found that the effects of price were more pronounced. Wheatley and Chiu (1977), in a similar study, found significant effects of store image, although price was still the most dominant cue. Note that we are focusing on an informational interpretation of the effects of store image on quality perception, not a normative approach (Burnkrant and Cousineau 1975); that is, the image of the store is seen in general as another information input that must be interpreted by the consumer, not as necessarily leading to some normative pressure to which the consumer complies when making choices.

Another interesting implication for distribution decisions is that different types of stores, with different arrays of information and alternative offerings available, may appeal to consumers with different information search strategies. For example, Dash, Schiffman, and Berenson (1976) compare consumers who shop at specialty stores for audio equipment with those who shop in department stores. They find that consumers who shop in specialty stores have greater prior experience and knowledge, and engage in much greater search. One might hypothesize that the consumer who shops in the department store, tending to be less knowledgeable about audio equipment, perceives the task of making a choice in the specialty store, with the vast amounts of information and alternatives available, to be extremely difficult. Hence, this type of consumer adopts a simplifying strategy of choosing from among the limited selection at the department store. Thus the marketer must determine to which segment the product appeals, and place the product in the type of outlet patronized by that segment. If the product is to be placed in specialty stores, then the marketer must also ensure that fairly complete information on the product is provided, through brochures or other means.

Howard (1977) generalizes this notion, arguing that the type of consumer decision process expected (extensive, limited, routine) influences the type of outlet that is most desirable. For an extensive problem solving process, the marketer desires an outlet which will provide heavy promotion and a great deal of information and explanation of the product to consumers. Specialty stores provide these services. For less complex decisions, coverage and price are more important, with outlets serving large numbers of customers and having lower prices being more suitable.

NEEDED RESEARCH

Several research needs have been identified above. First, the processing required by various forms of asking consumers for information needs to be studied (e.g., rating, ranking, sorting, or other comparison methods). Such studies should focus on the *processes* underlying the generation of the responses, not just differences in the responses under different conditions. The processing used in these information gathering tasks should then be compared with the processing required by the consumer choice tasks for which the information is relevant.

Research on the impacts of consumer information processing on promotional strategies is also needed. The most promising research areas have been discussed in earlier chapters to some extent, so only brief statements are made here. In general, the processing effort required by various modes of information provision needs to be examined. Also, research on consumers' levels of experience, the heuristics and implementation methods they use, and the interaction of these factors with the various methods for presenting information are necessary. Finally, research on influencing the choice heuristics used by consumers and on understanding consumers' reactions to messages should be undertaken.

A basic focus in future research on the effects of price should be how price is interpreted and utilized by consumers. One area worthy of study is the extent to which price ranges are used in the first stage of a phased choice process to eliminate alternatives. The extent to which price is used as opposed to other variables in this elimination stage should also be ascertained. A second broad area of interest is the interpretations consumers place on price and price changes. Of particular interest are studies of the conditions under which consumers infer quality from price, and of the conditions under which various interpretations of price changes are made.

One main area of research for product decisions, process studies of the product partitioning schemes used by consumers, has been discussed above in some detail. Finally, research on distribution decisions might focus on how the inferences about products made by the consumers vary as a function of the outlet carrying the product.

CHAPTER 12

Conclusions

In this final chapter, two topics are discussed. First, the relationship of the information processing theory presented in this book to other theories of consumer choice is considered. Second, based on the theoretical develop-ments in earlier chapters, those areas that seem to be most in need of future re-search are briefly outlined.

RELATIONSHIPS TO PREVIOUS CONSUMER CHOICE THEORIES

A broad comparison of the present theory with those of Nicosia (1966), Engel, Blackwell, and Kollat (1978), Howard and Sheth (1969), Howard (1977), and Hansen (1972) is presented in the following. A detailed comparison to these theories is not attempted. All of these theories are very complex. Each has many detailed elements that may be similar to or different from some ele-ments of the theory presented in this book, but in some cases these elements are not central or are mentioned only briefly. Thus only the broad similarities and differences are noted. For another comparison of Nicosia (1966), Engel, Kollat, and Blackwell (1973), and Howard and Sheth (1969) from a slightly dif-ferent viewpoint, see Zaltman, Pinson, and Angelmar (1973); for a comparison of a version of Howard and Sheth (1969) and Engel, Blackwell, and Kollat (1978), see Engel, Blackwell, and Kollat (1978, pp. 548–561).

COMMON ELEMENTS IN THE THEORIES

All of these theories have certain common elements (Lunn 1974). These elements include: (1) a focus on choice as a process, rather than choice as just the purchasing act itself (a major contribution of Howard [1963] and Nicosia [1966]); (2) a view of choice behavior as purposive, with the consumer's being an active information seeker and user, both of information stored internally and of information available in the external environment; (3) a belief that behavior is caused and hence can in principle be explained (although other authors such as Bass [1974] believe behavior contains an essentially stochastic component); (4) a belief that consumers limit the amount of information taken in, and move over time from general notions to more specific criteria and preference for alternatives; and (5) the notion that feedback based upon outcomes from choices affects later choices. Since the theories all are based on a common set of observed phenomena, some similarities would be expected. The range of consumer choice behaviors covered is fairly broad for all of the theories, although Howard and Sheth (1969) may apply more to frequently purchased items.

DIFFERENCES AMONG THE THEORIES

Despite the general similarities, there appear to be important specific differences between the proposed information processing theory and the earlier theories. These differences center on the information processing focus of the current theory; the role of motivation; conflict and responses to conflict; use of the scanner and interrupt mechanisms; the role of memory; the treatment of choice heuristics and implementation methods; and the focus on analyses of consumer choice task properties. The major differences discussed below are summarized in Table 12.1.

The information processing focus

The theory of this book is the first attempt to present a comprehensive information processing theory of consumer choice, using an integrated treatment of recent results in cognitive and information processing research. Although it is often difficult to distinguish clearly the meaning of information processing as a distinct concept, in Chapter 1 it was noted that any information processing system has a memory, a processor, and input/output mechanisms. As shown below, the proposed theory emphasizes the role of memory and allows for flexible processing heuristics and choice mechanisms to a much greater extent than the other theories.

In addition, the view of information processing espoused in the present theory is that processing mechanisms should be studied, with *detailed* consideration given to consumers' interpretations of information and their responses to those interpretations (Newell and Simon 1972). The proposed theory is thus at a more detailed level than were the previous approaches, with more concern shown for specification of such processing mechanisms. For example, the proposed theory explicitly includes the construct of processing capacity and discusses specific processing limitations and heuristics in detail, while the other theories do not. Nicosia (1966) is very general, concentrating on reviews of past research and not on specific mechanisms. Engel, Blackwell, and Kollat (1978) examine several information processing notions, including memory and attention. However, their treatment is less detailed than that of the present approach. Howard and Sheth (1969) also examine some information processing notions, mainly in the area of information search. However, one major basis of their approach is Hull-Spence (Hull 1952; Spence 1956) learning theory, a stimulus–response (S–R) approach, not cognitive. Howard and Sheth also tend to focus on constructs rather than on process mechanisms. The current theory places less emphasis on constructs and more on processing.

Hansen (1972) is quite cognitive in his treatment, but is less detailed in most of his discussions of mechanisms. Finally, Howard's (1977) recent work attempts to deal more extensively with information processing notions, and represents an important step. Howard also tempers the earlier S–R approach considerably. However, the information processing theory proposed here appears to treat several areas more comprehensively than does Howard (e.g., memory, attention, heuristics).[1]

The role of motivation

The information processing theory presented in this book uses motivation and the goal hierarchy notion as central concepts. Consumer choice is seen as purposive and goal-directed. Attention to stimuli and further processing of these stimuli are seen as being determined by the consumer's goals to a major extent (voluntary attention). The environment also plays a role, of course, in that some novel or surprising stimuli elicit attention (involuntary attention). In general, however, the attempt is made to recognize the active nature of the consumer, and make the theory less stimulus-bound (i.e., not view the stimulus as the sole source of energy, but also include the consumer's pursuit of goals as a source of activity). Nicosia (1966) seems to use motivation differently, seeing it as a specific driving force, and as the culmination of a process starting with a broad disposition and narrowing to attitude and then motivation. The notion of a goal hierarchy is not considered.

Howard and Sheth (1969) use Motives and Choice Criteria as two of their constructs. Motives represent more general needs or values, with Choice Criteria relating to more detailed attributes of a product. This differentiation of different levels of detail in goals is similar to the information processing theory notion of different levels of goals in a goal hierarchy. Motives are seen as influencing the direction of search. Howard and Sheth also consider the concept of a goal hierarchy, discuss the use of plans (pp. 105–109, 132–43), and view intention as the uncompleted portion of a plan whose execution has al-

---

1. In fairness to these other theories, it should be noted that many of them present a broader range of topics than does the present theory, discussing areas such as social class, culture, life-style, brand loyalty research, and so on, areas not covered in the present book. The purpose of the present effort is to provide a focused presentation of information processing issues, whereas several of the other theories attempt to provide treatments of many different areas of consumer research. Hence, their discussion of any single area may tend to be less detailed.

TABLE 12.1
A comparison of consumer choice theories[a]

ASPECTS COMPARED	THEORIES					
	PROPOSED INFORMATION PROCESSING THEORY	NICOSIA	ENGEL, BLACKWELL, AND KOLLAT	HOWARD AND SHETH	HANSEN	HOWARD
Information Processing Focus						
Level of detail	Very detailed	Very general	Some detail	Some detail	Some detail	Moderate detail
Consideration of specific processing notions	Extensive	Very limited	Some detail	Some detail	Some detail	Some detail
Role of Motivation						
Emphasis in theory	Central	Central	Central	Central	Not integrated	Central
Use of goal hierarchy	Extensive	Not considered[b]	Very limited	Limited	Very limited	Limited
Nature of consumer	Active	Stimulus-bound	Active	Stimulus-bound	Active	Active
Role of Conflict and Responses to Conflict						
Concept of conflict used	General	Not considered	Not considered	Perceptual and choice distinguished	General	Perceptual and choice distinguished
Determinant of reactions	Assessment of meaning	Not considered	Not considered	Optimal-level theory	Optimal-level theory	Optimal-level theory and assessment of meaning

TABLE 12.1 (cont'd)

Role of Interrupts and Reactions to Interrupts						
Specification of interrupt mechanisms	Extensive	Not considered	Limited	Limited	Extensive	Extensive
Determinants of reactions	Assessment of meaning	Not considered	Limited	Not considered	Assessment of meaning	Limited
Consideration of specific reactions	Extensive	Not considered	Limited	Not considered	Some detail	Limited
Role of Memory						
Treatment of memory phenomena	Extensive	Very limited	Some detail	Very limited	Limited	Moderate detail
Treatment of semantic structure, language	Not considered	Not considered	Not considered	Limited	Not considered	Extensive
Treatment of Choice Heuristics and Implementation Methods						
Range of heuristics considered	Very wide	Narrow	Moderate	Narrow	Narrow	Narrow
Specification of implementation methods	Extensive	Not considered	Not considered	Not considered	Not considered	Not considered
Specification of form of processing	Extensive	Not considered	Very limited	Not considered	Not considered	Not considered
Summary of choice research	Extensive	Limited	Limited	Limited	Limited	Limited
Is attitude a necessary component of choice?	No	Yes	Yes	Yes	Yes	Yes
Analysis of Choice Task Properties						
Treatment of task properties	Extensive	Very limited	Very limited	Limited	Some detail	Some detail

[a] This comparison focuses on some selected aspects for which the theories appear to differ. Similarities are considered in the text.

[b] "Not considered" means that the phenomenon is either not mentioned at all or is mentioned so briefly that it is not a central part of the theory.

ready begun. It appears, however, that Howard and Sheth's use of plans and information processing rules is based more on a stimulus–response framework than is the theory of this book (Howard and Sheth 1969, pp. 135, 138, 142).[2] Strictly speaking, one can show that some types of plans can be equivalently expressed in stimulus–response or in information processing terms (Millenson 1967), as Howard and Sheth point out (1969, p. 138). Thus it might be possible to study plans and some information processing rules from a stimulus–response perspective. However, the theory of this book emphasizes the active nature of processing and the interpretation and assessment of possible responses to outcomes. Such phenomena are probably more difficult to include in a stimulus–response based treatment. Thus the use of an information processing framework seems to allow more flexibility in treating choice phenomena. In any case, as operationalized, research based on the Howard–Sheth theory does not seem to directly relate to processing (e.g., Farley and Ring 1970). Finally, although feedback loops exist and the starting place may be to some extent arbitrary, the Howard and Sheth model (1969, p. 54) seems more stimulus-bound than does the current approach. In their model, Motives follow stimulus input and attention. Thus although on the surface there seem to be substantial similarities between the proposed theory and the Howard–Sheth approach, there appear to be some major differences in detail and in the underlying basic assumptions.

Engel, Blackwell, and Kollat (1978) postulate that motives affect the ideal state desired by consumers, and hence impact problem recognition. Motives are also hypothesized to influence the more detailed evaluative criteria used in choice. Thus this distinction, similar to Howard and Sheth's separation of Motives and Choice Criteria, implicitly acknowledges that there are different levels of goals. However, the goal hierarchy notion is not explicitly considered.

Howard (1977) also uses Motives and Choice Criteria. He appears to reduce the emphasis on stimulus–response notions. He does not explicitly emphasize the goal hierarchy notion to the extent the theory of this book does, although this notion would be quite compatible with his theory.

Hansen (1972, p. 68) uses the same source for his motivational concept as the present theory, Simon's (1967) notions of motivation in information processing systems. The concepts of plans and goal hierarchies are noted (Hansen 1972, p. 127) but these motivational elements do not seem to play an integrated role in Hansen's theory. Hansen uses an expectancy–value attitude model approach to choice, and uses conflict as a central notion, but it is not clear how the motivation and goal hierarchy concepts are integrated with these aspects of his theory.

---

2. An example of this S–R approach is "If she has solved the problem once and made a purchase, the strength of the plan in guiding her succeeding purchase behavior will be determined, to a great extent, by the number of times the plan is repeated." (Howard and Sheth 1969, p. 142)

The role of conflict and responses to conflict

Conflict is viewed as a major element in attention, perception, and choice processes in the proposed information processing theory. Reactions to conflict are not viewed as being automatic, but as requiring interpretation of the meaning of the conflict and choice of an appropriate response. Nicosia (1966) and Engel, Blackwell, and Kollat (1978) do not seem to consider intrapersonal conflict. Howard and Sheth (1969) and Howard (1977) use the constructs of Stimulus Ambiguity (lack of clarity of perceptual input) and Confidence (degree of certainty about the estimation of net payoff from a brand). Stimulus Ambiguity seems to relate to perceptual conflict, and the inverse of Confidence to choice conflict (i.e., the uncertainty component of choice conflict). Thus perceptual and choice conflict seem to be viewed as distinct phenomena by Howard and Sheth and Howard. In the proposed information processing theory and in Hansen (1972), conflict is viewed as a general phenomenon. Given the fuzziness and lack of specification in the entire concept of conflict (see the discussion in Chapter 4), it may be premature to divide the concept into subconcepts. We do not know how to develop a criterion measure for conflict, and have no research on how consumers perceive conflict, or whether forms of conflict are differentiated.

The present theory, Howard and Sheth, Howard, and Hansen all view conflict as related to intensity or degree of information search; however, Howard and Sheth and Howard see arousal as the actual determinant of search. The proposed theory is in opposition to Howard and Sheth and Hansen regarding responses to conflict (or arousal). Howard and Sheth (1969, pp. 156–168) and Hansen (1972, pp. 147, 156) use optimal-level theories. As noted above, such theories postulate prescribed responses, with the particular response observed depending on whether conflict or arousal is above or below the optimum level.[3] The present theory does not assume a single mechanistic response strategy, but hypothesizes that consumers will assess the meaning of a conflict and the situation in which it occurred and respond accordingly.

Howard (1977) appears to use an optimal-level theory, but it is not entirely clear. He also appears to postulate general mechanisms for assessing the meaning of conflict and making inferences, but does not make explicit propositions about such responses to conflict.

The role of interrupts and reactions to interrupts

The proposed information processing theory attempts to account for the fact that behavior can be interrupted, that consumers are distractible. This is accomplished by postulating scanner and interrupt mechanisms that allow disruption of ongoing goal-directed behavior if other events in the environment occur that are more pressing or are somehow perceived as having higher

---

3. Hansen (1972) uses an optimal-level theory both for arousal (to determine whether excitement will be sought or problem solving performed); and for conflict (to determine when a problem solving process will terminate).

priority by the consumer. Nicosia (1966) proposes a broader theory and does not appear to consider these notions. Howard and Sheth (1969, p. 105) consider interrupts only briefly, although their notion of inhibitors, or constraints on choice, may be related to the interrupt idea.

Engel, Blackwell, and Kollat (1978) discuss the concepts of problem recognition and unanticipated circumstances, both of which may be related to interrupts. Problem recognition seems to be related to interrupts that imply current choice rules are inadequate, and is triggered either by new information and experience or by motives. Determinants of problem recognition are considered (Engel, Blackwell, and Kollat 1978, pp. 219–230). However, as described by Engel, Blackwell, and Kollat, the process of problem recognition is much more general in nature and extensive in scope than is the notion of interrupt used in this book. Unanticipated circumstances refer to out-of-stock conditions, price changes, and other factors that might lead to interrupts in the store. Although these related notions are considered, the notion of interrupt is not explicitly developed.

Hansen (1972) explicitly uses the interrupt concept, since his motivational notions derive from Simon (1967). Hansen notes that changes in the environment help to keep behavior from becoming totally habitual, since interrupts occur and responses to these interrupts are often changed behaviors. Hansen (1972, p. 148) sees interrupts as the major cause of conflicts: "Situational novelty, change, surprise, and complexity generate an orienting response and, depending upon the salient cognitive structure, the choice process will either terminate immediately or take the form of more or less complex problem solving. Once the conflict has been aroused, the cognitive conflict is the crucial variable." Hansen also notes that interrupts often present clues as to what the appropriate response alternatives are likely to be, and that internal plans and self-instructions may be used to carry out responses to interrupts. Thus Hansen comes very close to the notions used in the present theory. Finally, Howard (1977) also explicitly incorporates Simon's interrupt notions into his theory. Only limited discussions about responses to various kinds of interrupts are presented, although there is nothing in Howard's theory which appears to limit the range of responses that might be considered.

The role of memory

Memory parameters and functioning are treated in some detail in the current theory, especially how various aspects of memory may be involved in choice processes. Nicosia (1966) and Howard and Sheth (1969) do not use a model of memory functions to any appreciable extent. Hansen (1972, p. 105) mentions an activation notion of memory, but does not apply it in any detail in the functioning of his theory. As noted in Chapter 7, most current views of consumer choice thus implicitly assume very powerful memory and retrieval capabilities, more powerful than seems justified by memory research.

Engel, Blackwell, and Kollat (1978) briefly discuss short-term and long-term memory, an activation model of memory, and depth of processing. Factors influencing the entry of new information into long-term memory are also considered, but they do not present detailed treatments of memory parameters or functioning.

Howard (1977) considers memory to a much greater extent than do these other models, discussing short-term and long-term memory and some of the memory parameters presented in Chapter 6. However, he does not go into detail beyond these areas, and thus his coverage of memory phenomena is not as comprehensive as that presented in this book. Also, the specific application of memory notions to choice tasks attempted in Chapter 6 goes beyond Howard's treatment. However, Howard (1977) also suggests an area in which the theory in this book is not as detailed as it might be. Howard provides a much more extensive treatment of the impacts of semantic structure and language on choice than is available in this book. Analysis of language, meaning, and semantic structure would be useful additions to the current theory.

The treatment of choice heuristics and implementation methods

The information processing theory presented seems much more flexible in its treatment of choice heuristics, and introduces the concept of implementation methods. The earlier theories do not seem to consider implementation methods at all. There is no notion presented, for example, that states explicitly how such processes as extensive problem solving, limited problem solving, or routinized response behavior (Howard and Sheth 1969) might be carried out, although Howard (1977) characterizes these types of processing more thoroughly. The distinctions between constructive and stored rule; in-store and prior processing; and use of recognition and use of recall are not made in these other theories. The previous theories appear to implicitly assume a stored rule rather than constructive approach in many situations (e.g., in situations other than extensive problem solving), and do not seem to consider the other implementation methods.

The current theory also delves more deeply into the alternative choice heuristics potentially used by consumers, and the determinants of usage of these heuristics. A wide range of potential heuristics is considered. Also, detailed analyses, such as the distinction between brand and attribute processing, are made for the first time in a consumer choice context. The present theory also provides a comprehensive summary of recent research on consumer choice heuristics and the factors influencing the use of these heuristics, something not attempted in previous theories, and discusses methods for studying choice processes in some detail. Nicosia (1966) is not specific about choice heuristics. However, Howard and Sheth (1969) and Hansen (1972) both use expectancy—value attitude models or variations of these models.[4] These heuristics are linear, compensatory, and assume processing by brand.

---

4. Howard and Sheth (1969, p. 136) do discuss decision nets, but it is not at all clear how these are integrated into their overall theory.

Howard (1977) proposes that decision nets are used in routinized response behavior, with linear compensatory models used elsewhere. Finally, Engel, Blackwell, and Kollat (1978) mention linear compensatory, conjunctive, disjunctive, and lexicographic models; and briefly cite the distinction between brand and attribute processing made in this book. However, their major focus is on linear compensatory attitude models.

Thus the theory proposed in this book treats many more alternative choice heuristics than do these previous theories. These previous theories also seem to assume that attitude is a necessary component of choice processes. The current theory, on the other hand, views attitude formation and choice as two distinct tasks, which may go on in parallel but are not necessarily related.

Finally, Howard and Sheth (1969), Howard (1977), Hansen (1972) and Engel, Blackwell, and Kollat (1978) appear to have more limited notions of the contingency of choice processes on task properties than does the present theory. All of these models have as their main contingency the notion that the choice process differs as a function of stage of learning (e.g., routinized response behavior, limited problem solving, and extensive problem solving (Howard and Sheth 1969; Howard 1977) or clue-guided choice, semicomplex choice, and rational choice (Hansen 1972). Form of the choice task to be performed is not considered in any detail, although Howard (1977) considers how the way information is presented may affect choice. However, as suggested in Chapters 7, 8, 10, and 11, the influence of choice task properties on the processing observed may be very great.

Analysis of consumer choice task properties

In general, the present theory concentrates on task parameters and the need for analyses of consumer tasks much more than do the previous approaches. Hansen (1972) and Howard (1977) are the previous models most similar to the present model in this regard. Hansen distinguishes types of consumer choice situations (1972, pp. 53–54), some of which are also differentiated in this book. For example, Hansen separates information acquisition (seeking) from forced learning (confronted) situations. Hansen also describes consumer situations in terms of factors relating to presence of product, degree of marketer control, and type of communication (1972, p. 57). This departs somewhat from the notion of task analysis used in this book, which concentrates mainly on processing factors (e.g., mode of presentation, type of memory involved, and so on). Howard's (1977) main task consideration is how the structure of information (speed of presentation, simplicity, abstractness) impacts choice.

Thus the proposed information processing theory seems to provide a more detailed approach to understanding consumer choice processing. In the application chapters, an attempt was made to show how various public policy and marketing decisions may require this detailed level of analysis. The proposed theory attempts to provide a fairly comprehensive framework that could be used to develop further implications of these information processing notions.

MAJOR AREAS FOR FUTURE RESEARCH

In preceding chapters, several research areas appeared repeatedly. An attempt is made here to bring together those areas seemingly most in need of study. The areas are mentioned only to provide an emphasis and general notion of priority; specific details were included in earlier chapters. Three general sets of topics are considered: general concepts of the theory, individual difference variables, and task factors.

Those general aspects of the theory in need of most research are: (1) the nature of motivation and the formation and processing of goal hierarchies; (2) measures of conflict, specification of the factors underlying conflict, and measures of conflict responses; (3) the operation of the scanner and interrupt mechanisms; (4) measures of internal information search; (5) studies of methods for implementing choice heuristics; (6) work on process measurement methods; and (7) the process of forming inferences from outcomes and from information in general.

The major individual difference variables needing study are: (1) the degree to which various implementation methods (e.g., in-store versus prior, recognition versus recall) are used; (2) the types of self-regulatory systems (self-instructions, etc.) used; (3) the reaction strategies used to respond to interrupts in general and to conflict in particular; (4) processing abilities and limitations, (5) the particular heuristics or rules of thumb known; and (6) the amount and organization of product-related information in memory.

Finally, analysis of consumer tasks emerged as a crucial need in discussing the theory. In particular, (1) consumer perceptions of their tasks; (2) memory and other processing requirements for tasks; (3) total effort requirements of tasks as a function of such factors as time pressure, information load, and rate of processing required; and (4) effects of task structure on form of processing and use of various implementation methods are important topics.

The information processing theory presented above is an extensive yet incomplete view of the consumer as an adaptive choice processor. I believe it describes some of the major mechanisms accounting for choice behavior. However, it is clear that advances, extensions, and undoubtedly substantial changes in many areas are needed. My hope is that presentation of an integrated view of consumer information processing will stimulate others to attempt those advances.

Bibliography

Abelson, Robert P., 1968. A summary of hypotheses on modes of resolution. In Robert P. Abelson *et al.*, (eds.), *Theories of cognitive consistency: a sourcebook.* Chicago: Rand McNally, pp. 716–720.

_____, 1976. Script processing in attitude formation and decision making. In John S. Carroll and John W. Payne, (eds.), *Cognition and social behavior.* Hillsdale, N.J.: Lawrence Erlbaum, pp. 33–45.

Alexis, Marcus, George H. Haines, and Leonard Simon, 1968. Consumer information processing: the case of women's clothing. In Proceedings of the Fall Conference, *Marketing and the new science of planning.* Chicago: American Marketing Association, pp. 197–205.

Alf, Edward F., and Norman M. Abrahams, 1974. Let's give the devil his due: a response to Birnbaum. *Psychological Bulletin* **81:** 72–73.

Allison, Ralph I., and Kenneth P. Uhl, 1964. Brand identification and perception. *Journal of Marketing Research* **1** (August): 80–85.

Anders, Terry R., and James L. Fozard, 1973. Effects of age upon retrieval from primary and secondary memory. *Developmental Psychology* **9**: 411–415.

_____, James L. Fozard, and Timothy D. Lillyquist, 1972. Effects of age upon retrieval from short-term memory. *Developmental Psychology* **6:** 214–217.

Anderson, John R., and Gordon H. Bower, 1972. Recognition and retrieval processes in free recall. *Psychological Review* **79** (March): 97–123.

_____, 1973. *Human associative memory.* Washington, D.C.: Winston.

Anderson, Norman H., 1971. Integration theory and attitude change. *Psychological Review* **78** (March): 171–206.

_____, 1974a. Methods for studying information integration. Technical Report No. 43, San Diego: Center for Human Information Processing, Department of Psychology, University of California.

_____, 1974b. Basic experiments in person perception. Technical Report No. 44. San Diego. Center for Human Information Processing, Department of Psychology, University of California.

_____, 1976. Social perception and cognition. Technical Report No. 62. San Diego. Center for Human Information Processing, Department of Psychology, University of California.

_____, 1978. Integration theory applied to cognitive responses and attitudes. In Richard Petty, Thomas Ostrom, and Timothy Brock, (eds.), *Cognitive responses in persuasion*. New York: McGraw-Hill.

_____, and James Shanteau, 1977. Weak inference with linear models. *Psychological Bulletin* **84** (November): 1155–1170.

Anderson, Rolph E., 1973. Consumer dissatisfaction: the effect of disconfirmed expectancy on perceived product performance. *Journal of Marketing Research* **10** (February): 38–44.

Antes, James R., 1974. The time course of picture viewing. *Journal of Experimental Psychology* **103**: 62–70.

Arch, David C., James R. Bettman, and Pradeep Kakkar, 1978. Subjects' information processing in information display board studies. In H. Keith Hunt, (ed.), *Advances in Consumer Research,* Volume 5. Chicago: Association for Consumer Research, 555–560.

Atkinson, John W., 1964. *An introduction to motivation.* Princeton, N.J.: Van Nostrand.

Atkinson, Richard C., and Richard M. Shiffrin, 1968. Human memory: a proposed system and its control processes. In K.W. Spence and J.T. Spence, (eds.), *The psychology of learning and motivation: advances in research and theory,* Volume 2, New York: Academic, pp. 89–195.

_____, 1971. The control of short-term memory. *Scientific American* **225** (August): 82–90.

Baddeley, Alan D., 1978. The trouble with levels: a re-examination of Craik and Lockhart's framework for memory research. *Psychological Review* **85** (May): 139–152.

Baker, Frank B., 1967. The internal organization of computer models of cognitive behavior. *Behavioral Science* **12**: 156–161.

Bandura, Albert, 1978. The self system in reciprocal determinism. *American Psychologist* **33** (April): 344–358.

Bartlett, F. C., 1932. *Remembering.* Cambridge, England: Cambridge University Press.

Bass, Frank M., 1974. The theory of stochastic preference and brand switching. *Journal of Marketing Research* **11** (February): 1–20.

Beatty, Jackson, and Daniel Kahneman, 1966. Pupillary changes in two memory tasks. *Psychonomic Science* **5**: 371–372.

Belk, Russell W., 1975. Situational variables and consumer behavior. *Journal of Consumer Research* **2** (December): 157–164.

Bennett, Peter D., and Robert M. Mandell, 1969. Prepurchase information seeking behavior of new car purchasers—the learning hypothesis. *Journal of Marketing Research* **6** (November): 430–433.

Berlyne, D. E., 1957. Uncertainty and conflict: a point of contact between information-theory and behavior-theory concepts. *Psychological Review* **64** (November): 329–339.

_____, 1960. *Conflict, arousal, and curiosity.* New York: McGraw-Hill.

_____, 1961. Conflict and the orientation reaction. *Journal of Experimental Psychology* **62**: 476–483.

_____, 1968. The motivational significance of collative variables and conflict. In Robert P. Abelson et al., (eds.), Theories of cognitive consistency: a sourcebook. Chicago: Rand McNally, pp. 257-266.

Bettman, James R., 1969. Applying a new methodological approach to a problem of information processing model validation. Working Paper No. 152, Western Management Science Institute, Los Angeles: University of California.

_____, 1970. Information processing models of consumer behavior. Journal of Marketing Research 7 (August): 370-376.

_____, 1971a. A graph theory approach to comparing consumer information processing models. Management Science 18 (Part II, December): 114-128.

_____, 1971b. The structure of consumer choice processes. Journal of Marketing Research 8 (November): 465-471.

_____, 1973. Perceived risk and its components: a model and empirical test. Journal of Marketing Research 10 (May): 184-190.

_____, 1974a. Decision net models of buyer information processing and choice: findings, problems, and prospects. In G. David Hughes and Michael L. Ray, (eds.), Buyer/consumer information processing. Chapel Hill: University of North Carolina Press, pp. 59-74.

_____, 1974b. A threshold model of attribute satisfaction decisions. Journal of Consumer Research 1 (September): 30-35.

_____, 1974c. Toward a statistics for consumer decision net models. Journal of Consumer Research 1 (June): 71-80.

_____, 1975a. Information integration in consumer risk perception: a comparison of two models of component conceptualization. Journal of Applied Psychology 60: 381-385.

_____, 1975b. Issues in designing consumer information environments. Journal of Consumer Research 2 (December): 169-177.

_____, Noel Capon, and Richard J. Lutz, 1975a. Cognitive algebra in multiattribute attitude models. Journal of Marketing Research 12 (May): 151-164.

_____, Noel Capon, and Richard J. Lutz, 1975b. Information processing in attitude formation and change. Communication Research 2 (July): 267-278.

_____, Noel Capon, and Richard J. Lutz, 1975c. Multiattribute measurement models and multiattribute attitude theory: a test of construct validity. Journal of Consumer Research 1 (March): 1-15.

_____, and Jacob Jacoby, 1976. Patterns of processing in consumer information acquisition. In Beverlee B. Anderson, (ed.), Advances in consumer research, Volume 3. Chicago: Association for Consumer Research, pp. 315-320.

_____, and Pradeep Kakkar, 1976. Consumer information processing mechanisms and product class experience. Paper No. 44. Center for Marketing Studies, Graduate School of Management. Los Angeles: University of California.

_____, and Pradeep Kakkar, 1977. Effects of information presentation format on consumer information acquisition strategies. Journal of Consumer Research 3 (March): 233-240.

_____, and Michel A. Zins, 1977. Constructive processes in consumer choice. Journal of Consumer Research 4 (September): 75-85.

_____, and Michel A. Zins, 1978. Information format and choice task effects in consumer decision making. Paper No. 54, Los Angeles: Center for Marketing Studies, Graduate School of Management, University of California.

Bilkey, Warren J., 1951. The vector hypothesis of consumer behavior. *Journal of Marketing* **16** (October): 137–151.

———, 1953. A psychological approach to consumer behavior analysis. *Journal of Marketing* **18** (July): 18–25.

———, 1957. Consistency test of psychic tension ratings involved in consumer purchasing behavior. *Journal of Social Psychology* **45**: 81–91.

Birnbaum, Michael H., 1973. The devil rides again: correlation as an index of fit. *Psychological Bulletin* **79**: 239–242.

Blackwell, Roger D., James S. Hensel, and Brian Sternthal, 1970. Pupil dilation: what does it measure? *Journal of Advertising Research* **10** (August): 15–18.

Bobrow, Daniel G., and Donald A. Norman, 1975. Some principles of memory schemata. In Daniel G. Bobrow and Allan Collins, (eds.), *Representation and understanding: studies in cognitive science.* New York: Academic, pp. 131–149.

Bogart, Leo, B. Stuart Tolley, and Frank Orenstein, 1970. What one little ad can do. *Journal of Advertising Research* **10** (August): 3–13.

Bower, Gordon H., 1970. Organizational factors in memory. *Cognitive Psychology* **1** (January): 18–46.

———, 1972. A selective review of organizational factors in memory. In E. Tulving and W. Donaldson, (eds.), *Organization of memory.* New York: Academic, pp. 93–137.

———, 1975. Cognitive psychology: an introduction. In William K. Estes, (ed.), *Handbook of learning and cognitive processes,* Volume I, Hillsdale, N.J.: Lawrence Erlbaum, pp. 25–80.

———, Michael C. Clark, Alan M. Lesgold, and David Winzenz, 1969. Hierarchical retrieval schemes in recall of categorized word lists. *Journal of Verbal Learning and Verbal Behavior* **8**: 323–343.

———, and Fred Springston, 1970. Pauses as recoding points in letter series, *Journal of Experimental Psychology* **83**: 421–430.

———, and David Winzenz, 1969. Group structure, coding, and memory for digit series. *Journal of Experimental Psychology Monograph* **80** (May, Part 2): 1–17.

———, and David Winzenz, 1970. Comparison of associative learning strategies. *Psychonomic Science* **20**: 119–120.

Branscombe, Art, 1975. Checkout on consumer math. *American Education* **11** (October): 21–24.

Bregman, Albert S., 1977. Perception and behavior as compositions of ideals. *Cognitive Psychology* **9** (April): 250–292.

Brehm, J. W., 1962. Motivational effects of cognitive dissonance. In M. R. Jones, (ed.), *Nebraska Symposium on Motivation, 1962,* Lincoln: University of Nebraska Press, pp. 51–77.

Broadbent, D. E., and Alastair Heron, 1962. Effects of a subsidiary task on performance involving immediate memory by younger and older men. *British Journal of Psychology* **53**: 189–198.

Brock, Timothy C., and Howard L. Fromkin, 1968. Receptivity to discrepant information. *Journal of Personality* **36** (March): 108–125.

Bruno, Albert V., and Albert R. Wildt, 1975. Toward understanding attitude structure: a study of the complementarity of multiattribute attitude models. *Journal of Consumer Research* **2** (September): 137–145.

Bucklin, Louis P., 1966. Testing propensities to shop. *Journal of Marketing* **30** (January): 22–27.

Bugelski, B. R., 1962. Presentation time, total time, and mediation in paired-associate learning. *Journal of Experimental Psychology* **63**: 409–412.

Burnkrant, Robert E., 1976. A motivational model of information processing intensity. *Journal of Consumer Research* **3** (June): 21–30.

———, and Alain Cousineau, 1975. Informational and normative social influence in buyer behavior. *Journal of Consumer Research* **2** (December): 206–215.

Buschke, Herman, 1976. Learning is organized by chunking. *Journal of Verbal Learning and Verbal Behavior* **15**: 313–324.

Calder, Bobby J., 1975a. The cognitive foundations of attitudes. In Mary Jane Schlinger, (ed.), *Advances in consumer research,* Volume 2. Chicago: Association for Consumer Research, pp. 241–247.

———, 1975b. Some methodological considerations in investigating consumer information processing. *Proceedings of the American Marketing Association Fall Conference,* pp. 167–169.

———, 1978. Cognitive response, imagery, and scripts: what is the cognitive basis of attitude? In H. Keith Hunt, (ed.), *Advances in consumer research,* Volume 5. Chicago: Association for Consumer Research, pp. 630–634.

———, Thomas S. Robertson, and John R. Rossiter, 1975. Children's consumer information processing. *Communication Research* **2** (July): 307–316.

Campbell, Donald T., and Donald W. Fiske, 1959. Convergent and discriminant validation by the multitrait–multimethod matrix. *Psychological Bulletin* **56** (March): 81–105.

Capon, Noel, and Marian Burke, 1977. Information seeking behavior in consumer durable purchase. In Barnett A. Greenberg and Danny M. Bellenger, (eds.), *Contemporary marketing thought.* Chicago: American Marketing Association, pp. 110–115.

———, John U. Farley, and James Hulbert, 1975. Pricing and forecasting in an oligopoly firm. *Journal of Management Studies* **12** (May): 133–156.

———, and James Hulbert, 1972. Decision systems in industrial marketing: an empirical approach. In *Proceedings, American Institute for Decision Sciences* **4** (November): 112–117.

———, and James Hulbert, 1975. Decision systems analysis in industrial marketing. *Industrial Marketing Management* **4** (Summer): 143–160.

Cardozo, Richard N., 1965. An experimental study of consumer effort, expectation, and satisfaction. *Journal of Marketing Research* **2** (August): 244–249.

Carroll, John S., John W. Payne, Irene H. Frieze, and David L. Girard, 1975. Attribution theory: an information processing approach. Unpublished manuscript. Carnegie–Mellon University.

Chabot, Robert J., Timothy J. Miller, and James F. Juola, 1976. The relationship between repetition and depth of processing. *Memory and Cognition* **4**: 677–682.

Chapman, Loren J., and Jean P. Chapman, 1967. Genesis of popular but erroneous psychodiagnostic observations. *Journal of Abnormal Psychology* **72**: 193–204.

———, 1969. Illusory correlation as an obstacle to the use of valid psychodiagnostic signs. *Journal of Abnormal Psychology* **74**: 271–280.

Chase, William G., 1978. Elementary information processes. In W. K. Estes, (ed.), *Handbook of learning and cognitive processes,* Volume 5, Hillsdale, N.J.: Lawrence Erlbaum.

_____, and Herbert A. Simon, 1973. Perception in chess. *Cognitive Psychology* **4** (January): 55–81.

Chervany, Norman L., and Gary W. Dickson, 1974. An experimental evaluation of information overload in a production environment. *Management Science* **20** (June): 1335–1344.

Chestnut, Robert W., 1976. The impact of energy-efficiency ratings: selective vs. elaborative encoding. Paper No. 160. Purdue Papers in Consumer Psychology.

_____, and Jacob Jacoby, 1976. Time costs and information-seeking behavior. Paper No. 155. Purdue Papers in Consumer Psychology.

_____, and Jacob Jacoby, 1977. Consumer information processing: emerging theory and findings. In Arch G. Woodside, Jagdish N. Sheth, and Peter D. Bennett, (eds.), *Consumer and industrial buying behavior.* New York: North Holland, pp. 119–133.

Chiang, Alice, and Richard C. Atkinson, 1976. Individual differences and interrelationships among a select set of cognitive skills. *Memory and Cognition* **4**: 661–672.

Clarkson, Geoffrey P. E., 1962. *Portfolio selection: a simulation of trust investment.* Englewood Cliffs, N.J.: Prentice-Hall.

_____, 1968. Decision making in small groups: a simulation study. *Behavioral Science* **13**: 288–305.

Claxton, John D., Joseph N. Fry, and Bernard Portis, 1974. A taxonomy of prepurchase information gathering patterns. *Journal of Consumer Research* **1** (December): 35–42.

Clay, Hilary M., 1954. Changes of performance with age on similar tasks of varying complexity. *British Journal of Psychology* **14**: 7–13.

Cofer, Charles N., 1973. Constructive processes in memory. *American Scientist* **61** (September–October): 537–543.

Cohen, Arthur R., 1961. Cognitive tuning as a factor affecting impression formation. *Journal of Personality* **29** (June): 235–245.

Cohen, Dorothy, 1972. Surrogate indicators and deception in advertising. *Journal of Marketing* **36** (July): 10–15.

Cohen, Joel B., and Marvin E. Goldberg, 1970. The dissonance model in post-decision product evaluation. *Journal of Marketing Research* **7** (August): 315–321.

_____, and Ellen Golden, 1972. Informational social influence and product evaluation. *Journal of Applied Psychology* **56** (February): 54–59.

Collins, Allan, M., and Elizabeth F. Loftus, 1975. A spreading-activation theory of semantic processing. *Psychological Review* **83**: 407–428.

_____, and M. Ross Quillian, 1969. Retrieval time from semantic memory. *Journal of Verbal Learning and Verbal Behavior* **8**: 240–247.

Coombs, Clyde H., and George S. Avrunin, 1977. Single-peaked functions and the theory of preference. *Psychological Review* **84** (March): 216–230.

Cooper, Elaine H., and Allan J. Pantle, 1967. The total-time hypothesis in verbal learning. *Psychological Bulletin* **68** (October): 221–234.

Cox, Donald F., 1967a. Risk handling in consumer behavior: an intensive study of two cases. In Donald F. Cox, (ed.), *Risk taking and information handling in consumer behavior.* Cambridge, Mass. Harvard Business School, pp. 34–81.

_____, (ed.), 1967b. *Risk taking and information handling in consumer behavior.* Cambridge, Mass.: Harvard Business School.

Craik, Fergus I. M., 1971. Age differences in recognition memory. *Quarterly Journal of Experimental Psychology* **23**: 316–323.

_____, and Robert S. Lockhart, 1972. Levels of processing: a framework for memory research. *Journal of Verbal Learning and Verbal Behavior* **11**: 671–684.

_____, and Endel Tulving, 1975. Depth of processing and the retention of words. *Journal of Experimental Psychology: General* **104**: 268–294.

_____, and Michael J. Watkins, 1973. The role of rehearsal in short-term memory. *Journal of Verbal Learning and Verbal Behavior* **12**: 599–607.

Cramer, Phebe, 1976. Changes from visual to verbal memory organization as a function of age. *Journal of Experimental Child Psychology* **22**: 50–57.

Cunningham, Scott M., 1967. The major dimensions of perceived risk. In Donald F. Cox, (ed.), *Risk taking and information handling in consumer behavior.* Cambridge, Mass.: Harvard Business School, pp. 82–108.

Cyert, Richard M. and James G. March, 1963. *A behavioral theory of the firm.* Englewood Cliffs, N.J.: Prentice-Hall.

Dalbey, Homer M., Irwin Gross, and Yoram Wind, 1968. *Advertising measurement and decision making.* Boston: Allyn and Bacon.

Dansereau, Donald F., and Lee W. Gregg, 1966. An information processing analysis of mental multiplication. *Psychonomic Science* **6**: 71–72.

Dash, Joseph F., Leon G. Schiffman, and Conrad Berenson, 1976. Information search and store choice. *Journal of Advertising Research* **16** (June): 35–40.

Dawes, Robyn M., 1966. Memory and distortion of meaningful written material. *British Journal of Psychology* **57**: 77–86.

_____, 1976. Shallow psychology. In John S. Carroll and John W. Payne, (eds.), *Cognition and social behavior,* Hillsdale, N.J.: Lawrence Erlbaum, pp. 3–13.

_____, and Bernard Corrigan, 1974. Linear models in decision making. *Psychological Bulletin* **81** (February): 95–106.

Day, George S., 1975. Full disclosure of comparative performance information to consumers: problems and prospects. *Journal of Contemporary Business* **4** (Winter): 53–68.

_____, 1976. Assessing the effects of information disclosure requirements. *Journal of Marketing* **40** (April): 42–52.

_____, and William K. Brandt, 1974. Consumer research and the evaluation of information disclosure requirements: the case of truth in lending. *Journal of Consumer Research* **1** (June): 71–80.

Day, Ralph L., 1977. Extending the concept of consumer satisfaction. In William D. Perreault, (ed.), *Advances in consumer research,* Volume 4, Chicago: Association for Consumer Research, pp. 149–154.

Dennett, Daniel C., 1968. Machine traces and protocol statements. *Behavioral Science* **13**: 155–161.

Dichter, Ernst, 1964. *Handbook of consumer motivations,* New York: McGraw Hill.

Diamond, Daniel S., 1968. A quantitative approach to magazine advertisement format selection. *Journal of Marketing Reseach* **5** (November): 376–386.

Dirlam, David K., 1972. Most efficient chunk sizes. *Cognitive Psychology* **3** (April): 355–359.

Donnermuth, William P., 1965. The shopping matrix and marketing strategy. *Journal of Marketing Research* **2** (May): 128–132.

Donohew, Lewis, and Leonard Tipton, 1973. A conceptual model of information seeking, avoiding, and processing. In Peter Clarke, (ed.), *New models for communications research.* Beverly Hills, Calif.: Sage, pp. 243–268.

Dosher, Barbara Anne, and J. Edward Russo, 1976. Memory for internally generated stimuli. *Journal of Experimental Psychology: Human Learning and Memory* **2** (November): 633–640.

Driscoll, James M., and John T. Lanzetta, 1964. Effects of problem uncertainty and prior arousal on pre-decisional information search. *Psychological Reports* **14**: 975–988.

———, and John T. Lanzetta, 1965. Effects of two sources of uncertainty in decision making. *Psychological Reports* **17**: 635–648.

———, Jerome J. Tognoli, and John T. Lanzetta, 1966. Choice conflict and subjective uncertainty in decision making. *Psychological Reports* **18**: 427–432.

Driver, Michael J., and Siegfried Streufert, 1964. The "General Incongruity Adaptation Level" (GIAL) hypothesis: an analysis and integration of cognitive approaches to motivation. Paper No. 114. Krannert Graduate School of Industrial Administration, Purdue University.

Duffy, Elizabeth, 1957. The psychological significance of the concept of "arousal" or "activation." *Psychological Review* **64** (September): 265–275.

Dyer, Robert F., and Philip G. Kuehl, 1974. The "corrective advertising" remedy of the FTC: an experimental evaluation. *Journal of Marketing* **38** (January): 48–54.

Eagle, Morris, and Eli Leiter, 1964. Recall and recognition in intentional and incidental learning. *Journal of Experimental Psychology* **68**: 58–63.

Ebbesen, Ebbe B., and Vladimir J. Konečni, 1975. Decision making and information integration in the courts: the setting of bail. *Journal of Personality and Social Psychology* **32**: 805–821.

Einhorn, Hillel J., 1970. Use of nonlinear, noncompensatory models in decision making. *Psychological Bulletin* **73**: 221–230.

———, 1971. Use of nonlinear, noncompensatory models as a function of task and amount of information. *Organizational Behavior and Human Performance* **6**: 1–27.

Engel, James F., Roger D. Blackwell, and David T. Kollat, 1978. *Consumer behavior,* (3rd ed.), Hinsdale, Ill.: Dryden.

———, David T. Kollat, and Roger D. Blackwell, 1973. *Consumer behavior,* (2nd ed.). New York: Holt, Rinehart, and Winston.

Ernst, G. W., and Allen Newell, 1969. *GPS: a case study in generality and problem-solving.* New York: Academic.

Estes, William K., (ed.), 1975. *Handbook of learning and cognitive processes,* Volume 1. Hillsdale, N.J.: Lawrence Erlbaum.

Eysenck, Michael W., 1976. Arousal, learning, and memory. *Psychological Bulletin* **83** (May): 389–404.

Farley, John U., and L. Winston Ring, 1970. An empirical test of the Howard–Sheth model of buyer behavior. *Journal of Marketing Research* **7** (November): 427–438.

Feather, N. T., 1967. An expectancy–value model of information-seeking behavior. *Psychological Review* **74**: 342–360.

Feigenbaum, Edward A., 1963. Simulation of verbal learning behavior. In Edward A. Feigenbaum and Julian Feldman, (eds.), *Computers and thought.* New York: McGraw-Hill, pp. 297–309.

Feldman, Jack M., 1974. Note on the utility of certainty weights in expectancy theory. *Journal of Applied Psychology* **59**: 727–730.

Feldman, Julian, 1963. Simulation of behavior in the binary choice experiment. In Edward A. Feigenbaum and Julian Feldman, (eds.), *Computers and thought*. New York: McGraw-Hill, pp. 329–346.

Fischhoff, Baruch, 1976. Attribution theory and judgment under uncertainty. In J. H. Harvey, W. J. Ickes, and R. F. Kidd, (eds.), *New directions in attribution research*, Vol. 1, Hillsdale, N.J.: Lawrence Erlbaum, pp. 421–452.

_____, Paul Slovic, and Sarah Lichtenstein, 1978. Fault trees: sensitivity of estimated failure probabilities to problem representation. *Journal of Experimental Psychology: Human Perception and Performance* **4** (May): 330–344.

Fishbein, Martin, and Icek Ajzen, 1975. *Belief, attitude, intention, and behavior: an introduction to theory and research*. Reading, Mass.: Addison-Wesley.

_____, and Rhonda Hunter, 1964. Summation versus balance in attitude organization and change. *Journal of Abnormal and Social Psychology* **69**: 505–510.

Flaherty, E. G., 1975. The thinking aloud technique and problem solving ability. *Journal of Educational Research* **68** (February): 223–225.

Freud, Sigmund, 1948. *Collected papers*. London: Hogarth.

Friedman, Monroe P., 1966. Consumer confusion in the selection of supermarket products. *Journal of Applied Psychology* **50**: 529–534.

_____, 1967. Quality and price considerations in rational consumer decision making. *Journal of Consumer Affairs* **1** (Summer): 13–23.

Friendly, Michael L., 1977. In search of the M-Gram: the structure of organization in free recall. *Cognitive Psychology* **9** (April): 188–249.

Frieze, Irene H., 1976. The role of information processing in making causal attributions for success and failure. In John S. Carroll and John W. Payne, (eds.), *Cognition and social behavior*, Hillsdale, N.J.: Lawrence Erlbaum, pp. 95–112.

Frijda, Nico H., 1967. Problems of computer simulation. *Behavioral Science* **12**: 59–67.

_____, 1972. Simulation of human long-term memory, *Psychological Bulletin* **77** (January): 1–31.

Frost, Nancy, 1972. Encoding and retrieval in visual memory tasks, *Journal of Experimental Psychology* **95**: 317–326.

Gardner, Meryl P., Andrew A. Mitchell, and J. Edward Russo, 1978. Chronometric analysis: an introduction and an application to low involvement perception of advertisements. In H. Keith Hunt, (ed.), *Advances in consumer research*, Volume 5. Chicago: Association for Consumer Research, pp. 581–589.

Gaumnitz, Jack E., Robert L. Swinth, and John O. Tollefson, 1973. Simulation of water recreation users' decisions. *Land Economics* **49**: 269–277.

Goldberg, Lewis R., 1968. Simple models or simple processes? Some research on clinical judgments. *American Psychologist* **23**: 483–496.

_____, 1971. Five models of clinical judgment: an empirical comparison between linear and nonlinear representations of the human inference process. *Organizational Behavior and Human Performance* **6**: 458–479.

Goldberg, Marvin E., and Gerald J. Gorn, 1974. Children's reactions to television advertising: an experimental approach. *Journal of Consumer Research* **1** (September): 69–75.

Goldwater, Bram C., 1972. Psychological significance of pupillary movements. *Psychological Bulletin* **77**: 340–355.

Grass, Robert C., and Wallace H. Wallace, 1969. Satiation effects of TV commercials. *Journal of Advertising Research* **9** (September): 3-8.

———, 1974. Advertising communication: print vs. TV. *Journal of Advertising Research* **14** (October): 19-23.

Green, Bert F., 1968. Descriptions and explanations: a comment on papers by Hoffman and Edwards. In Benjamin Kleinmuntz, (ed.), *Formal representation of human judgment.* New York: Wiley, pp. 91-98.

Green, Paul E., 1966. Consumer use of information. In Joseph W. Newman, (ed.), *On knowing the consumer.* New York: Wiley, pp. 67-80.

———, and Vithala R. Rao, 1972. *Applied multidimensional scaling: a comparison of approaches and algorithms.* New York: Holt, Rinehart, and Winston.

———, and Yoram Wind, 1973. *Multiattribute decisions in marketing: a measurement approach.* Hinsdale, Ill.: Dryden.

Greeno, James G., 1976. Indefinite goals in well-structured problems. *Psychological Review* **83** (November): 479-491.

———, and Robert A. Bjork, 1973. Mathematical learning theory and the new "mental forestry." *Annual Review of Psychology* **24**: 81-116.

———, and D. L. Noreen, 1974. Time to read semantically related sentences. *Memory and Cognition* **2**: 117-120.

Gregg, Lee W., 1974. Perceptual structures and semantic relations. In Lee W. Gregg, (ed.), *Knowledge and cognition,* Potomac, Md.: Lawrence Erlbaum, pp. 1-16.

Haber, Ralph N., 1964. Effects of coding strategy on perceptual memory. *Journal of Experimental Psychology* **68** (November): 357-362.

Haines, George H., 1974a. Information and consumer behavior. In Jagdish N. Sheth, (ed.), *Models of buyer behavior: conceptual, quantitative, and empirical.* New York: Harper & Row, pp. 108-125.

———, 1974b. Process models of consumer decision making. In G. David Hughes and Michael L. Ray, (eds.), *Buyer/consumer information processing,* Chapel Hill: University of North Carolina Press, pp. 89-107.

Haire, Mason, 1950. Projective techniques in marketing research. *Journal of Marketing* **14**: 649-656.

Haley, Russell I., 1968. Benefit segmentation: a decision-oriented research tool. *Journal of Marketing* **32** (July): 30-35.

Hansen, Flemming, 1972. *Consumer choice behavior: a cognitive theory.* New York: Free Press.

Harary, Frank, Robert Z. Norman, and Dorwin Cartwright, 1965. *Structural models: an introduction to the theory of directed graphs.* New York: Wiley.

Hass, Jane W., Gerrold S. Bagley, and Ronald W. Rogers, 1975. Coping with the energy crisis: effects of fear appeals upon attitudes toward energy consumption. *Journal of Applied Psychology* **60**: 754-756.

Hawkins, C. K., and J. T. Lanzetta, 1965. Uncertainty, importance, and arousal as determinants of pre-decisional information search. *Psychological Reports* **17**: 791-800.

Hayes-Roth, Barbara, 1977. Evolution of cognitive structures and processes. *Psychological Review* **84** (May): 260-278.

Hebb, D. O., 1955. Drives and the C.N.S. (conceptual nervous system). *Psychological Review* **62**: 243-254.

Heeler, Roger M., Michael J. Kearney, and Bruce J. Mehaffey, 1973. Modeling supermarket product selection. *Journal of Marketing Research* **10** (February): 34–37.

Hendrick, Clyde, Judson Mills, and Charles A. Kiesler, 1968. Decision time as a function
of the number and complexity of equally attractive alternatives. *Journal of
Personality and Social Psychology* **8**: 313–318.

Henry, Walter A., 1976. Cultural values do correlate with consumer behavior. *Journal of
Marketing Research* **13** (May): 121–127.

_____, and Robert V. Stumpf, 1975. Time and accuracy measures for alternative multi-
dimensional scaling data collection methods. *Journal of Marketing Research*
12 (May): 165–170.

Heslin, Richard, Brian Blake, and James Rotton, 1972. Information search as a function
of stimulus uncertainty and the importance of the response. *Journal of Personality and Social Psychology* **23**: 333–339.

Hess, Eckhard, H., 1965. Attitude and pupil size. *Scientific American* **212**: 46–54.

_____, and James M. Polt, 1960. Pupil size as related to interest value of visual stimuli.
Science **132** (August): 349–350.

_____, and James M. Polt, 1964. Pupil size in relation to mental activity during simple
problem solving. *Science* **143**: 1190–1192.

Hilgard, Ernest R., and Gordon H. Bower, 1966. *Theories of learning,* (3rd ed.) New York:
Appleton-Century-Crofts.

Hintzman, Douglas L., and Richard A. Block, 1970. Memory judgments and the effects
of spacing. *Journal of Verbal Learning and Verbal Behavior* **9**: 561–566.

Hoffman, Paul J., 1960. The paramorphic representation of clinical judgment. *Psychological Bulletin* **57** (March): 116–131.

_____, 1968. Cue consistency and configurality in human judgment. In Benjamin
Kleinmuntz, (ed.), *Formal representation of human judgment.* New York: Wiley,
pp. 53–90.

Hollan, James D., 1975. Features and semantic memory: set theoretic or network
model? *Psychological Review* **82**: 154–155.

Howard, John A., 1963. *Marketing management,* (2nd ed.). Homewood, Ill.: Irwin.

_____, 1977. *Consumer behavior: application of theory.* New York: McGraw-Hill.

_____, and William M. Morgenroth, 1968. Information processing model of executive
decisions. *Management Science* **14** (March): 416–428.

_____, and Jagdish N. Sheth, 1969. *The theory of buyer behavior.* New York: Wiley.

Hughes, G. David, and Michael L. Ray, (eds.), 1974. *Buyer/consumer information processing.* Chapel Hill, N.C.: University of North Carolina Press.

Hulbert, James, 1975. Information processing capacity and attitude measurement.
Journal of Marketing Research **12** (February): 104–106.

_____, John U. Farley, and John A. Howard, 1972. Information processing and decision
making in marketing organizations. *Journal of Marketing Research* **9**
(February): 75–77.

Hull, Clark L., 1952. *A behavioral system.* New Haven: Yale University Press.

Hunt, Earl B., 1971. What kind of computer is man? *Cognitive Psychology* **2** (January):
57–98.

_____, Clifford Lunneborg, and Joe Lewis, 1975. What does it mean to be high verbal?
Cognitive Psychology **7** (April): 194–227.

_____, and Walter Mackous, 1969. Some characteristics of human information pro-
cessing. In J. Tou, (ed.), *Advances in information processing,* Volume 2. New
York: Plenum, pp. 282–335.

Hunt, H. Keith, 1972. Source effects, message effects, and general effects in counter-advertising. In M. Venkatesan, (ed.), *Proceedings of the Third Annual Conference*. Chicago: Association for Consumer Research, pp. 370-381.

Hunt, J. McV., 1963. Motivation inherent in information processing and action. In O. J. Harvey, (ed.), *Motivation and social interaction — cognitive determinants*. New York: Ronald, pp. 35-94.

Jacoby, Jacob, 1974. Consumer reaction to information displays: packaging and advertising. In Salvatore F. Divita, (ed.), *Advertising and the public interest*. Chicago: American Marketing Association, pp. 101-118.

————, 1975. Perspectives on a consumer information processing research program. *Communication Research* **2** (July): 203-215.

————, 1977. The emerging behavioral process technology in consumer decision-·making research. In William D. Perreault, (ed.), *Advances in consumer research*, Volume 4. Chicago: Association for Consumer Research, pp. 263-265.

————, Carol K. Berning, and Thomas F. Dietvorst, 1977. What about disposition? *Journal of Marketing* **41** (April): 22-28.

————, Robert W. Chestnut, Karl C. Weigl, and William Fisher, 1976. Pre-purchase information acquisition: description of a process methodology, research paradigm, and pilot investigation. In Beverlee B. Anderson, (ed.), *Advances in consumer research*, Volume 3. Chicago: Association for Consumer Research, pp. 306-314.

————, and David B. Kyner, 1973. Brand loyalty vs. repeat purchasing behavior. *Journal of Marketing Research* **10** (February): 1-9.

————, and Jerry C. Olson, 1977. Consumer response to price: an attitudinal information processing perspective. In Yoram Wind and Marshall Greenberg, (eds.), *Moving a head with attitude research*. Chicago: American Marketing Association, pp. 73-86.

————, Donald E. Speller, and Carol A. Kohn, 1974a. Brand choice behavior as a function of information load. *Journal of Marketing Research* **11** (February): 63-69.

————, Donald E. Speller, and Carol A. Kohn, 1974b. Brand choice behavior as a function of information load: replication and extension. *Journal of Consumer Research* **1** (June): 33-42.

————, George J. Szybillo, and Jacqueline Busato-Schach, 1977. Information acquisition behavior in brand choice situations. *Journal of Consumer Research* **3** (March): 209-216.

Jenkins, Herbert M. and William C. Ward, 1965. Judgment of contingency between responses and outcomes. *Psychological Monographs* **79** (Whole No. 594).

Jenkins, James J., 1974. Remember that old theory of memory? Well, forget it! *American Psychologist* **29** (November): 785-795.

John, E. Roy, 1972. Switchboard versus statistical theories of learning and memory. *Science* **177** (September): 850-864.

Johnson, Eric, J., 1978. *What is remembered about consumer decisions?* Unpublished manuscript, Department of Psychology, Carnegie-Mellon University.

————, and J. Edward Russo, 1978. The organization of product information in memory identified by recall times. In H. Keith Hunt, (ed.), *Advances in consumer research*, Volume 5, Chicago: Association for Consumer Research, pp. 79-86.

Johnson, Stephen C., 1967. Hierarchical clustering schemes. *Psychometrika* **32** (September): 241–254.

Just, Marcel A., and Patricia A. Carpenter, 1976. Eye fixations and cognitive processes. *Cognitive Psychology* **8** (October): 441–480.

Kahneman, Daniel, 1973. *Attention and effort.* Englewood Cliffs, N.J.: Prentice-Hall.

———, and Jackson Beatty, 1966. Pupil diameter and load on memory. *Science* **154**: 1583–1585.

———, and Jackson Beatty, 1967. Pupillary responses in a pitch discrimination task. *Perception and Psychophysics* **2**: 101–105.

———, and Amos Tversky, 1972. Subjective probability: a judgment of representativeness. *Cognitive Psychology* **3** (July): 430–454.

———, and Amos Tversky, 1973. On the psychology of prediction. *Psychological Review* **80** (July): 237–251.

Kalwani, Manohar U., and Donald G. Morrison, 1977. A parsimonious description of the Hendry system. *Management Science* **23** (January): 467–477.

Kanouse, David E., and L. Reid Hanson, 1971. Negativity in evaluations. In Edward E. Jones et al., (eds.), *Attribution: perceiving the causes of behavior.* Morristown, N.J.: General Learning Press, pp. 47–62.

Kassarjian, Harold H., 1971. Personality and consumer behavior: a review. *Journal of Marketing Research* **8** (November): 409–418.

———, 1973. Field theory in consumer behavior. In Scott Ward and Thomas S. Robertson, (eds.), *Consumer behavior: theoretical sources.* Englewood Cliffs, N.J.: Prentice-Hall, pp. 118–140.

———, Cynthia J. Carlson, and Paula E. Rosin, 1975. A corrective advertising study. In Mary Jane Schlinger, (ed.), *Advances in consumer research,* Volume 2. Chicago: Association for Consumer Research, pp. 631–642.

Katona, George, and Eva Mueller, 1955. A study of purchase decisions in consumer behavior. In Lincoln H. Clark, (ed.), *Consumer behavior: the dynamics of consumer reaction,* Volume 1. New York: New York University Press, pp. 30–87.

Kelley, Harold H., 1967. Attribution theory in social psychology. In David Levine, (ed.), *Nebraska Symposium on Motivation, 1967.* Lincoln: University of Nebraska Press, pp. 192–238.

———, 1971. Causal schemata and the attribution process. In Edward E. Jones et al., (eds.), *Attribution: perceiving the causes of behavior.* Morristown, N.J.: General Learning Press, pp. 151–174.

Kelman, Herbert C., and Reuben M. Baron, 1968a. Determinants of modes of resolving inconsistency dilemmas: a functional analysis. In Robert P. Abelson et al., (eds.), *Theories of cognitive consistency: a sourcebook.* Chicago, Rand McNally, pp. 670–683.

———, and Reuben M. Baron, 1968b. Inconsistency as a psychological signal. In Robert P. Abelson et al., (eds.), *Theories of cognitive consistency: a sourcebook,* Chicago: Rand McNally, pp. 331–336.

Kerr, Beth, 1973. Processing demands during mental operations. *Memory and Cognition* **1** (October): 401–412.

Kieras, David, 1978. Beyond pictures and words: alternative information-processing models for imagery effects in verbal memory. *Psychological Bulletin* **85** (May): 532–554.

Kiesler, Charles A., 1966. Conflict and number of choice alternatives. *Psychological Reports* **18**: 603–610.

———, 1975. A motivational theory of stimulus incongruity, with applications for such phenomena as dissonance and self-attribution. Unpublished manuscript.

King, Robert H., 1969. A study of the problem of building a model to simulate the cognitive processes of a shopper in a supermarket. In George H. Haines, (ed.), *Consumer behavior: learning models of purchasing.* New York: Free Press, pp. 22–67.

Kintsch, Walter, 1970. Models for free recall and recognition. In Donald A. Norman, (ed.), *Models of human memory.* New York: Academic, pp. 331–373. ·

Koffka, F., 1935. *Principles of gestalt psychology.* New York: Harcourt and Brace.

Kohan, Xavier, 1968. A physiological measure of commercial effectiveness. *Journal of Advertising Research* **8** (December): 46–48.

Kohn Berning, Carol A., and Jacob Jacoby, 1974. Patterns of Information acquisition in new product purchases. *Journal of Consumer Research* **1** (September): 18–22.

Kolers, Paul A., 1973. Remembering operations. *Memory and Cognition* **1**: 347–355.

———, 1975. Memorial consequences of automatized encoding. *Journal of Experimental Psychology: Human Learning and Memory* **1**: 689–701.

Kollat, David T., and Ronald P. Willett, 1967. Customers' impulse purchasing behavior. *Journal of Marketing Research* **4** (February): 21–31.

Korchin, Sheldon J., 1964. Anxiety and cognition. In C. Scheerer, (ed.), *Cognition: theory, research, promise.* New York: Harper & Row, pp. 58–78.

Kosslyn, Stephen M., and Steven P. Shwartz, 1977. A simulation of visual imagery. *Cognitive Science* **1** (July): 265–295.

Krugman, Herbert E., 1964. Some applications of pupil measurement. *Journal of Marketing Research* **1** (November): 15–19.

———, 1965. The impact of television advertising: learning without involvement. *Public Opinion Quarterly* **29** (Fall): 349–356.

———, 1968. Processes underlying exposure to advertising. *American Psychologist* **23** (April): 245–253.

———, 1971. Brain wave measures of media involvement. *Journal of Advertising Research* **11** (February): 3–9.

———, 1972. Why three exposures may be enough. *Journal of Advertising Research* **12** (December): 11–14.

———, 1977. Memory without recall, exposure without perception. *Journal of Advertising Research* **17** (August): 7–12.

Kukla, Andy, 1972a. Attributional determinants of achievement-related behavior. *Journal of Personality and Social Psychology* **21**: 166–174.

———, 1972b. Foundations of an attributional theory of performance. *Psychological Review* **79** (November): 454–470.

Lambert, Zarrel V., 1977. Nutrition information: a look at some processing and decision making difficulties. In William D. Perreault, (ed.), *Advances in Consumer Research,* Volume 4. Chicago: Association for Consumer Research, pp. 126–132.

Landauer, Thomas K., 1975. Memory without organization: properties of a model with random storage and undirected retrieval. *Cognitive Psychology* **7** (October): 495–531.

Lanzetta, John T., 1963. Information acquisition in decision making. In O. J. Harvey, (ed.), *Motivation and social interaction-cognitive determinants*. New York: Ronald, pp. 239–265.

_____, and James M. Driscoll, 1968. Effects of uncertainty and importance on information search in decision making. *Journal of Personality and Social Psychology* **10**: 479–486.

_____, and Vera T. Kanareff, 1962. Information cost, amount of payoff, and level of aspiration as determinants of information seeking in decision making. *Behavioral Science* **7**: 459–473.

Lappin, Joseph S., 1967. Attention in the identification of stimuli in complex visual displays. *Journal of Experimental Psychology* **75** (November): 321–328.

Lehtinen, Uolevi, 1974. A brand choice model: theoretical framework and empirical results. *European Research* **2** (March): 51–68.

Lewin, Kurt, 1938. *The conceptual representation and measurement of psychological forces*. Durham, N.C.: Duke University Press.

Lindsay, Peter H., and Donald A. Norman, 1972. *Human information processing*. New York: Academic.

Lindsay, Robert K., and Jane M. Lindsay, 1966. Reaction time and serial versus parallel information processing. *Journal of Experimental Psychology* **71**: 294–303.

Locander, William B., and John P. Burton, 1976. The effect of question form on gathering income data by telephone. *Journal of Marketing Research* **13** (May): 189–192.

Locke, Edwin A., 1968. Toward a theory of task motivation and incentives. *Organizational Behavior and Human Performance* **3**: 157–189.

Looft, William R., 1971. The unimodal preference-for-complexity function: artifact? *Journal of General Psychology* **85**: 239–243.

Lord, Frederic M., 1962. Cutting scores and errors of measurement. *Psychometrika* **27** (March): 19–30.

Lunn, J. A., 1974. Consumer decision-process models. In Jagdish N. Sheth, (ed.), *Models of buyer behavior: conceptual, quantitative, and empirical*. New York: Harper & Row, pp. 34–69.

Lussier, Denis A., and Richard W. Olshavsky, 1974. An information processing approach to individual brand choice behavior. Paper presented at the ORSA/TIMS Joint National Meeting. San Juan, Puerto Rico, October.

Lutz, Kathy A., and Richard J. Lutz, 1977. Effects of interactive imagery on learning: application to advertising. *Journal of Applied Psychology* **62** (August): 493–498.

Lutz, Richard J., and James R. Bettman, 1977. Multiattribute models in marketing: a bicentennial review. In Arch G. Woodside, Jagdish N. Sheth, and Peter D. Bennett, (eds.), *Foundations of consumer and industrial buying behavior*. New York: North Holland, pp. 137–149.

_____, and Pradeep Kakkar, 1975. The psychological situation as a determinant of consumer behavior. In Mary Jane Schlinger, (ed.), *Advances in consumer research*, Volume 2. Chicago: Association for Consumer Research, pp. 439–453.

_____, and Patrick J. Reilly, 1974. An exploration of the effects of perceived social and performance risk on consumer information acquisition. In Scott Ward and Peter Wright, (eds.), *Advances in consumer research*, Volume 1. Chicago: Association for Consumer Research, pp. 393–405.

_____, and John L. Swasy, 1977. Integrating cognitive structure and cognitive response approaches to monitoring communications effects. In William D. Perreault, (ed.), *Advances in consumer research*, Volume 4. Chicago: Association for Consumer Research, pp. 363–371.

McGhie, Andrew, James Chapman, and J. S. Lawson, 1965. Changes in immediate memory with age. *British Journal of Psychology* 56: 69–75.

McGuire, William J., 1969. The nature of attitudes and attitude change. In Gardner Lindzey and Elliot Aronson, (eds.), *The handbook of social psychology*, (2nd ed., Volume III). Reading, Mass.: Addison-Wesley, pp. 136–314.

_____, 1976. Some internal psychological factors influencing consumer choice, *Journal of Consumer Research* 2 (March): 302–319.

MacKay, David M., and Richard W. Olshavsky, 1975. Cognitive maps of retail locations: an investigation of some basic issues. *Journal of Consumer Research* 2 (December): 197–205.

McKeachie, Wilbert, J., 1976. Psychology in America's bicentennial year. *American Psychologist* 31 (December): 819–833.

McLaughlin, Barry, 1965. "Intentional" and "incidental" learning in human subjects: the role of instructions to learn and motivation. *Psychological Bulletin* 63: 359–376.

McLuhan, H. Marshall, 1964. *Understanding media: the extension of man*. New York: McGraw-Hill.

Maloney, John C., and Bernard Silverman, (eds.), 1978. *Attitude research plays for high stakes*. Chicago: American Marketing Association.

Mandler, Jean M., and Richard E. Parker, 1976. Memory for descriptive and spatial information in complex pictures. *Journal of Experimental Psychology: Human Learning and Memory* 2 (January): 38–48.

March, James G., and Herbert A. Simon, 1958. *Organizations*. New York: Wiley.

Markus, Hazel, 1977. Self-schemata and processing information about the self. *Journal of Personality and Social Psychology* 35 (February): 63–78.

Martineau, Pierre D., 1957. *Motivation in advertising*. New York: McGraw-Hill.

Maslow, Abraham H., 1954. *Motivation and personality*, New York: Harper & Row.

Massy, William F., David B. Montgomery, and Donald G. Morrison, 1970. *Stochastic models of buying behavior*. Cambridge, Mass.: M.I.T. Press.

May, Kenneth O., 1954. Intransitivity, utility, and the aggregation in preference patterns. *Econometrica* 22 (January): 1–13.

Mazis, Michael B., 1972. Decision-making role and information processing. *Journal of Marketing Research* 9 (November): 447–450.

Millenson, J. R., 1967. An isomorphism between stimulus–response notation and information processing flow diagrams. *Psychological record* 17: 305–319.

Miller, George A., 1956. The magical number seven, plus or minus two: some limits on our capacity for processing information. *Psychological Review* 63: 81–97.

_____, Eugene Galanter, and Karl H. Pribram, 1960. *Plans and the structure of behavior*. New York: Holt, Rinehart, and Winston.

Miller, Stephen J., and William G. Zikmund, 1975. A multivariate analysis of prepurchase deliberation and external search behavior. In Mary Jane Schlinger, (ed.), *Advances in consumer research*, Volume 2. Chicago: Association for Consumer Research, pp. 187–196.

Mintzberg, Henry, Duru Raisinghani, and Andre Theoret, 1976. The structure of "unstructured" decision processes. *Administrative Science Quarterly* **21** (June): 246–275.

Mischel, Walter, 1973. Toward a cognitive social learning reconceptualization of personality. *Psychological Review* **80** (July): 252–285.

_____, and Charlotte J. Patterson, 1976. Substantive and structural elements of effective plans for self-control. *Journal of Personality and Social Psychology* **34** (November): 942–950.

Monroe, Kent B., 1973. Buyers' subjective perceptions of price. *Journal of Marketing Research* **10** (February): 70–80.

Montague, William S., and Joseph S. Lappin, 1966. Effects of coding strategy on perceptual memory. *Journal of Experimental Psychology* **72** (November): 777–779.

Montgomery, David B., 1975. New product distribution—an analysis of supermarket buyer decisions. *Journal of Marketing Research* **12** (August): 255–264.

Montgomery, Henry, and Ola Svenson, 1976. On decision rules and information processing strategies for choices among multiattribute alternatives. *Scandinavian Journal of Psychology* **17**: 283–291.

Morrison, Bruce J., and Marvin J. Dainoff, 1972. Advertisement complexity and looking time. *Journal of Marketing Research* **9** (November): 396–400.

Myers, John G., 1977. An interactive computer approach to product positioning. In Yoram Wind and Marshall Greenberg, (eds.), *Moving a head with attitude research.* Chicago: American Marketing Association, pp. 157–164.

Nakanishi, Masao, 1974. Decision net models and human information processing. In G. David Hughes and Michael L. Ray, (eds.), *Buyer/consumer information processing.* Chapel Hill, N.C.: University of North Carolina Press, pp. 75–88.

_____, Lee G. Cooper, and Harold H. Kassarjian, 1974. Voting for a political candidate under conditions of minimal information. *Journal of Consumer Research* **1** (September): 36–43.

Neches, Robert, 1977. Process and representation in modifying strategies. Unpublished working paper, Department of Psychology, Carnegie–Mellon University.

_____, and John R. Hayes, 1978. Progress toward a taxonomy of strategy transformations. In Alan M. Lesgold, James W. Pellegrino, and Robert Glaser (eds.), *Cognitive Psychology and Instruction.* New York: Plenum, pp. 253–267.

Neisser, Ulric, 1963. The imitation of man by machine. *Science* **139** (January): 193–197.

_____, 1967. *Cognitive psychology.* New York: Appleton-Century-Crofts.

Nelson, Thomas O., 1977. Repetition and depth of processing. *Journal of Verbal Learning and Verbal Behavior* **16**: 151–171.

Newell, Allan, and Herbert A. Simon, 1958. Elements of a theory of human problem solving. *Psychological Review* **65** (May): 151–166.

_____, "GPS, a program that simulates human thought. In Edward A. Feigenbaum and Julian Feldman, (eds.), *Computers and thought.* New York: McGraw-Hill, pp. 279–293.

_____, 1972. *Human problem solving.* Englewood Cliffs, N.J.: Prentice-Hall.

Newman, Joseph W., 1957. *Motivation research and marketing management.* Cambridge, Mass.: Harvard University Press.

———, 1977. Consumer external search: amount and determinants. In Arch G. Woodside, Jagdish N. Sheth, and Peter D. Bennett, (eds.), *Consumer and industrial buying behavior*. New York: North Holland, pp. 79–94.

———, and Bradley D. Lockeman, 1975. Measuring prepurchase information seeking. *Journal of Consumer Research* **2** (December 1975): 216–222.

———, and Richard Staelin, 1971. Multivariate analysis of differences in buyer decision time. *Journal of Marketing Research* **8** (May): 192–198.

———, and Richard Staelin, 1972. Prepurchase information seeking for new cars and major household appliances. *Journal of Marketing Research* **9** (August): 249–257.

Nicosia, Francesco M., 1966. *Consumer decision processes: marketing and advertising implications.* Engelwood Cliffs, N.J.: Prentice-Hall.

———, 1974. *Summary report. Technology and consumers: individual and social choices.* In Francesco M. Nicosia et al., (eds.), *Technological change, product proliferation, and consumer decision processes.* Washington, D.C.: National Science Foundation.

Nisbett, Richard E., and Eugene Borgida, 1975. Attribution and the psychology of prediction. *Journal of Personality and Social Psychology* **32**: 932–943.

———, and David E. Kanouse, 1968. Obesity, hunger, and supermarket shopping behavior. *Proceedings, 76th Annual Convention,* American Psychological Association, pp. 683–684.

———, and Timothy DeCamp Wilson, 1977. Telling more than we can know: verbal reports on mental processes. *Psychological Review* **84** (May): 231–259.

Norman, Donald A., 1969. *Memory and attention.* New York: Wiley.

———, and Daniel G. Bobrow, 1975. On data-limited and resource-limited processes. *Cognitive Psychology* **7** (January): 44–64.

Nystedt, Lars, and David Magnusson, 1975. Integration of information in a clinical judgment task: an empirical comparison of six models. *Perceptual and Motor Skills* **40**: 343–356.

Oliver, Richard L., 1977. Effect of expectation and disconfirmation on post-exposure product evaluations: an alternative interpretation. *Journal of Applied Psychology* **62** (August): 480–486.

Olshavsky, Richard W., 1971. Search limits as a function of tree size and storage requirements. *Organizational Behavior and Human Performance* **6**: 336–344.

———, 1973. Customer-salesman interaction in appliance retailing. *Journal of Marketing Research* **10** (May): 208–212.

———, 1976. Consumer decision making in naturalistic settings: salesman–prospect interaction. In Beverlee B. Anderson, (ed.), *Advances in consumer research,* Volume 3. Chicago: Association for Consumer Research, pp. 379–381.

———, and Lee W. Gregg, 1970. Information processing rates and task complexity. *Journal of Experimental Psychology* **83**: 131–135.

———, and John A. Miller, 1972. Consumer expectations, product performance, and perceived product quality. *Journal of Marketing Research* **9** (February): 19–21.

Olson, Jerry C., 1977. Price as an informational cue: effects on product evaluations. In Arch G. Woodside, Jagdish N. Sheth, and Peter D. Bennett, (eds.), *Consumer and industrial buying behavior*. New York: North Holland, pp. 267–286.

_____, 1978. Theories of information encoding and storage: implications for consumer research. In Andrew Mitchell, (ed.), *The effect of information on consumer and market behavior.* Chicago: American Marketing Association.

_____, Daniel R. Toy, and Philip A. Dover, 1978. Mediating effects of cognitive responses to advertising on cognitive structure. In H. Keith Hunt, (ed.), *Advances in consumer research,* Volume 5. Chicago: Association for Consumer Research, pp. 72–78.

Organ, Dennis W., 1977. Intentional vs. arousal effects of goal setting. *Organizational Behavior and Human Performance* **18** (April): 378–389.

Orvis, Bruce, R., John D. Cunningham, and Harold H. Kelley, 1975. A closer examination of causal inference: the roles of consensus, distinctiveness, and consistency information. *Journal of Personality and Social Psychology* **32**: 605–616.

Osterhouse, Robert A., and Timothy C. Brock, 1970. Distraction increases yielding to propaganda by inhibiting counter-arguing. *Journal of Personality and Social Psychology* **15**: 344–358.

Pachella, Robert G., 1974. The interpretation of reaction time in information processing research. In Barry H. Kantowitz, (ed.), *Human information processing: tutorials in performance and cognition.* Hillsdale, N.J.: Lawrence Erlbaum, pp. 41–82.

Paivio, Allan, 1971. *Imagery and verbal processes.* New York: Holt, Rinehart, and Winston.

_____, 1975. Perceptual comparisons through the minds-eye. *Memory and Cognition* **3**: 635–647.

Palmer, John, and Jean-Phillipe Faivre, 1973. The information processing theory of consumer behavior. *European Research* **1** (November): 231–240.

Park, C. Whan, 1976. The effect of individual and situation-related factors on consumer selection of judgmental models. *Journal of Marketing Research* **13** (May): 144–151.

_____, 1978. A seven-point scale and a decision-maker's simplifying choice strategy: an operationalized satisficing-plus model. *Organizational Behavior and Human Performance* **21** (April): 252–271.

_____, and Jagdish N. Sheth, 1975. Impact of prior familiarity and cognitive complexity on information processing rules. *Communication Research* **2** (July): 260–266.

Parker, Richard E., 1978. Picture processing during recognition. *Journal of Experimental Psychology: Human Perception and Performance* **4** (May): 284–293.

Patterson, Charlotte J., and Walter Mischel, 1975. Plans to resist distraction. *Developmental Psychology* **11**: 369–378.

_____, 1976. Effects of temptation-inhibiting and task-facilitation plans on self-control. *Journal of Personality and Social Psychology* **33**: 209–217.

Payne, John W., 1976a. Heuristic search processes in decision making. In Beverlee B. Anderson, (ed.), *Advances in consumer research*, Volume 3. Chicago: Association for Consumer Research, pp. 321–327.

_____, 1976b. Task complexity and contingent processing in decision making: an information search and protocol analysis. *Organizational Behavior and Human Performance* **16** (August): 366–387.

_____, and E. K. Easton Ragsdale, 1978. Verbal protocols and direct observation of supermarket shopping behavior: some findings and a discussion of methods. In H. Keith Hunt, (ed.), *Advances in consumer research,* Volume 5. Chicago: Association for Consumer Research, pp. 571-577.

Penney, Catherine G., 1975. Modality effects in short-term verbal memory. *Psychological Bulletin* **82** (January): 68-84.

Phillips, Lynn W., and Brian Sternthal, 1977. Age differences in information processing: a perspective on the aged consumer. *Journal of Marketing Research* **14** (November): 444-457.

Piaget, Jean, and B. Inhelder, 1973. *Memory and intelligence.* New York: Basic Books.

Platt, John R., 1964. Strong inference. *Science* **146** (October): 347-353.

Pollay, Richard W., 1970a. A model of decision times in difficult decision situations. *Psychological Review* 77: 274-281.

_____, 1970b. Only the naive are transitive decision makers. *Journal of Business Administration* **2** (Fall): 3-8.

_____, 1970c. The structure of executive decisions and decision times. *Administrative Science Quarterly* **15** (December): 459-471.

Posner, Michael I., 1973. *Cognition: an introduction.* Glenview, Ill.: Scott, Foresman.

_____, and Robert A. Warren, 1972. Traces, concepts, and conscious constructions. In A. Melton and E. Martin, (eds.), *Coding processes in human memory.* Washington: V. H. Winston, pp. 25-43.

Postman, Leo, 1975. Verbal learning and memory. *Annual Review of Psychology* **26**: 291-335.

Pras, Bernard, and John O. Summers, 1975. A comparison of linear and nonlinear evaluation process models. *Journal of Marketing Research* **12** (August): 276-281.

Preston, Ivan L., and Steven E. Scharbach, 1971. Advertising: more than meets the eye? *Journal of Advertising Research* **11** (June): 19-24.

Pribram, Karl H., and Diane McGuinness, 1975. Arousal, activation, and effort in the control of attention. *Psychological Review* **82**: 116-149.

Pryor, John B., and Mitchel Kriss, 1977. The cognitive dynamics of salience in the attribution process. *Journal of Personality and Social Psychology* **35** (January): 49-55.

Quillian, M. R., 1968. Semantic memory. In M. Minsky, (ed.), *Semantic information processing.* Cambridge, Mass.: M.I.T. Press, pp. 216-270.

Rados, David L., 1972. Selection and evaluation of alternatives in repetitive decision making. *Administrative Science Quarterly* **17** (June): 196-206.

Ray, Michael L., and Allan G. Sawyer, 1971. Repetition in media models: a laboratory technique. *Journal of Marketing Research* **8** (February): 20-29.

_____, and William L. Wilkie, 1970. Fear: the potential of an appeal neglected by marketing? *Journal of Marketing* **34** (January): 54-62.

Rayner, Keith, 1978. Eye movements in reading and information processing. *Psychological Bulletin* **85** (May): 618-660.

Reitman, Judith S., 1976. Skilled perception in go: deducing memory structures from inter-response times. *Cognitive Psychology* **8** (July): 336-356.

Reitman, Walter R., 1965. *Cognition and thought.* New York: Wiley.

_____, 1970. What does it take to remember? In Donald A. Norman, (ed.), *Models of human memory*. New York: Academic, pp. 469–509.

_____, Richard B. Grove, and Richard G. Shoup, 1964. Argus: an information processing model of thinking. *Behavioral Science* **9** (July): 270–281.

Restle, Frank, 1965. Significance of all-or-none learning. *Psychological Bulletin* **64**: 313–325.

Rieger, Chuck, 1977. Spontaneous computation in cognitive models. *Cognitive Science* **1** (July): 315–354.

Robertson, Thomas S., 1976. Low-commitment consumer behavior. *Journal of Advertising Research* **16** (April): 19–24.

_____, and John R. Rossiter, 1974. Children and commercial persuasion: an attribution theory analysis. *Journal of Consumer Research* **1** (June): 13–20.

Robinson, Patrick J., Charles W. Faris, and Yoram Wind, 1967. *Industrial buying and creative marketing*. Boston: Allyn and Bacon.

Rogers, Everett M., 1962. *Diffusion of innovations*. New York: Free Press.

Rorer, Leonard G., 1974. What, can the devill speake true? *Psychological Bulletin* **81**: 355–357.

Roselius, Ted, 1971. Consumer rankings of risk reduction methods. *Journal of Marketing* **35** (January): 56–61.

Rosen, Larry D., and Paul Rosenkoetter, 1976. An eye fixation analysis of choice and judgment with multiattribute stimuli. *Memory and Cognition* **4**: 747–752.

Ross, Ivan, 1974. Applications of consumer information to public policy decisions. In Jagdish N. Sheth and Peter L. Wright, (eds.), *Marketing analysis for societal problems*. Urbana, Ill.: University of Illinois, pp. 42–77.

Rossiter, John R., 1975. Cognitive phenomena in contemporary advertising. Paper presented at the 1975 Conference on Culture and Communication, Temple University, March.

_____, 1976. Visual and verbal memory in children's product information utilization. In Beverlee B. Anderson, (ed.), *Advances in consumer research,* Volume 3. Chicago: Association for Consumer Research, pp. 523–527.

Rumelhart, David E., Peter H. Lindsay, and Donald A. Norman, 1972. A process model for long-term memory. In E. Tulving and W. Donaldson, (eds.), *Organization of memory*. New York: Academic, pp. 197–246.

_____, and Donald A. Norman, 1978. Accretion, tuning, and restructuring: three modes of learning. In J. W. Cotton and R. L. Klatzky (eds.), *Semantic factors in cognition*. Hillsdale, N.J.: Lawrence Erlbaum, pp. 37–54.

Russ, Frederick A., 1971. Consumer evaluation of alternative product models. Unpublished doctoral dissertation. Carnegie–Mellon University.

Russo, J. Edward, 1974. More information is better: a reevaluation of Jacoby, Speller, and Kohn. *Journal of Consumer Research* **1** (December): 68–72.

_____, 1975. An information processing analysis of point-of-purchase decisions. Unpublished paper. San Diego: University of California.

_____, 1977. The value of unit price information. *Journal of Marketing Research* **14** (May): 193–201.

_____, 1978a. Adaptation of cognitive processes to the eye movement system. In J. W. Senders, D. F. Fisher, and R. A. Monty, (eds.), *Eye movements and the higher psychological functions*. Hillsdale, N.J.: Lawrence Erlbaum.

_____, 1978b. Eye fixations can save the world: a critical evaluation and a comparison between eye fixations and other information processing methodologies. In H. Keith Hunt, (ed.), *Advances in consumer research,* Volume 5. Chicago: Association for Consumer Research, pp. 561–570.

_____, and Barbara A. Dosher, 1975. Dimensional evaluation: a heuristic for binary choice. Unpublished working paper. San Diego: Department of Psychology, University of California.

_____, Gene Krieser, and Sally Miyashita, 1975. An effective display of unit price information. *Journal of Marketing* **39** (April): 11–19.

_____, and Larry D. Rosen, 1975. An eye fixation analysis of multialternative choice. *Memory and Cognition* **3** (May): 267–276.

_____, and Robert A. Wisher, 1976. Reprocessing as a recognition cue. *Memory and Cognition* **4** (November): 683–689.

Ryans, Adrian B., and Terry Deutscher, 1975. Children and commercial persuasion: some comments. *Journal of Consumer Research* **2** (December): 237–239.

Sawyer, Alan G., 1974. The effects of repetition: conclusions and suggestions about experimental laboratory research. In G. David Hughes and Michael L. Ray, (eds.), *Buyer/consumer information processing.* Chapel Hill: University of North Carolina Press, pp. 190–219.

Scammon, Debra L., 1977. "Information load" and consumers. *Journal of Consumer Research* **4** (December): 148–155.

Schachter, S., and L. Gross, 1968. Manipulated time and eating behavior. *Journal of Personality and Social Psychology* **10** (October): 98–106.

_____, and J. E. Singer, 1962. Cognitive, social and physiological determinants of emotional state. *Psychological Review* **69**: 379–399.

Schmidt, Frank L., 1973. Implications of a measurement problem for expectancy theory research. *Organizational Behavior and Human Performance* **10** (October): 243–251.

_____, and Terry C. Wilson, 1975. Expectancy value models of attitude measurement: a measurement problem. *Journal of Marketing Research* **12** (August): 366–368.

Schneider, Walter, and Richard M. Shiffrin, 1977. Controlled and automatic human information processing: I. Detection, search, and attention. *Psychological Review* **84** (January): 1–66.

Schroder, Harold M., Michael J. Driver, and Siegfried Streufert, 1967. *Human information processing.* New York: Holt, Rinehart and Winston.

SCIMITAR V: a market research system, 1975. London: David Beaumont, Ltd.

Scott, Jerome E., and Peter Wright, 1976. Modeling an organizational buyers' product evaluation strategy: validity and procedural considerations. *Journal of Marketing Research* **13** (August): 211–224.

Seibel, Robert, Richard E. Christ, and Warren E. Teichner, 1965. Short-term memory under workload stress. *Journal of Experimental Psychology* **70**: 154–162.

Shepard, Roger N., 1964. On subjectively optimum selection among multiattribute alternatives. In Maynard W. Shelly and Glenn L. Bryan, (eds.), *Human judgements and optimality.* New York: Wiley, pp. 257–281.

_____, 1967. Recognition memory for words, sentences, and pictures. *Journal of Verbal Learning and Verbal Behavior* **6**: 156–163.

Sheridan, John E., Max D. Richards, and John W. Slocum, 1975. Comparative analysis of expectancy and heuristic models of decision behavior. *Journal of Applied Psychology* **60**: 361–368.

Sheth, Jagdish N., and M. Venkatesan, 1968. Risk-reduction processes in repetitive consumer behavior. *Journal of Marketing Research* **3** (August): 307–310.

Shiffrin, Richard M., 1970. Memory search. In Donald A. Norman, (ed.), *Models of human memory*. New York: Academic, pp. 375–447.

———, and R. C. Atkinson, 1969. Storage and retrieval processes in long-term memory. *Psychological Review* **76**: 179–193.

———, and Walter Schneider, 1977. Controlled and automatic human information processing: II. Perceptual learning, automatic attending, and a general theory. *Psychological Review* **84** (March): 127–190.

Shwartz, Steven P., 1976. Capacity limitations in human information processing. *Memory and Cognition* **4**: 763–768.

Sieber, Joan E., and John T. Lanzetta, 1964. Conflict and conceptual structure as determinants of decision-making behavior. *Journal of Personality* **32**: 622–641.

Simon, Herbert A., 1964. On the concept of organizational goal. *Administrative Science Quarterly* **9**: 1–22.

———, 1967. Motivational and emotional controls of cognition. *Psychological Review* **74**: 29–39.

———, 1969. *The sciences of the artificial*. Cambridge, Mass.: M.I.T. Press.

———, 1974. How big is a chunk? *Science* **183** (February): 482–488.

———, 1975. The functional equivalence of problem solving skills. *Cognitive Psychology* **7** (April): 268–288.

———, and Michael Barenfeld, 1969. Information processing analysis of perceptual processes in problem solving. *Psychological Review* **76**: 473–483.

———, and Edward A. Feigenbaum, 1964. An information-processing theory of some effects of similarity, familiarization, and meaningfulness in verbal learning. *Journal of Verbal Learning and Verbal Behavior* **3**: 385–396.

———, and Kevin Gilmartin, 1972. A simulation of memory for chess positions. *Cognitive Psychology* **5** (July): 29–46.

———, and John R. Hayes, 1976. The understanding process: problem isomorphs. *Cognitive Psychology* **8** (April): 165–190.

———, and Glenn Lea, 1974. Problem solving and rule induction: a unified view. In Lee W. Gregg, (ed.), *Knowledge and cognition*. Potomac, Md.: Lawrence Erlbaum, pp. 105–128.

Slovic, Paul, 1972a. From Shakespeare to Simon: speculations—and some evidence—about man's ability to process information. *Oregon Research Institute Research Monograph* **12** (3).

———, 1972b. Information processing, situation specificity, and the generality of risk-taking behavior. *Journal of Personality and Social Psychology* **22** (April): 128–134.

———, 1975. Choice between equally valued alternatives. *Journal of Experimental Psychology: Human Perception and Performance* **1**: 280–287.

———, Baruch Fischhoff, and Sarah Lichtenstein, 1977. Behavioral decision theory. *Annual Review of Psychology* **28**: 1–39.

———, and Sarah Lichtenstein, 1968. Relative importance of probabilities and payoffs in risk taking. *Journal of Experimental Psychology* **78** (3, part 2): 1–18.

_____, and Douglas MacPhillamy, 1974. Dimensional commensurability and cue utilization in comparative judgment. *Organizational Behavior and Human Performance* **11**: 172–194.

Smith, Edward E., Edward J. Shoben, and Lance J. Rips, 1974. Structure and process in semantic memory: a featural model for semantic decisions. *Psychological Review* **81**: 214–241.

Spence, Kenneth W., 1956. *Behavior theory and conditioning.* New Haven: Yale University Press.

Stafford, James E., and Ben M. Enis, 1969. The price–quality relationship: an extension. *Journal of Marketing Research* **6** (November): 456–458.

Standing, Lionel, 1975. Learning 10,000 pictures. *Quarterly Journal of Experimental Psychology* **25**: 207–222.

Sternberg, Robert J., 1977. Component processes in analogical reasoning. *Psychological Review* **84** (July): 353–378.

_____, and Endel Tulving, 1977. The measurement of subjective organization in free recall. *Psychological Bulletin* **84** (May): 539–556.

Sternberg, Saul, 1969. Memory scanning: mental processes revealed by reaction time experiments. *American Scientist* **57**: 421–457.

Sternthal, Brian, and C. Samuel Craig, 1974. Fear appeals: revisited and revised. *Journal of Consumer Research* **1** (December): 22–34.

Stigler, George J., 1961. The economics of information. *Journal of Political Economy* **69** (June): 213–225.

Streufert, Siegfried, Peter Suedfeld, and Michael J. Driver, 1965. Conceptual structure, information search, and information utilization. *Journal of Personality and Social Psychology* **2**: 736–740.

Summers, John O., 1974. Less information is better? *Journal of Marketing Research* **11** (November): 467–468.

Svenson, Ola, 1974. Coded think aloud protocols obtained when making a choice to purchase one of seven hypothetically offered houses: some examples. Unpublished paper. University of Stockholm.

Swan, John E., 1969. Experimental analysis of predicision information seeking. *Journal of Marketing Research* **6** (May): 192–197.

_____, 1972. Search behavior related to expectations concerning brand performance. *Journal of Applied Psychology* **56**: 332–335.

Swinth, Robert L., 1976. A decision process model for predicting job preferences. *Journal of Applied Psychology* **61** (April): 242–245.

_____, Jack E. Gaumnitz, and Carlos Rodriguez, 1975. Decision making processes: using discrimination nets for security selection. *Decision Sciences* **6** (July): 439–448.

Takeuchi, Lawrence R., 1975. The structural analysis of a consumer information processing model. In *Proceedings of the Fall Conference.* Chicago: American Marketing Association, pp. 156–161.

Thomson, Donald M., 1972. Context effects in recognition memory. *Journal of Verbal Learning and Verbal Behavior* **11**: 497–511.

_____, and Endel Tulving, 1970. Associative encoding and retrieval: weak and strong cues. *Journal of Experimental Psychology* **86**: 255–262.

Thorelli, Hans B., Helmut Becker, and Jack Engeldow, 1975. *The information seekers.* Cambridge, Mass.: Ballinger.

Tolman, Edward C., 1932. *Purposive behavior in animals and men.* New York: Appleton-Century.

———, 1955. Principles of performance. *Psychological Review* **62**: 315–326.

Tulving, Endel, and Donald M. Thomson, 1971. Retrieval processes in recognition memory: effects of associative context. *Journal of Experimental Psychology* **87**: 116–124.

Tversky, Amos, 1969. Intransitivity of preferences. *Psychological Review* **76** (January): 31–48.

———, 1972. Elimination by aspects: a theory of choice. *Psychological Review* **79** (July): 281–299.

———, and Daniel Kahneman, 1971. Belief in the law of small numbers. *Psychological Bulletin* **76**: 105–110.

———, and Daniel Kahneman, 1973. Availability: a heuristic for judging frequency and probability. *Cognitive Psychology* **5** (September): 207–232.

Tversky, Barbara, 1973. Encoding processes in recognition and recall. *Cognitive Psychology* **5** (November): 275–287.

Udell, Jon G., 1966. Prepurchase behavior of buyers of small electrical appliances. *Journal of Marketing* **30** (October): 50–52.

Underwood, Benton J., 1969. Attributes of memory. *Psychological Review* **76**: 559–573.

———, 1971. Recognition memory. In H. H. Kendler and J. T. Spence, (eds.), *Essays in neobehaviorism.* New York: Appleton-Century-Crofts, pp. 313–335.

Valins, S., 1966. Cognitive effects of false heart-rate feedback. *Journal of Personality and Social Psychology* **6**: 458–463.

Valle, Valerie A., and Irene H. Frieze, 1975. Stability of causal attributions as a mediator in changing expectations for success. *Journal of Personality and Social Psychology* **33**: 579–587.

———, and Melanie Wallendorf, 1977. Consumers' attributions of the causes of their product satisfaction and dissatisfaction. In Ralph L. Day, (ed.), *Consumer satisfaction, dissatisfaction, and complaining behavior.* Bloomington, Ind.: Division of Business Research, Indiana University.

Van Raaij, W. Fred, 1976a. A contingency approach to consumer information processing. Unpublished paper. Tilburg University.

———, 1976b. Direct monitoring of consumer information processing by eye movement recorder. Unpublished paper. Tilburg University.

Venkatesan, M., 1973. Cognitive consistency and novelty seeking. In Scott Ward and Thomas S. Robertson, (eds.), *Consumer behavior: theoretical sources.* Englewood Cliffs, N.J.: Prentice-Hall, pp. 354–384.

Vinson, Donald E., Jerome E. Scott, and Lawrence M. Lamont, 1977. The role of personal values in marketing and consumer behavior. *Journal of Marketing* **41** (April): 44–50.

Ward, Scott, and Daniel B. Wackman, 1972. Children's purchase influence attempts and parental yielding. *Journal of Marketing Research* **9** (August): 316–319.

———, 1973. Children's information processing of television advertising. In Peter Clarke, (ed.), *New models for communications research.* Beverly Hills, Calif.: Sage, pp. 119–146.

———, Daniel B. Wackman, and Ellen Wartella, 1977. *How children learn to buy: the development of consumer information processing skills.* Beverly Hills: Sage.

Ward, William C., and Herbert M. Jenkins, 1965. The display of information and the judgment of contingency. *Canadian Journal of Psychology* **19**: 231–241.

Waterman, D. A., 1970. Generalization learning techniques for automating the learning of heuristics. *Artificial Intelligence* **1**: 121–170.

————, and Allan Newell, 1971. Protocol analysis as a task for artificial intelligence. *Artificial Intelligence* **2**: 285–318.

Waugh, Nancy C., and Donald A. Norman, 1965. Primary memory. *Psychological Review* **72**: 89–104.

Weiner, Bernard, 1972. *Theories of motivation: from mechanism to cognition.* Chicago: Markham.

————, 1974. An attributional interpretation of expectancy–value theory. In Bernard Weiner, (ed.), *Cognitive views of achievement motivation.* New York: Academic, pp. 51–69.

————, H. Heckhausen, W. U. Meyer, and R. E. Cook, 1972. Causal ascription and achievement motivation: a conceptual analysis of effort and reanalysis of locus of control. *Journal of Personality and Social Psychology* **21**: 239–248.

Weitz, Barton, and Peter L. Wright, 1978. Verbal reports about subjective evaluation strategies, Paper No. 63. Los Angeles: Center for Marketing Studies, Graduate School of Management, University of California.

Welford, A. T., 1962. On changes of performance with age. *Lancet* (February 17): 335–339.

Wells, William, D., 1975. Psychographics: a critical review. *Journal of Marketing Research* **12** (May): 196–213.

Westbrook, Robert A., 1977. A study of consumer dissatisfaction before purchase. In William D. Perreault, (ed.), *Advances in consumer research,* Volume 4. Chicago: Association for Consumer Research, pp. 142–148.

Wheatley, John J., and John S. Y. Chiu, 1977. The effects of price, store image, and product and respondent characteristics on perceptions of quality. *Journal of Marketing Research* **14** (May): 181–186.

Whipple, Thomas W., 1976. Variation among multidimensional scaling solutions: an examination of the effect of data collection differences. *Journal of Marketing Research* **13** (February): 98–103.

Wilcoxon, Hardy C., Warner R. Wilson, and Dale A. Wise, 1961. Paired-associate learning as a function of percentage of occurrence of response members and other factors. *Journal of Experimental Psychology* **61**: 283–289.

Wilde, Louis L., and Alan Schwartz, 1977. Equilibrium comparison shopping. Unpublished manuscript. California Institute of Technology, June.

Wilkie, William L., 1974. Analysis of effects of information load. *Journal of Marketing Research* **11** (November): 462–466.

————, 1975a. *How consumers use product information: an assessment of research in relation to public policy needs.* Washington, D.C.: United States Government Printing Office.

————, 1975b. New perspectives for consumer information processing research. *Communication Research* **2** (July): 216–231.

————, and Paul W. Farris, 1975. Comparison advertising: problems and potential. *Journal of Marketing* **39** (October): 7–15.

————, and David M. Gardner, 1974. The role of marketing research in public policy decision making. *Journal of Marketing* **38** (January): 38–47.

_____, John M. McCann, and David J. Reibstein, 1974. Halo effects in brand belief measurement: implications for attitude model development. In Scott Ward and Peter Wright, (eds.), *Advances in consumer research,* Volume 1. Chicago: Association for Consumer Research, pp. 280–290.

_____, and Edgar A. Pessemier, 1973. Issues in marketing's use of multiple-attribute attitude models. *Journal of Marketing Research* **10** (November): 428–441.

Wilson, David T., 1975. Organizational buying: a man and machine information processing approach. *Communication Research* **2** (July): 279–288.

Winikoff, Arnold, 1967. Eye movements as an aid to protocol analysis of problem solving behavior. Unpublished doctoral dissertation. Carnegie–Mellon University.

Winter, Frederick W., 1975. Laboratory measurement of response to consumer information. *Journal of Marketing Research* **12** (November): 390–401.

Woodruff, Robert B., 1972. Measurement of consumers' prior brand information. *Journal of Marketing Research* **9** (August): 258–263.

Woodward, Addison, E., Jr., Robert A. Bjork, and Robert H. Jongeward, Jr., 1973. Recall and recognition as a function of primary rehearsal. *Journal of Verbal Learning and Verbal Behavior* **12**: 608–617.

Worell, Leonard, 1962. Response to conflict as determined by prior exposure to conflict. *Journal of Abnormal and Social Psychology* **64**: 438–445.

Wright, Peter L., 1972. Consumer judgment strategies: beyond the compensatory assumption. In M. Venkatesan, (ed.), *Proceedings of the Third Annual Conference.* Chicago: Association for Consumer Research, pp. 316–324.

_____, 1973a. The cognitive processes mediating acceptance of advertising. *Journal of Marketing Research* **10** (February): 53–62.

_____, 1973b. A common vocabulary for research on cognitive structure. Working Paper 93. College of Commerce and Business Administration, Urbana-Champaign: University of Illinois.

_____, 1973c. Use of consumer judgment models in promotion planning. *Journal of Marketing* **37** (October): 27–33.

_____, 1974a. Analyzing media effects on advertising responses. *Public Opinion Quarterly* **38**: 192–205.

_____, 1974b. The harassed decision maker: time pressures, distractions, and the use of evidence. *Journal of Applied Psychology* **59** (October): 555–561.

_____, 1974c. On the direct monitoring of cognitive response to advertising. In G. David Hughes and Michael L. Ray, (eds.), *Buyer/consumer information processing.* Chapel Hill: University of North Carolina Press, pp. 220–248.

_____, 1974d. Research orientations for analysing consumer judgment processes. In Scott Ward and Peter L. Wright, (eds.), *Advances in consumer research,* Volume 1. Chicago: Association for Consumer Research, pp. 268–279.

_____, 1974e. The use of phased, noncompensatory strategies in decisions between multi-attribute products. Research Paper 223. Graduate School of Business, Stanford University.

_____, 1975. Consumer choice strategies: simplifying vs. optimizing. *Journal of Marketing Research* **11** (February): 60–67.

_____, 1977. Decision times and processes on complex decision problems. Unpublished manuscript. Stanford University.

_____, 1978. Cognitive responses to mass media advocacy and cognitive choice pro-
    cesses. In Richard Petty, Thomas Ostrom, and Timothy Brock, (eds.), *Cognitive
    responses in persuasion.* New York: McGraw-Hill.
_____, and Frederic Barbour, 1975. The relevance of decision process models in
    structuring persuasive messages. *Communication Research* **2** (July): 246–259.
_____, and Frederic Barbour, 1977. Phased decision strategies: sequels to an initial
    screening. In Martin K. Starr and Milan Zeleny, (eds.), *North-Holland/TIMS
    studies in the management sciences,* Volume 6: *Multiple criteria decision mak-
    ing.* Amsterdam: North Holland, pp. 91–109.
_____, and Barton Weitz, 1977. Time horizon effects on product evaluation strategies.
    Journal of Marketing Research **14** (November): 429–443.

Yates, J. Frank, Carolyn M. Jagacinski, and Mark D. Faber, 1978. Evaluation of partially
    described multiattribute options. *Organizational Behavior and Human Per-
    formance* **21** (April): 240–251.

Zajonc, Robert B., 1960. The process of cognitive tuning in communication. *Journal of
    Abnormal and Social Psychology* **61**: 159–167.
Zaltman, Gerald, Christian R. A. Pinson, and Reinhard Angelmar, 1973. *Metatheory and
    consumer research.* New York: Holt, Rinehart and Winston.
Zielske, Hubert A., 1959. The remembering and forgetting of advertising. *Journal of
    Marketing* **23** (January): 239–243.

Author Index

Subject Index

for interrupts (scanner), 64–65, 71, 86, 103
in terminating processing on goals, 54, 71
Time pressure; *see also* Consumer choice environment properties, Difficulty of choice task, Processability, Processing time, Task influences on choice
and changes in choice heuristics, 274
and choice heuristics used, 189, 212–213
and choice process intensity, 63
and conflict reactions, 97
and degree of external search, 127, 305
and learning about the environment, 27

and memory, 159–160
and scanner threshold, 64–65, 86

Variety seeking, 63, 65, 129, 277; *see also* Conflict response strategies
Voluntary attention; *see also* Attention, Effort, Goal, Involuntary attention, Processing capacity
definition, 25, 74
and information provision by marketers, 326
and information provision by policymakers, 297–298, 302, 314
and looking behavior, 77
selectiveness, 77